Underground Music from the Former USSR

edited by

Valeria Tsenova

translated from the Russian by
Romela Kohanovskaya

harwood academic publishers
Australia • Canada • China • France • Germany • India
Japan • Luxembourg • Malaysia • The Netherlands • Russia
Singapore • Switzerland • Thailand • United Kingdom

Copyright © 1997 OPA (Overseas Publishers Association) Amsterdam B.V.
Published in The Netherlands by Harwood Academic Publishers.

Amsteldijk 166
1st Floor
1079 LH Amsterdam
The Netherlands

British Library Cataloguing in Publication Data

Underground music from the former USSR
  1. Composers – Soviet Union – 20th century – Biography
  2. Music – Soviet Union – 20th century – Censorship
  I. Barsky, V. II. Tsenova, Valeria
  780.9'22

  ISBN 3-7186-5821-6 (Paperback)

CONTENTS

PREFACE

This book profiles the most interesting and innovative composers from contemporary Russia and the former Soviet republics. In the West only three modern composers of Russian origin have become famous in their lifetime — Edison Denisov, Sophia Gubaidulina and Alfred Schnittke. This book presents those who may not be so conspicuous in their creative careers but whose music undoubtedly deserves our notice. It should also be borne in mind that some of these composers have won recognition primarily in the West and that the musical community is therefore likely to be interested in a detailed survey of their music.

The composers featured in this book come from different regions of the former USSR: from Russia — Nikolai Karetnikov, Roman Ledenyov, Vyacheslav Artyomov, Alexander Vustin, Alexander Raskatov, Vladislav Shoot, Victor Ekimovsky, Sergei Pavlenko and Vladimir Tarnopolsky representing the Moscow composition school; Sergei Slonimsky, Boris Tishchenko and Alexander Knaifel residing in St. Petersburg; from the Ukraine — Valentin Silvestrov and Leonid Grabovsky; from Azerbaijan — Faraj Karayev; and from the Crimea — Alemdar Karamanov. Some are now resident in Western Europe and the USA.

This volume opens with profiles of two of the most important figures in Russian musical culture — Andrei Volkonsky, the recognized leader of the Russian (back in the 1960s it was still Soviet) avant-garde, who left Russia many years ago, and Philip Gershkovich, a remarkable composer and music scholar, who also spent his last years in the West. The other composers are loosely ordered by generation — senior, middle, and junior.

In preparing this collection it was not my intention to outline a single creative trend, but I have tried to draw together the more contrasted personalities in both their artistic quests and their style. Some composers follow a truly Russian tradition while others are inclined to write in the West-European avant-garde style; some tackle large-scale genres aspiring to convey global messages, whilst others strive to achieve finesse in chamber music.

The diversity of the personalities presented explains the diversity of the styles in which the articles about them have been written. Eschewing uniformity, I have deliberately retained the authors' original styles. Some articles are written in the form of a profile of the composer and his philosophical views, while others offer a dialogue accompanied by the author's commentary. The contributing authors are leading Russian musicologists who for many years now have been engaged in research and study into the theory and history of modern music, with numerous relevant publications to their credit.

A wide range of creative trends in music is perfectly normal, attesting to an incessant and intensive spiritual quest. I hope that this book will expand the range of information about the musical processes current in the former USSR and develop the exchange of musical ideas across international borders.

Valeria Tsenova

Andrei Volkonsky the initiator: a profile of his life and work

Yuri Kholopov

*Andrei Volkonsky with the Madrigal Ensemble
(Second from left, with cigarette)*

The creative evolution of Andrei Volkonsky makes a fanciful curved line abruptly intersected by his re-emigration.

Vasily Kandinsky once offered his vision of the progress in arts as an acute-angled triangle moving "forward and upward," with the creators of new ideas being on its edge; later on, those moving behind catch up with the same ideas, turning them from the avant-garde into conventional ones. At the sources of the movement, which was to transform the image of Russian music in the second half of this century, there stood several talented young composers. Andrei Volkonsky was one of those who emerged on the edge of the shaft in the mid-fifties. His compositions became the watershed to outline a new period — "the Soviet avant-garde." Without paying due tribute to his activities as a composer, interpretative artist and musical figure we would get an incomplete picture of the postwar musical scene in Russia, a country that owes a lot to his ancestors as well. His career sheds a new and unexpected light on the specific aspects inherent in the musical development in Soviet Russia.

Andrei Mikhailovich Volkonsky comes of the oldest family of Russian princes whose origins go back to the legendary Ruriks[1]. Many offspring of this dynasty have left a noticeable imprint on Russian culture, arts, and social life. Nikolai Sergeyevich Volkonsky, grandfather of the writer Leo Tolstoy on the maternal side, a general, served as the prototype for Nikolai Andreyevich Bolkonsky in *War and Peace*. Nikolai's son, Andrei Volkonsky, is one of the main characters in Tolstoy's novel (not a historical person) and in Sergei Prokofiev's opera based on the novel. Princess Zinaida

---

[1] Yelena G. Volkonskaya. The Volkonsky Dynasty of Princes. St. Petersburg, 1900; 980-page genealogy, with commentary.

Alexandrovna Volkonskaya (1792–1862), a writer, composer and singer, was famous for her salon in the 1820s; in 1826–27 the great Pushkin used to visit her salon (and glorified her as "the queen of muses and beauty"). The folklore scholars recorded the Russian folk song "At Prince Volkhonsky's" (which came to be arranged by Pyotr Tchaikovsky). Sergei Mikhailovich Volkonsky (1860–1937), brother of the composer's grandfather, was a celebrated Russian theatre figure, director of the Imperial Theatres; in the 1930s, after Glazunov's decease, he replaced the latter in the post of managing director of the Russian Conservatoire in Paris.

Mikhail Petrovich Volkonsky (1891–1961), Andrei's father, was a professional singer, a soloist at the Belgrade Opera (appearing on the stage under the assumed name of Veron), later he sang in Paris. Andrei's mother, Kira Georgiyevna (1911–1995) née Petkevich, was also a gentlewoman by birth. She left Russia in 1924, met Mikhail Volkonsky in Paris, they got married in 1931, and on February 14, 1933 Andrei was born in Geneva. In the fall of 1947 Kira Georgiyevna with her family moved back to Russia.

Andrei showed his musical gifts at a very early age. When he was five, he began improvising on musical compositions. Sergei Rachmaninov was among those who listened to his children's pieces. He got his musical education first at home (private lessons), then at the Geneva Conservatoire in 1944–45 (piano with Johnny Aubert) and the Paris Conservatoire (1946–47). He studied piano with Dinu Lipatti (Geneva), who was a friend of the Volkonsky family and often visited their home ("What a talented boy!", he used to say about Andrei). When they came to the USSR, Andrei attended music classes in Moscow and Tambov, and in 1950–54 he became a student of Yuri Shaporin, a composer of works on heroic and patriotic subjects, at the Moscow Conservatoire.

The young musician came to face the horrible atmosphere in the USSR as a result of several ideological resolutions passed by the Central Committee of the Communist Party on literature & arts. The "nationwide" persecution of the writers Anna Akhmatova and Mikhail Zoshchenko, later the composers Sergei Prokofiev and Dmitry Shostakovich, the whole of 20th-century new music, particularly "bourgeois" Western and jazz music, the campaign unleashed against "Cosmopolitanism," the murder of Solomon Mikhoels, all of this set up the atmosphere of bans, terror and reprisals for any vital idea and thought.

Andrei Volkonsky's development proceeded in complete independence of the omnipotent party tenets. He was his own master in defining and expanding the sphere of his musical cognition. As early as during his conservatoire years he came to be primarily preoccupied with two domains — modern and preclassical music. In the hermetically sealed Soviet environment, behind the Iron Curtain, he managed to find and absorb modern music. He took every opportunity to bring out of his case the music by Myaskovsky or Bach and get down to playing it at sight.

His ability to do it was striking: he sat down at the piano, playing a modern score, asking only someone to turn the sheets for him; upon repeating it, he played as if it had been a well practiced piece.

As a matter of fact, he was self-teaching. Neither Shaporin nor any other conservatoire professor could teach him anything. Afterwards Volkonsky used to refer to the fact that all the innovators in music were self-taught men — Wagner, Stravinsky, and even Beethoven learned hardly anything new from Haydn. To adopt one's tutor's experience was a necessity in the Middle Ages when music was not an art but a trade. Feeling it as a burden to pass exams in the Marxist social school subjects and dissatisfied with the musical ones, Volkonsky left the Moscow Conservatoire before due time, without getting a diploma.

To gain a foot-hold in his life, Volkonsky outlined two objectives for himself: to enter the Composers Union and set up a performing body.

By the time he was admitted to the Composers Union (1955) Volkonsky had to his credit some quite mature compositions. According to his own words, at the time he was under the influence of Prokofiev and Stravinsky; dodecaphony and Schoenberg came a bit later. His one-movement Piano Sonata in B–flat major (1949), written before he became a conservatoire student and showing the rapid development of his talent, and the Piano Trio (1950–51) were followed by two major compositions which attracted universal attention — the cantatas *Rus* (after Nikolai Gogol) and *The Image of the World* to the text by Paul Eluard (both cantatas written in 1952). Instead of the traditional image of the Russian troika-bird *à la russe* (the customary attribute of the merry wintry festive riding in a carriage with three horses harnessed abreast) the composer produced sharp rhythms akin to jazz music and "impermissible" dissonant harmonies. By contrast, in the aria of the other cantata he indulged in a drawn out lyrical melody, though founded on voice-leading in the orchestra's accompaniment in the neoclassical style of Igor Stravinsky.

Ex. 1 *The Image of the World,* Aria

Andrei Volkonsky came to the notice of music lovers. The general public was touched by his inspired music, the vigilant authorities approved of the "moral intelligence" of the topical subject on "the fight for peace" (as it was called in those years), and the jealous colleagues looked quite appeased by his moderate innovations. Moreover, it was evident that the music of his conservatoire years could not be any longer regarded as immature.

These two cantatas were followed by two compositions for orchestra: the Concerto for Orchestra in 1953 and Capriccio in 1953–54. A concerto for orchestra was a new genre for Russia (though, it was not so for Stravinsky) and the fact that this novelty was produced by the same recently emerged composer consolidated the halo of innovator around his name.

The conception of his Concerto for Orchestra was associated with the forthcoming bicentenary of Moscow State University to be marked in 1955, the best school of higher learning in Russia, founded on the initiative of the great Russian scientist Mikhail Lomonosov after whom it was named and is still known. Volkonsky explained the neoclassical coloring of his score by his belief that a jubilee of this kind presumed a retrospective view into the 18th century and that a university as any school is invariably engaged in something old-time. The word "neoclassicism" is paramount nowadays to "conservatism." Back in the 1950s it was an ideological scarecrow, a sort of "formalism." For at that time such neoclassical Western composers as Hindemith and Stravinsky were forbidden and considered to be dangerous (for their music was ideologically harmful!). At the conference of musicians at the Central Committee of C.P.S.U. (B), which was held a month before the adoption of the notorious resolution on music, neoclassicism was declared to be "an outcome of the idealistic world outlook," with its "asceticism and cold rationality being alien to the spirit of the entire Soviet art"[2]; the influence of neoclassicism was rejected as being "harmful," for it "represented and allegedly insurmountable impact of the bourgeois West"[3].

As for that restless composer, any piece written by him contained something novel, though it was not always an advance into the banned "modernism." Thus, in his incidental score to the radio production "Little Song in the Forest" (1954) he revealed his love for the simple pure colours of the children's world.

Yet, the main guideline in his creative work was exploration of the modern music, though still under the formerly chosen angle, with the conspicuous role of neoclas-sicism. The principal genres he tackled at the time were chamber instrumental and, a bit later, chamber vocal music. To all appearances, under the influence of the Stravinsky style, Andrei Volkonsky's music often showed his striving for clear-cut outlines and finely wrought expressiveness. It is a curious coincidence that in his compositions written in the mid-fifties the number of instruments involved in an ensemble diminishes:

1954	Piano Quintet	(5)
1955	String Quartet	(4)
1955	Sonata for Viola and Piano	(2)
1956	Trio for Two Trumpets and Trombone	(3)
1957	Fantasia for Piano	(1)
	To the same years belongs Sonatina for Harp	(1)

---

[2]   The Conference of the Soviet Musical Figures at the Central Committee of C.P.U.S. (B). *Pravda* Press, Moscow, 1948, pp. 118–119 (from Yuri Keldysh's speech). "Idealism is a dangerous ideological invective in the Soviet time" (Zhdanov associated idealism with something ugly and false, Ibidem, p. 137).

[3]   Ibidem (from Dmitry Kabalevsky's speech).

The quintet for piano, two violins, viola and cello in D minor, Op. 5 in the traditional four movements – *Allegro moderato* – *Burlesca* – *Passacaglia* – *Fuga* by the cast of its movements reveals the neoclassical, Baroque type of its content. The stylistic treatment of the cycle is therefore reminiscent of some neoclassicist features of Dmitry Shostakovich's cycles (Passacaglia in the Eighth Symphony, a fugue in the Piano Quintet), though in a different stylistic character: Volkonsky feels alien to the austere pathetic expressiveness of Shostakovich's music. Thus, his final fugue is permeated with a highly vigorous rhythmical thrust, more in the vein of the energetic fugal finales of the Bach epoch, perhaps through the experience of Hindemith. The grave character of the third movement is overthrown by a citation from "Dubinushka," a popular Russian folk song of barge haulers, (Figure 4) in its polytonal statement.

In his quartet for two violins, viola and cello, Op. 6, Volkonsky does not resort to the ready-made old model of the cycle, either. The composer invents a form as a theme for each individual piece.

This quartet falls into four movements. Movement One, *Eine Kleine romantische Opernszene,* is in C-sharp minor (the leading melody, however, being reminiscent of Tchaikovsky's Sixth Symphony). Movement Two, *Fuga. Presto,* is in C major. The fugue is not extensive but extremely energetic, captivating by its forcefulness. Example 2 is an episode from this fugue.

Ex. 2 *String Quartet, Op. 6, Second movement*

Movement Three, *Danza in modo canonico,* is once again in D-flat (major). The canon on a prolonged melodic theme is unfolding against the background of the cello's measured fascinating *pizzicato* so that "Danza" is a passacaglia as well. The abundance of chromatic elements, the tonal duality (D-flat major — C major), and the refined polyphonic elaboration bring the composer's procedures into close proximity of the serial technique, though he has a lot to go before he tackles it directly. Movement Four, *Coda. Molto adagio,* is a highly original slow finale that discloses the cycle's message. Two tonal centres – c♯ and c – do not push out each other but remain beautifully inscribed into the "polytonal" combination of C–sharp minor and C major united exclusively in thirds. Volkonsky's string quartet ends poetically in this fading sonority. The combination of two contrasting spheres is akin to the way in which Mussorgsky brought together two tonal characters in the piece *Two Jews* from his *Pictures at an Exhibition*.

Another challenging conception manifested itself in his Sonata for Viola and Piano, beginning with the cast of its four movements: I. Prelude for solo viola, without piano; II. The fugal Allegretto; III. The sharply rhythmical Toccata. The sonata is rounded off by the deliberately encoded "Greek" title of its fourth movement — *Apolarerion*. Its meaning (derived from "apò" and "laleō") could be interpreted as "the ending of speech," which is quite appropriate for a finale; or burial song. But the main point is that the entire finale in the viola's part repeats the first movement played from the last note to the first in a retrograde inversion (similar to the idea underlying Hindemith's *Ludus tonalis*), but here with the piano in counterpoint. In this way the first movement played twice and formally rooted in C tonality, at the same time is based on the four-note group c – b – a – b♭ (reminiscent of the BACH lettered theme) in every possible combination of these tones. The systematic statement of the group is akin to the use of the four-note series. The shattering forcefulness of the Toccata's key theme is attained by the technique of sharp rhythms — a skip of small duration: having strained the ear for pulsation in four eights, the composer all of a sudden at the end of the figure provides thirds:

Piano

Ex. 3 *Sonata for Viola and Piano, Third movement, Toccata*

Some of Andrei Volkonsky's compositions written in the mid-fifties have already been distinguished for a high professional level, quite worthy of concert performance on a par with the quartets and sonatas by Nikolai Myaskovsky and Dmitry Shostakovich.

The year 1956 proved a turning point in Volkonsky's creative evolution. It was the year of Nikita Khrushchev's anti-Stalinist report and the beginning of the "Thaw", and the year of the Polish musical avant-garde. But it was his own creative maturity that gave the composer the main impetus. Far from reaching as yet the most radical forms of "new tonality" or "atonality," he turned then to dodecaphony and the serial technique. Though, some of his compositions were still written in his former style, among them the incidental scores to Sartre's play *Only the Truth (Nekrasov)* and the radio production of *Midnight in Rome*, both in 1956, and the Trio for brass instruments.

Musica stricta was a small cycle of piano pieces written in 1956 in which the composer decidedly parted with the tonal style. He defined its character as "strict." Indeed, concentration on the inner relationships, avoidance of vivid sensory sonoristic effects and immersion into the exquisite world of pitch microintervalics — all of this produced an absolutely novel musical impression. THE NEW MUSIC WAS BORN. Of course, it was just his first experience in this field. The first movement in this cycle represents a polyphonic prelude.

Ex. 4

Technically, this music is based on a four-note series acting within the twelve-semi-tone pitch system. The listener has no need to discern the number of notes in the series, perceiving the twelve-note tonality. Therefore, in its type such music belongs already to dodecaphony[4]. The subsequent movements are still more radical. The second movement represents a ricercare on a twelve-note theme with interludes in triple counterpoint of twelve-note melodies. Two twelve-note series form the basis of the third movement (*Lento rubato*). The toccata-like finale is a double fugue on the twelve-note themes. "Fantasia ricercata," the subtitle of the composition, is explicitly oriented on a Baroque sonata with its focus on the paired movements of the "prelude — fugue" type.

At present it is hard for a musician to imagine the impact the birth of New Music had in Soviet Russia in 1956. The unregulated dissonance or chromaticism was looked upon as ideological sedition. As for dodecaphony, it was lying completely outside the tenets of "socialist realism," even beyond the control of the party supervisors over the arts. This is how the composer reminisces about the emergence of his serial music: "At first nobody even understood what it was. For a few more years, my compositions

---

[4] It is noteworthy that the great Stravinsky took up the serial technique just three years before, starting also with the four-note series (*Three Songs from William Shakespeare*, written in the summer of 1953). But Volkonsky could hardly be aware of the fact, for he studied dodecaphony from Schoenberg (Op. 25). Perhaps Stravinsky paved his own way to the serial technique in the similar microseries in No. 11 "Pas d'action" in his ballet *Orpheus* (the three–tone pattern g#. a. c.).

went on to be performed. But since 1962 my music has been banned once and for all."[5] The latter words should not be taken to the letter, but on the whole that was what actually happened.

The emergence of Volkonsky's New Music ushered in a new period in Russian music — *the beginning of the Russian avant-garde.* Of course, it involved a number of other young composers, among them Nikolai Karetnikov, Edison Denisov, Alfred Schnittke, Sophia Gubaidulina and Rodion Shchedrin. But the destiny willed it so that it was Volkonsky who should be the first among them. For this reason precisely he came to be regarded as the father and leader of the postwar Russian avant-garde.

In the Soviet Union of those years the only way to go on living, to get one's compositions performed in concerts and published, if only occasionally, was to split one's personality: one side had to be suitable to the ideological authorities while the other side lived entirely for oneself. In describing such a kind of mentality George Orwell has coined a word which has already become part of the modern vocabulary: *doublethink.* Even the greatest musicians sometimes stood no chance to avoid it. Andrei Volkonsky was organically incapable of such doublethinking. But along with composing music he was almost equally engaged in *performing activities.*

As early as in 1955, together with the well-known viola player Rudolf Barshai, Volkonsky set up a new performing body — the Moscow Chamber Orchestra. His friendly relations with Barshai inspired him to write a sonata for viola. Afterwards, however, these two musicians parted. Since 1956 (up to his emigration in 1977) it was Barshai who directed the Moscow Chamber Orchestra. As for Volkonsky, he left the orchestra in 1957 to find himself in playing the harpsichord. Guided by the goal he set before himself — "to get away from the Viennese classics" — Volkonsky gave up the piano to take up the early masters and old-time musical instruments, going from the piano to the harpsichord and the organ. During the period from 1957 to 1972 Volkonsky made numerous concert appearances in Moscow and went on a tour of other cities.

The paradox of Andrei Volkonsky's artistic conception lay in the unity of two seemingly diametrically opposing and even mutually excluding trends. On the one hand, early as in the 1950s he became the leader of the most radical innovations in modern music; on the other hand, he turned to the preclassical art, and not only to Bach but even to the earlier composers of France, Germany, Italy and Great Britain. With Volkonsky, it was not a breach, contradiction or "neoclassicism", it was a novel perception of *the integrity of music in the historical time,* undoubtedly, an innovative experience sharply breaking from conventional tastes. Attachment to the customary repertoire ranging from Bach and Handel to Rachmaninov, Liszt and Wagner was universal, embracing concert programmes, radio, musical theatre and musical training (especially with performing musicians)[6]. The departure outside the framework of the

---

[5] From an interview given to Andrei Lischke. *La Pensée russe* newspaper, 1973.

[6] It is noteworthy that in his treatise Roman Gruber, an authority among the historians of Western music, while characterizing the fourteenth-century motet uses such terms as the scholastic approach", "scholastic sluggishness" and "abstract logicizing." The early music written during the Middle Ages and Renaissance was not considered to be alive.

established musical consciousness was naturally two-sided, "forward" and "back-ward" – both to his own forms inherent in mid-twentieth-century music and the Baroque, Renaissance, medieval music. But these two trends had something in common: the thinking based not on functional harmony but on polyphonic procedures. In this respect Volkonsky seemed to follow the ideas initiated by Sergei Taneyev and Igor Stravinsky.

Andrei Volkonsky played Bach, Telemann, the French harpsichordists and British virginalists. The harpsichord was looked upon then as an instrument gone and past. The modern piano was esteemed as an instrument that naturally replaced the harpsichord due to its performing qualities — the lively and noble tone, the ability to "sing" (overcoming its percussive nature), the dynamic scope comparable to a symphony orchestra, and a wealth of its tone-colours. Moreover, harpsichords were believed to be unavailable in this country. The message that Volkonsky had aspired to convey as a performer immediately convinced the general public of the harpsichord's full artistic value for early music. The audience discerned the historical adequacy of the harpsichord to the preclassical music. It had been created not for the piano but for other keyboard instruments, primarily for harpsichord.

Andrei Volkonsky's performance of pieces by the early masters attracted not only by the perception of *genuine music*. Out of the two main approaches to the performance of early music — the historico-protective and creatively interpretative, the latter was more close to his heart. To play not imitating the supposed performing manner inherent in the times of Bach or Purcell but in a style prompted by the modern perception of rhythm and harmony. "Bach is not a museum" was the underlying principle in Volkonsky's treatment of the Baroque music. Bach was modern at the stage of the 18th century. One should avoid any stylization *à la antique*. Thus, once playing Bach's Fourth French Suite in E – flat major in a concert at the Moscow Scientists Club, Volkonsky gave a Staccato – like rendering of the Sarabande through the rows of eighths moving along the scales (in Egon Petri's romantic edition it is marked as "legato egualmente" and "soave"). The contrast between the measured legato and this staccatissimo produced a striking effect owing to the sharply accentuated rhythmical division of the musical form. Volkonsky thus spoke about his attitude to early music: "I have never been interested nor engaged in stylization, for I regard it the worst thing that can be. No, the impact was rather the reverse: my own pursuit in composition reflected itself in my performance"[7].

Andrei Volkonsky appeared not only as a soloist but also in a ensemble with other Soviet musicians. Thus, the Melodia Recording Company released the discs carrying his rendering, together with the violinist Eduard Grach, of Six Sonatinas for Violin and Harpsichord by Georg F. Telemann (CM 02951–2), and three sonatas for viola da gamba by J.S. Bach (D-019115–6), in a duet with the cellist Daniil Shafran.

The chief achievement of Andrei Volkonsky in the sphere of interpretative art was the Madrigal Ensemble of Early Music, which he set up in 1964. Its foundation met the artistic requirements of the time, opening up therefore a new promising trend in the interpretative art. Volkonsky's artistic conceptions turned out to be most adequate in

---

[7] Cited from an interview given to the Paris-based newspaper *La Pensée russe* in 1973.

this domain. His musical gift, his knowledge of diverse preclassical compositions and his artistic authority contributed to the success of this new undertaking. A kind of "harmony" was also attained in his relationships with the Composers Union, which by this time had banned Volkonsky's modern music completely. Early music written by the universally recognized composers was free from any ideological suspicions and "bourgeois" influences and had nothing in common with the modern composition procedures. Besides, the Composers Union, as a rule, was on good terms with the interpretative artists.

The Madrigal Ensemble, not very constant in its membership, was based on a group of singers-soloists, a player (players) of keyboard instruments — harpsichord and organ (Volkonsky himself), players of bow and wind instruments, and a percussionist. Several musicians who over different periods of time had been engaged in the Madrigal Ensemble became the distinguished artists, among them the Singer Lydia Davydova, who later appeared on numerous occasions as an interpreter of modern music, Artistic Director of the Madrigal Ensemble in recent years; the three singers — Karina, Ruzanna and Ruben, children of Pavel Lisitsian (singing with the Madrigal since 1965); the remarkable pianist Boris Berman (a member of the Madrigal since 1970, who also gave frequent performances of modern twentieth-century music), and Mark Pekarsky, now a well-known percussion player.

The repertoire of the Madrigal Ensemble under Andrei Volkonsky included predominantly the music dating back to the 16th and 17th centuries. It often gave monographic concerts featuring some definite national schools of a certain period — in Italy, Spain, France, Germany, Flanders, England and Russia. It performed the works of celebrated and little-known composers, as well as quite a few anonymous pieces. Those were madrigals by Gesualdo, madrigals and the magnificat *(Vesperae)* by Monteverdi, the compositions of Orazio Vecchi, Luca Marenzio, Palestrina's mass, the ballades by Guillaume de Machaut, chansons by Janequin *(Bird-Song)*, the pieces by Tomas Luis de Vittoria, Luis de Milan, Antonio de Cabezon, Diego Ortiz; "Spanish Music Under the Castilian Kings," Schütz, Purcell, and "Russian Music of the Period Prior to Peter the Great." Andrei Volkonsky was the first to take the challenge and turn to the early Russian church music, which was virtually under an official ban.

The performing style of the Madrigal fully reflected its director's artistic conception: no "historical" stylization, with the material of early music being treated as the alive modern melody. To quote Volkonsky once again, "The notations of medieval music are quite conditional, for up to Monteverdi any definite orchestration was non-existent. This music cannot be played monotonously and without nuances, as many ensembles do it, particularly where it concerns secular music. It is enough to look at the pictures by Flemish painters, for instance, by Bruegel to see that the austere and monotonous manner of performance could hardly be adequate to such merry and unconstrained people." Lively rhythms accentuated by the percussions added according to one's taste and the expressive tonality of human speech used to impart the licentious character to the performance of early music. Sometimes this approach led even to some risky liberties. Thus, while playing the early music for the organ Andrei Volkonsky could make use of the effect of strong overtones with their too colourful and almost false sounds. Indeed, there is something behind the "con stranezza e durezza" notes occasionally provided by the past masters of Baroque music.

The Madrigal Ensemble scored a great and well-deserved success. The young musicians made a frequent tour of the country, giving nearly a hundred concerts a year. The Madrigal went on tour in the other countries as well — East Germany, Romania, Poland and Czechoslovakia. The Madrigal turned out to be safety valve for Volkonsky in the Soviet musical life, without him having to give up his ideological convictions.

Meanwhile, his musical creativity was developing according to its own laws. The external circumstances failed to exert any effect on him, and he was confidently advancing into the novel domains of New Music. Though in each of his new compositions he mastered a novel technique, devoid of any apprenticeship. As a truly modern composer, Anderi Volkonsky was striving for novel content in every one of his new pieces.

Along with his film and theatre scores (he wrote the incidental scores to the film *Wishes Coming True*, directed by V.S. and Z.S. Brumberg, 1957, together with Nikolai Sidelnikov; to the film *Puss in Boots* by Sergei Mikhalkov, 1958; and to Bernard Shaw's tragedy *Saint Joan,* 1957), Volkonsky composed *Music for Twelve Instruments,* Op. 12, 1957 and *Serenade to an Insect* for chamber orchestra, 1958.

The year 1959 brought forth his song-cycle *Suite of Mirrors,* a setting of Federico Garcia Lorca for soprano and ensemble of the following instruments: flute, violin, guitar, piccolo organ, percussion (triangle, temple-block, wooden drum, drum, cymbals, gong). This composition proved a milestone in Russian music. The vivid sunlit gentle colors combined with the piquant agile sonority of the instruments predominantly in the medium-pitch register, and the enchanting "mirror-like" reflections in melodies and harmonies, all of this distinguished Volkonsky's cycle out of a large amount of pieces written by his contemporaries. The prevailing tone in Soviet music around 1960 was either austere, dramatic, earthly or frivolous.

Andrei Volkonsky came to serialism through refined polyphony corresponding with neoclassicism. But you find no trace of the latter in his *Suite of Mirrors*. His music has now delivered itself from the ballast of the Baroque-type polyphonic themes, from the impressive but encumbering fugues and triple counterpoints in favour of the microthemes adequate to the modern music. Furthermore, the eight-note series $e\flat$ -$g\flat$ -f- d-$a\flat$ -$c\flat$ -$b\flat$ -g has been structured à la Webern, with repetition enclosed within repetition. His music has brought to the fore a new trend which in its evolution has left far behind the predominating folklore–neoclassical style of the majority. The normal development abreast of the times was viewed as ideological sabotage. Besides, Lorca's verse selected by the composer was a challenge to the Marxist-Leninist precepts of the Soviet art, with its initial line reading as follows: "Christ holds a mirror in each hand." The tonal reflections were expressive of the idea that the mirrors multiplied Christ's appearance (using the series $e\flat$ -c-$d\flat$ -$f\flat$ -$b\flat$ -g-$a\flat$ -$c\flat$).

The composition he wrote the next year, in the same genre of song-cycle, revealed the rapid progress made by the young composer. In contrast to the *Suite of Mirrors,* which is a transparent and graphically clear-cut piece despite its certain refinement, *Shchaza's Laments,* his new song-cycle, is an intricate piece in its style and message, marked even for its too keen expressiveness. The contrast between the style of the text

Ex. 5 *Suite of Mirrors, First movement, Symbol*

and the music is striking[8]. The unsophisticated folk style of the verses enters into interaction with the music, sometimes reminiscent of Pierre Boulez, with their artlessness being completely absorbed by the subtlety of the music and its avant-gardist style.

Shchaza's Laments are intended for soprano and ensemble of the following instruments: cor anglais, violin, viola, marimbaphone, vibraphone and harpsichord (and tambourine in the second movement). The first movement is Vocalise (a wordless cantilena), *Lento ma non troppo*, flowing imperceptibly into the *Presto* cantilena of the gentlest sound, shadows of the second movement constantly broken down by the micropauses; while trying to describe the second movement, Stravinsky's words about Boulez's *Marteau sans Maître* come to one's mind: "the ice cubes seem to be ringing in a glass coming across one another." The third movement provides relaxation: in the space of medium tessitura there twinkle the varicolored dots of sounds; a play of time, which is now dragging slowly, then suddenly pressing, and again stretching. The finale is reminiscent of the second movement by its pointillistic cantilena, all the time cut across by the rests of various depth, though marked for the extremely rich texture built up out of the smallest fragments and dots, divided by micropauses. A kind of

---

8   Shchaza was a folk Lak poetess (Daghestan, the Caucasus) who used to recite her verses during festivities and weddings, acting as an improviser.

quintuple counterpoint of the mixed pitch lines in the twelve-note space leads to the recurrence of the first movement, rounding off the whole cycle in a wide and impressive way. Example 6 shows an episode from its final movement.

Before his compositions were finally banished, Andrei Volkonsky had at least got commissions for film scores, which allowed him to earn his living. Nevertheless, he went on composing and his artistic creations during that period included the aleatory *Play à trois*, 1961; *The Vagrant Concerto* for three soloists and twenty-six instruments, 1964–67; *Réplique* for chamber ensemble, 1969; and *Les mailles du temps* for three groups of instruments, 1969.

But this music had virtually no audience. The pressure of ideological bans was becoming universal and unceasing. The magazine *Sovetskaya muzyka*, that mouthpiece of Soviet ideology, wrote: "Somewhere, apart from a great life of our music, there exists a closed, narrow world of formal quests and fruitless experimentation."[9] "A great life" was associated with "the road towards communism," which was to arrive in 1980, as Nikita Krushchev had pompously pledged. The composers Andrei Volkonsky, Valentin Silvestrov and Arvo Pärt were staying away from this great life (Ibidem). Not only the party authorities persecuted the innovators. Many of their jealous colleagues, particularly officials of the Composers Union, took every chance to shove back their more successful and talented counterparts. Life is life... Later on Volkonsky spoke with bitter irony about the situation prevailing in the sixties: "I was a greasy spot on the marble monument of Soviet music."

The atmosphere of persecution for his music, which was aggravated by his collisions with the authorities of the Moscow Philharmonic Society, the official employers of the Madrigal Ensemble, and his feeling that his work as a composer held no promise in this country eventually made Volkonsky think about leaving Russia. One of the most feasible ways to leave his motherland was to join the widening exodus of Soviet Jews. The Russian composer decided to apply for emigration from the USSR.

The Volkonsky case was considered by the Board of the Moscow branch of the Composers Union. Here is an extract from the minutes of the session held by the Presidium of its Board on December 7, 1972: Upon hearing the matter on the expulsion of Volkonsky from the Composers Union "in view of his forthcoming departure for Israel," it was decided that the Moscow branch of the Composers Union "condemns the decision of A.M. Volkonsky and thinks it to be incompatible with the ideological and political position of a member of the Composers Union and therefore he is unworthy of remaining among its membership." In 1973 Volkonsky left for the West, to reside permanently in Western Europe.

This is one of the most burning problems in Russian culture: Russia and the West. And one of its vital aspects is the problem of totalitarian restrictions placed on creativity in the USSR and spiritual freedom in the West. The solution of the problem seems clear enough: leaving the USSR, a musician acquires at long last an opportunity to create without any obstacles, his compositions could now be performed and recorded. He is no longer instructed how he should develop a musical theme and what is the proper way to reflect the reality. But has the forty-year-old composer, one of the

---

[9] Tikhon Khrennikov. "On the Road to the Musical Culture of Communism," *Sovetskaya Muzyka* magazine, 1962, Issue, 6, p. 10.

Ex. 6 *Shchaza's Laments, Fourth movement*

most talented Russian musicians, achieved the peak in his creative quests? Yes, indeed, he has produced quite a number of works while living over there, still not repeating himself and discovering something novel in each of the following compositions. There are no weak pieces among them; written predominantly in the chamber genre, all of them are captivating by their diversity:

> Mugham for Tar and Harpsichord, 1974;
> *Lied* for four singing voices, 1977–78;
> *Immobile* for piano and orchestra, 1978;
> *Was noch lebt* for three mezzo-soprano and string trio, 1985;
> *Psalm 148* for three voices, organ and kettledrum, 1989.

The first half of the 1970s witnessed the upsurge of "the second avant–garde" in West–European music, marked for its movement towards greater simplicity and accessibility to the listeners. Andrei Volkonsky still held himself independent of the current fashions in musical progress, aspiring to go on his own way. He was even inclined to be somewhat critical in his attitude to the Western culture as well, discerning some signs of self-destruction in the Western civilization. He just wanted to write beautiful music. As a matter of fact, he remained the same person which he used to be in Russia. But in the situation prevailing in Soviet culture in the 1950s and 1960s he found a powerful impetus for his creativity in a sharp difference between the artistic perception of modern music in his soul and the spiritual atmosphere surrounding him, which had to be overcome, and he felt in himself plenty of creative forces for such overcoming. This powerful aspiration was also essential for the self–discovery of one's artistic individuality. Admittedly, the obstacles set before the talented composer for many years by the officials of the Composers Union (and therefore by the envious colleagues) interfered with his creative work. However, this could not sully his reputation, making the true musicians look up at him as the bearer of supreme values in art and the leader of modern Russian music. As for the West, no problems of such kind have ever arisen there.

Two of the above mentioned compositions are associated with German culture. *Lied* for four voices was commissioned by Westdeutsche Rundfunk for the Wittener Tage für neue Kammermusik festival. The text was borrowed from *Glogauer Liederbuch* (a collection of 15th century German songs)[10], presented as the interweaving of the initial words and song fragments (*Quodlibet*). Originally, Volkonsky even wanted to entitle his work in the same way: *Quodlibet*. According to the composer, after he had tackled serial music for so many years he felt a sudden urge to place three flats at the clef in the staves[11]. He tried his best to produce purely "German music" as far as it was possible, discarding any intellectual speculation. It should be understood as his refusal to follow the fashion which he believes to have exhausted itself[12].

The other work, *Was noch lebt,* was set to the text by the German writer Johannes Bobrowski whose biography had been closely tied with Russia. Bobrowski took part in Hitler's action on the Russian land during the last war, was taken prisoner and then came to live in East Germany. His verses reflected many Russian and Baltic motifs: *Nowgorod (Ankunft der Heiligen), Der Ilmensee 1941, Sergej aus Rjazan, Rostow am Don, Litauische Lieder,* and *Lettische lieder.* The three poems by Bobrowski selected for setting are marked for their highly expressive lyricism, polysemantic imagery fraught with many things untold, and intricate metrics. The song–cycle has three movements: I. Strandgänger, II. Ebene, and III. Sprache. The first song begins with the following lines:

---

[10] In the edition: Das Erbe deutscher Musik, Bd. 4, Kassel, 1954.

[11] See the annotation to this composition in the edition: "Musik der Zeit IY. Begegnung mit der Sowjetunion," März 1979, Westdeutsche Rundfunk, Köln, [1979, S. 16].

[12] Ibidem.

The midday flame is still over the edge of reeds
And no rustle of swans heard as yet over the dunes.

And it ends with the following invocation:

— What is my name? Who am I? How long am I to stay here?

Ex. 7 *Was noch lebt, Third movement, Sprache*

The setting of Bobrowski's cycle was conceived in the traditions of German vocal lyrics dating back to the Romantic period, reminiscent sometimes of Brahms, of Mahler and slightly of the early Schoenberg. The three pieces are united by the kindred melodic turns based on the "sighing tone" and characteristic parallel thirds, all of them delivered in the transparent soft tone-colors of the accompanying bow instruments.

Having abandoned the serial technique, which he used in his own, non-orthodox manner, Andrei Volkonsky retained its allergic sensitivity of each, even the smallest, melodic line, here manifested in the imitative polyphonic texture of all the voices.

To discover something novel in each composition and not repeat himself has been the principle underlying nearly all of Andrei Volkonsky's works. In his *Psalm 148* he turns to the "eternal" Latin text where the Prophet calls for praising God and divine forces and all people, and all the dumb and even inanimate creatures. For His glory extends over the earth and the heavens. The musical conception in this case is modal. Three homogeneous voices (either female or male) are singing the ecstatic alleluia in a capricious fanciful rhythm akin to Stravinsky's. It is noteworthy that all the sounds of three voices from beginning to end belong to the same scale e-f#-g-g#-a#-b-c#-d.

The missing four pitches from the sole chord played *secco* by the organ and the kettledrum, repeated invariably throughout the piece and rounding off the composition by its triple statement.

Ex. 8 *Psalm 148*

In technical terms, it is a kind of complementary polymodality founded on the purely twelve-note basis. In the spirit of the preclassical music the composer does not provide for the signs of dynamics, leaving this to the discretion of the performers.

As before, Andrei Volkonsky is engaged in intensive performing activities, playing primarily the harpsichord and touring in France, Italy, Great Britain, Germany, Switzerland, and Finland. In 1981, he set up in Geneva an ensemble of early music, Hoc Opus, a sort of Western sequel to the Moscow-based Madrigal. As a harpsichordist and director of the Hoc Opus Ensemble, he has repeatedly recorded the music of early masters, among them the first volume of Bach's *Well-Tempered Clavier* in its original, "non-museum" treatment. For many years now Volkonsky has been a board member of the Belayev Relief Fund for Russian musicians. His latest composition is *Carrefour* for instrumental ensemble comprising a synthesizer, piano, oboe, two bassoons, two French horns, violin and double-bass (1992). "Carrefour" ("At the Crossroads") is the name of a café at Aix-en-Provence which the composer likes to frequent.

Fortunately, Andrei Volkonsky, though no longer young, is still in his prime, full of energy and creative plans in his work as a composer and interpretative artist.

PRINCIPAL WORKS

For Singers and orchestra

Rus, cantata to the text by Nikolai Gogol (1952)
The Image of the World, cantata to the text by Paul Eluard (1953)

For orchestra (including **chamber orchestra**)

Concerto for Orchestra (1953)
Capriccio for Orchestra (1953–54)
Serenade to an Insect (1958)
Les mailles du temps for three groups (13 instruments; 1969)

For piano and orchestra

Immobile (1977–78)

Chamber Instrumental Pieces

Trio for Piano, Violin and Cello (1950–51)
Piano Quintet (1954)
Sonata for Viola and Piano (1955)
String Quartet (1955)
Trio for Two Trumpets and Trombone (1956)
Play à trois, mobile for flute, violin and harpsichord (1961)
Replique for ensemble (1969)
Mugham for Tar and Harpsichord (1974)
Carrefour for instrumental ensemble: a synthesizer, piano, oboe, two bassoons, two French horns, violin, double-bass (1992)

Piano Works

Sonata B–flat major (1949)
Musica stricta (1956)
Fantasia (1957)

Chamber Vocal Music

Suite of Mirrors, song-cycle for soprano, flute, violin, guitar, piccolo organ and percussion, verses by Federico Garcia Lorca (1959)
Shchaza's Laments for soprano, English horn, violin, viola, marimbaphone, vibraphone and harpsichord, verses by Shchaza (1960)
The Vagrant Concerto for voice, flute, violin, and twenty-six instruments, verses by Omar Khayyam (1964–67)
Lied for four voices (1978)
Was noch lebt, song–cycle for mezzo–soprano and string trio, verses by Johannes Bobrowski (1985)
Psalm 148 for three homogeneous voices (either female or male; a version for three–voice homogeneous chorus) with the accompaniment of the organ chord and kettledrum, a biblical text (1989)

Incidental Scores to radio productions

Little Song in the Forest (1954)
Midnight in Rome (1956)

Incidental scores to plays

Jean-Paul Sartre's play *Only the Truth (Nekrasov,* 1956)
Bernard Shaw's tragedy *Saint Joan* (1957)

Film scores

Wishes Coming True, directed by V.S. and Z.S. Brumberg (1957)
Puss in Boots, directed by Sergei Mikhalkov (1957)
cartoons: *Man for Man* (1959), *The Mystery of a Distant Island* (1959), *A Pigeon-toed Friend* (1960), *Maria, a Skilful Girl* (1960), *Yaskhan* (1961), *Kiddie's Adventures* (1961).

Philip Gershkovich's search for the lost essence of music

Yuri Kholopov

Philip Gershkovich

"The Second Viennese School" in Moscow? During all the Soviet years "socialist realism" ruling in Russian music has been fighting against the Second Viennese School and its founders Schoenberg and Webern. Their compositions were neither performed, nor published, nor studied. Yet, paradoxically enough, in the course of 47 years there lived and worked in Russia an adherent of the Second Viennese School, a remarkable person, a theoretician of music, composer and pedagogue — Philip Moiseyevich Gershkovich. A man who has traversed the roads of three countries, all his life striving for his cherished goal — to get down to the essence of music.

Philip Gershkovich (Filip Herščovici) was born on September 7, 1906 in Romania. But he perceived Germany and Austria as his spiritual homeland, for there, as he believed, lay the sources of genuine music. In his declining years, in the 1980s, he wrote to Heinrich Böll: "The German people is a vessel for German music. And I'm not just a musician, but in a strange and bizarre way a *German* musician. I, who was born in Jassy, in the Jewish quarters, who in his childhood could hardly imagine that there were other people on earth but the Jews and Romanians"[1].

Upon graduation from the Jassy Conservatoire the young musician went to Vienna to study, in 1927–29, at the Music Academy with Joseph Marx in his class of musical theory and composition. Dissatisfied with his studies at the Academy, Gershkovich left it.

Philip Gershkovich's compatriot, composer Klepper, a pupil of Franz Schreker, advised him to go and study music with Alban Berg. Gershkovich thus describes his impressions from his first visit to Alban Berg's home in 1928: it "shakes a man without overwhelming him. (Webern *crushed* and destroyed a man in order to build then something *different*, new out of him.) Alban Berg was an incomparable personification

---

[1] Cited from the book: Philip Gershkovich on Music. Articles, Notes, Letters, and Memoirs. Moscow, Sovetsky Kompozitor, 1991, 346 pp. Published by Mrs. Gershkovich jointly with Leonid Hofmann (Chief Editor) and Alexander Vustin. The present article is based mainly on this remarkably extensive collection of materials and documentary evidence; hereinafter referred to only by indicating the pages. Another penetrating study of Gershkovich's views and inner world is offered in the article by Dmitry Smirnov "A Visitor from an Unknown Planet: Music in the Eyes of Filipp Herschkowitz / / Tempo, London, No. 173 (June 1990). Soviet ed., pp. 34–38. See also a feature article "Herschkowitz Encountered, Herschkowitz Remembered", Ibidem, pp. 39–43 (Victor Suslin, G. McBurney, D. Drew).

of *gentle beauty* spiced with a remarkable sense of irony" (p. 338). In his memoirs Gershkovich writes: "When I came to Alban Berg I hated the very word and concept of 'form'. In those years many musicians believed that the destruction of a form was the main lever in musical progress. When Berg started showing *Wozzeck* to his new pupil, it triggered off "a very-very slow revolution" in the latter's soul, whose "(semi)-end" took place half a century later during the Moscow period of his life (pp. 341–342).

In the summer of 1932 Gershkovich went on probation attending the conducting courses in Strasbourg under Hermann Scherchen, and in 1932–38 he was working at Universal Edition. Thus, after Berg's decease in 1935 Gershkovich took part, as a proof-reader, in the first publications of his tutor's Violin Concerto, the klavierauszug of his opera *Lulu* and the orchestral suite *Lulu*.

It was from Berg that Gershkovich for the first time heard the word-combination "the Second Viennese School." To elucidate the contributions made by this school to world music, Berg asked Anton Webern to take on Gershkovich as his pupil. Beginning in February 1934 and up to September 1939 Gershkovich took lessons from this "master of pianissimo," visiting his "modest and very clean little house" in Maria Enzersdorf in the environs of Vienna three times a month, with a lesson lasting two hours. Upon learning that the young musician could not pay for his lessons, Webern gave them free of charge[2]. What was this extremist and modernist teaching? Following in the traditions of his own tutor Schoenberg, Webern disclosed for his pupil the art of the great masters, primarily Beethoven whom he idolized and in whose work the musical form had reached the peak of its development. While Webern was as young as Gershkovich when the latter came to study with him on a recommendation of Alban Berg, who wrote in his letter to Berg that Beethoven's birthday should be celebrated in the same way as Christmas Day. It was with profound reverence that Webern analyzed Beethoven's piano sonatas. He believed that their understanding was the prime task in the science of composition. According to Gershkovich, Webern used to make his pupils study Beethoven's sonatas for five years before he passed on to dodecaphony. Main Webern's own theory was based primarily on the *fest* — *locker* (firm — loose) opposition in the structure of the classical form. He also taught development of a theme through splitting and "liquidation" — transformation of a theme into a great amount of small units devoid of self-sufficiency. Proceeding from Schoenberg's definition of a motive as part of a musical idea capable of self-contained independence and thereby of repetition, Webern developed this concept further, differentiating between the motive as belonging to the domain of rhythm and duration, and the pitch to that of thematic arrangement. Following in the footsteps of Schoenberg, Webern asked his pupils first to compose a theme (in the form of a period, a sentence or a three-part song) and only then whole forms in an increasing order of their structural development, logically deducing the next from complication of the previous one:

— a theme and variations;
— minuet with trio (and scherzo);
— Andante or small rondo, and a large rondo;
— Sonata form.

---

[2] Webern's archive kept in Basle (Paul Sacher Stiftung) contains the relevant evidence.

Probably, Webern introduced his pupils to dodecaphony much earlier than he actually tackled it in his lessons. In his reminiscences about the years of his study with Webern, Gershkovich thus spoke about his tutor: following my studies under Webern "I started to view the music of the great masters . . . as fundamentally differing from other music *in its essence.*" Webern "himself was music. Of course, he was in touch with the surrounding world as well. But on the whole he regarded it like a diver keeping contact with those staying on the shore. And the shore was out of Webern's element." "It is to Webern that I owe the meaning of my life: my attitude to music. He disclosed for me the value of such concept as 'Beethoven' . . . As a matter of fact, it is from him that *I learned the real meaning of music*" (pp. 62, 348, 347). Only once, during his studies in Vienna, Gershkovich had a chance to meet Schoenberg. On that day the teacher of Webern and Berg spoke about J.S. Bach: "Bach was the first composer with twelve notes."

And then on March 13, 1938 there came the *Anschluß* of Austria. The following May, at the exhibition of "degenerate art" held in Düsseldorf they were trying to allege that a triad was a German element in music while atonality meant "degeneration and cultural Bolshevism," with Schoenberg proclaimed to be "the father of atonality." Then on November 9/10, there came *Kristallnacht* in Germany. On January 30, 1939 in his speech Hitler declared: "Today I'm willing to make another prophecy. If the international financial Jewish community in Europe and outside it plunged the nations into another world war, it would result in the elimination of the Jewish race in Europe." On September 1, 1939 the second world war began and the same month Gershkovich had to leave Vienna ("as if running," as he said) and go back to Romania, Bucharest. In September 1940 the pro-German military dictators came to power in Romania and in November Gershkovich emigrated to the USSR where, up to June 22, 1941, he taught harmony in the town of Chernovtsy, in the western part of the Ukraine. On the first day of the war against Russia he moved eastwards and after four months of horror and hardships, having covered thousands of miles, found himself in Tashkent, Central Asia. Since 1946 he resided in Moscow. He earned his living by working as an editor and, since 1960, giving music lessons (among his pupils was Leonid Hofmann), composing and reading lectures in musical form and the theory of composition (in Leningrad, Kiev, Yerevan). It was a glimpse of the Second Viennese School in Moscow. Philip Gershkovich's remarkable musical gift, the originality of his views bearing the imprint of the mysterious (in those years) Second Viennese School, his captivating musical analyses, his extraordinary destiny of a pupil of Webern and Berg, and his fascinating personality — all combined to attract to him a lot of young musicians. One of them, Dmitry Smirnov, then a student at the Moscow Conservatoire, made notes of his lessons[3], part of which were to be published many years later[4]. In the mid-sixties the author of the present article, who was then working hard on his

---

[3]   Dmitry Smirnov. A Book about Gershkovich. MS (kept in the author's archive).

[4]   Dmitry Smirnov. "A Geometer of Tonal Crystals," *Sovetskaya muzyka* magazine, Nos 3–4, 1990.

monograph devoted to Anton Webern, in the course of nearly two years regularly visited Gershkovich at his flat in Moscow and had long talks with him about the musical theory, harmony, musical form and music analysis.

When Philip Gershkovich applied for emigration from the USSR, he met with a refusal. His name became officially banned, a ban which lasted for many years to come. In 1987, on an invitation of the Alban Berg Stiftung, Gershkovich left once again for Vienna where he died on January 5, 1989.

Most likely, it was his teaching musical theory in the sixties that prompted Gershkovich, who had at first regarded himself to be primarily a composer, to shift the centre of gravity in his activity into the domain of the musical science. Yet, in the 1970s and 1980s he still viewed *composition of music* as one of his prime tasks. In the recommendation letter given to him by Webern on their parting on September 9, 1939 the latter wrote: "I consider him (Gershkovich) first and foremost to be a remarkably gifted composer" (p. 351).

Indeed, the roads that a modern composer has to traverse are intricate and entangled. It seemed that Philip Gershkovich was destined to follow the Viennese tradition initiated by Beethoven and Brahms and developed by Berg and Webern. Yet, his life took a different course. During the first two decades of his residence in Moscow (the information about his previous life being unavailable; Gershkovich was in general not inclined to share the details of his creative work, both as a composer and musicologist) he tried occasionally to write music in the tonal style à la Bartok or Prokofiev. Once he played a short episode from his music in this style — it was indeed reminiscent of Prokofiev. But he took it not very seriously and in his legacy the opuses of this kind are missing. Example 1 is a sample of Gershkovich's free tonal style.

Ex. 1 *Five Piano Pieces*, No.1, Prelude

The first serial work produced by Andrei Volkonsky in 1956 gave rise to a new musical movement in Russia, which was to be known as "the Soviet avant-garde."[5]

---

[5] Gershkovich met Andrei Volkonsky on several occasions and they had talks. But the reports that Volkonsky studied dodecaphony with Gershkovich are invalid.

The musicians turned their attention to the modern composition procedures, including the serial technique cultivated by the adherents of the Second Viennese School. It turned out that one of them. . . lived quite nearby, in Moscow. Philip Gershkovich soon became famous, even fashionable. The fact that the authorities of the Composers Union were invariably fierce in their opposition to dodecaphony and the Schoenberg school and that the *Sovetskaya muzyka* magazine, a mouthpiece of the red-and-brown ideology was tireless in its criticism of the advanced musicians served only to enhance their unofficial esteem with the general public. Gershkovich, who taught harmony after Schoenberg's *Harmonielehre*, in the mid-sixties turned to the study of dodecaphony as a musical system. He made the profound analyses of Schoenberg's Suite, Op. 25, later (together with the Bulgarian musicologist Kipriana Drumeva) of Webern's cantata *Das Augenlicht (Eyesight)*, Op. 26, and Schoenberg's Violin Concerto. The final stage of a good analysis, according to Gershkovich, was the time when one could take up composing *one's own* music. Through the analysis of Viennese dodecaphony Philip Gershkovich opened up the new vistas in his own creative work.

Once Gershkovich remarked that Berg and Webern had learned from Schoenberg how to proceed further on independently. The modern music written by the Moscow-residing adherent of the Second Viennese School followed the tradition initiated by Schoenberg, rather than by his own tutors. Naturally enough, Gershkovich stood aloof from the growing influx of avant-garde music written in the 1960s and 1970s. He chose for himself the road of serious, strict, and profound art. The spectacular colors and inventions of the fiery contemporary avant-gardists left him sceptically cold and indifferent. He used to say: "All of them are Liszts," adding "Do you get me?" (that was one of his favorite phrases). He sharply criticized Olivier Messiaen's 3 *Petites Liturgies de la présence divine*. It was quite understandable: orienting on Arnold Schoenberg's aesthetics and procedures, he felt himself to be alien to the avant-gardists following the "Beethoven — Liszt" model. The last named composer was not in the line of the spiritual tradition initiated by the Second Viennese School to which Gershkovich belonged.

His earliest compositions have been lost. Most likely, the composer himself thought it unnecessary to preserve them. The available MSS[6] date back to the 1960s, all of them written in the chamber genre. It is during this time, approximately since the mid-sixties, that he began using dodecaphony as the sphere of musical thinking in his compositions. The list of his principal works, regrettably not too long, dates back to that period, among them Three Songs of Ion Barbu for voice and piano (Ion Barbu was a Romanian poet and mathematician[7], Four Pieces for Cello and Piano, Four Piano Pieces, and Four Songs of the German poet Paul Celan for voice and chamber orchestra. The last named song-cycle is the most revealing of Gershkovich as a

---

[6]   Gershkovich's compositions have remained unpublished, with their originals being currently kept in Vienna, except for his Capriccio for piano duet, released in 1957 by the Sovetsky Kompozitor Publishers in Moscow.

[7]   In one of his notes Gershkovich cites the idea advanced by Barbu: there is a close relationship between mathematics and a poetical metaphor.

composer. It is the music marked for deep inner concentration and emotionality of reminicent the early Schoenberg (à la *Das Buch der hängenden Gärten*), the tone of his music characterized by a grave and sensitive treatment of each sound sparsely chosen for his work.

The attempt to pinpoint the tradition followed by Philip Gershkovich in his music will undoubtedly reveal the line initiated by Arnold Schoenberg, inherent not so much in the affinity of their musical language but rather in the artistic conception as a spiritual orientation. To the same line belong his Four Pieces for Cello and Piano (another cycle written in the 1970s) in the strict twelve-note technique based on the series c-d♭ -f-e-b-g♯ -a-d-e♭ -g-f♯ -b♭ .

Ex. 2 *Four pieces for Cello and Piano, No. 2*

One of Gershkovich's best pieces is his Small Chamber Suite for mezzo-soprano, violin, two violas, cello, two clarinets and piano, set to the verses by Federico Garcia Lorca and Rainer Maria Rilke, written in 1979. Retaining the above described general tone of Gershkovich's music (it would be quite appropriate to define it as his individual style), this Suite is distinguished for diverse sonority and melodic expressiveness.

Philip Gershkovich's last composition was also a song-cycle — *Madrigals* for voice and chamber ensemble, set to the verses by Rainer Maria Rilke, Federico Garcia Lorca and Guillaume Apollinaire, written in 1983.

During his lifetime the composer's works were hardly ever performed. The Soviet system failed to accept them as it rejected the New Music written by Andrei Volkonsky, Edison Denisov, Sophia Gubaidulina, and Alfred Schnittke. Philip Gershkovich's musical compositions are marked for one precious quality: it is good music which is undoubtedly to find eventually its way to the listeners.

However, it is not his compositions but musicological works and his impact as a music teacher that have left the most noticeable imprint. His scholarly papers (all to be found in the above mentioned collection) include: "Tonal Sources of Schoenberg's Dodecaphony" (its translation was published in *Nuova Rivista Musicale Italiana*, No. 4 for 1974); "One of Johann Sebastian Bach's Inventions (On the Origins of the Classical Sonata Form)"; "Webern and His Teaching, Dodecaphony and Tonality"; "Mozart and Beethoven"; "Notes on Mahler's Work"; "One of Beethoven's Tonal Problems (*Kreutzer Sonata*)"; several analytic articles about Beethoven's sonatas — Op. 2 No. 1, Op. 2 No. 3, Op. 7, Op. 10, No. 1, Op. 10, No. 2, Op. 27 No. 1, Op. 81a, Op. 106, and about Beethoven's string quartets, etc.; all these articles were written over the period from the 1960s to the 1980s.

The musical theory cultivated by the Second Viennese School came into sharp contradiction with the official Soviet science, which served an additional impetus for the intensive musicological research studies undertaken by Webern's pupil. This opposition was especially acute as regards the problem of paramount importance for the Second Viennese School, Webern in particular and Gershkovich as his follower — that of *form*. Moreover, the very teaching of composition was primarily designed to master the classical musical form[8]. The ideological tenets of the Soviet art were based on such rigidly aggressive black-and-white antitheses as "idealism/materialism and "formalism/realism." The fatal linkage between the "anti-people's," "bourgeois" *formalism* and musical *form* [9] led to the treatment of "form" exclusively as "manifestation of content," which was positively appraised only in a case if it corresponded to the Soviet dogmas on "moral intelligence" and "popular spirit." Only those works that led "our people" to the bright future of communism were considered to be "morally intelligent." A "popular spirit" was allegedly inherent only in those works that bore the obvious traces of folk music, expressed the sentiments of common Soviet people and their leaders, and drew a truthful picture of the people's life. Philip Gershkovich's approach to music as a form was fundamentally alien to the Soviet official doctrine[10]. As is known, extremes meet. Gershkovich used to say: "This is right. Music is indeed

---

[8] Schoenberg's book *Fundamentals of Musical Composition* (published posthumously in 1967, London) is a kind of textbook in musical form

[9] "Anti-people's" was virtually identical with the term "an enemy of the people," which eventually entailed a prison, a camp or even execution. . .

[10] It is noteworthy that the Soviet musicologists obliterated the very science of "musical form" from the educational system.

formalism." "The form of a given work constitutes some *definite arrangement of certain quantity* of something, essentially *non-existent outside* the strict relationship between precisely *this* arrangement and *this* quantity. For this reason *a form is primary*. For this reason *a form makes the essence of a work."* "The point is that the word 'form', which has arisen under some definite historical conditions, has long lost its touch with the corresponding concept. What we call a form of a given phenomenon it is *its essence*. Thus, for instance, the essence of a chemical element determining the latter's *properties* and inherent in its atomic weight, quantity and arrangement of its electrones, etc represents, *from the positions of music*, the form of a given element" (p. 140). In its basic *essence* a form does not depend on an epoch during which a composition came into being. But the *level* of musical form's development does depend on the epoch (Ibidem, p. 190). Beethoven's work may be regarded as a powerful mountain ridge of epoch-making significance in the historical evolution of musical form.

For Gershkovich, as in the case of Webern, the science of composition was not divided into separate disciplines. But in its general outlines he distinguished three things: harmony, texture and form. He regarded texture as *Tonsatz*, an art of creating a tonal fabric of a work, which presumes all possible kinds of counterpoint and homophonic methods of its structuring. Harmony was treated not as a combination of chords or a play of cadences (he used to make fun of the latter when he recalled his student years at the Music Academy in Vienna). "In this composition form and harmony mutually determine each other" (p. 63). They are indivisible in the same way as pitch and duration of a sound, its indispensable attributes. "Musical form con-stitutes *musical time* without which harmony as *an exponent of the sound system* does not exist in nature" (p. 19).

In contrast to Beethoven viewed as the peak in the evolution of form, Bach repre-sents the highest point in the development of bimodal tonal system. Since with Bach the secondary dominants began gravitating towards the tonic center, his tonality came to embrace not seven but all twelve notes. Herein lay the stage of complete develop-ment achieved in the bimodal Major/Minor system. After Bach the development of harmony has been directed towards creating new harmonic categories of form, the most important of which is *modulation*. In contrast to the childish understanding of modulation as an introduction of any element alien to diatonics, the secondary dominants and the attendant departures have nothing to add to modulation. "Modulation as a phenomenon is characterized by a certain duality: belonging to harmony in the nature of its resources, in its function it is *a category of musical form*" (p. 22). Such concept of modulation fundamentally changes the harmonic picture of musical form. How many modulations in a form? Their number turns out to be no accidental, being inseparably linked with the main goal of harmony — form-building. *"The number of modulations in a composition is equal to the number of its secondary themes.* It means that, as a rule, *there cannot be more than two modulations* in a composition. But in the overwhelming majority of cases a composition has *a sole modulation* <...> And this is despite a countless number of sharps, flats and natural notes strewn throughout the entire piece !" (Ibidem). Thus, in Movement One of Beethoven's Sonata C major, Op. 2 No. 3, we have only one modulation: C major — G major (the development — a long return back). Its finale has two modulations: C major — G major (and a return) and C major — F major (also with a return). "The modulatory chromatic tones move with the earth escape velocity while all the rest with the orbital velocity" (p. 23).

Besides, according to the modulation-generating requirement of a form, tonal transitions in the bridge part (from the principal to a secondary theme) and in the development section (from a secondary to the principal theme) are opposite in their direction, having absolutely different goals and therefore stated in a different way. So the command of modulatory harmony is equal in this aspect to the mastery of a form. Modulation is opposed to the rigid monotonality of the principal theme. In this respect Gershkovich quotes Webern: "*As a rule*, the principal theme *fails to modulate*," and cadences within the theme, containing non-diatonic notes, are not yet indicative of a departure from the key tonality (p. 292). Thus, in the principal theme of the first movement in Beethoven's Sonata G major, Op. 31 No. 1, the cadences in D major and C major do not shake the power of the tonic center in G major and even intensify it, contradicting one another and agreeing only in their joint gravitation to the common key tonic unifying them.

Having borrowed the terms from German musicology and Schoenberg, Webern evolved the theory of contrasting two types of structure in a form — *fest (firm)* and *locker (loose)*. He used to say: "A musical composition is not like an unbending stick but resembles man's flexible leg or arm; it has its own joints. The function of joints in a composition is assigned to its *loose* parts alternating with the *firm* ones in its structure. Beethoven represents the highest point in the development of a form precisely because his work constitutes that moment in music history when the firm and the loose came to be completely differentiated" (p. 63). Gershkovich developed further this idea advanced by his teacher: "*The firm* embraces everything linked with the key tonality. The principal theme is best stated in the key tonality. The principal theme is always built up *firmly*. As for the rest — the bridge passages and the secondary themes, they should be *loose*." But the latter are also built up in a different way, all of them being loose, with these varying qualities of the loose being relative and depending on the quality of this given firm. Beethoven provided a clear-cut differentiation between the different qualities of the loose in a secondary theme and in the development section. This section was associated by Philip Gershkovich with the way God, on one of the days of Creation, according to the Bible, separated land from water (p. 167; "Fiat firmamentum" – Genesis, 1:6). Thus, in a secondary theme after a short, relatively firm passage, there comes "free fantasy," to quote Webern once again. Beethoven's Sonata C major, Op. 53, Movement One, mm. 50–72, may serve as an illustration.

Philip Gershkovich's study of *dodecaphony* proceeded in a highly original way. In his article "Dodecaphony and Tonality" he wrote: "The *main* point in the essence of dodecaphony lies not in the establishment of a certain sequence of twelve notes and not in their use in accordance with this order. In contrast to the contemporary avant-grade breaking away from the historical roots, Gershkovich was striving to find *the musical in dodecaphony*, viewing it as a natural stage in the development of *the tradition* inherent in the European art of the 18th and 19th centuries. This methodological approach was logically to lead to the treatment of "atonal" dodecaphony as a regular stage in the development of the tonal system. No doubt, Gershkovich followed the precepts of the Second Viennese School. In this lectures *Wege zur neuen Musik* Webern said (on January 15, 1932): "like a ripe fruit falls from a tree, music has merely discarded the formal principle of tonality." As for his own dodecaphony, he neverthe-less did not detach it from tonality: "A note-row in its initial form plays the role previously assigned to the key tonality; it is naturally reiterated in the recapitulation" (February 26, 1932). Gershkovich cites his talk with Webern, which apparently took place in 1936 (my retelling it seems to be more authentic, for I had a chance to hear it from Gershkovich himself): "Once Webern, upon showing me, before our lesson, the composition which he completed on the previous day [11] said, 'it looks like E-flat minor, dosen't it?... Isn't it perceived as ending at the 6th step? Well, it means that we have nowhere departed from tonality" (p. 214)[12]. Drawing on these words he personally heard from Webern, Gershkovich comes to the conclusion that Webern, as early as in the mid-thirties, sensed the relationship between the latest composition procedure and the tonal system[13], and he makes the following query: "how far more acute should be this relationship felt a decade earlier by Schoenberg when he had just taken up the composition procedure based on the twelve mutually coordinated notes?" (Ibidem)[14]. According to Gershkovich, the old tonal law of sounds has become outdated, but it is still present in the subsequent system of sounds as one of its essential elements — *harmonic functionality*. Hegel termed such kind of quality transformation law as *Aufhebung* (German; obliteration and preservation at the same time) — when the essential properties of the previous evolutionary stage in a mediated form pass over into the new quality of the following stage. Of course, the new lease of life given to tonal harmony in dodecaphony does not necessarily imply the utilization of its former structural patterns and models.

It is no accident that Gershkovich devoted a whole article to the tonal sources of dodecaphony. His article, though in its underlying idea being similar to that of Webern's lectures delivered in 1932–33, in its point of departure is nevertheless based on the following three premises borrowed from Schoenberg's *Harmonielehre*, which was released in 1911, "i.e. fifteen years before" Schoenberg came to write his Suite Op. 25 and Wind Quintet Op. 26 (p. 13): (1) the difference between consonance and dissonance lies in quantity but not in quality; (2) there is no eternal sound system, and all the sound systems coming to replace one another constitute the links in the same process of development; (3) the structure of tonality is determined by the hegemony of the tonics. The essence of the idea underlying the tonal sources of dodecaphony, according to Gershkovich, amounts to the following: the tonal system in its evolution passes through the requisite stage towards its crystallization in the form of the seven-step diatonic system (let us bring to mind the signs placed at the clef, invariably

---

[11] Evidently, the matter involved Movement Three of his Variations for piano Op. 27, mm. 56–66. Chronologically, the finale of the cycle was written earlier than its first two movements (the author's note).

[12] Gershkovich, however, made a reservation that he failed to remember exactly what tonality Webern actually mentioned.

[13] If the matter had involved Opus 25, Webern was more likely to have shown his pupil the purely tonal principle underlying cyclization of these three songs.

[14] Among his friends Schoenberg used to say sarcastically that "atonal" music was soundless.

fixing down seven notes located along the chain of pure fifths). But the moving force behind the development of the tonal system is *"the process of extending the hegemony of the tonic over all the twelve notes"* (p. 22). The matter is not in distribution of twelve notes in several tonalities under the predominance of one of them (the concept of "depar-ture" from tonality as a temporary exit into another tonality), but in the arrangement of the chromatic chords borrowed from other tonalities at the steps of a given one, i.e. within tonality. For instance, the secondary dominant four-note chords turn out to be in C major at the steps: YII–III–YI–II, I. Even then, irrespective of the noted key steps at the clef, the tonality comes to embrace twelve notes: C-c♯ -D-d♯ -E-F-f♯ -G-g♯ -A-b♭ -B (p. 24). "The second face" of tonal dodecaphony is determined by the functions, under the given tonic, of enharmonic tones stated in the following note-row: C-d♭ -D-e♭ -E-F-g♭ -G-a♭ -A-b♭ -B. "The third stage" of tonal dodecaphony is characterized by giving up intratonal oppositions which keep up the tonal balance under the juxtaposition of Dominant/Subdominant, flat and sharp spheres. This stage, as a rule, involves expan-sion of vagrant (*vagierende*)chords, according to Schoenberg, i.e. occupying one and the same step in different tonalities and different steps in one and the same tonality. To this category belong a diminished four-note chord and an augmented triad. The closing up of sharp and flat spheres and autonomic statement of vagrant chords decidedly upset the tonal balance and virtually remove the need for the tonic (with the royal honors still bestowed on it for a long time to come just from force of inertia, rather than out of necessity). But then it appears that all chords turn into the vagrant ones and any chord may be linked with any other one. The system becomes "atonal" and the harmonic process comes to be regulated on the absolutely different grounds, primarily by gravitation and progression of a step towards the nearest step lying at a distance of a semitone. The dominant-tonic relationship comes to be replaced by the principle based on "progression in semitones" (Webern). In case this principle predominates, tonal dodecaphony turns into the classical serial dodecaphony cul-tivated by the Second Viennese School. The road to the New Music has been dis-covered, but it has arisen from tonality. "A tree is known by its fruit." This saying should be kept in one's mind while treating dodecaphony *"as a tonal system elevated to a higher level"* (p. 44).

In contrast to the old tonality based on the tonic gravity, dodecaphony constitutes *"tonality in the state of weightlessness"* (p. 215). Harmonic functionality in dodecaphony is manifested first and foremost in the interrelationship of a series (in its four forms) and its transpositions. A series is treated as a structural *unit* (similar to the tonic triad being a unit in the old tonality) whereas its transpositions resemble the *steps* of the chromatic tonal system. Concluding his analysis of Schoenberg's Prelude Op. 25 from the positions of tonal dodecaphony, Gershkovich writes: "In this study I wanted to reveal *the obvious objective links* between Schoenberg's dodecaphony and ... music <...>. Those who perceived all the beauty of Schoenberg's Opus No. 25 did so only thanks to their conscious or subconscious grasping the links of this composition with the great past of musical art" (p. 246).

Gershkovich's musicological studies reveal his two key subjects: the music of Beethoven, Mozart, and Bach, on the one hand, and dodecaphony, as well as Schoenberg, Webern, Mahler, and Berg, on the other hand. But his conception remained unified and unchanged: for Gershkovich the old Viennese classics and the neo-Viennese classics

represented one and the same phenomenon at different stages of musical development. As Gershkovich reminisced, "as a result on my studies with Webern, I came to
understand that the words *'a great master'* is not an appraisal but a theoretical term
<...>. The main thing that I have understood that the great masters make up one single
chain" (p. 62).

When at the end of his life Philip Gershkovich closed the circle of his earthly
existence by the ascension to his spiritual homeland in Vienna and soon deceased
there, it seemed that the cause of this remarkable musician was destined to fall into
oblivion. But the genuine values are not to be lost, even in our unfavorable times.
Gershkovich has his consistent followers, such as Leonid Hofmann and Dmitry
Smirnov. The now celebrated composer Alfred Schnittke named Philip Gershkovich
among his spiritual god-fathers. The following words from the newspaper *Die Zeit*
(Hamburg) may still prove prophetic: "Though today he is virtually unknown in the
West, in the future quite a number of dissertations will undoubtedly be written about
his life."

PRINCIPAL WORKS
MUSICOLOGICAL RESEARCH STUDIES

Published:

Tonal Sources of Schoenberg's Dodecaphony // Works on the Notational Systems, Vol. 6. Transactions of Tartu University, Issue 308, Tartu, 1973; Italian translation: *Nuova Revista Musicale Italiana*, No. 4, 1974; Bulgarian translation. History of 20th-century Music, Sofia, Muzika Publishers, 1986. Some Thoughts on *Lulu* // The International Alban Berg Society, Newsletter No. 7, 1978.

One of Johann Sebastian Bach's Inventions (On the Origins of the Viennese Classical Sonata Form)//Works on the Notational Systems,–Vol. 11. Transactions of Tartu University, Issue 467, Tartu, 1979.

Collection: Philip Gershkovich on Music. Articles, Notes, Letters, and Memoirs. Moscow, Sovetsky Kompozitor Publishers, 1991, 353 pp. The collection includes the following articles: Tonal Sources of Schoenberg's Dodecaphony; The Development of Form as a Whole and That of the Principal Theme; Webern and His Teaching on Form; Some Notes on the Type of the Principal Theme in Sonata Form; The Anatomy of Movement Three in Beethoven's Piano Sonata No. 1 (non-systematized notes); Piano Sonata No. 3; Piano Sonata No. 4; Piano Sonata No. 5; Piano Sonata No. 6; Piano Sonata No. 13; Movement One of Piano Sonata No. 22 <Piano Sonata No. 26>; Piano Sonata No. 28 (Materials); <Piano Sonata No. 29>; Beethoven's Piano Sonatas; Opus 2; "N. B."; Most Significant Beethovenian Phenomena; Some Thoughts About a Supercycle; An Attempt to Disclose the Structural Essence of Movement One in Beethoven's String Quartet No. 12, Op. 127, E-flat major; String Quartet A minor; <String Quartet No. 7>; Formal and Harmonic Inversions in the Finale of Beethoven's Symphony No. 3 <...>; One of the Main Features in Beethoven's Creative Development; Beethovenian Paradoxes; Mozart and Beethoven; One of the Young Mahler's Songs; Movement One in Mahler's First Symphony; Tentative Notes on Mahler's Work; Gustav Mahler's Third Symphony, Movement one <...>; Some Notes on Gustav Mahler's Work; One of Johann Sebastian Bach's Inventions <...>; Dodecaphony and Tonality; Some Notes on *Kreutzer Sonata*; One of Beethoven's Tonal Problems (*Kreutzer Sonata*), <III>; <Notes, Letters, Rememberings>.

Unpublished:

<The Evolution of Form>;
<Mozart's Sonatas>;
Mozart's Sonata No. 7;
Mozart's Sonata No. 1;
Mozart's Sonata No. 2;
The teaching on Musical Form, 124 pp. (dated back to the 1960s);
Das Augenlicht, 70 pp. (dated back to the late 1960s — early 1970s);
<On Dodecaphony and the Origins of Multi-Part Writing and Polyphony>;
The Beethovenian Bach, 83 pp.;

Slow Movements in Two of Mozart's First Sonatas (1970s);
The Analysis of Schoenberg's Violin Concerto, 56 pp. (1979–80);
<The analyses of Bach's *Well-Tempered Clavier*>, 90 pp. (1970s–1980s);
The Bridges Passages in the First Movements of Beethoven's Piano Sonatas;
<On Rondo>;
Beethoven's Piano Sonatas. Odd Notes;
Two-Movement Sonatas;
Large Rondos in Beethoven's Piano Sonatas. The First Sixteen Sonatas;
The Analysis of "Irregular" Principal Themes;
One of Beethoven's Tonal Problems (*Kreutzer sonata*), <I-III>;
Beethoven. Seine fünfte Symphonie anders betrachtet (1980s); and some others.

MUSICAL COMPOSITIONS
Early Works (lost)

Waltz for Piano (1929). Planned as part of a larger work
Tulips. Melodrama (after Peter Altenberg; 1930.) Plan
Fugue for Chamber Orchestra (1930). Planned as part of a larger form

Chamber Instrumental Music

Capriccio for Two Pianos
Three Piano Pieces, Five Piano Pieces (the 1960s)
Four Piano Pieces (1969)
Four Pieces for Cello and Piano (1968)
Four Pieces for Cello and Piano (1970s)

Chamber Vocal Music

Three Songs of Ion Barbu for voice and piano (1960s)
Four Songs of Paul Celan for voice and chamber orchestra (1960s)
Small Chamber Suite in three movements for mezzo-soprano, violin, two violas, cello, two clarinets and piano, verses by Federico Garcia Lorca and Rainer Maria Rilke (1979)
Madrigals for voice and chamber ensemble, verses by Rainer Maria Rilke, Federico Garcia Lorca and Guillaume Apollinaire (1983).

SOME OF GERSHKOVICH'S APHORISMS

— Form is a harmony *in the crystalline state*.
— Harmony and form are interrelated in the same way as pitch and duration in a musical sound.
— Form is the spectrum of harmony.
— Harmony develops faster than musical form.
— The mind lies in the length, and the heart in the pitch of a musical sound.
— Form is what turns the content of a composition into its essence. The musical character arises from a form like steam from hot water.

—" How" amounts virtually to "what." This discovery is made in art, and it can make it thanks to its unique and exclusive quality — that of uselessness.

— Symmetry is the chief attribute, for it is the essential core of all things.

— Beethoven's grandeur is due to some kind of temporal geometry.

— *Towards music and from music.* Many years ago I learned the following thing: the three laws inherent in dreaming and discovered by Freud — density (*Verdichtung*), inversion (*Umkehrung*) and transposition (*Verschiebung*) — fully coincide with the three laws inherent in polyphony. *Umkehrung* (inversion) is the term used in music; *Verdichtung* (density) corresponds to the polyphonic phenomenon called *Engführung* in German, and in Russia we use the Italian word *stretta*; as for *Verschiebung* (transposition), it makes the core of polyphony-*imitation*.

— "Sonata form without a development section" (the term widely used in Soviet musicology) is like a Don Juan without his male accessories [*sine testiculis*].

— Webern used to say: "Music is German music first and foremost."

— Prokofiev is a sorcerer's pupil who eventually became Acting Sorcerer. Schoenberg was born a magician, a bald magician, with his hair growing later on straight out of his brain.

— Shostakovich's harmony is the tonic combined with pits and bumps.

— Hindemith's music is the music in bank notes. Here the gold bars of tonality turned into paper money (not guaranteed by anybody).

— Beethoven is a radioactive composer.

— Memory is the rhythm (the length of a sound) while thinking is a melody (the pitch of a sound).

— A genius and a talent have nothing in common; genius is not the superlative degree of a talent. To speak, for instance, about Beethoven as a talent of the highest level is the same as to treat Venus as a very nice-looking woman. A man of genius keeps his hands in his pockets; a talented person scratches someone's ass. At best, he scratches his own ass.

— It is better to be old in a new way than to be new in the old way.

— The most epigonic music is that striving for novelty.

— The great masters (and I mean the greatest ones whom there are very few) are several aristocrats who got into music history like in a pigsty.

— Upon consideration it turns out that in the human world there is only one genuine reality: it is theatre; all the rest is just amateur performance.

— When some people do anything inhuman, they do precisely what is intrinsic in human beings. A human being is indeed inhuman!!! Mankind and humanity are incompatible!

— Lupus lupo homo est[15].

— [Gershkovich speaking about himself]: "I'm sunny."

---

[15] This is a modified version of the famous Latin set expression Homo homini lupus est (Dog eat dog).

Sergei Slonimsky: the impetus to innovation and cultural synthesis

Valentina Kholopova

Sergei Slonimsky

Sergei Slonimsky is a versatile musical personality, known as a composer, a music scholar, a pedagogue, and a public figure. Slonimsky as a composer made a name for himself in modern Russian music as one of the leaders in the Soviet musical movement that came to the fore in the 1960s. As a musicologist, he has to his credit a great number of profound research papers, among them a large volume about Prokofiev's symphonies. As a music theoretician, he worked out a new system of rhythmical notation which he called "rhythmic neumes." As a Professor of the Leningrad (now St. Petersburg) Conservatoire, he has brought forth a school of composers and musicologists, and guided many of his students into successful careers in music, among them the conductors Vladislav Chernushenko, Vasily Sinaisky and Yuri Simonov. As a pianist, he often appears in concerts playing his own compositions. Besides, in the ensemble with the singer Nadezhda Yureneva, he took up the vocal pieces by Balakirev, Tchaikovsky, Brahms, and Mahler, attracting not only the academic audiences, but also giving concerts for workers and students. Being a pianist endowed with the gift for composition, Slonimsky gave a new lease of life to the old art of improvisation, still appearing in this role. As a musical figure and a member of the Committee for Nomination of the USSR State Prizes, he initiated the opening of a monument to Mussorgsky in St. Petersburg (with himself donating the receipts from his concerts for this purpose) and sponsored the foundation of the International Prokofiev Competition to be held regularly in St. Petersburg.

Sergei Mikhailovich Slonimsky (born on August 12, 1932 in Leningrad) comes from a family renowned in the cultural community. His father, Mikhail Slonimsky, was a writer who in the twenties, together with Vsevolod Ivanov, Mikhail Zoshchenko, Konstantin Fedin, Valentin Kaverin and Nikolai Tikhonov, stood at the sources of the young Soviet literature. He met Maxim Gorky, Yevgeny Shvarts, Olga Forsh, and was on friendly terms with Anna Akhmatova, Alexander Grin and Kornei Chukovsky. Nicolas Slonimsky, his uncle, is an eminent American music scholar. Among his close relatives is Anthony Slonimski, a Polish poet.

Since his early childhood the future composer, growing up in a circle of national literary notables, imbibed not only a love for belles-lettres, poetry and the theatre but also the progressive sentiments and zest for life inherent in the intellectual elite. Since he showed a gift for musical improvisation very early, he began taking lessons in piano and composition.

During the Second World War the Slonimsky family was evacuated to Perm, where for a time the famous Kirov Opera and Ballet Company was also active. The young musician could therefore come into close contact with the musical theatre and learn its repertoire. During the same period Sergei Slonimsky for the first time got to know the Russian peasant life and the folk song traditions. And these youthful impressions gave an impetus to his serious study of the Russian musical folklore. He was primarily preoccupied with operas and ballets, coming to learn, in addition to the classical Russian operas — Rimsky-Korsakov's *Snow Maiden* and *The Tsar's Bride*, and Tchaikovsky's *Queen of Spades*, also Prokofiev's *Romeo and Juliet*, a ballet hardly comprehensible to anybody in those days, and Shostakovich's opera *Lady Macbeth of Mtsensk District (Katerina Izmailova)*, to be banned by the notorious resolution on music adopted in 1948.

Sergei Slonimsky graduated from the Leningrad Conservatoire in two specialities: piano (1955) and composition (1958). He studied composition with Boris Arapov and Orest Yevlakhov, both eminent pedagogues at the Leningrad Conservatoire.

Upon getting a good academic training, Slonimsky turned his attention to a different domain — a thorough study of the Russian musical folklore. Throughout the sixties he regularly made extended trips to various parts of the USSR — the Urals, the Votkinsk Power Station, the Pskov and Novgorod Regions, collecting Russian folk songs. Some songs that had been recorded down by him during these trips were later on incorporated in his opera *Virineya*, his Piano Sonata and other compositions. All in all, he spent nearly two decades of his life on exploration of folk culture, calling it a "folkloric conservatoire." In 1958 Slonimsky completed his training at the postgraduate courses (also at the Leningrad Conservatoire) where he was majoring in musical theory. His master's dissertation was entitled *Sergei Prokofiev's Symphonies*, which was released several years later in a book form (Muzyka Publishers, Moscow — Leningrad, 1964). Prokofiev's work was then just coming to the notice of musicians. Because of the Resolution passed by the Central Committee of the Communist Party in 1948, Prokofiev was still officially banned when Slonimsky was writing his dissertation. He turned out to be not only one of the first among music theoreticians to rehabilitate that great master in 20th-century music, but also provide original research into Prokofiev's composition techniques. In particular, the music scholar brought into light his device of "thematic cohesion" owing to which the entire Prokofievian form looked like a "monumental exposition."

Simultaneously, Sergei Slonimsky worked on another major research, revealing again a novel theoretical approach to the phenomenon under his consideration — that of Mahler, a composer standing quite apart from Prokofiev. Taking Mahler's *Das Lied von der Erde* as an example, Slonimsky disclosed some specific features inherent in that composer's later orchestral polyphony, which proved a pioneering work in musicological literature (published in 1963).

Meanwhile Sergei Slonimsky's general musical interests were developing on an intensive scale, expanding his knowledge of 20th century music. Following Prokofiev and Shostakovich, beginning with the mid-fifties he got engaged in the study of Stravinsky, Hindemith, Honegger, Schoenberg, and Berg. He established contacts with the Moscow-based composers of his generation, also looking for novel musical devices — Edison Denisov, Sophia Gubaidulina, Roman Ledenyov *et al.* And all the time Slonimsky has remained loyal to his native city Leningrad-St.Petersburg where he is still living and working.

Sergei Slonimsky has to his credit more than 100 compositions, including numerous chamber vocal and instrumental pieces and works for orchestra, among them ten symphonies. *Operas* and *ballets* make a major part of his work. Though their list is not very extensive, the production of each proved a highlight in the cultural life. But his last opera, *Hamlet*, after Shakespeare, written in 1992, has not been staged yet.

In his musical style the composer, who has a perfect command of all Western composition procedures, a strong, and in many respects a decisive factor belongs to the traditions of the St. Petersburg composition school with its explicit striving for national singularity and heightened attention to rhythmic innovations. These traditions were conducive to the formation of Stravinsky's talent, and Sergei Slonimsky also reveals his objective kinship with Stravinsky.

Among Russian composers it was Mussorgsky who attracted Slonimsky most of all. During one of his folkloric trips he even visited the village of Karevo, where Mussorgsky was born, and recorded down there a song whose text made a refrain in his opera *Virineya*. Slonimsky the composer was interested in Mussorgsky's method of tackling the folk material, the type of opera as a "folk music drama" created by the composer of *Boris Godunov* and *Khovanshchina*, and the people as the opera's real protagonist.

It is the Russian, or to be more precise, the St. Petersburg soil that nourished such quality of Slonimsky's style as hegemony of chorus in an opera. In historical retrospection it was preceded by monumental scenic choruses in the operas by not only Mussorgsky but also by Borodin (*Prince Igor*) and Rimsky-Korsakov (*Snow Maiden, The Legend of the Invisible City of Kitezh*). None of the contemporary operatic composers but Slonimsky assigns such a major part to the chorus. Thus, in his opera *Mary Stuart* the chorus acquires a fundamentally new function — in many respects it replaces the orchestra.

The Russian national sources tapped by the composer who on his own will has passed "a folkloric conservatoire," are extremely wide, including in addition to the above mentioned 19th-century classics, the choral, so called *partes* concerto dating back to the 17th and 18th centuries, *horn* (brass) orchestra, and the old Russian ritual monody known as *Znamenny raspev*. As for the folkloric genres, these include songs, dances, and playing various folk instruments. For example, Slonimsky's *Novgorodian Dance* (written in 1980) is a piece in the style of "instrumental theatre" where all the performers, the conductor included, gradually join in dancing. The performance manner of the *horn* orchestra found its manifestation in his *Dialogues* for wind quintet (to be discussed below). Slonimsky's serious approach to folklore made the musicologists in the former USSR rate his music, on a par with that of Rodion Shchedrin residing in Moscow, as belonging to the "new folklore wave."

Sergei Slonimsky is a remarkable master of melodic writing, who produces easily remembered musical themes, a quality not very encountered in the composers living in the second half of the 20th century. Along with the vocal foundations in his music with an occasional use of folk citations, diatonics and tonality live side by side, with their part increasing as the time passed from the 1960s marked for the rise of novel composition procedures, to the 1970s and 80s with their tendency to "retro."

The traditional striving of composers residing in St. Petersburg for rhythmic innovations (Mussorgsky, Rimsky-Korsakov, the early Stravinsky) has found its worthy continuation in Slonimsky's work in this line. Some of his devices are akin to Stravinsky's, in particular his asymmetrical variation of phrases and motives. As a composer belonging to the second half of the 20th century, Slonimsky feels absolutely unconfined in metric "breathing" of his works: beats freely change their measure or may even be avoided altogether. But his major innovation as regards rhythm is the system of "rhythmic neumes" he has worked out, in which he comes close to the notation reforms carried out by other present-day composers. His system presents relative durations, without conventional stems up and down, with the changes in the traditional "cross-bars" in the notation of minor note values such as quavers, semi-quavers, etc. Example 1 shows one of the graphic versions of symbols used in his system of "rhythmic neumes".

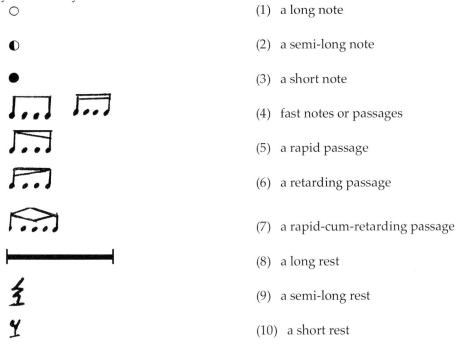

(1) a long note

(2) a semi-long note

(3) a short note

(4) fast notes or passages

(5) a rapid passage

(6) a retarding passage

(7) a rapid-cum-retarding passage

(8) a long rest

(9) a semi-long rest

(10) a short rest

Ex. 1

This system delivers musical rhythmics from the dictatorship of rigid measures, providing an opportunity for a modern use of non-classical, folk and ancient free musical time values.

Unrestrained rhythms in the Slonimsky style correspond with similarly free pitches. It may well be asserted that he was the first composer of his generation in the former USSR to employ microtones and quarter-tones. He mastered these microchromatic elements of the non-tempered system primarily in the Russian "folkloric conservatoire." For this reason, despite their outward similarity with the relevant Western avant-gardist innovations, their sonority stylistically differs from that of, say, Luciano Berio, Penderecki, and even Alfred Schnittke who has arisen to maturity in Moscow.

Another element in the Slonimsky style is the use of devices inherent in the "instrumental theatre." For such a truly theatrical composer as Sergei Slonimsky his bent for theatrical effects on the concert platform is quite natural. The idea of "instrumental theatre" made the basis of his First String Quartet, which he entitled *Antiphons*. It is noteworthy that this composition was written back in 1968, turning out to be the first experience in the former Soviet music in the "instrumental theatre." *Antiphons* aroused keen interest in other young composers while the officials of the Composers Union found them "controversial" and "experimental." It was so catching an example that in 1971 Sophia Gubaidulina also based her First String Quartet on the instrumental theatre. As for Slonimsky himself, following his *Antiphons*, he wrote a one-actor scenic piece for solo oboe, modestly called *Solo espressivo* (1975). In his preface to the published score the composer pointed out: "The important thing here is to perform this piece in motion." He outlined the following drawing of a concert hall, showing the trajectory of the oboe player's movement:

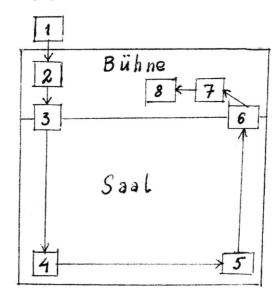

Ex. 2

We have already mentioned his *Novgorodian Dance* also featuring some theatrical elements. As for his *Evening Music* for a cappella chorus with the accompaniment of bell and tam-tam (written in 1973), it may serve as an example of the "choral" rather than "instrumental theatre."

The deep-going kinship of Slonimsky's musical language with the Russian traditions is complemented and counter-balanced in his work by a diametrically opposite aspiration: to cover as fully as possible the entire globe, all times and peoples in the plots, imagery, themes, and literary and poetical texts making the basis of his compositions. And here again come to mind the words used by Fyodor Dostoyevsky to characterize the people of Russian culture as endowed with "universal empathy." In the St. Petersburg composition school, which Sergei Slonimsky has inherited, the first to undertake such a conscious voyage around the countries of the world in his music was Nikolai Rimsky-Korsakov. In addition to Russia, his compositions embraced Spain, Italy, Ancient Greece, Poland, the Caucasus, and various regions of the Orient. Let us try to draw a similar list as regards Sergei Slonimsky: Russia, Slavic countries, Ancient Greece, England, Scotland, America, Poland, Bashkiria, Armenia, the Middle East, India, Ancient Judea, and the ancient Orient in general. And Slonimsky, like Rimsky-Korsakov in his time, is striving to recreate the local and historical atmosphere of a foreign culture which he tackles in his music. Thus, having chosen a plot about Mary Stuart, he collected all available material about Scottish music and made a deliberate use of characteristically Scottish melodic and rhythmic turns. Or, to convey his conception of *The Songs of Troubadours,* he first made a scholarly study of rhythmic structures inherent in the French music of the Renaissance period. Such stylistic *universality,* devoid nevertheless of so habitual polystylistics, corresponds to *pluralism* as an artistic quality of 20th-century culture. A blend of a modern musical language so naturally employed by Sergei Slonimsky with various national musical specifics is a hallmark of his compositions.

The cycle *The Songs of Freebooters,* consisting of nine settings of folk texts for mezzo-soprano and baritone (its piano score was written in 1959, and its full score in 1961) was the first composition to reveal Sergei Slonimsky's inimitable style. The appearance of this work on the eve of the stormy sixties, when the new generation of composers throughout the former USSR had not yet fully established themselves, anticipated the new trends in Russian music. *The Songs of Freebooters* overwhelmed the listeners by the agility of modern musical language and psychologically deep imagery based on folk poetry. Slonimsky seemed to retrace Mussorgsky's way, as if deriving his strength from the depths of *Khovanshchina* and *Boris Godunov* in the delineation of his own characters. This song-cycle set to popular verses dating back to the peasant uprisings against the tsar comprises, in addition to lyrical songs and ditties, some songs used to be sung by the robbers.

Since the 1960s turned out to be a time when the Russian and other composers in the former USSR were intensively grasping all the Western innovations in music, most of them, especially those residing in Moscow, began writing in the style of the Western avant-garde, following it to the letter. Sergei Slonimsky, being closely linked with the progressive artistic intelligentsia of Leningrad, felt himself mature enough spiritually to find his own, inimitable way to interacting with the West. The St. Petersburg traditions and his "universal empathy" made it possible for him to discover a synthesis of seemingly incompatible extremes — the elements of the avant-garde with the elements of Russian traditional culture just as the founder of the Russian classical music Mikhail Glinka had been striving to combine the Russian song tradition with the German fugue. In the course of the sixties he wrote several compositions, one after another in rapid succession, still regarded as his best opuses, among them his Piano Sonata, *Dialogues, Concerto-Bouffe,* and *Antiphons,* in which he demonstrated varied types of the Russian dialogue with Western Europe.

In his *Piano Sonata* (written in 1963) Sergei Slonimsky placed "under the same roof" the dodecaphonic principal theme and a genuine Russian folk theme, which he had recorded down himself; besides, he composed a wide variety of his own themes in the style of folk songs in diverse genres — drawn out, lyrical, and dirges. And therewith he employed in his own composition that principle of coupling a plurality of themes which he had earlier discovered in his research of Prokofiev's music. Such combination of folkloric themes with dodecaphony proved a unique artistic experience.

In his *Dialogues* (*Inventions*) for flute, oboe, clarinet, bassoon and French horn (written in 1964) Slonimsky solved another unique task of combining dodecaphonic-pointillistic texture with the manner of playing inherent in the Russian horn orchestra. This composition was intended expressly for the remarkable Leningrad wind quintet directed by Vitaly Buyanovsky. The Russian horn orchestra, which was in wide use in the 18th and 19th centuries, represented a combination of folk wind instruments, with each of them designed to produce only one note. Hence, an inevitable pointillism in the performance of any piece beginning with a folk song. Its subtitle *Inventions,* indicated in brackets, is reminiscent of the famous inventions from the opera *Wozzeck.* This work consisting of twelve short inventions abounds in the avant-garde procedures, ranging from a dodecaphonic series with its four forms, quarter-tones, and aleatory to glimpses of a rhythmic progression. Moreover, the techniques borrowed from *Wozzeck* include a "one-tone invention" and a "one-chord invention." That is one side of his dialogue with the West. The other side is represented by the diatonic Russian tunes in the popular style, but in a free intervalic and rhythmic nature (owing to quarter-tones and "rhythmic neumes") depicting the comic pointillism of a Russian horn playing one note in various octaves, colorfully conveying the pastoral landscape (through sonoristic whistles of the flute with its headpipe removed). The general effect is highly whimsical since none of the extreme stylistic poles seems ready to yield in its statement.

His *Concerto-Bouffe* for chamber orchestra (written in 1964) was a signal success, winning recognition for the composer in many respects — as a connoisseur of all the latest devices in Western composition procedures, as a continuer of the melodic principles inherent in the Russian composition school, and as a modern composer of a highly individual style. *Concerto-Bouffe* falls into two movements: I. Canonic Fugue and II. Improvisation. This work may well serve as an encyclopedia of the avant-gardist procedures, featuring dodecaphony, serialism, superpolyphony, aleatory, quarter-tones, clusters, pointillism, and the latest devices in playing the wind instruments in *glissando,* on vents (the flute), *frullato* (the trumpet), and on the piano's strings. At the same time it is marked for clear-cut melodic themes and energetic rhythms akin to Bartok and Stravinsky. The key moment in Slonimsky's dialogue with the West in this composition is psychological. Though dodecaphony emerged in the context of expressionism with its preponderance for gloom, estrangement and esotericism, Slonimsky takes the liberty of creating a piece with the fully inverted psychological content — life-asserting and vital. Herein, he follows the tradition of Russian symphonism initiated by Glinka in his *Kamarinskaya*. Slonimsky's *Concerto-Bouffe* proves the rarest sample of buoyant dodecaphony in 20th-century music.

Concerto-Bouffe presents a synthesis of many stylistic elements, ranging from the pointillism inherent in Webern's later compositions (Symphony Op. 21), the jazz trumpet playing solo with *frullato*, the neo-Baroque fugue, the aleatory of the Polish avant-garde type, a reminiscence of a Mozart theme, the simplest tunes of Russian folk ditties (short humorous improvised songs), and the sharply syncopated rhythms akin to Bartok's lapidary themes. The principal theme in the first movement, based on the dodecaphonic series No. 1 (all in all, there are three of them), is thoroughly elaborated stylistically.

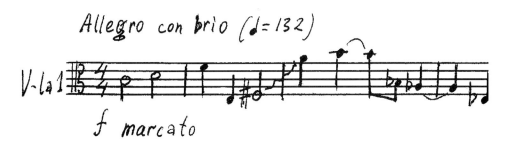

Ex. 3 *Concerto — Bouffe*

In this dodecaphonic series of major importance is the initial diatonic trichord: c-d-f. In contrast to Western composers using, as a rule, chromatic series, devoid of any pentatonic elements, Sergei Slonimsky makes a deliberate use of a sequence associated with Slavonic, in particular Russian, melodic turns. Moreover, the first four notes in this series are also associated with the theme in the final fugue of Mozart's symphony *Jupiter* — c-d-f-e. The composition is therefore rooted in the cultural soil of different countries.

Antiphons for string quartet, or one-movement String Quartet No. 1 (written in 1968), beginning with its title is another unusual "unity of opposites." The very title points to the widespread manner of church singing and the corresponding genre. But Slonimsky as an encyclopedist of the Russian folk art has a perfect command of a similar manner in the peasant singing when the singers call to one another from one bank of the river to the other, when the hay-makers listen to one another at a great distance, and of other similar cases. These sonorities of the Russian *plein air* of which the academic musicians are hardly aware served the basis for the musical "plot" in *Antiphons*. With a view to drawing these musical pictures Slonimsky made use of the devices inherent in the "instrumental theatre." Striving to convey the effects of choral singing through the timbres of stringed instruments, he *for the first time ever* treated a classical string quartet as oriented on the *chorus*. Some time later this idea of his colleague from Leningrad was taken up and further developed by Alfred Schnittke in his Second String Quartet coming in its finale to the sonority rendered by the seemingly invisible chorus. Slonimsky's *Antiphons* also end in the monolithic chorus but preceded by a chain of stereophonic contrasts of the voices involved in the string ensemble. The work begins with the following spatial contrast: as if reproducing the remote chorus backstage (quarter-tone heterophony of two violins and viola in a high register) and the solo male voice in the centre of the stage (céllo). Upon the entry of all the musicians onto the stage, there follow antiphons of the rhythmically well-coordinated "chorus" in a low register and the soloist (violin) in a high register, varied contrasts derived from the seemingly singing voices and the ringing background (quick passages in *glissando*). As a result, you hear a well-balanced monorhythmic playing of the quartet conveying the sonority of a monolithic hymn-like choral singing.

Sergei Slonimsky wrote his first opera *Virineya* in 1967. Based on the original plot of Lydia Seifullina's short novel, it depicts the revolution of 1917 not in the conventional way of glorifying the Great October Socialist Revolution but as a horrible nationwide cataclysm. The young composer was commissioned to write this opera by two opera companies simultaneously — the Nemirovich-Danchenko Opera House in Moscow and the Leningrad Maly Opera House, on the recommendation of Dmitry Shostakovich.

Like its literary source, Slonimsky's opera is full of gloom and tragedy. Thus, Scene One is entitled "The End of Power," Scene Two — "The End of the Family," and Scene Three — "The End of Faith." The main character, Virineya, a peasant woman, gets killed in the final scene by her infuriated fellow-villagers. While writing this opera Slonimsky followed the example set by Mussorgsky in his historical operas. Slonimsky's opera is also a folk music drama, with the people (peasants of the same village) acting as the real protagonist. In the musical terms it is based on numerous folk songs (here recorded down by the composer himself) which get a fresh rendering owing to Slonimsky's modern idiom. Its plot and music are somewhat reminiscent of *Boris Godunov*. It is also related to *Khovanshchina* in its correlation of the tragic plot and the drawn-out Russian songful music. The further enhancement of the part assigned to the chorus, in particular, the introduction of *choral entr'actes*, has made a major contribution to development of the national operatic traditions.

Sergei Slonimsky wrote his first and still his sole full-size ballet *Icarus* in 1971. It was dedicated to the memory of his father, Mikhail Slonimsky, with the libretto provided by Yuri Slonimsky, a noted ballet scholar from Leningrad (the composer's namesake). His *Choreographic Miniatures* were written a bit earlier in close cooperation with Leonid Yakobson, a talented choreographer from Leningrad. *Icarus* was marked by the appearance of a new image for Slonimsky — that of the wings capable of elevating man up to the sun, and even the inevitable death of the daring hero failed to destroy the flight-like quality and dynamism inherent in this music. To elucidate his idea of flight, the composer imparted the choral color to the ballet. In contrast to his opera *Virineya* abounding in melodic lines, in this ballet Slonimsky gave vein to his sense of rhythm. One of his fresh findings was rhythmic progression making the basis of the ballet number entitled "Forging the Wings" (Musical Example 4).

Its musical form is founded on the ostinato repetition of this original asymmetrical structure. The composer incorporated in his ballet the most spectacular, rhythmically agile themes from his *Concerto-Bouffe*, just asking for their embodiment in dance. In the musical form of this ballet Slonimsky came to realize his idea which was to become

Ex. 4 *Icarus*

his favorite — to provide in the finale a synthetic recapitulation of all the principal themes; this synthesis is elaborated here in the final scene called "Flight." The ballet *Icarus* also scored a signal success, like Slonimsky's first opera: it was produced on the huge stage at the Moscow Kremlin Palace of Congresses, which greatly increased the composer's official prestige.

Nevertheless, the official success of his revolutionary opera *Virineya* and his classical ballet *Icarus* proved too fragile, failing to help Slonimsky uphold his next operatic brainchild — *The Master and Margarita*, based on Mikhail Bulgakov's outstanding novel, perhaps, too outstanding to be accepted by the omnipotent musical "authorities" during the Brezhnev stagnation period of the 1970s. It was to acquire its full-fledged status only with the arrival of Gorbachev's perestroika in 1985. The opera had the same fate as the original novel: completed in 1972, it was first produced only in 1989 in Moscow, i.e., 17 years later, and even then on the humble concert stage.

The opera *The Master and Margarita* is intended for a non-traditional cast of performers: 20 singers-soloists, 20 solo instruments and two mimes. Besides, its ballet entr-acte involves a dance group. In the absence of the conventional opera orchestra the instrumentalists are to perform a singular part, acting as doubles of the opera's personages to carry their motto timbres. Thus, the voice of the main heroine, Margarita, is accompanied by the violin and the harp, the Master's by the cello, Yeshua's the oboe, Pontius Pilate's the bass clarinet, Judas's the trumpet, Korovyev's the bassoon, the Cat's by the piccolo, etc. As for its style, Sergei Slonimsky expanded here the range of his musical idioms boundlessly, coming to combine the archaic heterophonic choruses, lyrical cantilena arias, grotesque scherzos à la Shostakovich, piquant jazz elements, brutal pop and rock-rhythms, and subtle dodecaphony. The genre of this opera has become correspondingly synthetic, with its interweaving of the features inherent in the passion music, a lyrical psychological opera, a rock opera, an epic oratorio, as well as the 20th-century "instrumental theatre." In its correlation with Bulgakov's epoch-making novel, the composer managed to convey the intricate nature of its parallel planes: the modern hero-martyr Master — the crucified Yeshua, the Soviet literary officials and Pontius Pilate, Judas, etc. Slonimsky provided a profound rendering of the seemingly insoluble focal antithesis embodied, first and foremost, in the Great Ball at Satan's and in the final Flight of the Master and Margarita in the moonlight. Here are a few measures from the opera's epilogue in which, after the ascending "stairs" of the chorus's introductions, at the very climax there rings out Margarita's voice singing "I'll guard your sleep...".

Ex. 5 *The Master and Margarita*

The opera *The Master and Margarita* may well be regarded as the spiritual landmark in Slonimsky's creative career.

In his opera *Mary Stuart*, based on the novel by Stefan Zweig and written in 1980, Slonimsky revealed an absolutely different approach to a musical performance. Having called it an opera-ballade, the composer strictly adhered, from beginning to end, to this genre characterization. The opera's libretto was written in verse stylized after Burns songful poetry. And its measured, symmetrical rhythms are telling throughout on the music and the scenic action. The entire opera is to be sung (it has neither recitatives nor speech dialogues) in a manner the early verses used to be sung. It abounds in conventional old-time genres such as songs of the Sad Skald, songs of the Merry Skald, Pantomime of the Merry Skald with jesters, Bothwell's ballades, Torchlight Procession, Scottish March and so on. The music is permeated with the Scottish national coloring — its characteristic syncopated rhythms and pentatonic elements. The agile rhythms vitalize the general tone of the opera's production so that it may well compete, in the context of an academic genre, with the emotional energy inherent in a rock opera. In *Mary Stuart* Slonimsky carried out his yearning for vocalization of an operatic performance to the utmost: assigning the functions of the opera orchestra to the chorus, relegating the former to the minimal supporting role in the *basso continuo* type. The choruses got therewith doubled and tripled in size, with their technique becoming extremely complicated. *Mary Stuart* from the first day of its production has become a favorite opera with the general public at St. Petersburg, and it delighted the audiences in Scotland, too.

    Sergei Slonimsky's music is multifaceted in the same way as his whole personality. It would be hard to find the musical sources that had escaped his interest. It would be equally hard to name another composer who could embrace such contrasts as his *Songs of the Troubadours* refinedly stylized after the French music of the Renaissance period and involving the singing voices, recorders (the old-time instruments of the flute family used in the 15th century), and a lute, the dashing Cossack songs to the accompaniment of a snare drum in his choral cantata *Quiet Flows the Don* (after Mikhail Sholokhov), the combination in one piece of authentic old Russian church chants and twelve-note themes (*Dramatic Song* for orchestra), as his experience in artistic recon-struction of pre-historical singing (with alternation of great skips and the smallest quarter-tones) in *Taking Leave of a Friend*, written to the texts of the Sumerian-Accadian epic poem about Gilgamesh, and his Third Symphony dedicated to the Leningrad Philharmonic Orchestra, demonstrating the virtuosic finesse of a modern symphony orchestra, as his rendering of bell pealing by the orchestra's resources (in his cantata *A Voice from the Chorus* set to the verse by Alexander Blok), as his symphonic treatment of the traditional Russian folk instruments (*Festive Music* for balalaika, Russian wooden spoons and symphony orchestra) and the conception of a symphony with the final funeral march in the spirit of Mahler (Fourth Symphony), and his turn to jazz and rock-'n'-roll idioms (Concerto for orchestra, three electric guitars and solo instruments, *Exotic Suite* for two violins, two electric guitars, saxophone and percussion) and his *Hamlet*, that *dramma per musica* after Shakespeare. Indeed, the soundscape of Sergei Slonimsky's music comes to embrace the cultural space of the entire world.

PRINCIPAL WORKS

Musical Theatre

Choreographic Miniatures, libretto by Leonid Yakobson (1964)
Virineya, opera based on Lydia Seifullina's short novel (1967)
Icarus, ballet, libretto by Yuri Slonimsky (1971)
The Master and Margarita, chamber opera after Mikhail Bulgakov's novel (1972)
Mary Stuart, opera-ballade after Stefan Zweig's novel (1980)
Hamlet, dramma per musica after Shakespeare's tragedy (1990–1991)
King Ixion, monodic drama (chamber opera) after Innokenty Annensky's tragedy and the ancient myths (1993)
Ivan the Terrible, Russian tragedy, libretto by Yakov Gordin based on 16th-century historical documents (1994–1995)

Works for Voice and Orchestra

The Songs of Freebooters, vocal-symphonic cycle for mezzo-soprano, baritone and symphony orchestra, traditional words (1961)
A Voice from the Chorus, cantata for soloists, chorus, organ and chamber orchestra, verse by Alexander Blok (1965)

Works for Orchestra

Concerto-Bouffe for chamber orchestra (1964)
Dramatic Song for symphony orchestra (1973)
Concerto for symphony orchestra, three electric guitars and solo instruments (1973)
Festive Music for balalaika, Russian wooden spoons and symphony orchestra (1976)
Symphonic Motet for symphony orchestra (1976)
Symphony No. 2 (1978)
Symphony No. 3 (1982)
Symphony No. 4 (1982)
Concerto primaverile (*Spring Concerto*) for violin and string orchestra (1983)
Symphony No. 5 (1983)
Symphony No. 6 (1984)
Symphony No. 7 (1984)
Symphony No. 8 for chamber orchestra (1985)
Symphony No. 9 (1987)
Concerto for oboe and chamber ensemble or chamber orchestra (1987)
Slavonic Concerto for organ and string orchestra (1988)
Apollo and Marsyas, symphony with the solos of flute and harp (1991)
Symphony No. 10 *The Inferno's Circles* [*Cerchii dell inferno*] after Dante. Dedicated to all those living and dying in Russia (1992)
Overture to the opera *Ivan the Terrible* (1993)
Petersburg visions, fantasy for orchestra (1995)
Symphonietta (1996)

Chamber Instrumental Pieces

Piano Sonata (1963)
Dialogues (Inventiona) for wind quintet (1964)
Antiphons, or String Quartet No. 1 (1968)
Chromatic Poem for organ (1969)
Coloristic Fantasia for piano (1972)
Solo espressivo for oboe (1975)
Exotic Suite for two violins, two electric guitars, saxophone and percussion (1976)
Roundelay and Fugue for organ (1976)
Novgorodian Dance for clarinet, trombone, cello, piano, percussion and magnetic tape (1980)
Intermezzo in Memory of Brahms for piano (1980)
Dithyramb for cello ensemble and piano (1982)
In the Animal World, suite for cello and piano (1982)
Monody "Upon Reading Euripides" for solo violin (1984)
Variations on a Mussorgsky Theme for piano (1984)
Sonata for Cello and Piano (1986)
Sonata for Violin and Piano (1986)
American Rhapsody for two pianos and harpsichord (1989)
Recitativ, aria e Burlesca for flute, piano and percussion (1991)
Twenty-Four Preludes and Fugues for piano (1994)
Chechen Rhapsody for harp (1996)

Chamber Vocal Pieces

For voice and piano

Polish Strophes, song-cycle to the verse by Anthony Slonimski (1963)
Lyrical Strophes, song-cycle to the verse by Yevgeny Rein (1964)
Taking Leave of a Friend after the Sumerian epic poem about Gilgamesh (1966)
Four Poems of Osip Mandelstam (1974)
Ten Poems of Anna Akhmatova (1974)
Four Settings of Fyodor Tyutchev (1984)
Five Settings of Mikhail Lermontov (1985)
Rubaiyat — Five Poems of Abdurrakhman Jami (1987)
Nadira's Ghazals (1988)
Six Settings of Osip Mandelstam (1990)
Romances to verses by Russian poets (1993)
On Sabbath Day, vocal novella to verses by Evilina Shchats (1993)

Ensembles

Monologues for soprano, oboe, French horn and harp, set to David's psalms (1967)
Merry Songs, song-cycle for soprano, piccolo, trumpet and percussion, set to verse by Daniil Kharms (1971)
The Songs of Troubadours for soprano, tenor, four recorders and lute, set to verses by the old-time German and French poets (1975)
Dhammapada's Strophes for soprano, harp and percussion (1983)

Failure's songs for bass, guitar, jazz band and piano, set to verses by Yevgeny Rein (1995)
Moscow seen through the Eyes of Its Pubs for bass, guitar and piano, set to verses by Sergei Esenin (1996)

Choruses

Evening Music for a cappella chorus, bell and tam-tam (1973)
Quiet Flows the Don, concerto for mixed chorus, set to traditional Cossack lyrics (1977)
Four Stasima from Sophocles' tragedy *Oedipus at Colonus* for mixed chorus (1983)

Boris Tishchenko: striking spontaneity against a rationalistic background

Valentina Kholopova

Boris Tishchenko

The emergence of Boris Tishchenko on the musical scene was so spectacular that many musicians believed him to be a second Prokofiev. It was due to his combining in one person the qualities of bright, highly original composer and no less remarkable, uncommon pianist playing the most complicated opuses by Prokofiev; furthermore, his keen interest in the musical theatre, ballet in particular and the conspicuous, easily remembered utterances were equally captivating. Tishchenko won the attention of the general public while he was still a conservatoire student when owing to his strikingly early maturity (according to the current standards) he, at the age of 19, wrote his First Violin Concerto Op. 9 (later to be revised) and when he was 20-his Second string Quartet, a work still considered to be one of his best opuses. During the year he graduated from the Leningrad Conservatoire (1962) he wrote the song-cycle *Sad songs*, unforgettable to date, and by the time he completed a postgraduate course (also at the Leningrad Conservatoire, in 1965) he had to his credit the ballet *The Twelve* after Alexander Blok, included by several ballet companies into their repertoire; the First Cello Concerto for which the great Shostakovich provided his own version of orchestration; a work for orchestra, *Suzdal* (the name of an old Russian town famous for its remarkable architectural monuments), which captured the attention of music-lovers by a new type of synthesis of modern musical idioms and the Russian archaics; *Twelve Inventions for Organ*, to become a staple item in the concert programmes of organ-players; and the Third Piano sonata whose performance by the composer himself revealed his singularity as a pianist.

The cultural context in which his talent developed was most diverse. And it is quite valid as regards a galaxy of composers who came to the fore in the 1960s in the former USSR, including on a par with Tishchenko such names as Alfred Schnittke, Edison Denisov, Sophia Gubaidulina, Giya Kancheli, Avet Terteryan, Bronislavas Kutavicius and many others. The fact that Tishchenko as a composer grew up in Leningrad (now bearing its original name of St. Petersburg) left an imprint on his work, which is hardly noticeable in the composers coming from Moscow (Alfred Schnittke, Edison Denisov, *et al.*). It is true that St. Petersburg in its artistic traditions is a city more Russian in its spirit than Moscow with its international contacts. It was St. Petersburg that was the residence-place of the celebrated "Five Russians" (Balakirev, Borodin, Mussorgsky, Cui, and Rimsky-Korsakov) claiming for a singular road of Russia in music. Their aesthetics gave rise to the Russian foundations in Stravinsky's talent. These "Five Russians" from the very start of their creative careers were known for combining the deep-going national traditions with the extremely novel musical idioms. This kind of the Russian spirit made a major element in the Tishchenko style, too.

Boris Ivanovich Tishchenko was born on March 23, 1939 in Leningrad where he passed all the levels in his musical education and where he is still residing. As early as in a music college he was lucky enough to study composition with Galina Ustvolskaya, a talented composer herself, a pupil of Dmitry Shostakovich. Though hardly known as a composer, Ustvolskaya nevertheless is distinguished for her own musical style, austere and non-lyrical, most "unwomanly" as compared to others. The tragic severe spirit, devoid of any sweetish romanticism and sentimentality, turned out to be a common quality of the teacher and her pupil. At the Leningrad Conservatoire Tishchenko studied composition with Vadim Salmanov, Victor Voloshinov (to whose memory Tishchenko dedicated his first Symphony), and Orest Yevlakhov. When he was twenty-two, Tishchenko met Dmitry Shostakovich, under whose guidance he completed his postgraduate studies.

In this way the young composer's association with Dmitry Shostakovich came to be two-fold: through Galina Ustvolskaya and through his personal contacts with the great composer. The acknowledged master and the budding composer were strongly attracted to each other. While he was making his own orchestration version of Tishchenko's First Cello Concerto, Dmitry Shostakovich used to emphasize that he knew that score by heart. In his turn, Tishchenko dedicated his Third Symphony, a highly original work, to Dmitry Shostakovich. And after the master's death in 1975 Tishchenko expressed his shock and grief in his most dramatic Fifth Symphony, also dedicated to Dmitry Shostakovich (1976). All the five movements in this composition are permeated with the monogram DSCH, rendered in varied musical versions. As for its musical imagery, Tishchenko deliberately built up his work on a contrast between two, most characteristic types of sonority intrinsic in Shostakovich's symphonies: slow poignant meditations (the prolonged solo of the wind instruments) and catastrophic culminations (the orchestral *tutti* with the energetic part assigned to the percussion group).

The first movement in Boris Tishchenko's Fifth Symphony is wholly based on an alternation of long monologic solos and tragic *tutti*, with the strongest one coming at its end. And the entire symphony is developing along the line of the ever mounting tragic culminations, up to their climax in the fourth movement, preceding the finale, where the whole orchestra resounding in *ffff* shakes the listeners with its trills and glissandi. The "universal outcry" brought forth by shostakovich in his symphonies is the type of sonority that characterizes Tishchenko's symphonies, too. And this outburst is stronger and more desperate than the one produced, for instance, by the (20th) century Viennese expressionists. We have just mentioned his Fifth Symphony. This type of sonority got its excessive treatment in his Fourth Symphony, where the visions of terror make up a whole movement, entitled *Sinfonia di rabbia* ("symphony of violence," "symphony of evil"). The same imagery is manifested in his Second *Marina*

Symphony (written in 1964), set to the lyrics of Marina Tsvetayeva, a remarkable Russian poetess of the 20th century; in its third movement there ring out the frenzied outcries of the chorus (with glissando): "The heart's betrayal!," "Grishka! Dmitry!" (the names of the notorious impostors to the Russian throne), whereas in its first movement there are passages presenting a direct sequel to "the episodes of evil" with the solo of the snare drum in Shostakovich's so called "wartime symphonies."

In his tribute to the memory of his great teacher Boris Tishchenko revived Shostakovich's incomplete Trio Op. 8, finishing it off and revising it (1980). He also orchestrated Shostakovich's song-cycles *Satires* to the verses by Sasha Chorny (1980) and *Four Poems by Captain Lebyadkin* after Fyodor Dostoyevsky (1986).

As a truly Russian intellectual, Boris Tishchenko is sensitive to the civic principles in art, which was a characteristic trait of Shostakovich as man and composer. Throughout the history of national culture Russian writers, poets, painters and composers used to consistently follow the tradition of introducing in their works the motives of social protest and struggle against the current rulers: indeed, a poet in Russia is more than just a poet. The satirical challenge inherent in the works of composers belonging to the St. Petersburg school such as Mussorgsky with his musical lampoon *Rayok* (*The Peepshow*), and Rimsky-Korsakov who wrote *Le Coq d'or*, an anti-tsarist opera, passed over to the following generations of composers. Shortly after Shostakovich's decease his successors discovered in his archive files the micro-opera *The Antiformalist Peepshow*, a piece of biting satire against Stalin, which had it been found at the time of its writing, would have led to the composer's immediate execution. In 1989 Tishchenko scored this composition for an orchestra. As for his own work, its was a high act of civic spirit to write *Requiem* to the lyrics of Anna Akhamatova, another remarkable Russian poetess of the 20th century.

Requiem for soprano, tenor and orchestra was written by Boris Tishchenko in 1966 as a wittingly underground piece to be shelved until the more favorable times. It was set to the poem by Anna Akhmatove, remaining unpublished for political reasons, whose copies were kept in secret places throughout the homes of Leningrad-residing intellectuals. Akhamatova's poem is a requiem of the mother, who was also an outstanding poetess, for her missing son lost without a trace in the torture-chambers of the Stalinist camps. When with the coming of perestroika in the USSR this poem was at long last published, it made a sensation in the literary circles and was recognized as a major poetic work of the century. Tishchenko's *Requiem*, whose score was published in 1989 after having been shelved for nearly two decades, also won recognition of the musical community as one of the most profound compositions of his generation.

The creator of this *Requiem* set before himself an exceptionally hard task: to carefully convey to the listeners the entire poetical text of Anna Akhmatova without turning his music into an illustration to her verse. The following titles of separate items reveal the content of Tishchenko's *Requiem*: *"Not under the alien skies,* "Before such grief the mountains could bend," "You were taken away at daybreak," "This happened when only the dead were smiling," (Movement One); "I have been crying for seventeen months," "Away to death," "The verdict," and "Crucifixion" (Movement Two); "I learned how the faces fell," and "The funeral hour once again is drawing near" (Movement Three). And the final Coda ends in "Amen."

The poetical text is sung not by a large chorus, but exclusively by two soloists-the soprano and the tenor. The vocal parts written for the soloists are clearly discernible either in one-voice leading or in a duet with monorhythmic or variational correlation of the voices. Neither is the full symphony orchestra to tone down the bearers of the verse, with the composer allowing it to resound in-between the vocal lines, i.e. in the introductions and the concluding sections of the items, between the phrases, and as the emotionally colored background or as variations of the vocal parts. The vocal and orchestral resources so carefully employed with a view to producing an integral musical entity were thoroughly elaborated by the composer in their structure. Let us keep in mind that in the mid-sixties, when Boris Tishchenko was writing his *Requiem,* the composers were universally infatuated with Webern and the honed crystals of his musical compositions. You could glimpse the composer's work on the series, intervalic groups (microseries) and various canons in this *Requiem,* too. Thus, in No. 2 ("Before such grief the mountains could bend") the twelve-note series is developing through the rotation of sounds, a retrograde canon, an augmented canon, motives in their retrograde inversion, and the like. The composition is permeated throughout with an intervalic group consisting of a second and a third in all possible versions. As a whole, Tishchenko's *Requiem* makes a work of great inner expressiveness, well balanced by the subtle beauty of its external sonority.

The formation of all Soviet composers of the sixties proceeded during the period when, owing to the current bans and uncertainty, any piece of music written by 20th century composers, including Prokofiev, Stravinsky, Stockhausen, Boulez, and those producing electronic music, was perceived with extremely keen interest. Naturally enough, Boris Tishchenko with his wide range of interests was drawn into this process. The Prokofiev style captured his tenacious mind by the character of its melodic lines, both songfully Russian and excessively modern, with its unheard-of wide progressions fraught with chromatic tension in each motion. The line of modern songfulness discovered by Prokofiev proved fruitful for almost all contemporary Russian composers, Tishchenko included, be it his First Violin Concerto or the last of his piano sonatas.

The Prokofiev style turned out to be equally captivating for Tishchenko as a pianist. One of the specific features inherent in Prokofiev's piano pieces is the character of a musical sound. His scores are covered with the indications for all kinds of performance: *staccato, staccatissimo, martellato, legato,* accents, double accents, even *col pugno,* etc., so that in most cases each note has its own sign to indicate the performing manner. For Tishchenko the articulation palette of a piano tone has become a major domain of his work not only as a pianist but also as a composer. Along with the traditionally romantic approach to piano playing, he has always been interested in all other expressive resources inherent in this instrument. Those include the Prokofievian sharp *staccato,* the accents with a *staccato,* the Rachmaninovian bell-like beats, the piano overtones of the early Schoenberg, the avant-garde elbow clusters, and his own fanciful polyphony of various notes, contrasting registers, and textures of varied sound density. The contrasts of sound production, constantly discovered by Tishchenko, help him produce the so called "piano theatre" or "a drama on the keyboard."

The "piano theatre" created by Tishchenko as a composer is so specific in the world of piano music that it needs one actor alone-first and foremost, the composer himself as a pianist. And when the composer appears with the "stage" premieres" of his own piano sonatas, it gives an impression that anybody else could hardly be able to reproduce this music (through), naturally other pianists also play his compositions). Undoubtedly, Tishchenko's piano work in its style stands apart in the music written in the second half of the 20th century.

It is noteworthy how the Tishchenko style correlates with the traditions initiated by Igor Stravinsky. It is no accident that it was Stravinsky, whose early years were spent in St. Petersburg, who turned out to be a revolutionary innovator in 20th-century rhythmics and who followed in the footsteps of his predecessor in this domain-Rimsky-Korsakov, another resident of St. Petersburg. In contrast to Stravinsky who had shaken the world by the agile rhythms in his relatively earlier compositions (*The Rite of Spring*, *Histoire du soldat*, and some others) but later on began toning down the rhythmic energy and forcefulness in his music, Tishchenko became the successor to and continuer of Stravinsky's most complicated asymmetrical rhythms.

As early as in his Second String Quartet, written during his student years (1959), Boris Tishchenko made use of the refined changes in metre ($3/16 + 3/4$) and polymetrics ($3+3+2/8 : 2/4$). In his Third String Quartet (written in 1970) he came to employ (in its third movement entitled "Robusto") a system of mixed measures /2+2+2+3, 3+2+2+2, 3+2+3+2+2, 3+2+2, 2+2+3, 2+2+3+2+3+2, and so on/, given in the continual variation of metre and asynchronous polymetrics noted down with the help of broken bar-lines. The effect produced by such quartet "scherzo" is somewhat akin to the effects of Bartok's sharp polyrhythms, but in its structure it is more intricate in quality than in the composers belonging to the first half of the 20th century. Even in his compositions intended for children Tishchenko took up the challenge of experimentation in splitting the conventional measures into two units. Thus, in his symphonic tale *The Golden-Bellied Fly* after Kornei Chukovsky's fairy tale (written in 1968) he made use, perhaps, for the first time in Russian music, of the following measures and groupings: $5 1/2 : 8$, $1/4+5/16+7/8$ (to the words, "come black-beetles, I'll treat you to a tea") and $10 1/2 : 8$ (to the words "Little fleas used to visit the golden-bellied fly"). In his Second *Marina* Symphony (written in 1964) the rhythmic refinement reached the ratio of $2/4 + 5/28 + 3/20 + 2/4$ and the like.

One of the most involved matters as regards Boris Tishchenko's musical language concerns his correlation with the Western avant-garde and its compositional innovations. In contrast to some other composers of his generation, who had quite easily and naturally assimilated the quests of their Western counterparts (for instance, Edison Denisov), Boris Tishchenko seemed to face in this respect an invisible boundary-line, which made his work more typically Russian than European in general or Western in particular.

At the same time a deeper study of Tishchenko's work and his musical language reveals a multitude of elements which have much in common with the findings of the Western avant-garde. But all separate moments in this community only stress the qualitative differences in their employment. Boris Tishchenko tackles the pitched series, rhythmic progressions, rhythms with the added small duration, measured rhythmic structure of whole forms, pointillism, "torn textures" and the like. Making use of all these techniques, he nevertheless in a purely Slavonic, Russian style softens the mathematically strict approach to the composition procedures, always ready to produce a variation of any a priori chosen technical element. Let us consider, for example, his treatment of pitched series. The above mentioned No 2 ("Before this grief the mountains could bend") from his *Requiem* contains a series made up of not twelve but nine notes, and in his Fifth Piano Sonata the series has merely five notes. The treatment of such series is based on the classical dodecaphonic principle to use its following four forms: O, I, R, IR. Thus, in the third movement of his Third Piano sonata against the background of flitting phrases in *Allegro leggiero* as the imperative *cantus firmus* there come in distinct utterance, in large durations, the four forms of the five-note series recurred from the sonata's first movement: O, I, RI, R. And each series of such kind used by Tishchenko, not taking under its control all the twelve chromatic notes, is soon to subjected to rotation (transposition) of notes, then to reductions and repetitions of notes, i.e. it starts developing like a classical melodic line.

While using rhythmic progression, Tishchenko softens its mathematical automatic nature intrinsic in, say, Messiaen's progressions, by imparting to it the spontaneity of natural singing, a free and easy melodic phrasing. Thus, the first phrase of the French horn at the beginning of his Third Symphony involves the following durations: ♩ ♩ ♪. ♪ ♪³ But, first, this rhythmic progression lacks the "round" mathematical number 12 or 16; second, the durations got repeated and alternating so that the general effect turns to be opposite to that of the Western samples: not an artificial , forced augmentation or diminution, but a free, easy singing (this movement is called "Meditations").

Ex. 1 *Third Symphony*

The above mentioned refined structures such as 5 1/2:8 or 10 1/2:8 are similar to Messiaen's tense "rhythms with the added small duration," probably, evoked by this theory. But with this Russian composer such structures are placed into a different context — in the smoothing over division of musical phrases.

The second movement of Tishchenko's Fourth Symphony (written in 1974) exemplifies rhythmic calculation of a whole musical form. It may be compared with the composition of Boulez's *Structures* 1 for two pianos, written exclusively in the serial technique. In his monumental symphonic opus Tishchenko employs a system of rhythmic series combined into blocks. But his "series" widely encountered in the music devoid of series and serialism, such as: ♫♫♫ ♫♫♫ ♫♫♫ ♫♫♫ ♫♫♫ ♫♫♫ and some others.

The example of the most conspicuous pointillism used by Boris Tishchenko can be found in his song-cycle *Sad Songs*, No. 1 "Time" (written in 1962). Its piano part features separate dotes of sounds scattered throughout in all registers. But these dotted notes, first, are neither played in *staccato*, nor dried up in rests but rendered in their full-weight sonority and, second, they are stated in a strictly uniform rhythm, being grouped into pseudo-measures containing twelve fractions. Such a clear-cut rhythmic pointillism is not at all characteristic of the Western avant-garde known, on the contrary, for combining the progressions of dots with keen aperiodicity. Another, still more spectacular transformation of pointillism is to be found at the beginning of Tishchenko's Third Piano Sonata where the scattering of large durations over the pedals produces the effect close to that of the monumental Rachmaninovian piano bell-pealing. What had arisen as an abstract technique in the West turned into a visible image with the Russian composer.

The picture of Boris Tishchenko's style and musical language should be complemented with two more significant elements — the folk and Oriental aspects in his work.

The educational system, which is still in force in the Russian Federation, has invariably provided for the folkloristic trips to be made by the students majoring in composition. Within this compulsory programme all future composers, including Edison Denisov and Alfred Schnittke (from Moscow) and Boris Tishchenko and Sergei Slonimsky (from Leningrad), went on such trips around the country. Their task was to record down folk songs in the countryside, with their subsequent deciphering from a tape recorder. As a result, the fledging composers had access to the folk layer in musical culture and could absorb the folk timbres, the non-tempered tuning and a singular character of polyphony. As a rule, the budding musicians included the folk tunes they had happened to record down personally into their compositions written during their conservatoire studies.

In the case of Boris Tishchenko, the same as with Sergei Slonimsky, with their Russian line rooted in the St. Petersburg tradition, such contact with authentic folk culture made an indelible impression and exercised an powerful influence on his musical thinking and world outlook. He came to discover not only the previously unknown folk pieces, but also a peculiar logic underlying the train of folk "musical thought," which differed from the classical European one, and the folk philosophy inherent in this art.

The matter is not only in the fact that Tishchenko in his *Sad Songs* included several settings of traditional texts and that he left some melodies without harmonic accompaniment and bar-lines. The most important discovery lay in his apprehending the essence of folk improvisation, its spontaneous, free and easy nature, and in the composer's personal perception of this singular plainsong Russian folk musical form. Listening to such singing usually brings to one's mind the thoughts of the most general philosophical character about the eternity of these tunes as imperishable as earth itself.

As for the Eastern culture, Boris Tishchenko got interested in *gagaku,* Japanese ritual music, with its majestic measured motion and the tense heterophony of microtones. Others composers of his generation, following Tishchenko's example, made it a rule for themselves to learn the principles of *gagaku* music. As for Tishchenko, he deciphered and scored separate parts of this ritual music (1972).

Let us try to identify the inimitable qualities of the Tishchenko style. To do this, it would be insufficient to provide characteristics for separate elements of his musical language, which we have partly covered above. Further appraisal will be based on the criteria underlying *the inner models of his musical compositions*, which should help in understanding the specific features of the composer's musical thinking.

One of the inner models in Tishchenko's work is associated with the natural philosophical idea about the organic growth of all the living creatures. Such model presumes the exceptional gradualness of as musical process, imperceptible changes in quality, and formation of contrasts exclusively at a distance. The traits of such kind of a process are discernible both in the prolonged "meditative" solos of separate instruments in Shostakovich's symphonies and in the spontaneous improvisatory unfolding of the Russian folk drawn-out songs. Tishchenko's First Cello Concerto (written in 1963) provides one of the most spectacular examples of embodying the model of gradual organic growth in his music. In this composition Tishchenko discards the road of classical form-building, which presumes the exposition of a complete theme and its development. He employs here a special technique of growing a theme out of a tiny grain, doing it directly in front of the audience. In his First Cello Concerto this grain contains the note "A" alone. The composer repeats this sole note, varying it rhythmically, enveloping it from the bottom and the top, detaching a short scale-like progression from it, repeating it once again, varying, and so on. The listeners could watch the prolonged process of seemingly involuntary growing of a large structure out of the simplest impetus, and this process constitutes Tishchenko's extraordinarily broad singular theme, which is further varied and developed in the same gradual way.

Another technique of spontaneous unfolding, seemingly "artificial improvisation" in front of the audience, is founded on rhythmics, which can be exemplified by the key section in the finale of Tishchenko's Third Piano Sonata.

The composer seems to be modelling here a free and easy, but lengthy folk tune unfettered by the academic measures and tonality. The quality of spontaneity thus achieved gives an impression of no technique ever used. But the technique consists in varying several chosen note values. The composer starts with the simplest durations such as crotchets and minims and states them in all possible combinations.

Ex. 2 *Third Piano Sonata*

Further on, Boris Tishchenko adds also the simplest durations — two quavers, combining the latter with the previous ones in all possible ways. The Character of development thus attained turns out to be reminiscent of slow intensification inherent in the Russian folk choral polyphony. Of course, there could never exist such a choral folk piece, since it is the style of composer living in the second half of the 20th century. But the composer reveals the extremely sensitive attitude to reproducing the process of Russian folk singing in his music.

A model of spontaneity of a different kind is presented in Tishchenko's Seventh Piano sonata, which involves the participation of bells, (natural and tubular bells, and handbells). The inner imagery of this composition is based not on a folk tune but on another characteristic acoustic element from the Russian life, which has been inherent in it for several hundreds of years, — bells and their pealing. Each of the three movements in the Seventh Sonata in its development is moving to the bell-like polyphony of the piano, towards the dissonances produced by the bells. And only in the final Coda the grave and powerful character of the "bell-like piano" is suddenly removed by th seemingly childish music in the spirit of Prokofiev's gavottes by using the handbells.

The spirit of spontaneity and unpremeditation reigning supreme in Boris Tishchenko's music turned out to be the composer's conception and inner aspiration, which he defined in the following words: "... music is not to recreate the emotions and states but to depict their mutual cohesion. Therefore genuine music invariably gives the impression of being born on its own, without the outside help. It just had to be delivered"[1].

A number of other models inherent in Tishchenko's compositions appear to be related to a problem common for the entire 20th century — the philosophical problem of time. It is manifested in the first song "Time" to the verse by Shelley, which opens his early song-cycle *Sad Songs*. Its initial words "Ocean of Time, whose waters of deep woe are brackish with the salt of human tears!" may be regarded as programmatic. The capacious concept of Time for a musician embraces the acoustical, physical aspect of a musical work (vibration frequency of a sound, duration of a musical piece), the parameters of rhythm and tempo of the musical language, the ontological time of human history (past, present, and future), and the traditional artistic symbol of human mortality and transitory nature of a human life. All these aspects of Time proved to be highly topical for Boris Tishchenko.

A kind of "musical investigations" of Time is evident in his Third Symphony and Fifth Piano Sonata, with these musical moments being, as a matter of fact, unique in modern music. To apprehend the inner models of these moments, one ought to bring to mind Stockhausen's theoretical treatise *Wie die Zeit vergeht* in which he treated all parameters of music as a slice of musical time, building up a unified temporal scale and dividing it into "macrotime" and "macrotime" (pitches and rhythms).

---

[1] Cited from the article by V. Syrov: A Profile of Boris Tishchenko // Muzykalnaya Zhizn magazine, 1989, Issue No. 5, p. 10.

We have already discussed the beginning of Tishchenko's Third Symphony in relation to its specific rhythmic progression marked for its spontaneous character (see Musical Example 1). This spontaneity seems to take the listener's mind back to the archaic time when it was not measured by mechanical alternation of minutes and seconds: the music is not divided into either even measures or even fractions of a measure. Its texture is woven out of separate phrases and their pulsation makes up the organic rhythm of the music. The symphony falls into two large movements: Movement One — "Meditations" (consisting of four sections) and Movement Two — "Post scriptum". "Meditations" are developing from the rarefied phrases in the first section to the "Shostakovichian" tension in the second one, with energetic pulsation of musical time. In the third section the composer gradually passes from "microtime" (melody and harmony) to "macrotime" (rhythm), more and more slowing down the vibration frequency and leading the orchestra to the unnaturally slow, already purely acoustical pulsation of "sound waves." And at the point of such complete decomposition of the music into physical vibrations Tishchenko introduces an unforgettable contrast-the inspired musical integrity. As an image arising in the depths of one's memory, just for a few bars, there appear the allusions of Schubert's song "Margarita at the Spinning-Wheel" with the use of female and male voices (backstage or on tape) and the piano. This moment of reminding of the old imperishable music instantly depreciates the modern acoustical innovations, reinstating the entire system of values in this symphony. The subsequent stages of development are colored in gloomy tones.

His Fifth Piano Sonata (written in 1973) from the very beginning states "the struggle of times" as a "struggle" of motions contrasting in speed — fast movement in semiquavers and slow movement in semibreves and minims. The breakdown into "sound waves", comparable to the Third Symphony, but nevertheless quite different again, begins in the second movement. Taking two rows of uniformly repeated notes, the composer shifts the time of introducing the notes of one row in relation to the other, creating the asynchronous pulsation of the "macrotime" units (according to Stockhausen); it brings to mind the plot of Salvador Dali's famous picture "Running Time".

And like in the Third Symphony in contrast to the acoustical imagery you have the illusion of Schubert's inspired song, in the Fifth Sonata there arises a glimpse of the dear past in an arpeggio reminiscent of Bach and Beethoven ("Intermezzo" before the finale). And it also brings forth the reappraisal of current values.

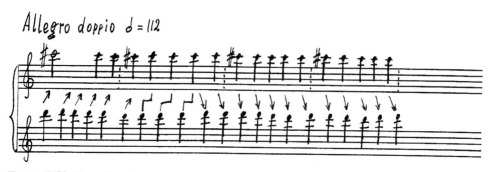

Ex. 3 *Fifth Piano Sonata*

Boris Tishchenko expressed his approach to historical time in his ballet *Yaroslavna* (*Eclipse*, written in 1974) based on the plot of *The Lay of Igor's Campaign*, the celebrated old Russian chronicle dating back to the 12th century, which had inspired Alexander Borodin to write his *Prince Igor* destined to become a classical Russian opera. It was a great challenge for a Russian composer of the 20th century to use the plot that seemed to be inevitably associated with the well-known Borodin music. But Tishchenko in his ballet, first of all, gave the plot quite a different interpretation by selecting the plot lines untouched by Borodin and, secondly, his music was so dissimilar in its style that there was no mention of any competition with the great classic. In contrast to Borodin who in his opera was primarily interested in the heroic epos and the picturesque Orient, Tishchenko was inspired by the goal of recreating the spirit of the austere archaics, the gloomy pictures of the battles, and the bitterness of defeat. In contrast to the melodic breadth of Borodin's arias, Tishchenko's music is permeated with the declamatory nature of the chorus introduced into this ballet and variations of short tunes rendered by the chorus and the orchestra.

Boris Tishchenko managed to draw the atmosphere of the Russian archaics primarily through the choral part based on the old Russian language, with the chorus conveying therefore the lines of the oldest chronicle. In the choral sonority a major part is assigned to basses, a characteristic timbre of the Russian singing. Besides, the full orchestra is used not as a traditional symphony orchestra, but based on a non-classical selection of various groups of instruments such as, for instance, horns, tubas, cellos, double-basses, and a male chorus (the number entitled "Svyatoslav"), the oboe and the clarinet used as the Russian horns (the number "Yaroslavna"), clarinet and solo violin ("Weeping for the killed"), and wooden drums with a male chorus ("Igor's Escape"). The classical orchestra is employed only in *tutti*, in particular, in all numbers depicting the battlefield: "First Battle with Polovtsians," "Second Battle" and others. The archaic sonority is also achieved owing to a special selection of harmonic combinations, with deliberate avoidance of thirds, based on fourths, seconds and dissonant polyphony. As a matter of fact, the harmonic system devoid of thirds existed in Russian up to the 17th century, before it came into contact with Western Europe. But Tishchenko imparted to it the chromatic agility inherent in 20th-century harmony. The variational development of short phrases and motives carried on Stravinsky's experience in his work on microthemes of the Russian type. Another manifestation of 20th-century characteristic idioms is the ostinato nature of microthemes, for instance, in the number "Eclipse" (with a gradual increase of the orchestral voices).

The archaically gloomy, singularly Russian and the tense spirit of 20th-century music is so evenly sustained throughout this three-act ballet that its separate numbers present themselves as individual facets of this singularity. For instance, "Glory to Igor" is accompanied by the dissonant two-voice leading of the male chorus, delivered in the Old Russian language, with the sonorous orchestral "vignettes" in-between the choral lines. The numbers "Steppe" and "The steppe of Death" with their "howling" strings playing the ostinato motives in *glissando* are picturesque and at the same time psychologically sinister. In the number "Night Premonitions" the male chorus has the sonorous, sound-imitating text, and against its background the solo violin delivers the phrases of despair. In the number "Arrows", to convey the spatial dimensions, Tishchenko once again brings into a clash various planes of musical time by resorting to the polytempo device: the tempo of the strings ♩=100, whereas the tempo of piccolo and wooden drums ♩=180. The composer concludes his ballet with "Prayer" delivered by the chorus and the strings, rendering the finale in the old, centuries-long Russian Christian tradition as opposed to the notorious official "Soviet optimism."

For all the unusual novel models of his compositions, Tishchenko takes a keen interest in such universal European musical model as a drama. The composer conceals in himself the hallmarks of a born actor and stage director. Paradoxically enough, as an "actor," he seems to be more attracted to comedy, or to be more precise, to animalist comedy, beginning with his *The Golden-Bellied Fly* and *The Giant Black-Beetle (Tarakanishche)*, written in 1968 on the subjects of Kornei Chukovsky's tales for children, and ending with *The Chelom Wise Men* to verse by Ovsei Driz (for adults; written in 1991), with their comic scenes involving mice, cats and dogs. As a stage director, he is striving for the diametrically opposite messages-the embodiment of tragic paradoxes in human existence and the search for a way out of hopelessness. And his sense of acute dramatic contrast, a sudden turn of events overthrowing the layout of the narrative, and his ability for the arrangement of opposite forces are the inborn traits of this composer who has to credit numerous symphonies, concertos and sonatas.

Some of his best and highly original compositions reveal his most characteristic dramatic pattern, which includes the following stages. The first one constitutes the ripening of an inner contrast within the organically growing homogeneity. The second stage amounts to attaining a culmination point through piling up or, conversely, the decomposition of his musical material. The third stage involves the alienation of this material, its comparison with something too remote and unpredictable (like the allusion to Schubert's "Margarita at the Spinning-Wheel" in his Third Symphony or the arpeggio in the style of Bach and Beethoven in his Fifth Piano sonata). The fourth stage brings about the reappraisal of values, a transition into another dimension, as if making a transfer from the world of objective realities to the world of purely ethical notions.

Out of his symphonies, Tishchenko's Fourth Symphony for a superlarge orchestra of 145 players is most theatrical in its spirit. The instruments include even an in-fragenerator affecting the mind in the strongest and imperceptible way. And there is a recitalist who narrates Ivan Turgenev's prose (through a microphone or on a tape recorder). The declamation of artistic prose in the Fourth Symphony makes an integral part of its general culmination within its fourth movement ("Sinfonia di crudelta," "symphony of cruelty") and it is linked with the general turn of developments, when the narration is suddenly interrupted by the deafening sound of a pistol shot.

Tishchenko's Third and Fifth Sonatas present a true "drama on the piano." The finale of his Third Piano Sonata is most dramatically striking. Its very first bars bring into an acute clash the two fundamental principles: the "aggressive" willpower, cruel force (octaves in the bass *marcatissimo forte-fortissimo*) and the quiet, almost lifeless aloofness (gentle lingering notes in a high register). In the middle of the finale there occurs the spontaneous ripening of a quasi-folk tune, unfolding into a broad multi-voice "chorus," which we have mentioned above (see Musical Example 2). As soon as the culmination stage is over, the aggressive, negative force recedes from the scene, whereas the gentle, static voice in its high register, without changing its outward character, becomes the voice of purity and enlightenment: the quiet has outlived all the loudest, thereby changing diametrically the ethical message of the composition.

In the Fifth Piano Sonata, following the phantasmagoria of "running time" (see Musical Example 3) and a sudden allusion to the imperishable old-time music (Bach, Beethoven), there comes the finale in which for the first time you hear the piano voice full of live human feelings, sufferings, and desires-the eternal emotions to accompany a human being on earth. Herein, lies the ethical catharsis of this piano drama.

The final catharsis is the summit point in the aspirations of this composer, a modern muscan-philosopher striving for not merely writing interesting music but in his innermost hoping, with the help of his music, to improve and change this world. And in this respect a 20th-century artist can follow the greatest examples set in the Russian art by Leo Tolstoy, Fyodor Dostoyevsky, and Alexander Scriabin. To improve and to change means to raise hopes for something immortal, intransient and having the greatest ethical value. The cathartic moments are particularly extended in Boris Tishchenko's symphonies. In his Third Symphony the finale "Post scriptum" is rendered in a new ethical vein, and his monumental Fourth Symphony is marked for prolonged static motion in the second half of its finale entitled "Sinfonia di risorgimen-to e tenerezza" ("Symphony of Revival and Tenderness"). The composer draws the imagery of these final ethical truths from the philosophy of early, but still living music — both Russian and foreign, folk and ritual, the music which the composer imbibed from the authentic Russian folklore, the ancient Oriental culture and the old West, striving for a global synthesis of musical sources. To quote Boris Tishchenko's own words when he spoke about Shostakovich, in his music "You can find the answers to the most vital questions: what is the message of a human life and where lies the light of truth..."

PRINCIPAL WORKS

Musical Theatre

The Twelve, ballet after Alexander Blok (1963)
The Golden-Bellied Fly, ballet after Kornei Chukovsky's tale (1968)
The Stolen Sun, opera after Kornei Chukovsky (1968)
The Giant Black-Beetle (*Tarakanishche*), operetta after Kornei Chukovsky (1968)
Yaroslavan (*Eclipse*), ballet based on the old Russian chronicle *The Lay of Igor's Campaign* (1974)

Orchestral Works

Violin Concerto No. 1 (1958; 2nd version, 1964)
Symphony No. 1 (1961)
Piano Concerto (1962)
Concerto No. 1 for cello, 17 wind instruments, percussion and harmonium (1963; Dmitry Shostakovich's version for cello and orchestra, 1969)
Symphony No. 2 *Marina* for mixed chorus and symphony orchestra to verses by Marina Tsvetayeva (1964)
Symphony No. 3 for chamber orchestra (1966)
Pushkin's Death, dramatic music (1967)
Concerto No. 2 for cello accompanied by 48 cellos, 12 double-basses and percussion (1969; version for string orchestra and percussion, 1979)
Sinfonia robusta for symphony orchestra (1970)
Concerto for flute, piano and string orchestra (1972)
Symphony No. 4 for full symphony orchestra and a recitalist, prose by Ivan Turgenev (1974)
Symphony No. 5 for symphony orchestra (1976)
Concerto for Harp and Orchestra (1977)
Violin Concerto No. 2 (Violin Symphony, 1981)
Symphony *The Chronicle of the Siege* for full symphony orchestra (1984)
Symphony No. 6 for soprano, contralto and symphony orchestra to verses by Anatoly Naiman, Anna Akhmatova, Marina Tsvetayeva, Osip Mandelstam, and Vladimir Levinzon (1988)
French Symphony, a new version of the like-named early composition (1993)
Symphony No. 7 (1994)

Works for Voice and Orchestra

Suzdal (songs and tunes), suite for soprano, tenor and chamber orchestra (1964)
Requiem for soprano, tenor and symphony orchestra to verse by Anna Akhmatova (1966)
Severe Cold, aria for mezzo-soprano and orchestra to verse by Vladimir Tendryakov (1974)

Chamber Instrumental Works

Piano Sonata No. 1 (1957–1995)
String Quartet (1959)

Twelve Inventions for Organ (1964)
Piano Sonata No. 3 (1965)
String Quartet No. 3 (1970)
Piano Sonata No. 4 (1972)
Piano Sonata No. 5 (1973)
Piano Sonata No. 6 (1975)
String Quartet No. 4 (1980)
Sonata No. 7 for piano and bells (1982)
String Quartet No. 5 (1984)
String Quintet (1985)
Piano Sonata No. 8 (1986)
The Heart of a Dog, novellas for chamber ensemble (1988)
Concerto for Clarinet and Piano Trio (1990)
Twelve Portraits for organ (1992)
Piano Sonata No. 9 (1992)
Fantasia for Violin and Piano (1994)

Chamber Vocal Music

Sad Songs, song-cycle for soprano and piano to verses by different poets and folk texts (1962)
Five Settings of Ovsei Driz for voice and piano (1974)
Testament for soprano, harp and organ to verse by Nikolai Zabolotsky (1986)
To the Brother for soprano, flute and harp to verse by Mikhail Lermontov (1986)
The Garden of Music, cantata for three soloists-singers and piano trio to verse by Alexander Kushner (1987)
The Chelom Wise Men, vocal-instrumental quartet for violin, soprano, bass and piano to verse by Ovsei Driz (1991)
The Devildraft, vocal cycle for middle voice and piano (1995)

Incidental Scores to Plays and Films

Music to Chekhov's play *"The Three Sisters"* (1987)
Music to Molière's comedy *Georges Dandin, ou le mari confondu* (1993)
Orchestrations (Monteverdi, Grieg, Mahler, Prokofiev, and Shostakovich)

Valentin Silvestrov's lyrical universe

Svetlana Savenko

Valentin Silvestrov

Valentin Vasilyevich Silvestrov was born on September 30, 1937 in Kiev (Ukraine). He started his musical training in 1952, first by taking private lessons and then attending the evening music courses for adults, completing them in 1958. Upon graduating from a higher school as a civil engineer, he entered the Kiev Conservatoire in 1958, where he studied composition with Boris Lyatoshinsky. Upon graduation from the conservatoire, from 1963 to 1970, he taught music in the elementary music schools of Kiev. The composer lives in Kiev together with his wife, a musicologist by education, and their married daughter and her two children.

Valentin Silvestrov, a talented modern composer, belongs to the postwar generation of artists who embarked upon their careers in the late 1950s and early 1960s, a time of radiant hopes and an upsurge in Soviet social life. His formation proceeded in the intricate social context with its struggle between the innovative artistic quests and the conservative official policies whose oppression in Kiev, as compared to Moscow and Leningrad, was particularly hard. The young composer's natural striving for novel expressive means turned under these conditions into a dissident-like opposition to the totalitarian regime. The label of "avant-gardist," which had been pinned on Silvestrov in the mid-sixties, greatly complicated his creative and human life; in his native land his opuses for a long time were hardly performed anywhere but at the informal concerts (for instance, in the clubs of scientists), rarely published, with himself being expelled for a time from the membership of the USSR Composers Union, which in those years deprived him of the official civil status (if the authorities so willed, criminal proceedings could be instituted against Silvestrov on the grounds of leading a parasitic life, like in the case of Joseph Brodsky).

Few people could withstand such long-lasting pressure. But Silvestrov managed even in these conditions to retain the dignity and inner freedom of a true artist who could be guided exclusively by the laws of his own creative nature, with the social environment failing to dictate him and impose upon him its dogmatic doctrines. To quote the composer himself, "I have to write what I like but not what the others like, nor what is dictated by the times, to use a conventional cliché. Otherwise, it will be time-serving that cripples one's mind"[1].

The spiritual independence is naturally not to exclude, but more likely to presume the community of stylistic processes that involve the artists of the same generation. In the early sixties Valentin Silvestrov, as Alfred Schnittke, Andrei Volkonsky, Arvo Pärt, Edison Denisov, and Sophia Gubaidulina, began the intensive assimilation of the avant-gardist musical idioms. That "Sturm und Drang" of the young composers allowed within a short span of time to overcome the local confinement of Soviet music and disrupt its actually existing isolation despite the world-wide recognition of Dmitry Shostakovich, Sergei Prokofiev and Aram Khachaturyan.

Valentin Silvestrov was quick at grasping the avant-gardist spectrum of expressive means: first, classical dodecaphony (which is evident in his compositions written during his conservatoire years, such as *Quartetto piccolo* for string quartet, 1961; or his *Triad* for piano, 1962), then the post-Webern pointillistics, sonoristics, and aleatory (*Mystery* for alto flute and six percussion groups, 1964; or *Monody* for piano and orchestra, 1965). It is noteworthy not only how speedy was the young composer in his evolution but also how early he revealed his highly individual treatment of the latest techniques. The mastery of the avant-gardist devices was marked in Silvestrov by new expressiveness, for he seemed to be not much interested in the self-sufficing beauty of rational structures. Therefore it is no accident that his music aroused some criticism on the part of the avant-gardists, which got its indirect evidence in Theodor Adorno's following remark: "My impression of Silvestrov was that he was a very talented man. The objection of some purists that his music is too expressive I could not share, and would find it unfortunate if he now, more or less mechanically, wanted to repeat himself what has happened in Western Europe for the last 20 years"[2]. Silvestrov was fortunate, though he has indeed "repeated" the experience of the West-European avant-garde, to do it "for himself," in his own inimitable style.

Elegy for piano (written in 1967), a piece lasting five minutes, entitled in a characteristically paradoxical way, is sustained throughout in a quite strict serial-pointillistic manner akin to Webern and Boulez. The salient features of this type of writing are obvious: twelve-note atonality, register isolation of sound elements-dots, metric equilibration of rhythmical units, microagogics and microdynamics, up to the finest pedal gradations.

However, the pointillistic isolation of its components are partly overcome through the quasi-melodic combination of sound dots owing to the register and phrasing nuances. Thus, the first four notes of the right hand rapidly outline the BACH motto theme, whose highest sounds, $e^3 — f^3$, fix down the interval of a major second, very essential for further development of the piece (in the cited fragment a major second is

---

[1] Cited from the book by T. Frumkis *Valentin Silvestrov's "Landscapes for Ear"*//Works by Modern Composers: Alemdar Karamanov, Valentin Silvestrov and Philip Glass. Moscow, Informkultura, p. 2. Hereinafter all the composer's utterances are to be cited according to this publication, without any reference.

[2] Cited from Virko Baley's *"Triada" by Valentin Silvestrov*: Notes from the program of M. Kriesberg's concert of piano music. N.Y. 1980.

Ex. 1 *Elegy*

skipped only in mm. 4 and 5). Later on this interval becomes a bridge between the melodic and sonoristic texture. And, in general, the type of texture is not rigid, with an easy interchange of the melodic, pointillistic and sonoristic lines. This specific feature is still more evident in Silvestrov's compositions for orchestra, written in the 1960s and called by him "cosmic pastorales": a live changing nature of the texture is invariably perceived as the boundless motion of matter. There is no room here for any subjective personal emotions, and it is no accident that the acute expressiveness inherent in the early neo-Viennese compositions, "stiffened" later in the serial structures, with their predominance of a semitone as a constructive and expressive unit, fails to find a continuer in Silvestrov, in contrast to, say, Alfred Schnittke.

Of major importance is Valentin Silvestrov's aspiration for interpreting the novel musical idioms as symbols. A contrast between the strictly notated and aleatory-im-provisatory material in his Third Symphony and in his earlier *Mystery* is treated by the composer as a conflict between the "cultural" and the "magical." The philosophical understatement of the Third Symphony, having the subtitle *Eschatophony*, "the last sound," is most significant, bringing to mind "eschatology" — "the last word" about the destinies of the world. As it may well be concluded, the assimilation of the avant-garde experience by Silvestrov was based on the semantic interpretation of its separate elements: using the linguistic terms, language was turning into speech, with the avant-garde innovations and discoveries being eventually included in a tradition and adapted by it.

Apparently, by the late 1960s Silvestrov felt a need for a fresh approach to the experience he had accumulated, and at the same time for a departure outside the limits of the purely avant-gardist spectrum of composition devices. After a year of keeping silence he began writing his *Drama* for three performers, a supercycle consisting of a sonata for violin and piano, a sonata for cello and piano and the final trio. The *Drama* and his next work, *Meditation* for cello and chamber orchestra (written in 1972), revealed for the first time in Silvestrov's music the elements of polystylistics, which were then gaining ground in European music (as is known, Luciano Berio's Symphony appeared in 1968, and Alfred Schnittke's First Symphony in 1972). The polystylistic conflict as a manifestation of the cultural apocalypse is embodied by Silvestrov with extreme sharpness. The musical "dialects" clashing in his *Drama* are so incompatible that their violent opposition transcends the framework of the purely acoustic sphere. The sound modulates into a gesture whereas the latter transforms into music: the matter involves wordless utterances about the dangers facing the very existence of art.

The signs of the instrumental theatre, which are evident in his *Drama* and *Meditation*, impart to these two compositions a considerable degree of the avant-gardist extravagance, perhaps, the most conspicuous in his entire creative output. The participants in the trio move around the stage, handling their instruments in the most unusal manner, sometimes treating them like the live creatures. The first sonata ends with the violinist's gesture lighting a match and immediately blowing it out. A similar action takes place at the culmination point in the *Meditation*: the orchestra players are prescribed to light and blow out matches in complete darkness, and only following this break the musical texture is restored and the light is switched on again. However, these actions, which are still shocking the general public and opposed to by most musicians, turn out to be just outwardly akin to the scenic innovations of the avant-garde happenings or the ideas inherent in the theatre of the absurd. Their message is highly symbolic and almost plot-like. It is no accident that the composer introduces here a polysemantic motif of the blazing up and dying out fire, one of the fundamental symbols in the world treasury.

In his *Meditation* the juxtaposition of different realms — musical essential elements (which can be defined as the individual, natural and cultivated) is perceived at first as their neutral coexistence in time and space. But gradually it stands to reason that these are not merely different "styles" but the incompatible, mutually excluding realms whose clash is fraught with a worldwide catastrophe. These realms have to be reconciled and "reduced to an identity" by restoring the broken chain of times-spaces-and herein lies the ultimate goal of meditation. The tension is so great that it leads to a rupture of the musical matter as it were, to the downfall into "the anti-world." The flashes of light and its tracers signify the otherworldliness of motives that flared up earlier in time and broke through the confines of the globe, to somewhere "where pass the shadows of other worlds, like the shadows of nameless and soundless ships"[3].

Valentin Silvestrov treats the polystylistics not only as a cultural-historical, "human" conflict but as a global collision of cosmic magnitude. It involves "on a par" the human and the natural, the cultivated and the spontaneous, the earthly and the universal. The supreme goal of the artist's effort is to wed Man and Nature and to reconcile the life's contradictions, which is paramount to Orpheus' mission. The conception underlying *Drama* and *Meditation* is typologically reminiscent of the utopias inherent in the late romantic period and the artistic and philosophical constructs of Mahler and Scriabin, despite the overall dissimilarity of the concrete forms of sound production during that period (later the situation is to change).

The stylistic range of Silvestrov's music in his new compositions is quite naturally expanding. The atonal pointillistic texture and the twelve-note vertical and horizontal relationships go hand in hand with the diatonic motives associated with the folk tunes and melodic turns in the Renaissance music. Beginning with *Meditation*, these are usually rendered by the French horn or the woodwind instruments, which produces the atmosphere of the Romantic *plein air*. The timbre semantics of "natural voices" are to be retained by Silvestrov up to his latest compositions. Another "traditional" element of polystylistic compositions are the classical Viennese cadence-like turns acting as the symbol of culture; in *Meditation* these turns are most distinct owing to the timbre of the harpsichord. Moreover, both spheres are elaborated by the composer during that period as the self-contained ones: in this vein is written his *Music in the Old-Time Style* for piano (1973), two episodes of which are cited below. The first one is distinguished by Silvestrov's maximal approximation to the prototype, verging on precise stylization; the second episode presents an interesting combination of quasi-folk tunes and "Gothic" cadences with the gently dissonant "echo" chords.

At the same time Silvestrov is not striving for a clear-cut delimitation of the contrasting stylistic spheres: the word "collage" often associated with the polystylistics and implying the emphasis on junctions, a confrontation of heterogeneous elements, can be hardly applied to his music, even to his *Drama* and *Meditation*. The term coined by Stockhausen — "symbiotic polystylistics" — is more suitable to it, for in many respects it corresponds to Silvestrov's approach to the process of meditation as reduction to an identity. The resolution of the conflict occurs as if in overcoming the concrete nature of the style, on "no man's land" — in the prolonged coda section of static character wherein thematic elements gradually lose their stylistic, "limitedness", being perceived as parts of a harmonious entity. The coda section, an "afterword" to the composition, gradually becomes its more and more weighty part.

When asked about the periodization of his creative career, Valentin Silvestrov pointed out that the year 1974 had marked a new stage in his evolution: "a 'metaphorical' style in the vein of new traditionalism or neoromanticism." In those days stylistic surprises were quite in vogue. But Silvestrov's *Kitsch Music* for piano and especially his song-cycle *Quiet Songs* (written in 1974–77) shocked many listeners, in

---

[3] Vladimir Nabokov. Nikolai Gogol // Novy mir, 1987, Issue 4, p. 225.

Ex. 2a *Music in the old-time style: Morning Music*

particular professional musicians, who regarded them as a betrayal of the avant-gardist ideals and as renunciation of his own individuality. However, as was stressed above, dogmatism of any kind was ever alien to Silvestrov, and this time the truly avant-gardist creative daring and the spiritual independence manifested themselves in his denial of the outdated musical clichés.

Ex. 2b *Contemplation*

Valentin Silvestrov turned his attention to the previously "non-topical" romantic stylistics: in *Kitsch Music* it is Schumann, Brahms and Chopin, in *Quiet Songs* – the Russian romances of the 19th century with all their numerous overtones, from Glinka and Schubert to the home music-making. The immersion into "the magnificent past" seems to be absolute: the composer goes to an extreme, risking to sacrifice his own style. However it is not imitation, but a "weak style," to quote him once again; in other words, his is a contextual style, based not so much on its own matter as on a metaphor, an allegory, and an allusion. The composer's poetic programme finds its indirect evidence in his noted remarks for the performers: "It should be played in a very tender and heartfelt way, as if gently stirring up the listener's memory so that the music would ring inside one's mind" (*Kitsch Music*); "To sing as if listening to himself. All the songs should be sung very quietly, in an easy, transparent and lucid tone, with restrained expressiveness and rigidly, without any psychological pressure. It is desirable to perform the whole cycle without interruption, as *a single song*" (*Quiet Songs*).

At first sight the classical verses, most of them known to almost all Russian listeners from the school years, selected by Silvestrov for setting in this extensive song-cycle (consisting of 24 songs whose performance takes nearly two hours) seems to indicate that he confined himself to a very modest task — "to let poems sing," to use the composer's own words, i.e. to reveal in a poem its own inner melody. However, there is no need to prove how much this task involves. The more so as the first impression of complete identity with the classical sample is short-lived: the ear gradually begins differentiating the details and nuances that lend individuality to this composition. A rarely encountered melodic wealth is sustained by the intensive vibration of textural voices, unexpected turns of harmony, asymmetrical rhythms and, last but not least, by the unique agogic mobility. The smallest details for interpretation are noted down in the most precise way, which has been obviously borrowed from the early pointillistic manner.

However, all these details constitute nothing else but separate nuances of the common tone of "quiet" intoning which is not to change the general spirit of elegiac contemplation reigning supreme throughout the work. The whole cycle sung as "a single song," as the composer stresses, draws a portrayal of the resplendent world past and gone, which was guided by the laws of perfect beauty; an integral world in which there coexisted in full concord the voices of the most different, unlike poets — Alexander Pushkin and Fyodor Tyutchev, Sergei Yesenin and Yevgeny Baratynsky, Mikhail Lermontov, Vasily Zhukovsky, Osip Mandelstam, as well as John Keats and Percy Bysshe Shelley (in Russian) and Taras Shevchenko (in Ukrainian). The inner unity is attained through the direct thematic relationships (for instance, by a bridge connecting the initial song with the last but one) and numerous melodic and genre recurrences. The inner musical "rhymes" are conceptional, concealing the secret affinity of remote poetical essences, a sign of the unity inherent in a tradition to be revived.

The experience gained in writing *Quiet Songs* was expanded further afield in his other song-cycles: *Steps, Simple Songs,* and Four Settings of Osip Mandelstam. As a whole, the years from 1973 to 1983 saw the flourishing of vocal music in Silvestrov's creative output: in addition to the above mentioned opuses, he produced three solo cantatas and a large-scale work for a cappella chorus to verses by Taras Shevchenko, the great Ukrainian poet.

A comparison of Silvestrov's cantatas and chamber vocal pieces reveals a difference in the interpretation of the poetical word. His cantatas are not so obviously resting on the classical archetypes of intoning as compared to his songs, even in those cases when the verses of the same poet are set to music (Fyodor Tyutchev in the first cantata). The most revealing in this respect is his *Ode to a Nightingale* to verse by John Keats (Russian translation by Yevgeny Vitkovsky), a cantata for soprano, piano and chamber orchestra. The meaning of each word is flexibly reflected in the turns of melody, based

on syllabic recitative, embellished occasionally by the arioso-like passages and extensive instrumental leaps. The melody develops with almost improvisatory freedom,
without any stylization or apparent genre prototypes.

The psychological embodiment seems to be almost naturalistic, and the melodic
line — fractional. At the same time any shade of naturalism is eliminated by the
elevated style of declamation: it is the actor's solemn singing utterance, "intensive and
contrasting" (according to the composer's remark). A similar, equally "ode-like"
interpretation of the poetical text is characteristic of Silvestrove's symphony *Exegi
monumentum*, written much later in 1987, for baritone and symphony orchestra to verses
by Alexander Pushkin, the great Russian poet.

On the whole, Valentin Silvestrov's interpretation of the poetical word is notable
for its "anti-avant-gardist" character. It is quite natural that in the sixties the composer
did not virtually tackle the vocal genres, using the novel expressive means exclusively
in his instrumental opuses. Both in his songs and cantatas Silvestrov retains the
semantic integrity of a word, being not inclined to divide it into pointillistic microelements and anatomize its phonetics in seeking sonoristic effects. However, it is not to
imply that the composer remains indifferent to the musicality inherent in verses and
their instrumentation (by the way, he never uses prose for setting). The musicality of
a word is concealed in its meaning in the same way as noise is hidden in a definite
pitch. It is another idea that is very important to Silvestrov. Fading away, the tone is
imperceptibly modulated into rustles, strings squeaks, bell breathing of the wind
instruments (Silvestrov's favorite device). Such moments of the dissolving musical
fabric are most impressive in his music; but in general his works, particularly the
large-scale ones are never ending in some "material" sonority, the more so, in the
imperative *tutti* chord. The composer values the phenomenon of acoustic "aftereffect"
very high: "If the form comes to its close in all parametres and, nevertheless, it is still
ringing in some invisible and inaudible space, it attests to the undisputable value of a
composition, meaning that it could be recognized as the established ontological fact."
The concluding sections in Silvestrov's works are of exceptional importance, often
competing with the principal section even in their duration. To this category belong
the codas in his cantatas, many songs, and in his symphony *Exegi monumentum*. As a
matter of fact, these are not codas at all, but something more significant; it is no accident
that in the early eighties in his work you can clearly distinguish the self-contained
genre of *postlude*, most likely to traced back to these extended finales. This genre has
not been invented by Valentin Silvestrov; as is known, it was Witold Lutoslawski who
wrote the first postlude as a self-contained musical piece. But Silvestrov treats this
genre in an absolutely inimitable way, lending it the profound philosophical and
culturological connotations.

At first there appeared the chamber versions of this genre: *Postlude DSCH* for
chamber ensemble, Postlude for solo violin, and Postlude for cello and piano. The first
one, *Hommage to Dmitry Shostakovich*, as most of such musical offerings, is based on its
motto theme, the great master's monogram, which is intoned, however, not in the
habitual dramatic but in a serene and concentrated "afterword" style. The sonority of
the Postlude for cello is akin to the tone of the composer's *Quiet Songs*, being reminiscent of the coda in one of them (afterwards Silvestrov included it in his Sonata for Cello
and Piano). But this genre turns out to be truly conceptual in Valentin Silvestrov's

three large-scale compositions written in the mid-eighties, though only one of them is called unambiguosly *Postlude* for piano and orchestra (1984).

The idea of a postlude epitomizes for Silvestrov the core of current cultural problems. To quote the composer once again, "There has now arisen a new situation in music, perhaps we are on the threshold of the all-embracing universal style. Having reached, to a large extent thanks to the avant-garde, the boundaries of the acoustic world, we have perceived and even overstepped them... The author's text blends with the world that is incessantly speaking. Therefore, I believe that in the advanced artistic consciousness there can hardly emerge now the texts beginning, figuratively speaking, 'from the beginning'. A postlude, to my mind, represents a collection of reverberations, a form which presumes the existence of a certain text not actually included in a given context but interrelated with it. Therefore, a form is exposed, not at the end, which is more habitual, but at the beginning.

"A postlude is something else. It is virtually a certain state of culture when the forms reflecting a life-music by analogy with a life-novel, for instance, a music drama, come to be replaced by the forms commenting on it. And this is not the end of music as an art, but *the end of the music* in which it may stay for a very long time. It is precisely in the zone of a coda that a gigantic life could unfold..."

And it is "in the zone of a coda" that Silvestrov built up his most significant composition of those years — the Fifth Symphony (1982).

Outwardly, his Fifth Symphony looks quite ordinary: a one-movement poem in a slow tempo, lasting for approximately an hour, written for the customary cast of symphony orchestra (in contrast to, say, his previous Symphony No. 4 for strings and brass instruments). But the degree of inner renovation of the conventional scheme here is most considerable; the weighty message of the Fifth Symphony makes one to discern in it an artistic and human declaration and a confession of one's faith, rendered not in the imperative oratorical style but in a "quiet," concentrated, lyrical and meditative tone.

This symphony is based on the songful themes that can be traced back to Silvestrov's song-cycles, primarily to his *Quiet Songs*. The similarity seems to be associated with citations, but the fact is that there are no direct quotations in it, and only assimilation and analogy.

The musicality of classical poetry penetrates the symphony as a symbol of the ideal, as a kind of cultural Eliseus.

Another type of thematic material also has its prototypes and sequels in Silvestrov's music. These are "the voices of nature" which are already familiar to us: literal (noises, booming, and light breathings) and metaphorical — figural patterns, folk tunes, and the brass chorales, which are associated in our minds with vast open-air expanses.

The natural and the cultivated in this symphony are not confronted at all but closely blended, with one growing out of the other and dissolving in it. The unity of two fundamental principles, formerly often conflicting, carries the profound philosophical message: two facets of the resplendent being appearing as if for the last time in the resigned tension of a parting.

The reflection of a serene farewell underlies the music of this "postsymphony," as the composer defined his work. The Fifth Symphony is devoid of the conventional dramatic contrasts and collisions, lending therefore no sensation of the development in its process directed from the point A (exposition) to the point B (finale). In other words, in this case we have a *static composition*.

The idea of statics, overcoming the vectorial nature of time, as is known, gained wide currency in the postwar avant-garde music. However, the static compositions, "forms of a staying," as a rule, involve homogeneous material whose "infinite" duration is perceived as a physiological reality. As for its semantics, such material is usually neutral, for it is the "new reality" of a sonoristic composition (Ligeti's *Atmosphères* or Stockhausen's *Stimmung*). As for Silvestrov, his themes are extremely semantic, widely ranging in their associations and quite diversified. Moreover, one can easily discern in his symphony the contours of sonata form, which is commonly regarded as one of the most processual forms. Nevertheless, the static character of this symphony can hardly be questioned.

The point is that in the Fifth Symphony there reigns supreme the coda and postlude-like character of statement, with its predominance of retardation over development. Silvestrov makes use of a ramified system of devices inherent in the coda, the most important of which are repetitions, cadences, and the slowing of tempo and dramatic development. But this coda in the listener's mind should be associated not with the text of a really existing work which it concludes, but with the extratextual phenomena, remaining "off screen": with the themes of the songs, which had got their full-blooded and integral rendering somewhere in the imperceptible past, and with the "natural voices" which had left only repercussions of a vague humming. In other words, here we have the coda of a tradition, a postlude of culture.

The materialization of this profound poetical conception involves an unusual technique, or to be more precise, the non-conventional treatment of the devices that have long been in use in European music. The most important of these devices are as follows:

(1) Of prime notice are the rests in the unfolding of the musical material. The melody "stands still" for a time being, and then you can hear the reverberative figurations of the harps (with their strings not to be muffled). Here you get just echoes and reverberations doubled and tripled in space.

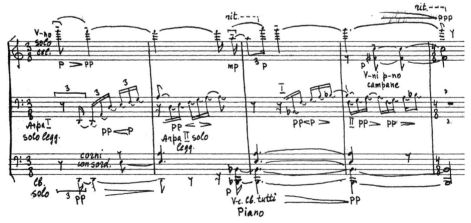

Ex. 3 *Fifth Symphony*

As a result of the rests, each motive exists as a self-contained unit, as a microwave of inhalation and exhalation — without an integral broad melodic line, without "flowing" song fulness. This device is employed predominantly in thematic exposition.

(2) Another device — "incoherence" in alteration of songful phrases — is also used in exposition. It is most distinct in the second theme, making one feel as if something has slipped or not everything reached one's ears…

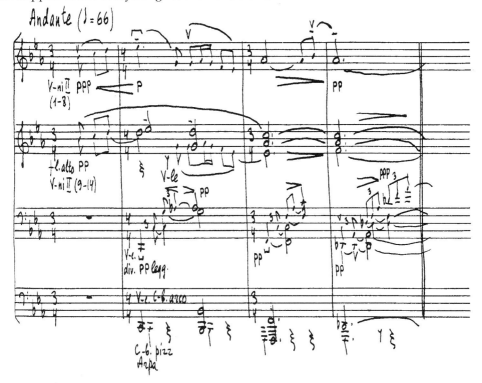

Ex. 4 *Fifth Symphony*

(3) Then the "incoherence" is overmastered, the rests become less noticeable, and to the fore comes another "developing" device of retardation-"infinite" variation, prolonged sequential arrangement to overcome the idea of repetition and its excessive growth. Outwardly the variation seems to be development, a forward movement, but in fact it "rotates" the material in one and the same place and state. This device is characteristic of all the thematic structures, but it is most distinct in the last, pastoral folk-tune theme: here we have no sequences but merely a multiple repetition with the smallest variations (for this episode Silvestrov used a fragment from his *Music in the Old-Time Style*, see Musical Example 2b).

This "freezing of time" (to use the composer's own expression) by asserting the idea of suspension in its pure form anticipates the forthcoming conclusion — and indeed there follows a framing recapitulation.

(4) But, perhaps, the most essential, though not immediately perceived, singular trait of these themes are their sonorities which seem to be not clearly and fully distinguished. It is partly due to their harmonization: conventional tonal chords accompany the melody somewhat "out of place," as if at a tangent (but without a sharp polyfunctional discrepancy), which gives an impression of latent atonality. The second reason lies in the textural specifics of the themes. The melodic line is constantly "spotlighted" by the kindred and resonant timbres: thus, the solo violin in the first theme is doubled by the celesta (see Musical Example 3), the violin in the second theme — by the alto flute, and the piano in the third theme — by a duet of clarinets and flutes. These textural "doubles," however, are not precisely following the principal voice, there arise heterophonic variants, with separate notes "being held up", among them the most "inadequate" ones, such as the subsemitonal and passing notes (see Musical Examples 3 and 4). In this way there arises an interesting type of texture, very characteristic of Valentin Silvestrov in general — sonoristic monody similar to the pedal "envelopment" of melody in *Quiet Songs*[4]. Owing to this device the themes seem to be vibrating, getting diffused in a certain halo — this is an aura incarnate, the materialized aura, a symbol of reminiscence and its unattainability[5].

The "natural elemental" themes have a different timbre character, with the prevalence of the brass sonorities, and the booming of the percussion instruments and the piano in a low register. The contrast of the strings and the brass instruments in the symphony is conventional: it is the same romantic semantics inherent in the melodic lines. But this contrast is not of conflicting character for, as we have pointed out above, Silvestrov treats the natural and the cultivated as just different facets of a certain entity. And all the more significant is the increasing proximity of timbres and their reconciliation that occurs at the end of the symphony when the trumpet and the French horn, upon turning into purely cantilena instruments, "finish singing" the counterpoints to the framing theme.

Postlude, a symphonic poem for piano and orchestra, was completed by Silvestrov shortly after his Fifth Symphony, in 1984. Here we have another model — a romantic piano concerto revived in its most important imagerial facets such as a passionate spirit, lyricism and pastorale. However the inner motion of its thematic material to embody these states is leading to its destruction and dematerialization. Thus, the initial impulse-declaration, reminiscent of the concertos by Liszt or Tchaikovsky, Schumann or Grieg, is immediately dispersed like breathing on a frosty day. The same happens to the second culmination point, which is still more spectacular and stylistically definite: the piano falls into a long-expected "grand" passage, but the climax immediately droops and "subsides" to never go through. The lyrical songful melody that emerges later also fails to form a stable theme. And finally, the trichordal figural theme

---

[4] A certain analogy with this "noted down reverberation" can be found, for instance, in the texture of Ligeti's *Lontano* or, in particular, in Berio's *O King*, despite the absolutely different type of thematic arrangement.

[5] The range of meanings inherent in this Greco-Latin word creates a remarkably precise resonance to the symphony's atmosphere: aura — breathing, blowing, air; the skies, heavenly heights; light breathing, flash, ghost, shadow; lusture, radiance, warmness; sound, voice, echo.

definite: the piano falls into a long-expected "grand" passage, but the climmax immediately droops and "subsides" to never go through. The lyrical songful melody that emerges later also fails to form a stable theme. And finally, the trichordal figural theme of the concluding section by its "infinite" repetitions, reminiscent of a folk tune in the Fifth Symphony, leads the musical matter to its exhaustion and complete dissolution . Paradoxically enough, the first emergence of this transparent pastoral theme is associated with the soloist's cadenza which turns here into an "anti-cadenza," for this solo playing is so far from the habitual virtuosity displayed in the development sections.

In his *Postlude* Silvestrov elaborates on the same type of "retardation technique" of which he has made an extensive use in his Fifth Symphony. But its employment here has quite a different goal — to reveal its extraordinary flexibility. The figural material, quite definite and well-shaped in the Fifth Symphony, turns in this case into a means of destroying, "washing out" the musical form. The chaotic atonal and ametrical roamings of the piano, as if gaps in the weakening memory, gradually become more and more noticeable until they force out the rest of the material once and for all. The natural train of the recurrence determining the dramatic pattern of the coda looks as if it is going to collapse irrevocably: herein lies the hidden tragic message of the lucid idyllic sonorities in this work.

Exegi monumentum, a symphony for baritone and orchestra to the verses by Alexander Pushkin, is written in the same style. Pushkin's poem "Unto myself I reared a monument not built by hands..." is one of the main poetical treasures in Russian culture, and it is no accident that its text has been engraved on the pedestal of Pushkin's monument erected in Moscow. These verses have their own tradition of reciting, be it on the concert platform or in their mental intoning "to oneself": they presume the solemn, outloud sonority, in a grand oratorical style. In this context Silvestrov's interpretation looks quite puzzling at first: the recitative of a baritone of medium range, dynamically modest, sometimes even close to psalmody (like in the last line: "O Muse, follow but the divine behests...") is deliberately devoid of any zeal. This is often encountered in Silvestrov's vocal music: the composer seems to be reading the verses for the first time, purifying them from the distorting extraneous strata to restore their original message. Pushkin's "Monument" sounds in the vocal part as an innermost private confession of an artist-creator, conveying his hope but not an imperative assertion of his own rightness. Only occasionally ("It will tower with its unsubdued head over the pillar to Alexander...") in the soloist's voice there arise the passionate tones. But, as a whole, the verses are presented in a clearly distinct and weighty manner owing to the chiselled formulas of the melodic turns and musical "rhymes" which enhance the poetical ones (Silvestrov's favorite device in vocal genres). However, the most important factor belongs here to the orchestra.

The ode-like solemnity is enhanced and stressed by the strict chorale chords of the trombones into which the soloist's recitative is "inscribed". These chords are so imposing that the singer's voice resounds not above them, as is the common practice in vocal music, but inside them. Of still greater interest is the orchestral accompaniment, the "background" of the chorale, which is ringing out in the vast, resonant space as if really "throughout the great Rus," in the universal natural and cultural scope, as the ancients used to understand it. This musical space is populated with the live every movement of tones has to be comprehended primarily as a mutual relation of sounds, of oscillatory vibrations, appearing at different places and times"[6]. The texture of the "background" is extremely unstable, the melodic polyphony interspersed with tonal chords, clusters of varying configuration, and heterophonic superpositions of figural patterns. And then, once the recitation stops, it is still "ringing" for a long time in the orchestral postlude, gradually dissolving in the space filled up with the reverberations fading away....

It can be easily observed that Silvestrov's musical language embraces the ideas of the avant-gardist nature but interpreted in a highly individual way. Sonoristics, atonality (both serial and free), a static form, and spatial effects — all of these devices have been elaborated by Silvestrov on the wave of the avant-garde and "restored" by him, enriched and "burdened" by the philosophical conceptuality and semantic significance, which are traditionally inherent in Russian art.

---

[6] Arnold Schoenberg. Composition with Twelve Notes // Style and Idea. N. Y. 1950, p. 113.

PRINCIPAL WORKS

Symphonic Compositions

Symphony No. 1 for full symphony orchestra, in three movements, 1963; new version 1974. Duration 18', MS

Classical Overture for small symphony orchestra, 1964, 5', MS

Symphony No. 2 for flute, percussion, piano and string orchestra, in one movement, 1965, 10'. Kiev, Muzychna Ukraina Publishers, 1978

Monody for piano and symphony orchestra, in three movements, 1965, 18', MS Released by Deutsche Schallplatten, Berlin, Space 315 222-2; Ural Philharmonic Orchestra, Andrei Borejko, conductor.

Spectra, symphony for chamber orchestra, in three movements, 1965, 15', MS

Symphony No. 3 (*Eschatophony*) for full symphony orchestra, in three movements, 1966, 22'. N.Y. Schott, 1969

Hymn for strings and wind instruments, piano, celesta, harp and bells, in one movement, 1967, 10', MS

Poem in Memory of Boris Lyatoshinsky for percussion, wind and stringed instruments, in one movement, 1968, 19', MS

Meditation, symphony for cello and chamber orchestra, in one movement, 1972, 31', MS

Symphony No. 4 for brasses and strings, in one movement, 1976, 28'. Kiev, Muzychna Ukraina, 1986. Released by Deutsche Schallplatten, Berlin, Space 315 222-2; Ural Philharmonic Orchestra, Andrei Borejko, Conductor.

Serenade for string orchestra, in one movement, 1978, 15', MS

Symphony No. 5 for full symphony orchestra, in one movement, 1980–82, 48'. Kiev, Muzychna Ukraina, 1990. Released by Melodia Recording Company, C10 27029 008, Symphony Orchestra of the Kiev Conservatoire, Roman Kofman, conductor; Deutsche Schallplatten, Berlin, Space 315 223-2; Ural Philharmonic Orchestra, Andrej Borejko, Conductor.

Intermezzo for chamber orchestra, in one movement, 1983, 7'30", MS the same CD 315 222-2

Postlude, symphonic poem for piano and orchestra, in one movement, 1984, 18', MS

Exegi monumentum, symphony for baritone and symphony orchestra to the verse by Alexander Pushkin, in one movement, 1985–87, 20', MS. the same CD, 223-2;

Dedication, symphony for violin and symphony orchestra, in three movements, 1991, 40', MS

Metamusic for piano and symphony orchestra, in one movement, 1992, 40', MS

Symphony No. 6 for full symphony orchestra, in four movements, 1994–95, 50'; MS

Cantatas

Cantata to Verses by Fyodor Tyutchev and Alexander Blok for soprano and chamber orchestra, in three movements, 1973, 10', Kiev, Muzychna Ukraina, 1990

Cantata to Verses by Taras Shevchenko for mixed a cappella chorus, in three movements, 1977, 20', MS

Forest Music to verses by Gennady Aigi for soprano, French horn and piano, in three movements, 1977–78, 25'. Kiev, Muzychna Ukraina, 1990

Ode to a Nightingale to the verse by John Keats (Russian translation by Yevgeny Vitkovsky) for soprano and chamber orchestra, in one movement, 1983, 19'. Kiev, Muzychna Ukraina, 1990

Diptych to the prayer "Pater noster" and to the verse by Taras Shevchenko, for mixed a cappella chorus, MS, 1995.

Elegy to verses by Taras Shevchenko for mixed a cappella chorus, MS, 1996

Chamber Ensembles

Piano Quintet in three movements, 1961, 21'. Kiev, Muzychna Ukraina, 1969

Quartetto piccolo for string quartet, in three movements, 1961, 5', MS. Released by ETCETERA Recordings, Amsterdam. The Lysenko String Quartet.

Trio for Flute, Trumpet and Celesta in two movements, 1962, 8', MS

Mystery for alto flute and six percussion groups, in one movement, 1964, 12', MS

Projections on Harpsichord, Vibraphone and Bells in one movement, 1965, 5', MS

Drama for violin, cello and piano, in three movements, 1970–71, 40', MS

String Quarter No. 1 in one movement, 1974, 18'. Kiev, Muzychna Ukraina, 1979. Released by Melodia, C10 17117 000, Lysenko String Quartet; Etcetera Recordings, Amsterdam.

Postlude DSCH for soprano, violin, cello and piano, in one movement, 1981, 6', MS

Postlude for solo violin, in one movement, 1981, 9'30", MS. Etcetera Recordings, Amsterdam.

Postlude for cello and piano, in one movement, 1982, 3'40", MS

Sonata for Cello and Piano in one movement, 1983, 22', MS

String Quartet No. 2. in one movement, 1988, 25', MS. Etcetera Recordings, Amsterdam, The Lysenko String Quartet

Post scriptum, sonata for violin and piano, in three movements, 1990, 15', MS

Piano Pieces

Sonatina in E minor in three movements, 1960; new version, 1965, 7'. Kiev, Muzychna Ukraina, 1985

Piano Sonata No. 1 in two movements, 1960; new version, 1972. 17'. Kiev, Muzychna Ukraina, 1987. Released by Melodia, C10 11429 000, Nikolai Suk, soloist

Five Piano Pieces, 1961, 8'. Kiev, Muzychna Ukraina, 1984.

Triad in three movements (13 pieces): 1. Signs. 2. Serenade. 3. Music of Silvery Tones. 1962, 10'. Kiev, Muzychna Ukraina, 1970

Classical Sonata in three movements, 1963, 8', MS

Elegy in one movement, 1967, 5'. Kiev, Muzychna Ukraina, 1982

Children's Music No. 1: 7 pieces, 1973, 15'. Kiev, Muzychna Ukraina, 1980. Released by Melodia, C10 11127 003, Yevgeny Rzhanov, soloist

Children's Music No. 2: 7 pieces, 1973, 12'. Kiev, Muzychna Ukraina, 1980. Released by Melodia, C10 11127 003, Yevgeny Rzhanov, soloist

Music in the Old-Time Style in four movements (11 pieces). 1973, 20'. Kiev, Muzychna Ukraina, 1981

Piano Sonata No. 2 in one movement, 1975, 17'. Kiev, Muzychna Ukraina, 1987

Kitsch Music, five piano pieces, 1977, 15', MS

Piano Sonata No. 3 in three movements, 1979, 15'. Kiev, Muzychna Ukraina, 1987
Naive Music, 1993, MS
Distant Music, 1993, MS

Works for Voice and Piano

Two Settings of Alexander Blok for middle voice and piano, 1968, 8'.
Kiev, Muzychna Ukraina, 1980
Quiet Songs, cycle of 24 songs to verses by classical poets for baritone or soprano and piano, 1974–77, 110'. Moscow, Sovetsky Kompozitor Publishers, 1985
Simple Songs, cycle of 6 songs to verses by the anonymous poet, Osip Mandelstam and Alexander Pushkin for middle voice and piano,
1974–81, 28', MS
An Old-Time Ballade to verse by Andrei Bely for baritone and piano,
1977, 5'. Kiev, Muzychna Ukraina, 1981
Steps, cycle of 11 songs to verses by the anonymous poet, Osip Mandelstam, Fyodor Sologub, Fyodor Tyutchev, John Keats, Alexander Pushkin and Yevgeny Baratynsky for soprano and piano, 1980–82, 50', MS
Four Settings of Osip Mandelstam for baritone and piano, 1982, 12', MS
Nocturne for soprano and piano to words by V. Kurinsky, 1982, 3', MS

Leonid Grabovsky: constants of style

Svetlana Savenko

Leonid Grabovsky

Leonid Alexandrovich Grabovsky was born on January 28, 1935 in Kiev (Ukraine). He started his music training in 1951 (piano and musical theory). The same year he entered Kiev University to major in economics, graduating in 1956. He studied composition at the Kiev Conservatoire (1954–59) with Lev Revutsky and Boris Lyatoshinsky. He also completed the postgraduate course there (1959–62). Over different periods of time (in 1961–63 and 1966–68) he taught at the Kiev Conservatoire. In 1982 he moved to Moscow where he worked as an editor with the Sovetskaya Muzyka magazine. Since 1990 he has been residing in New York.

Leonid Grabovsky embarked upon his artistic career in the early 1960s. The initial stage in his creative evolution was marked to a great extent by his adherence to the folkloric trend which was characteristic of the contemporary Ukrainian music in particular and the art of other former Soviet republics in general. This trend in those years had quite academic stereotypes. His first major work, *Four Ukrainian Songs*, written to traditional texts for mixed a cappella chorus, seemed to indicate that the young composer followed a well-trodden path. But it also displayed his highly talented approach to the national traditions. Along with his writing in the folk vein, Grabovsky early revealed his aspiration to tackle a wide spectrum of musical genres ranging from the large-scale orchestral compositions (*Symphonic Frescoes*) to chamber cycles and operas (*The Bear* and *The Proposal*, his diptych after Anton Chekhov). At that time he came under the influence, as most composers of his generation, of Prokofiev, Shostakovich, Stravinsky of the early Russian period, and also his teacher — Boris Lyatoshinsky. But his early compositions, nevertheless, show quite a few original traits, rather daring for Soviet music in those years. Leonid Grabovsky employed various types of clusters, including cluster-like *glissando*, ostinato forms, and mixed scales. Of special notice are his timbre innovations, which revealed the composer's interest in sonoristic effects. Later on Grabovsky pointed out that harmony and instrumentation had been the spheres of his greatest competence and prime preoccupation in his early years.

The period of apprenticeship did not last long with Grabovsky, and the year 1964 saw a radical change in his style. Within that year he wrote "at a gulp" several compositions which were in striking contrast to his previous works, such as the Trio for Violin, Double-Bass and Piano, *Microstructures* for solo oboe, *Pastels* for soprano and four stringed instruments, *From Japanese Haiku* for tenor, piccolo, double-bassoon and xylophone, and finally *Constants* for four pianos, six percussion groups and solo violin. This "outburst" in his creative activity has so far been the only period when he worked incessantly, moreover, afterwards he developed a habit of keeping silent for a long span of time, sometimes even for several years running.

In the mid-sixties Leonid Grabovsky, together with his colleagues — Valentin Silvestrov, Vitaly Godzyatsky and Vladimir Zagortsev, set up an unofficial creative association (known in the West as "the Kievan Group"). The young composers studied the works written by the adherents of the Second Viennese School (particularly Webern), Boulez, Stockhausen, Penderecki, and Lutoslawski, mastering the novel composition procedures and the new aesthetics. According to Grabovsky's own evidence, his contacts with the new Polish school with its cultivation of timbre-textural writing and aleatory proved to be most important for him. However, Grabovsky has never written purely cluster compositions, preferring, as a rule, a mixed techniques based on a wide range of elements. His opuses embrace the melodic lines, monody included, modality, and diverse metric and rhythmic structures.

As a matter of fact, Leonid Grabovsky's mature style developed very rapidly, its main characteristics taking shape virtually by the late 1960s. It is rooted in the anti-Romantic aesthetics, which was quite customary for the contemporary avant-garde with its focus on building up new acoustic objects. As is known, later on the situation has changed, but not for Grabovsky, a rational person by nature. Grabovsky's mature idioms are succinct, to the point of being ascetic, with a preference for pungent piercing sonorities. His music is far from being dispassionate, but its expressiveness carries a certain imprint of aloofness, being completely devoid of any outright emotionality.

Each composition of Grabovsky's, appearing after meticulous and painstaking polishing of every detail, forms a soundscape all its own, its singularity arising from an unorthodox combination of instruments, and a unique conception. In his Trio for Violin, Double-Bass and Piano the development rests on juxtaposition, contrasts and interchanges between different types of timbres, involving the definitely pitched elements, both horizontal and vertical.

The first movement in the nature of a fantasia unfolds as textural and dynamic variations of the principal pitch core — the note "A". A wide use is made of the non-conventional methods of sound production, such as playing beyond the bridge, uncustomary *glissandi*, playing the piano strings, at times with drum sticks and wire brushes; all kinds of tapping on the soundboard, the music stand, on the pedals, or on the piano lid. In this world of noises and half-whispers the tones of definite pitch either give a spur to the further development or emerge as an outcome.

In the second movement unfolding in a toccata-like motion there prevail the ostinato motorics with their successively sustained pointillistic texture — with the instruments playing strictly in turns. The binding element here are the piano's chords of stable pitch.

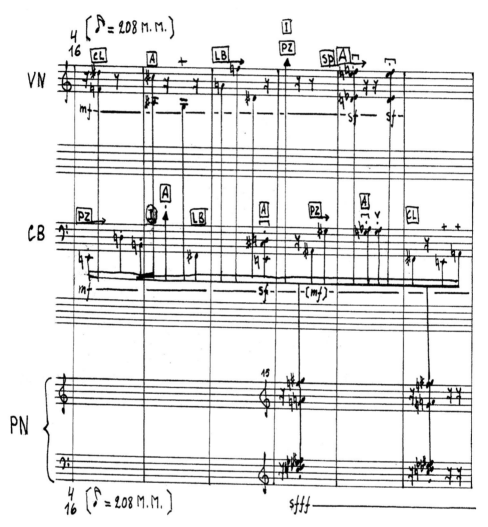

Ex. 1 *Trio*

In the second section the instruments play their solos in turn, in the manner of a sonoristic cadence. The third movement epitomizes the summing up of the melodic lines; the introduction of the fused chord vertical progressions flowing from the strings to the piano brings the composition to an impressive denouement. The main factor in creating an integral composition belongs to exposition and "investigation" of the basic, elementary qualities of the musical matter; statics — dynamics, motorics — aperiodicity, discreteness — fusion, density — rarefication.

Leonid Grabovsky's *Pastels* develops in a broad sense the same sonoristic line. This microsuite in four movements has been set to the early verses by Pavlo Tychina, written by this Ukrainian poet back in the twenties, a heyday of the young Soviet avant-garde. The four short poems depict the four parts of the day: morning, daytime, evening and night. The childish naive treatment of the forces of nature as living creatures, which is akin to folklore, combines in Tychina's elegant poetry with the aesthetically refined imagery and its musicality. The palette of *Pastels* is extremely rich in its sounds and colors. (For instance, the following extended metaphor is used to convey the daybreak: "The cocks stitching up the black cloak of night with flame-colored threads. . .").

In addition to direct illustrations encountered in the cycle, Leonid Grabovsky creates a subtle system of concords and assonances, stressing the word's phonetics, identifying its separate elements up to an individual note, i.e. treating the text in the sonoristic vein. The vocal part is therewith enriched by such instrumental effects as the guttural *frullato, tremolos* of different type and configuration, as is evidenced from the following episode taken from its third movement:

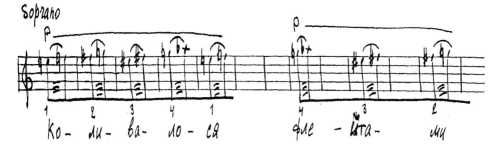

Ex. 2 *Pastels*

The vibrating melodic line subtly conveys the fine musicality of the poetical image ("The flute-like haze spread over the sunset...", translated from the Russian). The sonoristic impressionism of the vocal part accompanied by the flowing lines of violin, viola and cello (omitted in the above example) is combined with the rationalistic formula-like organization of intervals: a retrograde rotation takes shape here on the basis of semitonal microstructure (see the figures in the cited example).

Leonid Grabovsky's other vocal compositions written during that period are in a similar vein. It looks quite natural that Grabovsky should turn to the aphoristic form of *haiku*, a poetical source of inspiration for many composers in the sixties. The unorthodox combination of instruments used in the cycle *From Japanese Haiku* (tenor, piccolo, double-bassoon and xylophone) looks also quite typical of the contemporary avant-gardist poetical idioms. The voice and the instruments virtually form a unified timbre sphere, with Grabovsky developing the idea of an interplay of vocal and instrumental sonorities, which was actualized in those years in two main versions — a serial scale of timbres (by Stockhausen, in particular, in his electronic compositions) and free sonoristic mixtures (Ligeti, Penderecki and other composers of the Polish school). The later variety involving the non-conventional treatment of conventional instruments is much closer to Grabovsky. Each of the six pieces in this cycle is distinguished by a timbre all its own, with the maximal similarity of vocal and instrumental colors, the more so as the thematic material of the vocal and instrumental parts being common. Thus, in the first haiku ("Here is a butterfly slightly trembling with her wings... What are you dreaming of?") the piccolo's *frullato* almost impercep-tibly flows into the tenor's *frullato* catching up the same melody (to enhance the effect, the composer prescribes to tap rapidly on the breast with both hands). In the second haiku the singer's staccato syllables-sounds imitate the xylophone forming with it a kind of *hoquet*; in the third and sixth pieces a similar united tone-color is formed by the singer's voice and the double-bassoon. Of great interest is the fourth miniature — a dynamic centre of this microcycle. Three instruments are playing here the extremely loud figural passages, aleatorically repeated in-between the momentary rests; in this seething vortex of timbres there comes the "screwed-in" tenor's voice producing an A-effect, with the singer nearly crying out his text *falsetto*, with his nose squeezed. The text is also alienated, wit the composer combining the words and syllables of haiku in terms of pure phonetics, violating its semantics[1]. The purpose of this deformation, reminiscent of the Futurists' word formation, is to concretize the poetical imagery as much as possible to the point of onomatopoeia: the composer seems to offer here a new variety of *stile rappresentativo*.

Its traits are obvious in the other pieces of the cycle, too. Thus, in his *Pastels*, written within the same year, in 1964, Grabovsky is striving to perceive and stress in a poetical word its original meaning, the phonetic inner form, which is to a large extent shrouded in its concept. It was enough to hear these two vocal pieces to be able to predict the composer's future preoccupation with the absurdist poetry. And this is exactly what happened shortly afterwards, in 1967, when Grabovsky came out with his vocal-in-strumental composition *Marginalia to Heissenbüttel*. Three original German texts writ-ten by Helmut Heissenbüttel and selected for setting by Grabovsky represent a variety of graphic poetry: it is based on a certain simple, grammatically valid, entity, which is then divided into its components separated by blank spots of rests and therefore losing its semantic relationship. So looks, for instance, the poem "Kam" (according to the composer's remarks, three parts of the cycle "ein", "Wenn" and "kam" could be performed in an arbitrary order):

kam nachts		es war	Kino und	kein	Roman	
		es war	Kino und		Schnee	fiel
	nachts von oben		und	kein	Roman	
	von oben					fiel etwas
					Schnee	
kam nachts			und			
			und			
					Schnee	fiel
	von oben					

The discrete character of the poetical text is underlined to the utmost by its musical interpretation which in its vocal and instrumental parts can be defined as minimalist

---

[1] If we compare the original haiku:"On the jag of a hill / / there sat to rest / / a honking flock of birds of passage!" with the composer's version, we'll get something like that in English:"On the jag of a honking hill honk-sat-there-rest-pass-birds-age-of-flock!". Perhaps, sort of allusion is also made to the exotic character of the Japanese phonetics.

(though it has nothing to do with the style of minimal music). The text is intoned by a recitalist who is prescribed to keep strictly one and the same pitch, varying only the dynamic nuances of utterance, though in a very wide diapason (from fff to pppp), by its discreteness akin to the technique of total serialism. The same principle is used in the parts of the instruments — two trumpets, trombone and percussion, each of them playing one and the same note in the course of one piece and keeping up the same manner of sound production and dynamics (in contrast to the recitalist). The principle of *hoquet* finds it full manifestation in Grabovsky's *Marginalia*, since the "dotted" sounds of the voice and the instruments are completely isolated from one another, moreover, quite often they are separated by rather long rests corresponding to the "blank spots" in the verses. Apparently, the rigid formula-like structure underlying the relationship of sound elements is designed to give the impression of fully mechanical disunited coexistence of numberless fragments of the once integral world. The disintegration of links in the entity is stated with cool aloofness, as a purely aesthetic quality.

Marginalia to Heissenbüttel have so far been a unique experience of this kind in Grabovsky's creative output. It can be assumed that as a composer he is more interested in the interaction, "vibration" of semantics and phonetics, carrying its own "semantics," rather than asemantics as it were, which eventually deprives a word of its colors and dimensionality. The more so as Grabovsky is no less preoccupied with the other characteristics of the poetical text such as, for instance, its national coloring. Thus, in his cycle *From Japanese Haiku* the composer recreates the traits inherent in the European reflection of the Far-Eastern culture, and not only the general aesthetic one, such as aphoristic succinctness and transparent writing, but also quite concrete, modal ones. For example, in the first piece mentioned above he makes a successive combination of two pentatonic scales. It is noteworthy that in his *Pastels* the composer's native Ukrainian coloring is confined to the sonority of the poetical word, with the music practically devoid of any local traits. At the time Grabovsky's approach to the national principle was rather challenging. He counterposed the sentimentality of traditional Ukrainian lyrical poetry and the academic stereotypes with the indigenous, essential traits of folklore, rigorous asceticism, archaic austerity and intricate inventiveness. Grabovsky's method may be compared with that of Bartok who was striving to rid folklore of its later layers — urban, gypsy and the like — and bring it back to the purity of old-time peasant specimens. Grabovsky's quests had also much in common with those of his Russian, Armenian and Lithuanian colleagues belonging to the new folk wave. At the same time he avoids direct quotations, borrowing only the general principles and separate constructive ideas of folk art. This is evident in his *Ornaments* for oboe, viola and harp (written in 1969), inspired by the paintings of Katerina Bilokur, a folk artist, to whom Grabovsky later dedicated his *Concerto misterioso*.

The main idea behind this work is to "translate" folk decorative patterns into the language of music. Short musical phrases in this composition alternate with rests the way separate elements of these patterns alternate with blank spots on a canvas. The musical material, also reminiscent of folk art, is based on two pentatonic scales ascending and descending from the common centre d^2 and making up a major 9th in their total.

Ex. 3 *Ornaments*

The diatonics and the modal principles are reigning supreme: a stable unit here is a scale, not differentiated in its inner structure and therefore similar to a series. The motifs are mirroring one another (Grabovsky describes this variety of heterophony as counterorganum). The rhytmical units are also constant: the composition is based on a five-note group within which one and the same number of durations — three ♪, ♪. and ♪ — is freely rotated. A different number of such groups may proceed in succession, but this number should necessarily be odd — from one to fifteen, excluding eleven and thirteen. The groups are separated by "blank spots on a canvas" — rests of four durations /2, 6, 10 and 14 seconds/. Two structures equal in length are never going in succession, which concerns both the sounds and the rests. Since each five-note figure lasts approximately a second, on the whole, there arises alternation of sounds and silences, following the odd and even principles.

In addition to the rhythmic and pitched pattern, the timbres and the methods of sound production are also varying: here you can observe a strict set of devices too. Three instruments are never playing together, with the two-voice texture clearly predominating in the piece. There is actually no melodic development, instead the composer employs variations on a "frozen" melodic formula tune. As in the decorative patterns, real subjects remain "frozen" and abstracted, with flowers turning into circles and animals becoming geometrical figures.

The total variation makes the form of *Ornaments* infinite and open — its durations, according to the composer's indication, varies from 4'20" to 21'34". It is up to performers to decide when to stop, the end being marked by a harp's chord comprising all the notes of the formula tunes except for the tonal centre d^2.

The use of spatial methods in composing music, a temporal art by its nature, produces a kind of static composition arising on the borderline between folklore and the avant-garde (along with folk influences, Grabovsky himself acknowledges the impact of op-art upon his music). The new relationships arising between sound and silence became a distinct feature of modern music, and *Ornaments* are a fresh proof of this. But silence in Grabovsky's music is not "ringing" as in the works of some other composers; for instance, in the music by Alfred Schnittke or Giya Kancheli the rests, on the contrary, sharpen the sensation of time and its running process. In *Ornaments* a rest is a truly blank space since the motifs separated by it are complete and meaningful in their own right, and therefore not "flowing" into rests. Paradoxically enough, the folkloric *Ornaments* and the refinedly absurdist *Marginalia to Heissenbüttel* have something in common. These two opuses are evocative of the most essential features in Grabovsky's style.

The sources of Grabovsky's innovative treatment of folklore can be also traced back to the extramusical stimulus he got from writing incidental scores to films. In the 1960s–70s the Ukrainian cinema was thriving, mainly due to the impetus it received from folk art. A breakthrough was made by Sergei Parajanov in his film *The Shadows of our Forgotten Ancestors*, and later on by the films of Yuri Ilyenko. Grabovsky wrote the incidental score to the latter's film *The Midsummer Night* after Nikolai Gogol, which he subsequently converted into his *Symphony-Legend* for full symphony orchestra (written in 1976). One can judge about the style of this large-scale composition from one of its movements, used as a separate piece for organ and entitled "Pastorale" (as part of *Bucolic Strophes*). It is based on spectacular contrasts of sound densities, from one- or two-voice modal lines to the blocks of "organo pleno" resting upon the textural transformations of the same formula tunes. For all the diversity of the musical material, the very composition of this piece is reminiscent of Messiaen's "vitraux" with their static juxtoposition of blocks. It is evident that a static type of composition is of paramount importance for Grabovsky.

To the above category belongs the cycle *Homeomorphia* which Grabovsky started to write in 1968. The title implies the homogeneity of structural elements making up the material of the pieces. The first three of them, written for piano (The second one for two pianos), contain various types of figuration. As a matter of fact, Grabovsky develops the conventional genre of piano étude in these pieces. His first *Homeomorphia* is based on scale-like figures alternating in a fast tempo-varying intervalic structure, in different registers, of varied diapason and duration. Pedalization used to vary the sound intensity and outline separate tones and tonal groups is also of structural importance: its absence renders a contrasting color of "dry" sonority. The second *Homeomorphia* is made up of intervals and chords, also of diverse variety and separated by rests; the third piece of the cycle comes to combine three groups of *Homeomorphiac* elements: repetitions, melodically related notes, and tirati. These are virtually the same *Ornaments*, piano decorative patterns of various configuration and density.

The problems involved in performing new compositions, invariably facing any Soviet avant-garde composer, in the case of Grabovsky looked quite insurmountable. Most of his opuses were suspended from public performance for years. Thus, "*Homeomorphia IY* has been awaiting its premiere for eight years now; *Pastels* had to wait 13 years and *Epitaph in Memory of Rilke* — 19 years to be premiered, to name but a few compositions" (from the letter dated October 15, 1978, addressed by the composer to the author of the present article). In some cases Grabovsky himself cancelled the premieres which, in his view, had been badly prepared: his music is not simple and therefore it calls for meticulous care and concentrated effort on the part of the performers. Some of his compositions have been so far performed only abroad as, for instance, his *Concerto misterioso* presented in the USA under the baton of Virko Baley who does his utmost to promote Soviet music (its premiere took place in Las Vegas in November 1987).

Concerto misterioso ushered in a new period in his work, which was preceded, according to Grabovsky himself, by his prolonged reflections and theoretical preparation. The previous stage came to a close with his large-scale composition *La mer*, a melodrama for recitalist, chorus, organ and orchestra to the verses by Saint-John Perse. The sea element in the poem epitomizes not so much the picturesque imagery of natural forces as a symbol of human life: the sea as the depths of one's heart, as a metaphor to embody the changeability, motion, the beneficent life-giving chaos mythologically counterposed to the inert solid soil. Among Grabovsky's compositions this melodrama stands out as the most complete one in its sonoristic outlines akin to the cantata style of the Polish school.

The striving of many composers writing in the late 1960s — early 1970s for expansion of their styles and a synthesis of various composition systems in the case of Grabovsky revealed once again his rationalistic approach. The composer elaborated, according to his own words, "the systems, techniques and methods of a universal musical language, basing himself on the experience of music (Stravinsky, Stockhausen, Pousseur, *et al.*), literature (Velimir Khlebnikov, James Joyce) and structural poetics, regarding polystylistics as a means of enriching the musical idioms and musical semantics, and eventually deepening the perspective and multidimensionality of musical space" (from the letter dated April 9, 1978 and addressed to the author of the present article). Grabovsky substantiated the theory of "stylistic modulation" designed to secure smoothness and gradualness in a passage from one "stylistic tonics" to another and counterbalance the sharp collage collisions. The technique of such modulation involves an alternate change in the components of the musical style in a given composition (melody, harmony, rhythm, etc.), with "the stylistic hybrids arising at the intervening stage of modulation (so called 'stray stylistic chords') serving an extra source for enriching the stylistic expressiveness" (Ibidem). The emergence of this theory, according to Grabovsky, dates back to the summer of 1973, i.e. it appeared approximately at the same time as the idea of Stockhausen's *Weltmusik* and "symbiotic polystylistics" marked for a similar rationalistic character. Grabovsky's initial project, not realized so far, was to produce a musical scenic composition, sort of "total theatre", in which the motives of varying historical and cultural origins were to be fancifully combined on the basis of Nikolai Gogol and Thomas Mann, ("While reading Dmitry Merezhkovsky's *Gogol's Destiny* and *Gogol and the Devil* I was struck for the first time — and really shocked — at the similarity in the destinies of Gogol and Leverkühn. Then I found out that Thomas Mann might well be familiar with Merezhkovsky's books" (from the letter cited above).

Unfortunately, this large-scale project failed to be ever implemented, and the principles of stylistic modulation found their expression only in 1977 in the above mentioned *Concerto misterioso* and *Concorsuono*, a piece for solo French horn.

Concerto misterioso for nine instruments in one movement proved a landmark in Grabovsky's work. It is based on thematic arrangement of tunes akin to Ukrainian folk music and built up according to the principle of mosaic. These tunes are diverse in character ranging from cantilena, playful to dance-like. Here prevails the melodic writing: monody, pure or with an accompaniment, heterophony (including the counterorganum earlier employed in *Ornaments*), and polyphony, including that of heterophonic blocks). Use is made of imitations, both rhythmical (without the imita-tion of a melody) and melodic (without the imitation of a rhythm), reminiscent of the techniques of *talea* and *color*. The structure is based on polymodality, polyrhythmics and polymetrics governed by the principle of limited aleatory (employing the method of random numbers). The random character is involved here in the very process of composition, but the results of this process are fixed down most precisely.

The contrasting features inherent in diverse tunes are subdued and the succession of episodes is built up not on juxtaposition but on subtle variational changes in "stylistic modulations." Evident is the genetic kinsip of this opus with the tradition of basing compositions on short tunes initiated by Stravinsky, a composer who had exercised a great influence of the formation of Grabovsky's individual style. The shadow of Stravinsky's *Symphonies of Wind Instruments* in memory of Debussy seems to be hovering over Grabovsky's *Concerto misterioso*, but it is indeed only a shade and not its live embodiment in sounds. The folk material used here assumes a particular coloring from its context where elementary diatonic melodies are treated polytonally and atonally, from refined ingenuous timbres and restrained dynamics fluctuating between *p* and *pppp*. This serene score justifies its title, for it depicts a glimpse of insight into the earthly, full-blooded indigenous imagery, the message Grabovsky has dis-cerned in the "mystical paintings" by the folk artist Katerina Bilokur and which he has tried to portray in this work dedicated to her memory.

In its composition procedure *Concerto misterioso* is rather refined and intricate. The "overflowing" from the initial tonal centre (*D*) to the final one (*G#*) proceeds strictly by stages, with the degrees of tonal decentralization being carefully designed. Its rhythmical organization is based on differentiation of 17 groups formed by kindred rhythmical figures. The score indicates merely three types of principal measures 3/8, 4/8 and 5/8, but owing to a great number of their subdivisions there arises an intricate, changeable life of rhythms, abounding in an interplay of accents.

The refinement of *Concerto misterioso* somehow makes it hard to perceive it a polystylistic composition. The subtlety and the occasional indistinctness of "stylistic modulations" make it impossible to grasp the transitions and, the more so, apprehend separate portions in the composition as stylistically heterogeneous. It is likely due, primarily, to its themes, homogeneous in their make-up, with their clear orientation on the folk prototypes.

A slightly different type of polystylistic composition is offered by Grabovsky in his *Concorsuono* for solo French horn. The title of this opus, a conflation of three Italian words — *concorso, cor* and *suono*, indicates the "hybrid-like" character of the composition. As for its materialization in sounds, here we have a kind of "stylistic aleatory". Let us cite the composer's remarks to his score:

"The notational text consists of ten main versions, 'scored' down one under the other and arranged according to the nearly identical rhytmical outlines but in the following varied melodic styles:

1. In the form of segments of the so called chain scales comprised of different diatonic modes;
2. The same on the basis of separate notes therefrom;
3. On the basis of segments from the chromatic scale;
4. The same on the basis of separate notes therefrom;
5. In monointervalic progressions (e.g. exclusively in minor thirds; fourths, etc.);
6. The same as applied to diatonics (e.g. minor and major thirds, pure and diminished fifths, etc.);
7. In panintervalic twelve-note series;
8. On the basis of the *Znamenny* scale;[2]
9. Based on melodic models of classical music.
10. Based on melodic models of Ukrainian folk music.

Musical example 4 contains all the above mentioned models in their initial statement.

It is obvious that in his *Concorsuono* Leonid Grabovsky consistently elaborates on the above described theory of stylistic modulations. However, upon a closer analysis of these melodic models one can hardly fail noticing a somewhat speculative embodiment of the stylistic idea as it were: there are too many models not enough contrasting to make the listener, even if he or she stays confident of the composer's commentary, perceive them as such. But it appears that the composer neither regards his "stylistic modulations" as of paramount significance, which could be partly assumed from his indications to the performers. The piece could be played either according to one of the versions–the lines of the "score" and keeping up to it to the end; or passing from one to another version in the places designated by the arrows. The composer offers a third, "experimental" variety of performance–simultaneous presentation of all the versions by ten French-horn players, to be crowned by their joining together in an aleatory cadence. It is apparent that the first and the third versions of performance completely exclude the moment of a polystylistic contrast. But what is undisputable is the virtuosic nature of this piece designed, among other things, to be performed within the programme of contests for French-horn players. In *Concorsuono*, in addition to the conventional types of playing, the musicians have to employ a very fluent, almost clarinet-like technique; besides, a set of various mutes (made of five different materials: steel, glass, cardboard, plasticine, and ceramics) requires the help of an assistant. Many technical details involved in *Concorsuono* were elaborated by Grabovsky jointly with

---

[2] The Znamenny, or obikhodny, scale making the basis of the old Russian ritual chants (also encountered in folk music) has the following structure (in semitones): 221 221 ... (The author's note).

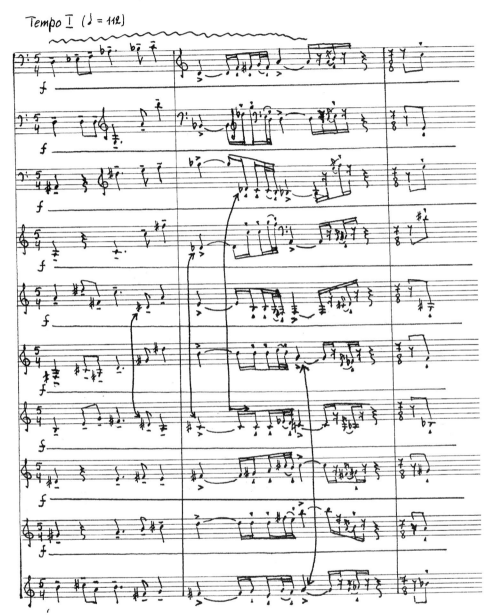

Ex. 4 *Concorsuono* for French horn (in F)

Vasily Pilipchak, a virtuoso French horn player, residing in Kiev, to whom the composer dedicated this piece.

Following his *Concerto misterioso* and *Concorsuono*, there came a break lasting for ten years in Grabovsky's creative work. His next opus, the song-cycle *When* to the verses by Velimir Khlebnikov, appeared in 1987. Then he wrote a piano piece, *To Elise* (1988).

A fresh impetus to his work was given by the musicians. The song-cycle *When* was commissioned by the Continuum Ensemble of New York, who played it in many cities throughout the USA and Europe. His cooperation with the American musicians proved most beneficial for Grabovsky as his career in the 1980s resembled in many ways the structure of his *Ornaments* abounding in long silences and "still fields." Perhaps his recent emigration to the USA will also give a fresh impetus to this talented composer who has by no means exhausted his creative resources, remaining as in his youth, far from the academic stereotypes.

In Soviet music of the postwar decades Leonid Grabovsky stands apart as one of the few composers who consistently followed the avant-garde type of creativity. The "building up" of a sound object, invention and discovery of the ever novel resources inherent in music, and the rational beauty of his structures make the essential traits of his poetics, which have withstood the test of time.

PRINCIPAL WORKS

Orchestral Compositions

Symphonic Frescoes inspired by the drawings of Boris Prorokov from the cycle *It is Never to Happen Again*, op. 10, 1961, duration 30'. Kiev, Muzychna Ukraina, 1968

Small Chamber Music No. 1 for 15 stringed instruments, 1966, 10'10. Kiev, Muzychna Ukraina, 1975

Homeomorphia IY for full symphony orchestra, 1970, 20', MS score

Meditation and Pathetic Recitative for string orchestra, 1972, 8'38". Moscow, Sovetsky Kompozitor, 1980.

The Midsummer Night, symphony-legend after Nikolai Gogol for full symphony orchestra, 1976, 35', MS score

Vocal Pieces

Four Ukrainian Songs for mixed chorus and orchestra to traditional words, Op. 6, 1959, 20'. Moscow, Muzyka, 1966

From Japanese Haiku for tenor, piccolo, double-bassoon and xylophone, 1964; new version, 1975. 4'25". MS

Pastels for soprano and four stringed instruments (violin, viola, cello and double-bass) to verse by Pavlo Tychnia, 1964; new version, 1975. 10'. MS

Epitaph in Memory of Rainer Maria Rilke for soprano, harp, celesta, guitar and bells, to verse by Rainer Maria Rilke, 1965; new version, 1975. 3'07". MS

La mer, melodrama for recitalist, chorus and orchestra, to verse by Saint-John Perse, 1966–70, 20'. MS

When, introduction and 9 miniatures for mezzo-soprano, three soloists-instrumentalists and 12 strings, to verse by Velimir Khlebnikov, 1987. 12'. MS

Temnere Mortem, Cantata on a text of Grigorij Skovoroda for a cappella chorus, 1991, MS

The Omen of Light, on poems of Barka, for soprano and ensemble, 1992, MS

Chamber Pieces

Trio for violin, double-bass and piano, 1964; new version, 1975. 8'10". MS

Constants for four pianos, six percussion groups and solo violin, 1964, 20'. MS

Marginalia to Heissenbüttel for recitalist, two trumpets, trombone and percussion, 1967; new version, 1975. 5'. MS

Ornaments for oboe, viola and harp, 1969; new version, 1987. Duration: from 4'20" to 21'34". MS

Concorsuono for solo French horn, 1977, 10'. MS.

Concerto misterioso for nine instruments (flute, clarinet, double-bassoon, ancient cymbals, harpsichord, harp, violin, viola, and cello), 1977, 16'. MS

Works for Piano and Organ

Homeomorphia I-III for piano (Part 3 for two pianos), 1968–69, 60', MS

To Elise for piano, 1988, 10'

Bucolic Strophes for organ, 1976. 8'20 Kiev, Muzychna Ukraina, 1980

A drama of non-recognition: a profile of Nikolai Karetnikov's life and work

Mikhail Tarakanov

Nikolai Karetnikov

Nikolai Nikolayevich Karetnikov (1930–1994) belongs to the ranks of Russian master musicians kept in the background for many years and even decades. The composer seemed to be haunted by the persistent neglect in his homeland and the indifference on the part of those in the West who promoted some of his fellow-countrymen. He did not share in the currently successful careers of the recognized leaders of the Soviet avant-garde represented by "the magnificent three": Edison Denisov, Alfred Schnittke and Sophia Gubaidulina. The ominous shadow of non-recognition has been cast upon his name, with his compositions remaining still unclaimed.

Could this sentence be valid and regarded as final and not subject to appeal? Guided not only by the sense of human justice but also by the real significance of Karetnikov's compositions whose invaluable merits are obvious to any unbiased person, I take the liberty of saying in full confidence *"no"* to the above posed question. His music is every bit as captivating as those modern pieces written by the composers who now receive universal recognition from the musical community both in present-day Russia and elsewhere.

But what is then hampering the rehabilitation of Karetnikov's work and why is it so hard for his compositions to find their way to the concert platform? There are a lot of reasons for this, among them a lack of the personal capacity without which a modern composer is unable to assert himself in life and shove aside his rivals — the lack of so called "go-getting power." Of course, a lack of businesslike qualities and the ability to establish contacts with people and push forward one's own compositions is far from being the prime reason. The more serious one lies in the "unspectacular" character of his music, devoid of any caressing allusions to the outdated romanticism and radical, challenging innovations to the point of the permissible in music and often intrepidly going beyond it. Nikolai Karetnikov's music is not striking by its extraordinariness, which may justify some reproaches of its being old-fashioned. At the same time it is unconventional enough to appeal to the habitual, sensually open outbursts in the "retro" style which is currently in vogue. His music is difficult and serious in the supreme sense of the word, calling for certain effort to comprehend it. And it happens too often that the listeners are not inclined, and in most cases just unable, to make such an effort. But as soon as the barrier of misunderstanding is overcome, this music is sure to reveal, for the unbiased mind, its unfathomed messages and the hidden depths.

The unhappy lot of his music was not due to circumstances; it turned out to be a result of his own free choice. For at the start of his creative career nothing indicated such a turn for the worse in the composer's life and work.

Nikolai Karetnikov belongs to the postwar generation of Russian artists who embarked upon their creative career in the 1960s. His student years coincided with the raging oppression that followed the adoption of the resolutions on art and literature initiated by the notorious party leader Zhdanov. He entered the Moscow Conservatoire in 1948, when the "historical" Resolution passed by the Central Committee of the CPSU concerning Vano Muradeli's opera *The Great Friendship* was made public (on February 10, 1948). That document shocked the young immature creative mind. Being a Komsomol member of firm ideological convictions, he failed to accept the fact that the most outstanding masters of Russian music, such as the composers Nikolai Myaskovsky, Sergei Prokofiev and particularly Dmitry Shostakovich whom he held in great esteem, were declared to be the anti-popular formalists, with their music proclaimed to be harmful and alien to the people. Neither could he understand how his own teacher with whom he studied composition, Vissarion Shebalin, a solid professional, a musician of high erudition, could be named in that Resolution among the six "formalists."

Nevertheless, in those years it could not occur to him that the Stalinist ideology and practices, including its doctrine on aesthetics, were completely absurd. It took some radical changes in the country's life, and another shocking experience from the dethroning of the former idol — the omnipotent "leader of the nations," to see things clearly. Of major importance for Nikolai Karetnikov became the glimpses of light and the safety valves which were opened during the period of Nikita Khrushchev's "thaw" in the previously soundproof "Iron Curtain."

But before that he had written quite a few works in many diverse genres, which revealed his proficiency in the fundamentals of composition, and won a warm response from musicians of most varied creative orientations. Karetnikov came to be acclaimed as a promising composer, who could eventually become a good professional and a master of conventional genres, such as cantatas, oratorios, chamber and especially symphonic opuses. He was regarded primarily as a young composer with a great gift for writing symphonic works in the traditions of Russian classical music. Some undesirable deviations in his music, which came to the notice of the musical officials, were explained by his immaturity and the inevitable "growing pains." In his memoirs Nikolai Karetnikov writes about his confrontation with Dmitry Kabalevsky, who came to establish himself in the post of the omnipotent secretary of the USSR Composers Union for many long years; that staunch champion of the official ideology found his young colleague's Second Symphony too gloomy, with its tragic theme looking suspicious to the adepts of the official "commanded optimism." Any references to the classics, in particular, to Tchaikovsky with his celebrated Sixth Symphony, failed to help, for the regime demanded of the musicians that they glorify the successes of the fairest socio-political structure in the world, wherein the personal had to be completely merged with the public needs.

And in this respect, it would be appropriate to mention the composer's own severe and uncompromising attitude to his early works. Karetnikov gave all of them up, treating these as non-existent and beginning to count the number of his opuses with his Third Symphony (written in 1959). Not agreeing to such unjust, in our view, appraisal of these compositions, one has to recognize the author's right to pass judgments on his own creations and respect them no matter how wrong he may be. Incidentally, these "discarded" compositions included an oratorio that had good notices in the press, two symphonies, choruses, arrangements of Russian folk songs, and the romances which used to be performed by Zara Dolukhanova, a noted chamber singer. Admittedly, these compositions differ quite conspicuously from his later opuses, nevertheless, the composer's extremely negative attitude to them, with no words spared to express it, seems to be too exaggerated. Without the experience he had gained while writing these not quite perfect works, a decisive leap that made itself evident in the composer's creative development in the late fifties and early sixties could have hardly been possible.

It proved, indeed, to be a discovery of the new world — the 20th century with its soundscape broke into the minds of the young and at times not so very young musicians who had never before even suspected of its existence. Despite the still persisting thoughtless speculations about the Soviet musical avant-garde as a certain counter-culture pitilessly suppressed by the party functionaries, including the composers who had seized the official posts in the Composers Union, the very existence of the avant-garde in Russian music at the turn of the 1960s could be questioned for the reason that the "daring" innovations of the young neophytes amounted in most cases to nothing more than the well (or not so well) learned lessons provided by such masters as Stravinsky, Bartok, Hindemith and, certainly, Shostakovich first and foremost. The latter's impact was indeed overwhelming: the numerous symphonies, instrumental concertos and string quarters revealed the Shostakovichian *marcato* forcefulness (in the spirit of the well-known "invasion episode" from his celebrated Seventh Symphony), endless melodies in which the habitual turns came to be exaggerated through introducing high and low steps and, finally, it was "to Shostakovich's measure" that the large-scale forms were cut out, which reflected in an indirect way the influence of Mahler's symphonies.

It should be reminded that by this time the Western musical community had already passed the stage of the universal infatuation with total serialism and overcome the irresistible temptations inherent in aleatory music, and started exploring the sonoristic effects and conducting experiments in the sphere of electronic music. All these trends found their expression in the music of Soviet "avant-gardists" as mere reverberations, being used in more than moderate, sometimes even in homoeopathic doses. As for the main attraction for the young composers, their hearts and minds were primarily preoccupied with the classical, Schoenberg's dodecaphony, which by that time had been a long stage past and gone for the Western musicians.

It should be admitted that no trend in 20th-century music came under such fierce castigation in Russia in those years as the one propagated by the three foremost representatives of the Second Viennese School — Schoenberg, Berg and Webern. As

Nikita Khrushchev declared at one of the conferences on artistic matters, "Dodecaphony is just cacophony." Of course, he had no idea about the subject of his attacks, being obviously prompted to utter this statement by some obliging person.

But as it had often happened in the history of arts, the severe banishments, even those occasionally initiated by persons endowed with an excellent taste, brought forth the reverse results; the subject of bitter criticism was given a fresh lease of life, rising like Phoenix from its ashes. The infatuation with dodecaphony turned out to be universal, involving even the well established and no longer young masters. Even Shostakovich himself used the twelve-note serial technique in some of his compositions (Symphony No. 14, String Quarters Nos 12 and 13). Nikolai Karetnikov also found himself among the most convinced adepts of the classical serial technique. Though, in his case dodecaphony proved to be not a temporary infatuation, soon to be overcome (as, for instance, with Alfred Schnittke) but a newly acquired faith to which he remained loyal.

Of course, from the standpoint of those seeking a striking novelty in music, who get involved in the movement from the ever new to the supernovel in the spirit of Hegelian notorious infinity, Nikolai Karetnikov's loyalty to the method of composition based exclusively on twelve, interrelated notes may seem a rather provincial, belated reproduction of outdated findings, well mastered and overcome. In this case there is no point in listening to Karetnikov's music.

But for those who look for something more in music than mere following of changeable, fast fleeting fashion, striving to discern and perceive behind the certain structures of sounds the inspirations of supersensitive aspects of human existence, for such persons the outwardly "old-fashioned" compositions may open the unheard-of and earlier inaccessible depths of the human spirit which is well aware of its kinship with the emanations of the living Cosmos. As for dodecaphony as it were, representing nothing more than a method of sound organization with its easily assimilated limitations, it leaves room for nearly the same diversity of stylistic solutions as the classical tonal system in which were written the compositions of such different masters as Haydn, Mozart, Wagner, and Mahler. And the value of Karetnikov's music is due not to the degree of his consistent employment of dodecaphonic technical devices, but to its artistic outcome, sometimes arising contrary to the conventional and rigorously observed limitations.

The 1960s became the time of Nikolai Karetnikov's vigorous creative work. One after another, in rapid succession, there appeared his compositions written in various genres, among them *Lento-variatione* for piano (1960), Sonata for Violin and Piano (1961), String Quartet (1962), Concerto for Wind Instruments (1965), and Chamber Symphony (1967) (Musical Example 1).

Two of the above mentioned compositions merit special consideration. Karetnikov's String Quartet and Concerto for Wind Instruments reveal the close attention given to a sound and sonority as it were, with the composer intently listening to such sonorities and demanding that the performers render them in their pure form, devoid of any sensuality, which is so characteristic of the habitual manner of sound production with its full-blooded *vibrato*. The texture of the String Quartet is deliberately discrete (disclosing Webern's obvious influence) but without the eventual loss of relationship between the adjacent notes and atomization of its fabric. As a result, the finale of this quartet may be perceived as a kind of dotted-lined cantilena.

In his Concerto for Wind Instruments the composer tackles another task: it resembles a rotating crystal ball illumined from the outside and from within by the rainbow colors playing on its facets. The incessantly ringing and constantly renovated block formed by the combinations of different tone-colors seems to transfer the music into a multidimensional space.

However, despite all the singularity of his chamber compositions written in the sixties, the true nature of Karetnikov's style is most explicit in his monumental works for full symphony orchestra, out of which his Fourth Symphony in one movement is still regarded as his best achievement.

The message of this symphony was defined by the composer himself in the following, most precise, terms: "I was to build up a composition based on the serial technique, being its consistent adherent, and at the same time to create within it a prolonged spatial structure which would allow to express myself as fully frankly as possible." (This statement is cited from the composer's annotation, the translation of which was published in the *Nutida Musika* magazine.) The composer considered it inadequate to regard symphony as a genre (as it was understood by Mahler and Schoenberg) losing its validity today; he believed that the genre will not die out, but acquire a new lease of life.

Then it would be valid to pose the following question: how one should organize quite a large-scale composition basing oneself on the procedure that presumes concentrated attention to building up a logical or coloristic structure? To intensify the conventional neo-Viennese scheme, Nikolai Karetnikov produced a one-movement composition whose sections (corresponding to the five movements of a symphonic cycle) simultaneously represent the structural units of the sonata *Allegro* (the first movement exposing the principal part, the second movement — the secondary part, the third movement representing the development section, the fourth movement — the episode before recapitulation, and the fifth movement — recapitulation comprising a coda). At the same time the symphony may be also viewed as a variational cycle containing 13 links (their number being distributed between the movements irregularly, with their bridge passages also acting as variations).

And how is this symphony perceived today, 25 years after it has been written? To my mind, it does not look like appearing from some remote past when the hearts of the then comparatively young generation of the thirty- and forty-years-olds were full of enthusiasm, inspired by a flicker, or in some cases by a spark, or hope for the better future, cherished by their faith in the ultimate triumph of the new. This triumph has come at long last and what then? How should one appraise the music written during the period of *Sturm und Drang,* a fruit of the true, and not faked, perestroika in its creator's musical consciousness?

Nowadays Nikolai Karetnikov's Fourth Symphony is still perceived as a serious work captivating by the powerful scope of its musical flow, up to its final culmination point. But now you find nothing strange in a combination of impressive symphonic declarations in the spirit of either Mahler or Berg with the refined explicitly chamber-like contemplations so akin to the creations of Webern, that universally recognized idol among the post-war music innovators. However, this music is far from being purely German, for its symphonic dramatic pattern is reminiscent (for all dissimilarity of the music!) of the Russian tradition, which was vividly represented by Shostakovich and which could be traced back to Tchaikovsky. But is this composition destined to be performed only within the programmes of historical concerts designed to remind us of the past of Soviet music, as a specimen of the music written by composers running against the mainstream, against the officially cultivated styles and standards? We hope that the Fourth Symphony by Nikolai Karetnikov still has a chance to win well-deserved recognition as one of the most valuable accomplishments in 20th-century Russian music, attracting the attention of music connoisseurs precisely by its unspectacular extraordinariness and becoming a ringing documentary evidence of thwarted hopes and incomplete undertakings.

However, Karetnikov's creative work was developing in another direction too, which reflected the deep-reaching Russian roots in his talent. He proved to be one of the first composers to find a new field for applying his creative resources — in the domain of sacred music inspired in his quests by the Orthodox teaching. Over the course of several decades he wrote ritual choruses intended, according to the age-old Russian tradition, for a cappella singing. But even in the extremely rigid confines of the orthodox canon the composer tried to revive the nearly dried up source of ecclesiastical chants: he was intent on restoring the tradition without too decisive violation of its conventional standards. Yet, the appraisal of the composer's orthodox choruses could hardly be one-sided. Perhaps, these choruses are too complicated, with their dissonaces, elliptic progressions and other intricate turns of harmony displaying the techniques of a modern master? Perhaps, this music could even disrupt the mood of serenity and peace of mind and abstraction from the daily chores and vanities which a person hopes to attain in a temple, having nearly lost the road to it? Or it may seem out of place under the vaults of a temple, carrying even the remotest echo of everything that worries and torments one's soul in our imperfect world?

One could hardly provide the answers to the above questions, for in this matter one should fully rely on the artist's conscience and the unbiased appraisal of his creations. But first of all, in doing so one must undoubtedly disregard the severe denunciations of certain clerics who imposed upon themselves to judge about the moral aspects in art, about what is pleasing or unpleasing to God in it.

The destiny of a professional composer is in the least determined by his accomplishments that remain wrapped in mystery. He may write as much as he wishes in the stillness of his cosy study room, enjoying to his heart's content his embodiment of the still inaudible musical sounds: but in order to live in this world he has to *serve*. This service implies not the literal holding of a certain post in the system of musical institutions concerned with music promotion or musical training, but the writing of music in conformity with the conventional rigid "rules of the game" prevailing in the various spheres of artistic activity.

Nikolai Karetnikov shirked no job of this kind to earn his living. Moreover, in certain circles he became known as a master of applied music, being capable of not merely following the whims of a film director or a choreographer but retaining therewith his own individuality in the successful solution of artistic tasks within the most rigidly "stipulated terms." This is what actually happened, for instance, with his ballet *Vanina Vanini* after Stendhal, when he managed to inspire with his ideas the notable choreographers Vladimir Vasilyov and Natalia Kasatkina. And the matter here is not only in the plot of this ballet with its love story conventionally complicated by social motives — the confrontation of love and duty, faithfulness and betrayal. The very music of this ballet, based on the standards of the dodecaphonic-serial technique, was perceived as a revelation for the mere reason that it got its rendering on the stage of the famous Bolshoi Theatre. But its success proved to be ephemeral and short-lived, for owing to the endeavors of the cultural officials and the intrigues of his secret enemies Karetnikov was banished for many years to come not only from the Bolshoi but also from any musical theatre, of which there were quite a lot in those years. It took several decades for his ballet *Baby Zaches* after E.T.A. Hoffman to be staged at home. This ballet produced by the composer in cooperation with the same choreographers and telling the story of the vicious dwarf coming into power looked too explosive and fraught with the undesirable allusions. But here also the sharply grotesque delineations of the main characters born of the great German taleteller's fantasy went hand in hand with the "strange world" of serial music associated with the image of the mysterious magician Prospero Alpanus (Musical Example 2).

A similar lot fell on the composer's best incidental score to the film *A Dirty Joke* directed by Alexander Alov and Vladimir Naumov, based on Fyodor Dostoyevsky's short novel. No doubt, the composer had to make forced and tormenting compromises when he, for instance, took part in such dubious venture as the production of the film *Flight* in which Mikhail Bulgakov's famous play turned out to be barbarously distorted along with Karetnikov's music. In these cases no obstacles arose for releasing such films (and others in the same vein) on the screen. Following a private review at the Cinema-Makers Club in Moscow, a strict ban was imposed on the film *A Dirty Joke*. By the way, the music to this film may be ranked not only as Karetnikov's best film score, but also as the most spectacular and highly important accomplishment in this sphere of applied sound creativity comparable, in its level, with Prokofiev's incidental scores to the films by Sergei Eisenstein.

It would be hard to name another Russian feature film where the music governs a synthesis of arts, places accents and renders its message in such a clear and easily perceptible way. Nikolai Karetnikov's music is full of bitter grotesque in exposing both a VIP condescending to make happy his grateful subordinates unctuously peeping into his eyes, and an infamous crowd of noneities and morally depraved persons in whose mind the outward servility and cowardice get along together with the hatred of slaves ready at the earliest convenience to trample upon the one whose boots they have just been licking. And this intricate sensation arises owing to the devices of indirect characterization: a sensitive ear, or to be more precise, the inner feeling of music, discerns it even in the rollicking quadrille performed by a random ensemble of musicians (by the way, its cast is indicated by Dostoyevsky himself). In this incidental score the composer captured the naked cruelty of people who could not stand one another but forced to coexist, even if they sank down to becoming completely wild.

The established system discarded Karetnikov's work, pushing it to the background of the country's musical life, with the composer remaining shrouded in the neglect directed by some experienced hand. Under such circumstances it is no wonder that the composer had to keep himself away altogether, having stopped work in serious genres not for years but for decades. And on the outside something like that was taking shape: at regular intervals the music festivals of "Moscow Autumn" featured separate compositions written by Nikolai Karetnikov, which failed, as a rule, to draw the public notice; there were also "passable" films with his music far inferior to his flight in *A Dirty Joke*.

Meanwhile, the composer was far from idling. It took him twenty years of hard work to complete two capital operas: *Till Eulenspiegel* and *Saint Paul's Mystery*. The latter one so far existing merely in the form of a score could be discussed here only in brief: it is a kind of musical-scenic composition combining the features of an opera and an oratorio-like mystery play. Its action takes place during the reign of the Roman emperor Nero, who initiated the persecution of Christians, and whose god-father, according to the legend, was Saint Paul. The confrontation between the heathen emperor epitomizing a bloody and uncontrolled tyranny and the greatest Father of the Church who made Christianity a world religion, without the involvement of the Jews and the ancient Greeks, may be accepted, of course, with certain reservations as a free artistic assumption. Nevertheless, it helped the composer to convey in the most revealing way the irreconcilable opposition of two fundamental principles — the absolute goodness and no less consistent embodiment of the destructive power of evil. A more adequate appraisal of this work would be possible only after it is presented at least in its concert version.

As for the opera *Till Eulenspiegel*, it can be discussed in greater detail and more confidence since we have at our disposal the recorded performance of this opera on the concert stage, which was prepared for production by the eminent stage director Anatoly Efros, who had to endure, up to his premature decease, the whole measure of official persecution unleashed against his innovative quests.

The opera *Till Eulenspiegel* reflects Karetnikov's views as a moralist artist. This composition stands apart in the progress of the Russian musical theatre. Nevertheless, the plot of this opera provides the grounds to regard it with apprehensive distrust. The fact is that the numerous Soviet operas on the subject of national liberation struggle have bored the listeners to death. And the plot of this opera presented plenty of gratifying material to the same effect: the people who rose in rebellion against the foreign invaders; the savage reprisal of the heretics who dared to pray God not in the way the merciful Mother, i.e. the Catholic Church, demands; the executions without a trial, the purple glow of impressive *autos-da-fé* and the like. It portrays the unbending heroes prepared to go through mortal tortures for the sake of their ideas and the villains exterminating the dissenters by fire and sword. In short, it has everything to assert the myths still ruling the minds of the people rushing in the wild-goose chase for the elusive ghost of freedom "at any cost."

However, upon a closer scrutiny of this composition the prejudiced opinions get dispelled. For this opera carries another understatement too, sometimes hidden in the background and at times quite obvious, which lends life-like authenticity to the well-hackneyed and artistically hardly inspiring conflict. As a result, this conflict presents itself not as an opposition of the righteous and the wicked but as a clash of far from perfect people hating their fellowmen only because the latter adhere to "another creed," the people headed by their grasping leaders who came into confrontation in their struggle for power. The romantically depicted Gueux of Charles de Coster act here as a crowd of envious ragamuffins greedily snatching away the other people's possessions and no less cruelly dealing with the vanquished than the self-conceited Spaniards whom they hold in such unmitigated contempt. The matter virtually involves the opposition of two truths — the old truth inherent in the age-old tradition and the new truth, destroying the so far unshakeable establishments in the merry, but bloodthirsty mischief. At the same time it is the opposition of two falsities: the stagnant inertness opposing any change and the spirit of renewal destroying the long-established standards without which the human community could hardly exist.

But the chief point upsetting the former socially oriented scheme lies in the interpretation of the opera's main protagonist. Till Eulenspiegel's image is multifaceted: he is possessed with the spirit of freedom, but his idea of freedom is genuine, not passing into arbitrary rule and self-destruction, freedom going hand in hand with justice. A convinced opponent to any reprisal and persecution from any side, he is at the same time a cheeky mocker and an impudent mischief-maker, somehow akin to a Russian buffoon, fond of joking and making fun. At the same time Till epitomizes truly Christian mercy for vanquished enemies; he is also a tender and faithful lover. And in the long run the great rebel feels himself an outsider in that renewed society where the foreign rulers came to be replaced by the domestic ones, no less mercenary, perfidious and cruel.

The other characters in the opera are not so multifaceted, acting as the bearers of some definite, prevailing human traits rather than live people: Lamme Goodzak, a gormandizer with a sweet tooth, is a kind of Sancho Panza to Till's Flemish Don Quixote; Nele, Till's unaging sweetheart, is a symbol of loyalty and boundless love; the courageous Claes ready to die for the sake of his cherished idea; the unwomanly staunch Soetkin, and many other taking part in that carnival of masks where everyone plays 'for real', with its non-imaginary dangers and real deaths. The opera's heroes are clearly reminiscent of the characters depicted in the classicist operas *seria* and *buffa*. And the decisive factor here belongs not so much to the opera's poetic underpinnings as to the devices employed by the composer in the interweaving of its fabric.

The first thing that strikes the listeners is the grotesque and parodic transformation of the habitual "musical idioms," for instance, the architraditional heroic fanfares which are devoid of any shade of elevation and enthusiasm inherent in oratorical declarations, as if an imaginary hero, invisibly assuming a cothurnal pose, is just going to make faces and put out his tongue at the public. The great sacrament invariably associated with the incoming of a new man into this world is also tackled in an ironical manner. And though the prayer-like sounds of the organ, appropriate only within the vaults of a temple, stress the solemnity of the moment, this elevation is removed by the deliberately prosaic cues of the clergyman dully and automatically performing, perhaps, in a thousandth time, the rite of christening, and by the outcries of the child's god-father with stupid pomposity parroting the endings of the phrases uttered by the former. It is precisely this "lowering" disbalance in the overall manifestation of the genre characteristics, the emotional imagery of the vocal parts and in the the background created by the instrumental accompaniment that becomes the key feature in the style of Karetnikov's opera. The orchestra acts mainly as the bearer of the serious developments in the action unfolding on the stage while the singing voices convey irony and parody.

In his musical portrayal of the characters from the remote past the composer is guided not so much by the striving for observing the museum and archeological authenticity as by his modern perception of the period music. And this is evident even in his treatment of the episodes based on the song-strophic structures. Thus, in the outwardly unpretentious tune sung by the kind-hearted Lamme one can discern the keen refinement of a modern musician feeling nostalgia for those immemorial times when even civil strife failed to violate the long-established order in a human life and one's peace of mind, with the people being able to indulge in their material welfare.

The same duality is felt in the monotonous scansion of the high-flown words opening a mass for the dead: it horrifies us to hear them as at the same moment a live person is being set on fire. And again a sharp contrast arises between the words sung by the male chorus and the desperate cries of a son witnessing the execution of his father. For the musical embodiment of the incorporeal imagery far removed from the daily vanities of this world, the composer employs the serial structures of classical dodecaphony: in this vein unfolds the musical apparition of Jesus Christ before Till, opposing in its style to everything that accompanied the previous developments in the opera's action.

The specific feature of this opera lies in the utmost importance attached here to the vocal tonality as the main and conceivably unique device of depicting its characters, the change in their moods and their response to the current developments. As for the orchestra and the chorus, they are often assigned the role of the stable background to express in sounds a certain situation. Even all kinds of skirmishes and scuffles are rendered in the extremely theatrical manner similar to the performances in a popular show-booth. Such is, for instance, the fight provoked by the restless Lamme rushing into the crowd of pilgrims, both men and women, that takes place against the background and in the rhythms of the rollicking impetuous tarantella. But the chief point lies in the other matter: this music, looking purely illustrative on the outside, serves in an indirect way to characterize Till, the main protagonist, which is manifest in his exclamations revealing in him an interested spectator cheering up a fighter and admiring his actions. Till as a mischievous person, an instigator of all kinds of tricks far from being harmless, looks extremely unbridled in these scenes. Such approach undermines the foundations of the officially cultivated Soviet canon of a popular leader, which could not be challenged by anybody. Instead of an impressive manne-quin there arises a live person incorporating all the human frailties and contradictions. And even depicting his state on the threshold of passing into the other better world the composer brings into a clash the austere concentration of a prelude in the nearly Bachian nature and a reckless dance of this great life-lover, as if combining in one character the grand nobleness of the Commendatore and the champagne-like spark-ling charm of his mortal enemy — Don Giovanni.

The above analysis discloses the mixed style of this opera, revealing a great number of truly incompatible sources interwoven in its texture. This is undisguised eclecticism elevated to a principle. But as far as we are concerned, we have been accustomed to mixing all sorts of things in music, this trend even getting its justification and definition and known in the musical theory as "polystylistics." During the period of summing up, on the eve of the third millennium since Christ was born, a time has come to gather stones together, and an artist living in the postmodernist age is fully entitled to take up any good thing lying nearby.

To sum it up, it would be apt to point out that in later years Karetnikov was still working in most diverse fields. In 1990 he completed his Piano Quintet in three movements, perhaps the best chamber piece written in Russia in recent years. This quintet attracted listeners by its graphically fine style, its chiselled texture and the uncommon consistency in the composition procedures of classical dodecaphony. In addition to this piece there appeared six new sacred chants (1992) in which the composer was striving to follow the standards of the orthodox canon, at the same time renewing as much as possible the strictly chordal style of a cappella singing.

And maybe the very fact that Karetnikov's compositions have not been fully appreciated as yet in his native land is the best evidence of the seriousness inherent in his artistic quests, his uncompromising nature and faithfulness to the truth in art as he understood it. Nikolai Karetnikov made his own choice in this world as a human being and as an artist, preferring to go his own way, without looking round and bypassing the numerous obstacles arising on this way. As for the future, let us hope that it would do justice to his accomplishments.

Ex.1 *Chamber Symphony Reproduced by permission of Boosey and Hawkes Music Publishers Ltd.*

PRINCIPAL WORKS

1943–1947	Childhood Pieces
1959	Third Symphony
1960	*Lento-variatione* for piano
1961	Sonata for Violin and Piano
1962	*Vanina Vanini,* ballet in one act
1962	String Quartet
1964	Fourth Symphony
1965	Concerto for Wind Instruments
1967	Chamber Symphony
1968	*Baby Zaches,* ballet
1969	*Kleinenachtmusik* for mixed quartet
1968–1989	Eight Sacred Chants in Memory of Boris Pasternak
1970	Piano Piece
1978	Two Piano Pieces
1985	*Till Eulenspiegel,* opera
1986	*From Sholom Aleichem.* Chamber suite
1987	*Saint Paul's Mystery,* opera
1990	Piano Quintet
1992	Concerto for Strings
1993	Six Sacred Chants

Ex.2 *Baby Zaches* (introduction)

Alemdar Karamanov:
an outsider in Soviet music

Yuri Kholopov

Alemdar Karamanov

For a long time the Crimean composer Alemdar Karamanov, virtually unknown to the Western musical community, has been consigned to oblivion in Russia. His compositions were neither performed nor even mentioned in the mass media. Karamanov remained an outsider in Soviet music, being alien to keeping abreast of the times and refusing to follow the conventional standards and the current fashions in music. But, as it often happens, the recluses turn out to be the bearers of some profound ideas of their time.

The composer's name reveals the Turkish origins of his father, who was called Sabit Temel Kagyrman. As time passed, this name assumed its Russian version of Karamanov. The senior Karamanov had to go through all the hardships involved in the repressive Soviet system. The composer's mother, Paulina Sergeyevna, was a Russian woman working as a head librarian. Their son, Alemdar Sabitovich Karamanov, was born on September 10, 1934 in Simferopol. The mother, an accomplished singer, became the first tutor in music for the future composer, who tried writing music when he was just six years old. He entered an elementary music school in Simferopol to learn piano playing. The war with Germany did not touch the family with its tragic side. Alemdar retained in his memory some curious details of wartime life: the German soldiers having no special liking for their "Fuehrer" were inclined to scold him (though in the battlefield they were, of course, the most honest warriors); they liked the boy playing the piano and used to bring for him Johann Strauss music and precious blank music sheets whenever they came back from their leave in Germany. Upon liberation of the Crimea from the Germans, his father as a man of non-Russian origins was banished from the Crimea to the city of Kemerovo in the western part of Siberia, never to return from his exile. . .

Upon graduation from the music college in Simferopol, Alemdar Karamanov entered the Moscow Conservatoire to study composition with Semyon Bogatyrev, a remarkable musician and pedagogue, and piano with Vladimir Natanson. In the mid-fifties the atmosphere of supressing any free thought and persecuting "formalists" and "cosmopolitans" was reigning in Russia's cultural life. In reality it meant the banishment of all the best accomplishments in modern music. As Karamanov reminisces, "In order to take a Shostakovich's score in the library you had to get a special permit from the conservatoire rector." In his student years Karamanov was far from being a "modernist," nevertheless his free-thinking proved enough to mount attacks against his musical language. Upon graduation from the conservatoire, Karamanov took a postgraduate course in composition, from 1958–63, formally under the tutorship of Dmitry Kabalevsky, an official composer and a man of conservative views in music. Having failed to find common ground with Kabalevsky he started attending the classes of Tikhon Khrennikov.

Meanwhile the budding composer was rapidly progressing and within a decade his creative development underwent a rapid evolution. He selected symphony as the main sphere of his endeavors. During the period from 1954 to 1963 he wrote ten symphonies and a number of chamber pieces. One trait of his artistic personality stood out immediately in the style of his compositions written in the 1950s: the emotional spontaneity in expressing himself, avoiding whenever the necessity arose the strict confines of academic forms. At first Karamanov was not drawn to the current com-position procedures used in the New Music. His themes, texture and orchestration seemed to be following the traditions of the Moscow composition school represented by Nikolai Myaskovsky, Vissarion Shebalin and Eugene Golubev. His rapidly progressing style came under the impact of the later styles in Russian music. To quote the composer himself, "My composition style has evolved on the basis of the profound ideas underlying the works of such great masters of Russian music as Rachmaninov, Scriabin, Prokofiev, and Shostakovich." The latter made a point of Karamanov's gift: "His is an interesting and highly original talent, and his individuality is apparent even in his student compositions."

Ex. 1 *Symphony No.7: The Moonlight Sea*

Example 1 is a sample of Karamanov's early music exemplified by an episode from his Symphony No. 7 subtitled *The Moonlight Sea*, written within his graduation year at the Moscow Conservatoire.

As Karamanov reminisces, "When I was a child my ear could not even bear the harsh dissonances of modern music . . . When I entered the Moscow Conservatoire, I came to embrace all the whole of great music on Earth. I found myself drawn to the modernist music and infatuated with Luigi Nono and Xenakis" (cited from his statements made on Moscow Radio in 1989). In the early sixties Alemdar Karamanov came to the fore among the most distinguished Soviet avant-gardists. His New Music attracted the attention of Luigi Nono during one of his visits to Moscow in the early 1960s. But the period of his "avant-gardism" proved short-lived: it lasted from 1962 to July 1964. Nevertheless, within this short span of time he wrote a number of highly impressive compositions running against the mainstream. Those years saw a fierce official campaign waged in the USSR against the novel composition procedures and those using the serial technique, sonoristic effects and novel instrumental sonorities. A shower of ideological accusations was levelled upon the composers of modern music, which was dangerous in a country based on the Marxist social system. Karamanov's turn to avant-garde music revealed once again the spontaneous nature of his creativity. He opened for himself a wide field of artistic activity in the domain of dissonances and twelve-tone chromatics.

Ex. 2 *Prologue, Thinking and Epilogue, 1st movement*

Example 2 is a piece from his small triptych for piano *Prologue, Thinking and Epilogue,* one of his first avant-gardist compositions.

The piercing sharpness of the chords, their burning dissonance, the spontaneous unbridled expressiveness and complete emotional freedom are the features that stood out in Karamanov's style. The way the flow of cantilena-like melodic lines used to characterize his earlier compositions. The technique of free atonality with rhythmically dynamic sonoristic effects is inherent in all the works dating back to his avant-gardist period, including all the four pieces of his *Music* — one for the cello, one for the violin, and two for the piano, also his String Quartet No. 3, his Second Violin Concerto, and Tenth Symphony. One quality unifies Alemdar Karamanov's musical thinking throughout his creative career, notwithstanding all of its sharp turnings — his tendency to use free structures. He builds up his forms out of microsections, interweaving them into a stretched structure guided exclusively by his innermost feelings and freely employing the method of passing from one note to its adjacent one on the scale of semitones. The semitonal system of a scale, hemitonics, is perceived by Karamanov as the indispensable presence of a semitone in its vertical or horizontal relationships. It is noteworthy that the composer did not start exploring the constructive resources inherent in the serial technique as did the other Russian composers of the early avant-garde — Edison Denisov, Alfred Schnittke, Nikolai Karetnikov, Sophia Gubaidulina and Leonid Grabovsky. For a free structure is a singular feature of Russian music.

Alemdar Karamanov's technique in his avant-gardist compositions of such kind may be defined as *non-serial dodecaphony*. His music produces the serial-dodecaphonic *effect* without resorting to repetitions of serial note-rows. What is actually acting in his music are small groups of notes with the constantly audible semitone (a major 9th, a major 7th). In contrast to the tradition-oriented compositions inherent in the Second Viennese School with their periods, fugato, rondo, *Hauptstimme* and *Nebenstimme*-counterpoint, Karamanov produces the "new one-voice leading" out of dots of notes, two dots, clusters, and the trembling and passing notes. In its form, it is a recitative rather than a song. In the Prologue cited above (Musical Example 2) the emotional and nervously jerky statement is divided into "lines" (only the first one of the four lines is cited in the musical example) of approximately the same length. At the end of the fourth line there rings out the glimmering cluster "nail-like" cadence rendered in the piano's high register. Two or more "new one-voice" lines come to be contrapuntally interwoven in his pieces intended for an ensemble of instruments.

The polyphonic thinking comes therewith to be fully delivered from the Baroque types of pitch-rhythm-line trinity. However, in contrast to the main tendency in the Western avant-garde to serialization of several parametres, Karamanov is more inclined to set free the rigid strong lines and rhythms. His *Music* for the cello abounds in melodic lines whereas its "lyrical form rejects the dissonance tuning" (to quote the composer). Even in a slow movement the melodic flowing is full of energy and forcefulness (Musical Example 3a). As for the climaxes, here it reaches its extreme stridency (Musical Example 3b).

During his avant-gardist period the composer wrote few vocal pieces, to be more precise, the following two works: *When You Are Passing By*, a ballade for tenor and piano set to the verse by L. Asmapur, and *The Crime at Grenada*, a three-part song-cycle for voice and instrumental ensemble to the verses by Antonio Machado y Ruiz. The

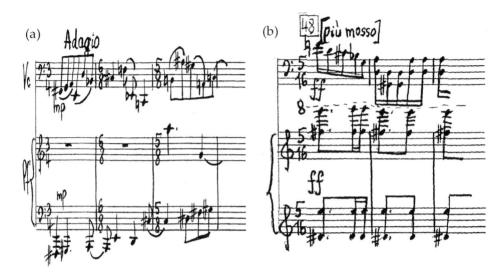

Ex. 3 *Music for Cello and Piano*

mood of the ballade is unusual for Karamanov, for it is imbued with frank Oriental eroticism:

> My desire like a jaguar's licking his gentle spotty female,
> My desire like an ass's playing with his love partner,
> My desire like an elephant's calling for his mate in the jungle.

Ex. 4 *When you are passing by*

    The other composition is diametrically opposite to this one. Dedicated to the memory of Federico Garcia Lorca killed by the Nazis in 1936, this triptych represents a spectacular and biting pamphlet full of high civic spirit: "He was killed at daybreak, with the first sunrays. None of his executioners dared to raise his eyes to watch it." The singing is accompanied by the violin, the flute and two pianos, the prepared one included. Below are two episodes from the cycle's outer parts:

Ex. 5a *The Crime at Grenada: I. The Crime*

Such music was in glaring contradiction with the tenets of the Soviet ideology. Naturally enough, it evoked a sharply negative response in Soviet musical circles. The professors at the Moscow Conservatoire gave an unsatisfactory mark to the composer for his Ninth Symphony which he played at one of his exams (by the way, they had to correct it soon to avoid the intereference on the part of the watchful higher "instances"). Any possibility of publishing his compositions, which had been slim enough before, were now excluded. The printing of such avant-garde music was out of the question. The performance of the young composer's works became also impossible despite the fact that some of them, reflecting the patriotic sentiments, bore the most appropriate titles (e.g. his Fifth Symphony subtitled *Lenin*, written in 1957; the overtures *Heroic* and *Festive*, written in 1964). Admittedly, there were few exceptions: in 1961 the ballet company of the Maly Opera House in Leningrad staged Alemdar Karamanov's early (pre-avant-gardist) ballet *Stronger Than Love* based on Boris Lavrenyov's short story *The Forty-First* (on the subject of the Civil War in Russia).

As a result, the composer found himself in an extremely hard situation. He had neither lodgings in Moscow, nor any job; his work as a composer, the more so as an avant-gardist composer provided him no means of subsistence. He was not a person to seek a successful career at the expense of his ethics, such as "to marry a Moscow-residing woman" (for instance, a daughter of some high-placed party functionary). The Soviet "doublethink" (the word coined by George Orwell) did not suit him either.

Ex. 5b *The Crime at Grenada: II. Made of Stone and Hope*

Karamanov was forced to take an unexpected decision: to throw everything away and leave for his native Crimea. It happened in 1965, opening up a new stage in his life.

The spiritual ferment in the composer's soul, which made itself evident in his turning to the contrasting trends and artistic ideas — neo-romanticism, Soviet patriotism, and avant-gardism — came to be centered now on Karamanov's main artistic conception. Let us call it, using his own words, *musical religion* in its basically Christian spirit. Once again it was a manifestation of the artist's running against the mainstream and of his non-conformist nature. God and Jesus Christ were even the greater enemies of the Soviet regime than Boulez and Webern. The late 1950s and the early 1960s saw a renewed persecution of the church in Soviet Russia, with fifteen thousand temples and many monasteries coming to be shut down. Nikita Khrushchev boasted that he would show "the last priest" on the national TV and pompously declared the year 1980 to see the coming of communist paradise in the USSR. At the same time it was in the sixties that the religious revival in Russia began. Karamanov was the first, though not the unique composer, to turn from the avant-garde to sacred music. The other two were Yuri Butsko (born 1938) and Vladimir Martynov (born 1946).

Alemdar Karamanov's turn to Christianity was, no doubt, due primarily to his hard and prolonged spiritual quests. But there are a few specifically Russian reasons for it. The exposed failure of the social ideology, the fictitious nature and falsity of the showy Soviet clichs and labels made many people to draw their attention to the solid and worthy principles in human life. And the official denunciation of his music, which left for the artist no chance to earn his living, all of a sudden revealed to him that God alone had been always supporting him in all his undertakings, irrespective of what the people around him were doing. Almost a quarter of a century later, speaking on the radio, Karamanov came to express his sentiments in the following words: "God is Our Lord and He is always with us. He grants me His spiritual protection. All the time I feel some powerful, supporting hand. And in this I see [the action] of some purposeful divine force."

Upon leaving for his native, albeit provincial town of Simferopol, Karamanov got ample time and opportunity for his creative work: "As an 'aborigene' of my country I came back to the southern sun, and it gave me a chance to take long walks in the faraway parts and conceive of some musical idea. But at the same time I have been invariably haunted by the following thought: it would be so nice to have someone in Moscow to look at it, for where I'm now residing there is nobody to show it to." The composer found himself "confined" in a remote place, far away from Moscow. In the Soviet reality a secluded life was paramount to oblivion. In some peculiar way Karamanov in this atheistic country became virtually a *musical monk*, a man from an outside world, who at his own will underwent the austere penance imposed by the Christian religion. Yet, his music written since 1965 has been secular, rather than sacred, though it is imbued with the religious spirit. He has rejected nothing done previously, though he regards now the spectacular avant-gardist period in his work as "a time of infatuations". As for the new, third period, he views it as "regeneration" of his creative spirit, as "purification and adoption of his own language" on the basis of the Russian tradition "engendered by the life-giving resources inherent in modern music" (from his radio interview).

Upon discarding hemitonics of his avant-gardist period, Karamanov has been now guided by the principles of expanded tonality (he calls it "expanded diatonics"), a mixture of modes, major and minor in particular, and polyharmonic extraneous layers termed by him as *supertonality* (stressing the supremacy of one predominating, usually lower, layer in his polyharmonic strata). As a matter of fact, it is *neo-romanticism* in harmony and tonality, i.e. the prevalence of the principles underlying the late Romantic music — written by Rachmaninov and Scriabin, but enriched with some idioms intrinsic in 20th-century New Music. It is characteristic of Alemdar Karamanov to mix major and minor modes simultaneously, which he terms as *absorption of minor*. Some elements of minor tonality are drawn into the orbit of major as an additional embellishing component. Hence, the predominance of major tonality in his compositions. It is in this lucid and emotionally joyous key that he perceives the ideas and plots depicted in the works written during the so called "Simferopol" stage in his creative work.

This period in Alemdar Karamanov's life is devoted to the New Testament and the Christian imagery. To quote the composer once again, "In contrast to the low biological force, the struggle for survival, there is another force — kindness, humanity, humaneness. Life is one's spirit. It alone enlightens and makes the chain of human existence infinite." Of course, Christianity constitutes for Karamanov the Russian Orthodox teaching first and foremost. However his world outlook appears not to be so orthodox. Somewhat in the spirit of modern "universal" religions he draws an analogy between Jesus Christ and other gods known to have descended upon Earth. "I understand the Christian idea in a very broad sense, not rejecting any of its historical manifestations," says the composer. He extends the sphere of orthdox manifestations, tracing them back to two millennia B.C., through the "Byzantine holiness" and bringing the Orthodoxy and the ancient Indian tradition closer to each other. Calling himself "an orthodox Christian," he nevertheless makes the following confession: "I'm very deeply touched by Hinduism and Vedic myths" (from his interview given to Moscow Radio in March 1993). Paraphrasing Fyodor Dostoyevsky's idea, Karamanov asserts: "Only art, spirit and human thought can save the world and oppose to all the destructive forces." And, of course, he would be happy to see his music, "if it starts ringing out," somehow contribute to the salvation of the world.

Since 1965 Alemdar Karamanov has been inspired by the above delineated set of ideas. In 1965–66 he wrote a cycle of symphonies under the general title *Sovershishasia* ("All things now accomplished"). This word in the Old Church Slavonic language, but not in modern Russian, sounds grand and very impressive. It was borrowed from the Gospel according to St. John (19:30), the last word uttered by Jesus Christ on the Cross (in the English translation of the Bible Jesus's last words being: "It is accomplished"). The full title of the cycle reads as follows: "All things now accomplished for the glory of God and Our Lord Jesus Christ." The cycle incorporates ten one-movement compositions for the superlarge cast of the orchestra, at the same time representing an extended symphony in ten movements, lasting 150 minutes. Its finale, the Tenth Symphony, involves also the chorus and soloists. The titles of the movements trace the history of Jesus's trials and his Resurrection according to the four Gospels:

1. "For God so loved the world"
2. "For theirs is the kingdom of heaven"
3. "In Hebrew, and Greek, and Latin"
4. "It is accomplished"
5. "They shall look on whom they pierced"
6. "And all the people...smote their breasts"
7. "Wound in linen clothes with the spices"
8. "He is not here: for he is risen from the dead"
9. "And were continually in the temple"
10. "In the glory of his Father"

Afterwards the movements of this grand symphony *Sovershishasia* in the list of the Karamanov's symphonies were to be designated as Symphonies Nos 11 through 14, the composer trying to make it look more like a conventional cycle. By and large, the religious programme is embodied in the music in a generalized way, without any details. The composer thus expressed his message: "I was striving to convey the mighty drive that urged the authors of the Scriptures to record down these religious texts and their deep-going inner symphonism." The title of this cycle also expresses the irrevocable nature of the world outlook attained by the composer as the most adequate one to reveal his individuality.

This third stage in Alemdar Karamanov's creative work is also marked by the novel principles in his musical *style*. There is no room in it now for the extreme tension of his avant-gardist sonorities, yet a return to the conventional academic optimistic depiction inherent in the conservative, neo-classicical trend is also out of the question. The composer's concentration on the spiritual and religious subjects guides his choice of the musical material. He is influenced by the moods and sentiments of the Orthodox sacred music which is distinguished for its lucid character and avoidance of extreme expressiveness; in ecclesiastical music, since it is applied but not autonomous, the purity of a depicted character dominates over the artistic refinement of the musical material. The principal genre characteristic of sacred music is its orientation to the easy perception, as in the popular genres; hence the simplicity of its musical language and purification of the music from any down-to-earth passions. In contrast to artistic music designed to impress the listeners by the singularity of its musical material and compositional structure, in applied ritual music a non-musical religious message comes first as compared to any acoustic factor. *Word is superior to sound.*

Karamanov, with his generous contribution made to the avant-gardist principles in art just behind him, came now to accept this conception of sacred music and extend it over non-ritual genres. In his output, where prevail concertos and symphonies, you would hardly find ritual music as it were, in contrast to, say, Vladimir Martynov's later works. It is significant that the composer prefers to write the large-scale cycles of programmatic symphonies. Bearing the habitual genre designation and being outwardly "simple" as regards their musical language, Karamanov's symphonies nevertheless outline some new genre of music for orchestra. According to the apt remark made by Svetlana Savenko, a notable Russian musicologist, his symphonies represent the late-romantic poems invested by the traditions initiated in the post-avant-gardist period. But in contrast to the late-romantic symphonic poems rooted in the genre of overture and often based on the sonata Allegro, Karamanov's religious symphonies may be well defined as *symphonic mysteries* directed by their programme the way an operatic act is built up to take the shape of scenic action. The composer gave up the classical conception of tense development within a one-movement form and dramatic gravitation of separate movements to the final culmination. This music, observing on the whole the motion towards local and general climaxes, nevertheless, is virtually inclined *to stay*, rather than to move. Listening to it is akin to meditation, prolonged concentration on the feelings and thoughts arising from the offered programme. A programme in Karamanov's compositions performs approximately the same function as Alexander Scriabin's celebrated *Poem of Fire* (*Prometheus*) for orchestra and chorus. Scriabin does not embody the plot of the myth but directs the listener's spirit into a higher world devoid of the earthly daily routine. These are religious dramas without the outwardly stated succession in the plot's developments.

It is no accident that the cycle *Sovershishasia* and *Stabat Mater* (written in 1967) stand side by side in Alemdar Karamanov's output. A purely symphonic work and a composition in the traditional oratorial genre are essentially close to each other in their musical principles. The orthodox composer is not loath to use the genre inherent in the Catholic music, for the Orthodox and Catholic teachings bear the same images of the Christian world outlooks. As a Russian composer, Karamanov feels *Stabat Mater* to be dear and close to his heart since it is dedicated to the Virgin Mary and the church feast known as "Seven Sorrows of the Mother of God at the Cross." Saint Mary is venerated by the Orthodox Church as a patroness of Russia; her Nativity on September 8 (according to the old calendar) is also celebrated in this country as the Birthday of the Russian State (in the year of 862).

Karamanov's *Stabat Mater*, despite its Latin text, is not following in the traditions of Pergolesi or Penderecki, but rather in that of Rachmaninov's orchestral cantata *The Bells* (according to the orthodox tradition, the Russian sacred music is invariably written for a cappella chorus, any instrumental accompaniment being excluded). As in his programmatic symphonies, the composer is not striving for detailed musical elaboration, rendering the text's images in a generalized way.

Ex. 6 *Stabat Mater, 5th Movement*

In 1968, Alemdar Karamanov wrote his Piano Concerto No. 3 subtitled *Ave Maria*. Like his symphonies, it is a pure mystery made up of some episodes to convey the dialogue between the angel Gabriel any Mary unfolding in a mysterious musical succession, with its strong climax leading to the enlightened finale to express the mood of Saint Mary: "Be it unto me according to the word."

The compositions written in the 1970s were also developing these lines in the composer's creative work, among them his *Requiem* for chorus, soloists and full symphony orchestra (1971), lasting for 65 minutes; a cycle of two Symphonies Nos 15 and 16 under the general title *Et in amorem vivificantem*, written in the mid-seventies; a number of song-cycles for mixed chorus, and the Symphony No. 17 subtitled *America*, dedicated to the bicentennial of the USA.

However, the unification of symphonies still remained his prime objective. In the second half of the 1970s Karamanov produced another grandiose cycle *Byst* ("It is done"), embracing six symphonies Nos 18 through 23. The new symphonic mysteries were inspired this time by the apocalyptic images arising in the Revelation. For the reasons of ideological security the composer had to disguise their authentic titles behind the Soviet clichés, hoping at least in this way to get them performed or published in this country based on the atheistic Marxian ideology[1]. Below are given the original and the disguised titles of the symphonies in this cycle:

"BYST" ("IT IS DONE")	THE POEM OF VICTORY
18. "Unto him that loved us"	"On the Road to Victories"
19. "By the blood of the Lamb"	"Born for a Victory"
20. "Blessed are the dead"	"A Great Sacrifice"
21. "The great city"	"Superior to All"
22. "It is done"	"Revenge"
23. "I Jesus"	"Risen from the Ashes"

All the original programmatic titles were provided once again not in modern Russian, but in the Old Church Slavonic language in which these words sound lofty, producing the stronger impression. Not used in daily speech, these titles are likely to stir the listeners and find a response in them particularly in combination with the programmatic plots borrowed from the Revelation of St. John the Divine. Thus, the title of the fifth symphony in this cycle, and that of the entire cycle, could be traced back to Chapter 16:17 which reads as follows: "And the seventh angel poured out his vial into the air; and there came a great voice out of the temple of heaven, from the throne, saying, It is done."

The striking pictures of the Judgment Day come to be unexpectedly associated with the "democratic Apocalypse," which took place in Russia 20 years later. Though, in these musical mysteries based on the New Testament you would hardly find any depiction of the end of the world, monstrous beasts and the synagogue of Satan. It is the major tonality that prevails in the music's emotional coloring. Thus, the initial symphony in this cycle subtitled *Unto him that loved us"* (Rev. 1:5) begins suddenly with the well-known melody from Dvořák's Gypsy song, which in Karamanov's symphony seems to glorify "Grace be unto you, and peace, from him which is, and which was, and which is to come," from Jesus Christ (Rev. 1:4–5), and "Unto-him that loved us, and washed us from our sins in his own blood ... to him be glory and dominion for ever and ever. Amen" (Rev. 1:5–6). The music is not designed to illustrate the programme, following the logic of purely musical dramatic pattern where the change of sections-"events" directs the flow of the musical idea. The cantilena of the principal theme comes to be replaced by a series of twelve-note harmonies (Figures 4–15) built up according to a variety of principles: as a cluster, as an outcome of pedalization in the trumpet's melody, as a five-note chord gigantic in its volume, as a natural twelve-note chord (Musical Example 7), as a polychord made out of four augmented triads, etc.

1
    The composer partly succeeded in this trick. His Symphony No. 19 was released in 1977 by the music publishers in Kiev, and in 1983 his Symphonies Nos 20 and 23 were performed in Moscow under the baton of Vladimir Fedoseyev.

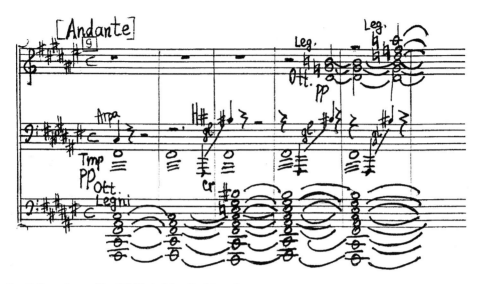

Ex. 7 *Symphony No. 18 Unto him that loved us*

As a matter of fact, Karamanov's twelve-note chords have little in common with dodecaphony, though its vertical relationships involve all the twelve pitches. Such progression of polyphonic vertical relationships is rooted back in the late-romantic chord elaboration technique, which was used by Nikolai Rimsky-Korsakov in the Prelude to Act One in his opera *Snow Maiden,* or in the entr'acte before Act Two in his opera *The Tsar's Bride*; the formation of a four-or five-note chord could be elaborated by Rimsky-Korsakov into a whole episode. The entire sphere of the secondary theme in Alemdar Karamanov's symphony (Figures 4–15) is engaged in a series of such harmonic progressions. But the emotions inherent in his music are akin not to 19th-century compositions but to the expressive forcefulness intrinsic in Rachmaninov's symphonies (you can clearly distinguish a direct quotation from Rachmaninov in Karamanov's symphony subtitled *The great city*). All the notes are delivered in their full sonority, with wide wave-like swellings, unhurried but strong enough, gradually unfolding in the orchestra. Herein lies one of the characteristic features evident in the composer's new style developed since 1965. The form of the symphony subtitled *Unto him that loved us* is also uncommon. Opening the cycle and acting as its first movement, this one-movement symphony combines the sonata form in its slow movement with the dramatic logic underlying a succession of episodes where the preceding passages motivate the following ones like in a succession of theatrical scenes. This approach to form-building in Karamanov's composition makes it akin to the structure of many avant-gardist works with their building up of an entity out of several "sections," each with its own organizing exposition. This principle is also reminiscent of Mahler's symphonic forms. Sometimes the succession of episodes is following in strict conformity with the programme. Thus, the symphony subtitled *I Jesus*, according to the composer, is "biographical as regards this saint ... offering the story of his heroic life and tragic death."

The entire cycle *"Byst"* was completed in 1980. After being neglected for fifteen years, some concert organizations little by little became interested in this composer of symphonies from Simferopol. Alemdar Karamanov's latest compositions came to the notice of Tikhon Khrennikov and were highly acclaimed by him. In 1979 his dramatoria *Lenin* (i.e. his Fifth Symphony written back in 1957) had its successful premiere in the Grand Hall of the Moscow Conservatoire. His musical *The Fount of Love* (after Alexander Pushkin) was staged in 1982 in Kiev. In December 1982 the USSR Radio and TV Symphony Orchestra under the baton of Vladimir Fedoseyev played his Symphony No. 23, naturally under its disguised title *Risen from the Ashes* in the Trade Union Hall of Columns (formerly used for the Nobility Assembly). This opened up some prospects for performing the other symphonies too, and the composer was commissioned to record his works. It seemed that fortune had smiled on him at long last. But than within an hour all the plans were frustrated by some officials in the Composers Union acting resolutely against the promotion of his music. An unlucky chance helped them, in 1983 during the session held by the secretaries of the Moscow branch of the Composers Union to discuss the Karamanov case a very distorted recording of one of his compositions was brought to their notice. It turned the opinion of many people against him. Immediately the planned performances and recordings of his music were cancelled, and he was even banned from writing film scores (which he intended to do to earn his living). True enough, the score of his symphony subtitled Risen from the Ashes was published (in a print run of 220 copies!) for the forthcoming 40th anniversary of Victory over Nazism.

Nevertheless, many distinguished musicians went on to encourage Karamanov. In the 1980s in one of his TV interviews Alfred Schnittke called him a phenomenally gifted person[2]. Yuri Butsko has invariably appraised his work very highly: "His talent for composition is singular and highly individual, not to be influenced by any trend arising around him"[3]. In 1988, in the height of Gorbachev's "perestroika," persecution of the Christian religion, which had lasted for more than 70 years, stopped in Russia. There was no need any longer to disguise the biblical plots behind the Soviet labels. For Alemdar Karamanov's 55th birthday Professor Vera Gornostayeva, of the Moscow Conservatoire, arranged,together with her students, a sort of music festival in the Smaller Hall of the conservatoire, which featured all of Karamanov's three piano concertos (with the piano accompaniment). In her introductory speech Professor Gornostayeva characterized the Karamanov phenomenon (using the words of his friend, Nektarius Chargeishvili, who had committed suicide during the gloomy years) as "a return to the religious type of mentality." She also gave high praise to Karamanov's piano playing technique.

In 1991 Karamanov for the first time had a chance to go abroad. Sharing his views about his visit to Czechoslovakia, he said, "Prague has made a tremendous impression

---

[2] Once Schnittke described Karamanov as "the genius of music" // The other art, Moscow, 1991, Issue 1, p. 302.

[3] Victoria Adamenko. Alemdar Karamanov // Rossiiskaya muzykalnaya gazeta, 1989, Issue 7–8, p. 12.

on me." There followed concerts of his compositions, among them his concert fugues for the piano. In 1992 he wrote the national anthem of the Crimean Republic. In 1993 the charity foundation named after Alemdar Karamanov started its activities in the Crimea. His latest compositions in many respects depart from the impassioned religiosity that marked his works written during the period from 1965 to 1980. These include *The True Legend of Ajimushkai* (the latter word being the name of the catacombs in the Crimean town of Kerch) for chorus, soloists, full symphony orchestra and brass band; *The Springtime Overture* for orchestra, the incidental scores to the films *The Strategy of Victory* in fifteen parts, and *A Privileged Love*. He also wrote a mystery play, entitled *Khersonese*, designed to employ both musical and theatrical means and to be performed on the excavated ruins in the amphitheatre of Khersonese in the open air. The performance took place in 1994 (a video film was made). This town, founded by the Greeks 2500 years ago and located now in the suburbs of Sevastopol, awakens today the images of the ancient life by its walls and towers, the contours of its temples and theatres, and the urban quarters. That imagery strikes the composer's fancy the way the programmes of his works stir up the souls of the listeners. As previously, his compositions bring forth serious and elevated reflections.

A concert of Karamanov's music in London, at Westminster Central Hall on 3 October, 1995, enjoyed great success. The piano concerto, *Ave Maria* (soloist — Konstantin Shcherbakov) and *Stabat Mater* were performed.

Alemdar Karamanov may be well regarded as one of the first composers to reveal the general post-avant-garde trend: departure from its extremes towards moderateness and greater traditionalism. His solution to the problem "What follows the avant-garde" crosses the roads of many other Russian composers such as Vladimir Martynov, Roman Ledenyov, Yuri Butsko, Sergei Slonimsky, and Georgy Sviridov. In the early sixties when avant-gardist innovations came into vogue, Karamanov, a true innovator, glimpsed a new road in the artistic negation of avant-gardism. Some time later the adherents of the avant-garde turned out to be assimilated by the establishment. Yet, Karamanov, like an extreme avant-gardist, is still standing apart from almost anybody else.

However, it is too early to indulge in generalizations in this case. Alemdar Karamanov is capable of rapid evolution, and for all we may know, we are soon to witness a new period in his style.

PRINCIPAL WORKS

Theatrical works

Stronger Than Love, ballet after Boris Lavrenyov, staged in 1961 by the ballet company of the Maly Opera House in Leningrad
Khersonese, mystery play, 1994

Works for Soloists, Chorus and Orchestra

The Song of a Married Soldier, text by Antonio Machado y Ruiz, 1963
Stabat Mater, 1967
Requiem, 1971
The True Legend of Ajimushkai, words by B. Serman, 1983

Works for Orchestra

Symphonies

No. 1 in five movements, 1954
No. 2 *Peace for the World*, in two movements, 1955–75
No. 3 in four movements, 1956
No. 4 *May*, in seven movements, 1956
No. 5 with chorus, in three movements, 1957
No. 6 (Sinfonietta) in four movements, 1957
No. 7 *The Moonlight Sea*, in three movements, 1958
No. 8 *Classical*, in four movements, 1960
No. 9 *Liberation*, in four movements, 1962
No. 10 in three movements, 1963
Nos 11–14 *Sovershishasia* (*"It is accomplished"*), a cycle of symphonies in ten movements, with chorus in the finale, 1966
Nos 15–16 *Et in amorem vivificantem*, 1974
No. 17 *America*, 1975
Nos 18–23 *Byst* (*"It is done"*), a cycle of six symphonies, 1976–80
No. 24 *Ajimushkai*, 1984
Symphony No.1 for Chamber Orchestra *Dedication*, 1996

Overtures

Heroic, 1964
Festive, 1964
Crimean, 1982
Springtime, 1984

Suite

Heroic Dances in five movements, 1961

Concertos

Piano Concerto No. 1, 1958
Piano Concerto No. 2, 1961
Piano Concerto No. 3 *Ave Maria*, 1968
Violin Concerto No. 1, 1961
Violin Concerto No. 2, 1964
Oriental Capriccio, for violin and orchestra, 1961
Concerto for Trumpet and Jazz Band (*Song of the World*), 1965

Chamber Instrumental Ensembles

Four Pieces for Clarinet and Piano, written in the 1950s
Music for Cello and Piano, 1962
Music for Violin and Piano, 1963
String Quartets Nos 1 and 2, written in the 1950s
String Quartet No. 3, 1963

Piano Pieces

Piano Sonata No. 1, 1953
Piano sonata No. 2, 1954–55 (MS lost; the finale's Rondo published in 1958)
Piano Sonatas Nos 3 and 4, 1960–61
Two Dances, published in 1959
Six Etudes, 1960–62
Prologue, Thinking and Epilogue, triptych, 1962
Music for Piano No. 1, 1962
Music for Piano No. 2, 1962
Window into Music, sixteen children's pieces, 1963
Nineteen Concert Fugues, 1964 (published in 1984 as "Fifteen Concert Fugues")

Chamber Vocal Pieces

Africal Songs, song-cycle for baritone and piano, 1962
When You Are Passing By, ballade for tenor and piano, text by L. Asmapur, 1963
Stars, song-cycle to verses by Stepan Shchipachov, for middle voice and piano, 1970s
Four Settings of Russian Poets for bass and piano, 1970s
For You, seven settings of A. Sampurova for coloratura soprano and piano, 1975
Song, vocalise with piano accompaniment, 1970s
The Crime at Grenada for soprano, violin, flute and two pianos in memory of Federico Garcia Lorca to verses by Antonio Machado y Ruiz, 1963

Choral Pieces

Choral Poem, 1957
Motherland, verse by Konstantin Simonov (in the late 1950s)
To Slavs, 1960
Autumnal, verse by Vladimir Firsov, 1964

Choral Cycles to verses by A. Sampurova (1975): *The Return, The Seasons, The Flying Leaves, Pictures-Images*

Musicals

A Glamorous World after Alexander Grin, staged at the Crimean Operetta, Simferopol, 1962–65
The Fount of Love after Alexander Pushkin, staged in Kiev, 1982

Film Scores

Common Fascism released in 1966
The Strategy of Victory, a TV film in 15 parts, 1985
A Privileged Love released by "Ekran" Film Studios, 1989
Anthem of the republic Crimea, 1992

The labyrinths of Roman Ledenyov's creative work

Valentina Kholopova

Roman Ledenyov

The 20th century has been marked by the emergency of unpredictable mixtures of styles, which owing to the global character of its culture has virtually brought together seemingly incompatible things. The creative work of Roman Ledenyov, a Moscow based composer, represents a case of such stylistic unpredictability, for he came to embrace such extremes as the spheres of Webern and Sviridov, Berg and Rachmaninov while all of these opposites in style could be traced back to Sergei Prokofiev.

Roman Semyonovich Ledenyov, born on December 4, 1930 in Moscow, belongs to that generation of Russian (and formerly Soviet) composers who back in the 1960s were striving for cultivation of the New Music in this country. Ledenyov took part in this progressive movement along with Alfred Schnittke, Edison Denisov, Sophia Gubaidulina, Boris Chaikovsky and other innovators among the Moscow based composers making up a cohort of like-minded persons. He graduated from the Moscow Conservatoire in composition in 1955 and completed a postgraduate course there in 1958. He entered the conservatoire in 1948, the unluckiest year for Soviet music, the year when the notorious, resolution on music was adopted on the initiative of Zhdanov, one of the party leaders, and which virtually banished all the Soviet music classics, beginning with Prokofiev and Shostakovich. As far as the budding composers were concerned, it implied a total ban imposed on their own innovations in music.

Ledenyov studied composition with Anatoly Alexandrov, a keen master of chamber music, who had been criticized some time back for his "decadence." In the fifties it was the banned Prokofiev who became the idol of the young composer, and when Prokofiev died (in 1953) Ledenyov, who was still a student, decided to dedicate his Piano Sonata to his memory. Completed in 1956, this sonata in three movements subtitled, In Memory of Sergei Prokofiev, became a true highlight in the musical life of Moscow. It proved to be a discovery of Roman Ledenyov as a highly individual composer, and its writing was regarded as an act of a civic courage.

Roman Ledenyov's Piano Sonata incorporated both the deliberate reflection of the Prokofiev style and the seeds of the young composer's own style, which were subsequently to give rise to a contrasting trends in his work. As regards Prokofiev, this sonata came to manifest the fiery energy of his Sixth Sonata, the wise restrained lyricism of his Eighth Sonata, and the indomitable rhythmical thrust inherent in the finale of his First Violin Sonata. Ledenyov's own musical themes — elaborate, stretched and abounding in dense chromaticism — came as a remarkable continuation of the Prokofiev style. A highly impressive article about Ledenyov's Piano Sonata was written by Alfred Schnittke. It appeared in 1962 under the title "Meeting the Listeners' Wishes" in the magazine *Sovetskaya muzyka;* among other things, this article carried the following lines: "As many of our contemporaries, Ledenyov has grown up 'under the Prokofievian sun' ... His Piano Sonata in Memory of Prokofiev is a kind of musical monument to that great composer"[1].

Anatoly Alexandrov thus characterized his pupil: "Roman Ledenyov is a talented Soviet composer who strives to write music capable of reflecting the inner world of our contemporaries. He is an artist of immaculate honesty, never interested in superficial flights of fancy. His conceptions are always serious and significant. He is not inclined to self-congratulation at his successes, and his critical attitude to his work impels him forward"[2].

His immaculate honesty and sincerity, and his faithful adherence to his attachments and musical tastes, which came to the notice of Anatoly Alexandrov, Alfred Schnittke and other musicians, proved far from conducive to a straight and smooth road in Roman Ledenyov's artistic career. Quite the opposite, these qualities led to unexpected turns and zigzags in his creative work.

His diploma work was the oratorio *The Lay of Igor's Campaign* (1954) based on the plot of the oldest Russian chronicle, and this theme generated his deep interest in Russian national traditions. In 1977 the composer made a new version of this early work. In the late 1950s — 1960s he was primarily preoccupied with all kinds of eulogy — odes, songs and hymns, which found its manifestation in his *Ode to Joy* to lyrics by Pablo Neruda and *Song of Freedom* to verses by Asian and African poets.

With the coming of the stormy sixties giving rise to a new generation of Soviet composers, there began an intensive study of Western music, primarily that of the Second Viennese School. Being a remarkable melodist, Ledenyov came to be infatuated with Alban Berg first and foremost, especially with the latter's Violin Concerto dedicated "to the memory of an angel." He was less interested in Schoenberg. But what seemed quite unexpected, he was also captivated by Webern's unspectacular music. The impressions made by Berg's Violin Concerto found their expression in Ledenyov's own Violin Concerto (written in 1964) dedicated to Mark Lubotsky. A series of Berg's ascending thirds that found their reflection in many of 20th-century compositions (in the former USSR — in the works of Shostakovich, Kara Karayev and Alfred Schnittke) came to bewitch Ledenyov too: either in the form of progressions in thirds or in the excessive progressions in fourths and tritones, this series imbued the whole of Ledenyov's Violin Concerto, which is marked for its explicit emotionality and tragic spirit.

---

[1] Alfred Schnittke. Meeting the Listeners' Wishes // Sovetskaya muzyka, 1962. Issue 1, p. 17.

[2] Anatoly Alexandrov. [A Few Words about Roman Ledenyov] // Sovetskaya muzkya, 1969, Issue 1, p. 10.

Roman Ledenyov's encounter with Webern's music calls for special consideration. The vital element of Ledenyov as a composer is his broad tuneful melodies in the Russian spirit, delivered in the traditions of Sergei Prokofiev and Nikolai Myaskovsky. As for Webern's vital element, it is the utmost compression of musical matter, devoid of any national shade. Ledenyov was impressed by Webern's concentration of expressive means, and the magnitude of each momentary sound, as well as by the pure, astral world of his music in general. As he wrote later on, "Each sound is full of imagery and substance, incorporating therefore a lot of facets"[3].

Remaining faithful to his attachments, Roman Ledenyov in the course of the second half of the sixties produced a whole series of compositions revealing his response to the Webern style: Six Pieces of Harp and String Quartet (1966), *Ten Sketches* for chamber ensemble (1967), *Seven Moods* for chamber ensemble (1967), and *Three Nocturnes* for chamber orchestra (1968). This manner of writing made itself also evident in his *Brief Tunes* for string quartet (1969) and *Four Drawings* for chamber ensemble (1972).

There was another reason, originating in Moscow, to turn to writing chamber pieces of such kind: a new chamber orchestra was set up in Moscow to be directed by the famous flutist Anatoly Korneyev, who gathered together a team of remarkable musicians and asked the innovative-minded composers to write chamber pieces expressly for his orchestra. On his commission Roman Ledenyov wrote first his *Ten Sketches* for ten musicians and then, in his other pieces, he came to vary this cast of interpretative artists.

Roman Ledenyov came to be particularly captivated by Webern's early atonal compositions, his quartets and orchestral cycles Op. 5, 6, 9, and 10. The entire series of Ledenyov's opuses à la Webern constitutes the cycles of miniatures for the chamber ensemble or chamber orchestra. This composer from Moscow tried his hand at "sketch-like writing," as he called it himself, with its brief leading themes, detailed articulation and microforms. But the message of his compositions revealed a trait traditionally inherent in Russian aesthetics — a striving for the realistically concrete embodiment of an artistic idea. The case in point is the usage of programmatic titles for his musical pieces. In contrast to Webern who only in his rough copies occasionally provided the titles for his pieces never to be mentioned in the printed scores, Ledenyov found it necessary to keep the titles of his cycles and separate pieces in most of their publications. As we can see, his cycles have been defined as "sketches," "moods," "nocturnes," "brief tunes," and "drawings." As for the titles of separate pieces in the cycles, his Six Pieces for Harp and String Quartet comprise: 1. Prelude, 2. Variations, 3. Repetitions, 4. *Tristesse*, 5. Anxiety, 6. Farewell; his *Four Drawings* fall into: 1. The Daybreak, 2. The Noon, 3. The Evening Shadows, 4. In the Moonlight; in his *Seven Moods* the composer placed the following titles at the end of each piece: "The Autumnal," "Merriment," "Premonitions","Melancholy," "Perturbation," "Reflections,", and "Reminiscences." At the same time the role assigned by Webern to rests surrounding the sounds was definitely associated in Ledenyov with Chekhov's short stories in

---

[3]   Roman Ledenyov. Contribution to the Renewal of Society. A Talk with Victor Licht //Sovetskaya muzyka, 1989, Issue 9, p. 4.

which the author used to place three dots both at the beginning and at the end of his narration.

The character of Roman Ledenyov's musical language is quite clearly revealed in the earliest of his cycles — Six Pieces for Harp and String Quartet. Like in Webern's music, in this cycle to the foreground come the pieces in slow and moderate tempo, with its final piece, Adagio, being the slowest one. Following in the traditions of Webern's early cycles, Ledenyov's musical texture brings into counterpoint trills, *tremolo, vibrato,* flageolets, *arco, pizzicato, col legno,* con sordino and other devices of sound production. But his compositions written in the sixties already contain some non-Webern elements. Thus, his first piece from this cycle shows a Russian composer looking for his own approaches to the serial technique. Ledenyov employs here a series of merely five notes, meanwhile using the diatonics and even some pentatonic elements — the so called "Russian trichords" combining major seconds and minor thirds (see the brackets below).

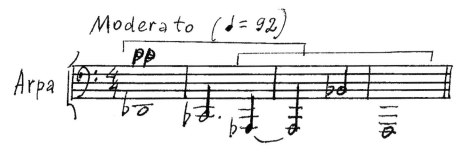

Ex. 1 *Six Pieces for Harp and String Quartet*

It should be noted that in some pieces of his next cycle *Ten Sketches* for chamber ensemble Roman Ledenyov also elaborated on twelve-note chromatic series, though he did so not à la Webern since the latter had written no cycles of miniatures during his dodecaphonic period.

In his second piece subtitled *Variations* (from the cycle of Six Pieces) Ledenyov used the strictly sustained retrograde form, which reveals the influence of Berg, in addition to Webern's, — *Presto delirando* from Berg's *Lyric Suite* for string quartet. In the third piece subtitled "Repetitions" the use was made of fortifying the notes within an octave, the techniques used by Webern in his Symphony Op. 21. However, the musical texture in this piece also involves clusters inherent in the post-Webern period. The Coda of the sixth piece subtitled "Farewell," which concludes the cycle, introduces a sonoristic effect of playing beyond the bridge (*dietro il ponticello*), a device that has also evolved much later in the musical practice.

Roman Ledenyov's chamber cycles written back in the sixties have another invisible but still fundamental difference from Webern's musical language, which is rooted in its rhythmics. Webern's rhythms are known to conspicuously deviate from the system of measures: his strong measures are hardly distinguished by the ear, and the abundance of triplets are reminiscent of the medieval Renaissance mensural rhythmics. As for Ledenyov's pieces, they are marked by quite stable measured rhythms, the rhythmic organization underlying tonality with its clear-cut basic and non-basic keys. Let us take his first piece "à la Webern" in the cycle *Ten Sketches* as an example (mm. 1–4 from the 13-measure form).

Ex. 2 *Ten Sketches*

The metrically clear-cut location of the notes b♭-f-d (in the measures 1, 2, 4) allows to capture the latent outlines of B-flat major tonality, which would have been impossible in the case of Webern's metrically irregular rhythmics.

The same *Ten Sketches*, so outwardly reminiscent of the microforms in Webern's orchestral cycles — Six Pieces Op. 6 and Five Pieces Op. 10, differ from Webern even in their number — ten pieces in lieu of five or six, owing to their composition structure. Ledenyov's prolonged cycle is definitely based on thematic arrangement. The final piece No. 10 in this cycle is composed as a synthesis of a new motto theme and the leading melodies from many previous pieces. This device has become favorite with other composers belonging to the second half of the 20th century, among them Sergei Slonimsky, Rodion Shchedrin and Alfred Schnittke. The whole series of Ledenyov's instrumental cycles à la Webern, though revealing the deep-rooted traits of his own style, with their semantic heavy weightiness, concentrated expressiveness, and ethical and acoustic beauty proved a milestone in the composer's creative evolution.

His departure from Webern's manner of writing proceeded gradually, bringing forth highly original results. His cycle *Brief Tunes* ("Popevki" in Russian) of five pieces for string quartet merits special consideration. "Popevka" is a Russian term used to mean a short turn of songful melody comparable to the Western concept of motive. Besides, this word used to define the melodic elements making up the old Russian church monodic chants. Therefore, the title selected by Ledenyov for his cycle of pieces for string quartet quite clearly explains his message. This cycle retains the same brevity of themes and the aphoristic style inherent in his previous chamber cycles, but its themes are now imbued with the specifically Russian, lyrical and melodious character. The diatonics are now more evident, the rhythms become still more measured, with use being made of mixed measures characteristic of 19th-century Russian music, and the melodies embellished by grace-notes inherent in Russian folk singing and so lovingly employed by Stravinsky in his *Les Noces* and *Renard*. Though the composer fails to provide programmatic titles for any piece in this cycle, the music's imagery is quite concrete, telling of some scenes from the Russian folk life: in Piece No. 1 it is an unhurried conversation of two voices (the viola and the cello); in Piece No. 2 — the merry festive games (with some popular "blank fifths"); No 3 is associated with spinning, with its fast rhythmic motion akin to the "humming" of spindles; No. 4 — the singing of a sad drawn-out song; No. 5 — singing to the "balalaika-like" accompaniment in *pizzicato*, though of a gloomy rather than a joyous nature. Such "unity of opposites" as presented in Ledenyov's Brief Tunes" forms a singular style which organically combines the Russian cantilena-like melodies with the refined colors of the string-quartet texture and expressionistic tension of the music in general.

Another step to the exit from "Webern's circle" was taken by Ledenyov in his *Four Drawings* for chamber ensemble (the programmatic titles of its pieces provided above), with each piece lasting much longer than in any of his previous cycles. The composer himself attributed great importance to the "Webernian" in particular and the "neo-Viennese" period in general for his creative work: "I believe it has given me a lot. It is common knowledge that the writing of chamber music helps to evolve the composer's individual style"[4].

The latent mechanism underlying the departure from the "neo-Viennese" procedures lay in the composer's wish to retract the initial roots of his creative individuality. Though, paradoxically enough, Ledenyov drew back not to the Prokofievian focal point in his style, but as if bypassing it, he moved forward "to the right," by taking a sharper turn than the one he had formerly made in his movement "to the left" — to Webern. To quote the composer himself, "At a certain moment the so called sketch-like manner of writing seemed to have exhausted to have exhausted itself, and I lost my interest in it. No matter how captivating it was to work with brief tunes, I felt myself drawn once again to what was probably closer to my nature — more definite national roots and wide melodic breathing. It so happened that precisely during this period, in the late sixties — the early seventies, I came to be closely associated with Georgy Vasilyevich Sviridov"[5].

However, even before his close association with Georgy Sviridov a new focal point arose in Roman Ledenyov's creative work, which made the composer shift his interests to somewhere else. His ballet *A Tale of Green Balloons*, written in 1967 after Vladimir Lugovskoi's poem, signified the composer's departure from the gloomy preoccupation with psychological factors and austere rational control to the childishly pure perception of the world, towards the broad melodious writing and stylistic freedom, up to introducing some elements of sympho-jazz. The message of this ballet may be

---

[4] Ibidem, p. 5.

[5] Ibidem, p. 4.

expressed by Vladimir Lugovskoi's following poetic lines: "I wish everybody to be happy everywhere... I wish nobody would ever die a horrible death."

Roman Ledenyov continued to elaborate on the musical line associated with the world of childhood and nature in the seventies when he produced a number of compositions for children, giving vein therein to his bent for concrete musical thinking, which is inherent in the Russian artistic mentality. It would be hard to name another composer of his generation who has invented such a great amount of titles, first for his children's pieces and then for his compositions intended for "adults" — their list makes hundreds of headings. His *Children's Album*, written in 1961, includes 98 titles, his *Pieces for Children*, written in 1977, comprises 99 titles. In 1972 he wrote the cycle *I Play the Clarinet* of eight pieces, each bearing its own subtitle ("What you See from the Mountaintop," "The Hooting of a Faraway Steamer," and so on). During the period from 1978 to 1990 Ledenyov composed a large-scale wordless choral cycle *The Seasons*, including twenty-four poems-pictures, each bearing its programmatic title. Thus, the group of his *Spring Tunes* carries the following headings: "The Awakening of Spring," "Languor," "Forest Echoes," "A Faraway Song," and "A Spring Roundelay"; his *Summer Nocturnes* include "The Night Call," "Before a Thunderstorm," "Games," "The Moonlight Idyll," and "On the Bank of the Sleeping River"; his *Autumnal Elegies* comprise "The Colors of the Autumnal Forest," "The Falling Leaves," "The Wintry Breath," and "The November Landscape." And this system of titles, poetical themes of his works, not prompted by the poetry or any other literary source but contributed by the composer himself, depicts the imagery that strikes his fancy.

To comprehend the dramatic change in Roman Ledenyov's creative career when he came to uphold Geórgy Sviridov's ideals, one should have a clear notion of the latter's place in Russian music. Georgy Sviridov represents a kind of "Russian Orff," who has found himself in the deliberate simplification of the modern musical language. This composer has to his credit quite a number of song-cycles, cantatas and choruses to verses by Russian poets and settings of Robert Burns and in general the impulse for his music comes from the sonority of measured rhythms inherent in verses. A taste for primitivism turned out to be so keen in Ledenyov that he became interested in minimal music, appraising it as the sole novel idea that had arisen lately in the avant-gardist quests. Though he finds the music written by minimalists to be somewhat artificial and unintelligible, Ledenyov regards it as being akin to the popular principles of such countries as Estonia, Latvia and Lithuania. His turn to Sviridov's ideals also signified his immersion into the Russian national elements and the respective vocal melodic principles. In the 1980s the composer was still sharing this view: "My general conviction is that the truly promising trends should be based on the national sources — be it Estonia, Latvia, Lithuania, Ukraine or Byelorussia"[6].

In the course of the 1970s and 80s Ledenyov wrote a great number of vocal pieces in a style close to Sviridov's melodic manner. These settings of Russian poets include *The Nekrasov Notebooks* comprising 20 songs, romances and poems for bass and piano to verses by Nikolai Nekrasov, and *"Three Poems"* to verses by Nikolai Rubtsov for

---

[6] Ibidem, p. 5.

bass and orchestra. But even on this "right" pole of his style, his own personal melodic element was still revealing itself. The composer gradually came to appreciate the self-sufficient musical material of good quality, which on its own could give rise to a certain musical work. In this way there appeared his Concerto-Elegy for Cello and Orchestra (1980); the theme he composed proved to be precisely suited to this kind of work. Along with a transition from concise to extended themes the composer turned from the chamber genres to writing concertos, with latter therewith acquiring novel genre nuances. In contrast to the year 1964 within which Ledenyov had written, in addition to his Violin Concerto in the vein of Berg, the Concerto-Poem for Viola and Orchestra and his Concerto-Nocturne for Flute, in the late 1970s and in the 1980s he wrote the Concerto-Elegy for Cello and Orchestra (1980), the Concerto-Romance for Piano and Orchestra (1981), and *Concert Recitative* for Cello and Orchestra (1990).

As we can see, Roman Ledenyov interpreted his numerous concertos in his own way, being least interested in their virtuosic, purely concertante style, except for his Violin Concerto. He approached them as pieces for a soloist and orchestra, with their own individual and concretized content whose idea he expressed in their title. Says the composer: "And I provide the titles for them to express more precisely the character of music I imply"[7]. His concertos written in the 1970s and '80s are primarily marked for their clear-cut melodic themes, for the composer is convinced that "there can hardly be a composition without vivid thematic material"[8]. He expressed his credo during this period in the following words: "Melodic structures, seriousness and the continuity in the tone-structure are the most invaluable characteristics of music"[9].

His attachment to the clear-cut melodies, their breadth and national coloring was inevitably to lead Ledenyov to the traditional values as regards both the structural and emotional aspects. In this way the composer came to the style reminiscent of "retro" and he was quite right when he pointed out thereby that many composers had occupied similar positions in their style. In 1980 he wrote: "In my latest works I turned to the modal organization of my musical material, to the diatonics, striving to produce clear-cut melodic lines. (To my mind, this trend has now come to reflect, so to speak, the spirit of the times in many works written by modern composers both Soviet and foreign")[10].

Thus, as many composers who had come of the avant-garde in the sixties, Ledenyov took up the key tonalities: E-flat major in his Concerto-Elegy for the cello, A minor — F major in the Concerto-romance for the piano, D major with the indicated keys in his *Elegiac Sextet* for two violins, two violas and two cellos (1982), etc. However, in his musical thinking he refused to treat it as "retro" or as an extreme case of collage when

---

[7] Composers About Their Work. Roman Ledenyov //Sovetskaya muzyka, 1987, Issue 3, p. 136

[8] Ibidem, p. 136.

[9] Ibidem, p 136.

[10] Composers Share Their Views. Roman Ledenyov //Sovetskaya muzyka, 1980, Issue 7, p. 135.

the entire composition represented a citation of someone else's style. In the case of Roman Ledenyov, with his characteristic frankness, it was his own self, with his own romantic feelings. And no matter how you perceive, at the close of the 20th century, Glinka's sentimental and lyrical outpourings (in *Elegiac Sextet* for the strings) or the quotations of Arensky and Rachmaninov (in Concerto-Romance for the piano), the musical language, the structure and the very spirit of these works reveal the pure harmony inherent in the composer's self-truthfulness and his incapability of any sham and a cold obliging approach to the current fashion.

This justification of all ups and downs in Ledenyov's creative career by his own inner sense secured for the composer the freedom of stylistic maneuverability in the subsequent years of his work. By 1987 one more sphere in his style took shape, which became obvious in his chamber composition entitled *Reminiscences*, intended for an unusual cast of four instruments from the clarinet family: piccolo clarinet, ordinary clarinet, basset horn and bass clarinet. Then followed *Four Choral Preludes* for the same instruments (1989). This new stylistic sphere came to incorporate the choruses from his monumental cycle *The seasons*, which he had started back in 1978 being still under Georgy Sviridov's influence; also some other choruses, including those of the sacred character, such as *Three Vocalises* for mixed chorus (1988), and *Four Sacred Chants* for mixed chorus (1991). It also includes *Epigraphs*, four pieces for flute and chamber orchestra (1989), *Concert Recitative* for cello and orchestra (1990), and some other works.

This new sphere in quite obviously associated with the writing of miniatures, which already happened two decades back in the mid-sixties. Perhaps, for this reason the initial work to usher in this stage in the composer's work has been entitled *Reminiscences*. Ledenyov believes that upon finishing some large-scale works a composer is inclined to withdraw, concentrating on the refined expressive means, which is vitally important to the composer's inner laboratory work. It is a miniature that suits perfectly such moments of seeking a secluded life. But since one miniature is too short for a full-fledged composition, the common practice is to write cycles of mininatures.

Roman Ledenyov got an impulse for writing his cycles for four clarinets from the colorful sonority produced by the ensemble of clarinettists, which had been set up by that time. He was struck by the combination of their timbre homogeneity (like in a string quartet) and the unusualness of separate parts, such as the part of basset horn, an instrument known for its usage in Mozart's ensembles, though failing to get its cultivation in Russia. The composer was captivated by the beauty of chordal, joint sonority of the uncustomary "chorus" of clarinets, and in his admiration he wrote, in addition to *Reminiscences*, *Four Choral Preludes* for the same quartet. No doubt, the clarinet's timbre has an enchanting power. From 20th-century music history we know that in 1915–16 Igor Stravinsky wrote *Cat's Cradle Songs* for alto and three clarinets. Upon hearing this composition, Anton Webern was captivated by the clarinets and started writing opus upon opus (14, 15, 16, 17, 18, 19, 21 ...) involving the participation of clarinet, bass clarinet, and piccolo clarinet. From the outset of his creative career Roman Ledenyov was also drawn to the clarinet; incidentally, his Opus No. 1 had been his Sonata for Clarinet and Piano (1952), later on, in 1972 he wrote *I Play the Clarinet*, and in 1975 and 1977 — *Recitative and Tune* and *Autumnal Pictures* respectively, also for the clarinet.

Ledenyov's *Reminiscences*, a cycle of six miniatures displays the expressive resources of the clarinets from different aspects. Thus, his miniature No. 1 brings into juxtaposition the leader (piccolo clarinet) and the "chorus" of the three other instruments in lower registers; No. 2, provided by the composer's remark *Tempo di valse*, is a grotesquely broken waltz with the piccolo clarinet's sharp solo in the spirit of Shostakovich, with its noteworthy intervening section with its minor triads delivered by all the four instruments in *pianissimo*. The miniature No. 3 conveys the quiet singing of several voices (*cantabile*) with the successive introduction of the clarinets' parts. The miniature No. 4 offers the ingenious contrasts of a scherzo-like type.

Ex. 3 *Reminiscences*

No. 5 presents a touching pastorale with the heaving fourths and fifths in the leading melodies.

Ex. 4 *Reminiscences*

The final miniature No. 6 provided by the composer's remark *semplice* embodies the idea of perpetual motion, most naturally combining diverse ostinato principles, polyrhythmics and polyphonic canon. This perfect naturalness is the key to understanding the entire latest sphere in Roman Ledenyov's creative work.

Devoid of the classical tonal organization, Ledenyov's musical idioms achieve logical clarity owing to his masterly use of the simplest musical turns in their unusual combinations. The above cited Musical Example 3 shows a combination of the repeated *gruppetto* figure and the repeated groups of the simplest intervalic progressions — by a minor second, a major second, a minor third, and an augmented fourth. Musical Example 4 displays a highly original pastorale playing in unisons, octaves, fifths and fourths. Ledenyov's most favorite turns are the trill-like figures, progressions along triads and four-note chords, the so called "repetitiveness" of separate notes and intervals, the obvious symmetry of motto themes, phrases and the other similar, easily discernible elements. These simplest, or to use Webern's expression, "vivid" microelements of a composition are perfectly getting along together with not only the diatonics but also with the most tense chromatics throwing light on the latter's "obscurity" through their clear-cut logic. Take, for example, the beginning of *Concert Recitative* where the theme of the solo cello playing up the tense chromatic intervals of an augmented prime and a diminished octave, owing to numerous repetitions of the microelements, illuminates the chromatics from within up to the nearly primitive degree. The orchestra responds by its sharply accentuated chromatic chords elucidated by the symmetry of framing intervals — major thirds or diminished fourths.

Ex. 5 *Concert Recitative*

In his cycle of pieces for flute and string orchestra entitled *Epigraphs* similar chromatic structures become most natural owing to the symmetrical melodic lines of their motto themes (in Piece No. 1) or rhythmical "repetitiveness" (repetitions in semiquavers in Piece No. 2):

Ex. 6a *Epigraphs*

Ex. 6b *Epigraphs*

Among Roman Ledenyov's latest compositions special mention should be made of his monumental choral cycle *The Seasons,* unique in its structure comprising twenty-four poems-pictures in six notebooks. The composer worked on this cycle for twelve years, completing it in 1990. He was inspired to write this large-scale composition by the outstanding Moscow-based choral conductor Valery Polyansky to whom it was dedicated[11].

The seasons are intended for chamber choir, full chorus and instrumental ensemble of varying cast for each of six notebooks of choral pieces. Six notebooks make up two parts, each containing three notebooks. Part One comprises the following three notebooks: 1. Four Preludes-Pastorales, 2. Wintry Etudes, and 3. Spring Motifs. Part Two includes: 4. Summertime Nocturnes, 5. Autumnal Elegies, and 6. Two Postludes. In this way the four middle notebooks (2–5) corresponding to the four seasons of the four seasons of the year make the basis of this composition, with the two outer notebooks framing it as an introduction and a conclusion. The introductory "Four Preludes-Pastorales" offer a cursory reminiscence of all the four seasons, with the pieces being subtitled respectively "Autumn," "Winter," "Spring," and "Summer."

---

[11] Valery Polyansky made a name for himself as a conductor of the choir celebrated for their immaculate performance of the most complicated preclassical and modern compositions. His executive talent and a wealth of resources inherent in his choir urged many composers to write choral pieces of extreme difficulty. In particular, thanks to his cooperation with this remarkable choral conductor Alfred Schnittke wrote his Choral concerto to words by Grigor Narekatsi, which is distinguished for its high spirituality and vocal complexities.

Since this large-scale cycle was expressly designed for the Polyansky Choir, the composer makes his musical language extremely complicated, rather than simplified, as compared to this instrumental pieces. The musical texture is based not on the classical four-voice but on the eight-voice leading which is then varied through the participation of soloists and with the addition of the wind and percussion instruments and the piano. Since the entire cycle is sung without words, the composer concentrates on the inner contrast between articulation and the devices of vocal performance — legato, staccato, accents, glissando, humming, singing with opened lips, a transition from humming to singing with opened lips, with the sound-imitative syllables (ta, pa, pom), etc. As is known, choral singing calls for the utmost naturalness in the structure of vocal parts, and the simpler the lines of polyphony, the more expressive is the sonority of an entity. Ledenyov showed himself to be a true master of choral writing in this lengthy suite of pieces imbued with pungent beauty of 20th-century chromatic harmony and at the same time with supreme naturalness of singing.

The technique Ledenyov discovered for himself in this composition has proved to be virtually "the technique of simple details." It imparted singular coloring to this choral work. Take, for instance, the choral trills embracing half of the amassed voices in "Autumn", Piece No. 1 from Notebook One.

Ex. 7 *The seasons*

In its score the harmony of this episode seems to present an indivisible conglomeration of dissonances, but owing to the elementary progressions in each voice it is discerned by the ear as the most natural succession of sounds. Thus, each miniature is built up out of natural and simple details interwoven into a field of chromatics and dissonances inherent in 20th-century music, while tens of miniatures make up the widest circle of songs glorifying nature, a kind of elevated pantheistic mass.

It is hard to define the stylistic sphere that took shape in Roman Ledenyov's creative work by the late 1980s — early '90s. It seems to be no accidental that the composer outlined minimal music as a creative initiative much to his liking. However, his music has become just more coherent through the employment of some devices smilar to those used by minimalists, remaining alien to the minimalist trend in its spirit. Ledenyov's latest style represents the quintessence of his own musical creativity, not to be associated with any other known styles. And in it you can clearly perceive the harmony of the composer's intrinsic self-truthfulness.

PRINCIPAL WORKS

Ballet

A Tale of Green Balloons after Vladimir Lugovskoi' like-named poem (1967)

Vocal-Symphonic Works

The Lay of Igor's Campaign, oratorio based on the old Russian chronicle (two versions, 1954 and 1977)
The Native Land, cantata for female singer, chorus and orchestra to verse by Nikolai Nekrasov (1977)
Three Poems for bass and orchestra to verse by Nikolai Rubtsov (1988)

Instrument Concertos. Symphony

Violin Concerto (1964)
Concerto-Poem for Viola (1964)
Concerto-Nocturne for Flute (1964)
Concerto-Elegy for Cello (1980)
Concerto-Romance for Piano (1981)
Concert Recitative for Cello (1990)
Rus the Green and Snow-White, symphony (1991)
Something unclear. . ., concerto fantasy for violin and orchestra (1996)
Variations on a Haydn theme for orchestra (1996)
Nostalgia for oboe and string orchestra (1996)

Chamber Instrumental Pieces

Six Pieces for Harp, Two Violins, Viola and Cello (1966)
Ten Sketches for chamber ensemble (1967)
Seven Moods for instrumental ensemble (1967)
Three Nocturnes for chamber orchestra (1968)
Brief Tunes, five pieces for string quartet (1969)
I Play the Clarinet, eight pieces for clarinet and piano (1972)
Four Drawings for chamber ensemble (1972)
Elegiac Sextet for two violins, two violas and two cellos (1982)
Reminiscences, six pieces for four clarinets (1987)
Serenade for ten wind instruments (1987)
Tristesse for basset horn and string orchestra (1989)
Four Choral Preludes for four clarinets (1989)
Epigraphs, four pieces for flute and chamber orchestra (1989)
The Evening Bells for percussion ensemble (1992)
Metamorphoses of a Johann Sebastian Bach Theme for viola and string ensemble (1993)
Self-portrait on the background of Russian landscape for bayan (1996)

Piano Pieces

Sonata In Memory of Sergei Prokofiev (1956)
Children's Album, 98 pieces (1961)
Pieces for Children, 99 pieces (1977)

Lyoka's Notebook, 59 easy pieces for piano (1993)
Easy pieces for piano, 129 pieces for children (1994)

Choruses

Three Vocalises for mixed chorus (1988)
The Seasons, twenty-four poems-pictures in six notebooks for chamber choir, full chorus and instrumental ensemble (1990)
Four Sacred Chants for mixed chorus (1991)
Vespers, six fragments for mixed chorus (1994)
Eichendorff Diptychon for mixed chorus (1996)

Chamber Vocal Music

The Nekrasov Notebooks, twenty songs, romances and poems for bass and piano in four notebooks to verses by Nikolai Nekrasov (1977)
Night and Day (From Russian Lyrical Poetry), five settings of Afanasy Fet and Fyodor Tyutchev for voice and piano (1994)
Seven German songs for soprano, tenore and chamber ensemble (1996)

Vyacheslav Artyomov: in search of artistic truth

Mikhail Tarakanov

Vyacheslav Artyomov

Vyacheslav Petrovich Artyomov (born 1940) belongs to that generation of Russian composers who embarked upon their creative careers during the period of the Thaw initiated by Khrushchev. His earliest compositions appearing in the sixties were soon to reveal that his road to the artistic truth was alien not only to those who served faithfully to the official ideology cultivated by the communist regime, but also to the tenets and aesthetic views of their implacable opponents. However, at first the opposition of Artyomov's style to the currently fashionable avant-garde and later to the post-avant-garde was not so obvious. He was regarded as one of the numerous adherents of the sonoristic trend which came to be pronounced so prominently in the early sixties by such Polish masters as Witold Lutoslawski, Krzysztof Penderecki, *et al*. Artyomov's early compositions were looked upon as conscientious reproduction of the previous findings in 20th-century modern music while he was treated as *one of the many*.

And as late as in the second half of the 1980s, and even then not universally but at least by many musicians and connoisseurs of genuine music, Vyacheslav Artyomov's *singular road*, as well as his true contribution to the development of Russian music at the close of the 20th century was at long last recognized. With the disappearance of the halo of *non-recognition* hovering over his name for many years, he may well be regarded now as the key figure in the main developmental trend in Russian music at its present-day stage.

The essence of Vyacheslav Artyomov's approach to art in general and music in particular lies in his treatment of these categories as acts of *faith*, with the composer viewing himself a servant to that ultimate truth that makes the human creativity sensible, justifying it before the Creator. In this respect he meets halfway his spiritual instructors — the great thinkers and founders of Russian religious philosophy, Nikolai Berdayev first and foremost. During the period when the night of non-spirituality and atheism had fallen over Russia, and a mere imitation of fashionable trends emerging in the postwar avant-garde, with their challenging rationalism and the cult of the self-sufficient value of sound structures, was in some cases treated as a kind of heroic deed, it was natural that Vyacheslav Artyomov turned out to be an "outsider" both for the composers acting as party functionaries, and those progressive innovators painstakingly mastering the techniques of 20th-century music — from the outdated dodecaphony through serialism, aleatory and sonoristic devices up to polystylistics and other post-avant-gardist trends.

Vyacheslav Artyomov remained unwavering in his loyalty to the traditions of Russian spiritual culture, which found their reflection in the works of Russian artists of the so called Silver Age, who had been looking for the religious purport of art and for a contact with the other worlds — the traditions that had been violently interrupted by the establishment of the Bolshevik dictatorship. Precisely for this reason Artyomov could neither embrace the tenets of the postwar musical avant-garde calling for complete severance of the Romantic tradition, nor agree with the idea about the self-contained value of a sound and sonority as it were, purified of any non-musical sense, nor accept the striving for the beauty of a sound structure asserting its own self-sufficiency. As for the great masters of the past, it was Alexander Scriabin who turned out to be the closest to him; Artyomov esteems him as the most significant of Russian masters, with his spiritual quests being akin to his own.

The faithfulness to the traditions, however, meant no complete renunciation of renewing the artistic means in the case of Vyacheslav Artyomov, for he could hardly be ranked among the champions of *traditionalism*, adherents of the protective, conservative trend. He had made a close study of all the latest trends in 20th-century music and in his quests of new musical idioms he sometimes appeared even more daring and consistent than many of the leaders of the so called "Soviet avant-garde". He rejected in modern music only those things that used to lead away from the spiritual essence of artistic creativity as a manifestation of a person's attitude to the infinity and prevented man to approach the supersensitive, a beauty that reveals itself beyond the confines of his earthly existence. Artyomov has been following his own way to attain the truth in art. Naturally enough, his style could not remain unchanged, undergoing a long evolution.

Vyacheslav Artyomov's biography is poor in spectacular events. He studied composition at the Moscow Conservatoire with Nikolai Sidelnikov, a highly experienced musician. His tutor was not a great master, but he enjoyed the respect of the people around him as a decent person, faithful to genuine music and uncompromising in the matters of principle. Besides, he was endowed with a priceless trait, which was most important for the talented young people — he never interfered with their free self-development nor fettered their initiative by his imperative instructions. Therefore, he arrived at an understanding with his student who had quite early showed his independent nature.

The above reflections, however, are hardly to imply that Artyomov did not have to face the problem of choice, most vital at the moment owing to the current situation that arose in Soviet music in the 1960s when Artyomov was entering on his artistic career. In those times a composer remaining loyal to the academic genres, such as symphony, instrumental concerto, opera or ballet, had a chance to quite promptly win recognition if he had accepted the official dogmas and the appropriate "rules of the game". It gave "the green light" to his compositions, with himself being promoted to the ranks of a functionary with the Composers Union and thereby safely insured against any criticism. Anything such time-server produced was immediately and "in the bud" obtained by the Ministry of Culture, which had substantial funds at its disposal to purchase musical compositions. The "obedient" composers could live fairly comfortably thanks to the state patronage guaranteed at a sacrifice of their talent and individuality.

However, there was another road, also quite promising, though not so promptly but sure to win recognition in the forthcoming future. A composer could pose as an opponent to the official art, following the whimsical fancy of the current avant-gardist fashion. It promised recognition and an earthly paradise already associated then with the faraway and inaccessible west located beyond "the Iron Curtain". It did not matter that this music was often of secondary nature, nor that it merely repeated the composition procedures discovered by such masters of the foreign cultural centers as Boulez, Nono, Stockhausen, Ligeti, Lutoslawski and other major and minor gods of the avant-garde. The prime value of this music for the west was due to the very fact that it had been written over there, in snow-white Russia and therefore it was entitled to indulgence on the part of strict arbiters making allowances for the inevitable provinciality of the neophytes who had emerged from this god-forsaken place.

The 1960s brought forth some peculiar illusions. Thus, the budding composers, who used from their early years to hear everybody repeating over and over again the words about the popular spirit and the necessary to rely on folklore, often sought for an impulse for their own composition in the music recorded down in the ethnographic expeditions and not infrequently took part themselves in such trips to collect the unheard-of masterpieces in the faraway villages scattered over the remote parts in this vast country. It gave rise to the so called *new folk wave* whose representatives looked for the ways to renewal in the deep-going, previously unexplored and artistically untouched strata of folk music. This road quite soon proved to be unpromising, since the real specimens of the renewed "Russian style" failed to be even compared in their level with the achievements of the classics from the past century (Mussorgsky in the first place) or, the more so, with the findings of Igor Stravinsky in his *Rite of Spring*. Yet, the current "neo-folkloric" experiments were in general treated with favor: from the viewpoint of the party functionaries a study of folk music by the avant-gardist composers could help in redeeming them and overcoming their errors.

The reason for a brief appraisal of this trend here is due to the fact that Vyacheslav Artyomov, at the outset of his career, also paid tribute to it in his early compositions, such as *Funny Songs* (1964) and *Northern Songs* (1966). But his approach to folklore, which became evident in these works, fundamentally differed from that of his fellow-students in his obvious failure to admire the exotic popular style and stress the "delightful roughness" inherent in the naive music-making. The folk model remained for him just an impulse for his own independent creativity, merely an initial point of departure and a cornerstone for erecting a building according to his individual design. He displayed the same approach to the old-time Georgian chants in his *Gurian Hymn* written much later, in *1986*.

Vyacheslav Artyomov's most significant work among those written in the 1960s (winning the notice of music critics) *Concerto of the Thirteen* (the figure in its title defining the number of performers but not the instruments), also reflected the composer's current quests. This composition was intended for a large non-standard ensemble (the woodwind and brass instruments without French horns, the piano and an extensive percussion battery) and in its dynamic style it was reminiscent of Bartok, Prokofiev and Stravinsky. It won warm response, for it revealed the youthful ardor, purposefulness and virtuosic finesse. It displayed to a full advantage the concertante style realizing the idea of contest between the instruments and their striving for leadership. In contrast to most of Artyomov's later compositions, the forcefulness and motorics in his *Concerto of the Thirteen* (1967) apparently prevail over contemplation and meditation (Musical Example 1).

His Violin Concerto in two movements, subtitled *In Memoriam* (1968), the most significant and definitive of his compositions, written back in the sixties as a gradua-tion work, was destined to be shelved for many years to come, getting no way to the concert stage partly because the composer himself had failed then to find time enough to bring through his message. Only in 1984 Artyomov took up this work once again and made its second version.

It was his first, "test of strength" in monumental symphonic composition to reveal Artyomov intrinsic striving for building up large-scale forms. Though the second movement of this Concerto surpasses in its scale the comparatively modest first movement, it is the latter that carries the qualities justifying its subtitle *In Memoriam*; it may be regarded as a kind of "musical memorial" in which the monologue of the solo violin is complemented and set off by the accompanying voices. As for its second movement, it depicts a prolonged road to the still vague ideal, glimmering somewhere in remote space and never to be attained in the long run. It discloses the leading idea underlying nearly all of Artyomov's compositions-the idea of a *road*, not in the sense of mere motion in space but in the other, higher spiritual sense — the road on which a person embarks in his striving for purification and transfiguration in his self-development. In a certain way *In Memoriam* became a model for the composer's own life and creative work, his difficult road in art.

By the late 1960s the initial period in Vyacheslav Artyomov's creative evolution — the period of formation of his own inimitable style came to a close. With the time of tentative trials gone into the past, there appeared his first works giving the clear idea of the composer's creative aspirations. Then followed a pause during which he wrote very few compositions. As a matter of fact, during this pause he produced just three pieces, namely: *Scenes* for mixed ensemble (1970), *Confession* for solo clarinet (1971), and variations for flute and piano bearing the exotic subtitle *Nestling Antsali* (1974).

And what was he doing during this pause in his creative work? One can easily imagine how the young composer had to spend many years of his life on the elemen-tary struggle for survival, trying his hand first at teaching, then working as an editor of symphonic scores in a music publishing house, and writing incidental scores to films though he felt no particular liking for this kind of job. Yet, the period of forced silence was not wasted in vain, with his talent maturing still further and his long-established world outlook and his unwavering interest in spiritual values asserting themselves.

At last, in the mid-seventies, there occurred a breakthrough, with his compositions appearing one after another in rapid succession and revealing Artyomov's finally established style. But separate components of this style seemed to be broken up and present themselves on their own in groups of the compositions focusing on some particular aspects of a synthetic integral entity.

An attempt at identifying these components shows that the matter involves those aspects of music which could be traced back to the customary and quite conventional concepts such as melody, harmony, rhythm, polyphony and, last but not least, form in its general artistic and specific musical meaning, and eventually a novel treatment of the eternal components of a musical entity.

Prime and detailed consideration should be given to melody and harmony. Since the mid-seventies Vyacheslav Artyomov wrote one after another the compositions that set in strong relief his style and the trend of his creative quests. True enough, in these works the composer disclosed only one of his facets — a bent for stretched, drawn out sonorities in which to the foreground came the finely differentiated *melodies* and their material basis represented in a musical *sound*. Admittedly, there was nothing particularly original in the striving to identify a separate musical tone, to discern in it a wealth of potential resources, and to disclose and actualize them. Neither was it innovative to tackle polyphonic and timbre-embellished blocks of sounds, for such sonorities had long been in use, beginning with Stravinsky's *The Rite of Spring*, Schoenberg's *Pierrot Lunaire* (*Moonstruck Pierrot*) and Scriabin's later compositions written in Russia. These complicated blocks of sounds got their novel treatment in the postwar sonoristic music, primarily by Lutoslawski in his *Three Poems* to verses by Henri Michaux, as well as by other leaders of the Polish avant-garde.

Yet, there was one fundamental difference. With Vyacheslav Artyomov a sound and sonority were important not for their material, sensory tangibility but for that spiritual essence perceived in the very process of spontaneous self-exposition. A separate tone incorporated, in a latent, "involuted" form, the polyphonic sonority to be delivered in the process of slow, gradual *ripening* like a grain giving rise to shoots, the root system, leaves, a flower, and finally a ripe juicy fruit. The composer was far from alienating himself from sensual beauty but he sought for the correspondences between the beauty as it is perceived *here* and the beauty as it is understood *there*, in those rarefied worlds inaccessible to the ordinary consciousness.

A musical instrument as a natural producer of sounds was treated by Artyomov not as a soulless hand-made artifact but as a spiritual creature — a mediator between man and the supreme spheres of his entity, illuminated by the emanations of one and indivisible divinity. And at first he was drawn to his favorite sphere of timbres, which he persistently developed in the second half of the 1970s. It primarily concerns his music written for the wind instruments, for solo instruments included.

Vyacheslav Artyomov discerned in these instruments their spiritual essence which had got obscured and distorted through its applied, "parade-ground" manifestations. And these centuries-old symbols of aggression and violence sanctified by law all of a sudden disclosed the potentials for his spiritual self-expression. One after another, within three years, from 1975 to 1977, he wrote the pieces making up a series of recitatives in which the wind instruments acted both in ensemble and in solo. In some compositions the use has been made of the archi-traditional duet of a wind instrument and the piano, among them: Five Pieces for Clarinet and Piano (1975), *Romantic Capriccio* for French Horn and Piano (1976), and *Sunday Sonata* for Bassoon and Piano (1977).

However, the composer's elaborate work on melody is likely to be most revealing in those pieces for the wind instruments which are intended for solo playing. For all the complexities involved in the pattern of a melodic line in these pieces, it retains its clear-cut phrasing and in a certain way each subsequent phrase is perceived as a free variation on the previous one, as a stage in the flow of an infinite melody extended in its horizontal relationship. All these stages are bound together through the homogeneity of the key structural idea: the correlation between the drawn out, clearly discernible full notes and quite elaborate "approaches" of a whimsical melodic pattern. The sonority of the rhythmically lingering tone seems to contain the inner vibration, which gives an impetus to the following, rhythmically broken motion. A contrast between such finely elaborate turns and rests on the lingering tones is sustained throughout to the end of each recitative, providing for the coherence of melodic motion based on an interplay of variations forming an endless chain. It gives eventually an impression of meditation, immersion into contemplation while the sounding matter, in addition to its purely acoustical, "audible" expression, also incorporates some "inaudible" but implied second supersensitive understatement. Separate tones do not become isolated but interwoven into a coherent melody of the new type wherein the importance attaches to the expressiveness of the sounds spotlighted "in a close-up" by the means of rhythm. And our mind is involuntarily drawn to such sounds, lending them an attentive ear and trying to capture the melody they carry. As for the approaches to such sustained tones, they seem to resemble the figures emerging in kaleidoscopic motion, displaying the most fantastic patterns.

The work on such kind of melody got Vyacheslav Artyomov prepared to write *A Symphony of Elegies* for two solo violins, string orchestra and percussion (1977), a composition that may be appraised in full justice as crowning his output in the seventies. This symphony in three movements expressed the composer's style most vividly as regards its essence, content and materialization in sounds.

A Symphony of Elegies is marked for the prevalence of lingering drawn out sonorities, and in this respect it follows the tradition of writing romantic Adagios, which is inherent in both Russian and German music represented by such names as Beethoven, Schumann, Mahler, Bruckner, and Berg, on the one hand, and Tchaikovsky, Scriabin, Prokofiev, and Shostakovich, on the other. And the point here is not at all in the similarity with the music of the above listed composers, but just in the fundamental principle of musical self-expression *in a slow tempo*, which gives scope for immersing into contemplative meditation, and not only in the Eastern, Indo-Aryan meaning of this word, but also in the western, Christian religious sense. *A Symphony of Elegies* proved conclusively that Vyacheslav Artyomov was an artist inspired by *faith* to be treated both as the Orthodox tradition kindred to him in his blood, and as the faith in the other, broader sense — the fundamental principle of a human life, justifying its message and purport.

The composer quoted D.T. Shuzuoka, a master and popularizer of Zen Buddhism, to define the message of his Symphony: "These are the moments in our inner life awakening and coming into contact with eternity".

Upon lending an attentive ear to this music, you would hardly fair perceiving in it not just the expression of some "lingering states" but also the obvious *motion"*, albeit extremely slow, in the process of which you feel the overcoming of the initial state and a transition from the temporary and transient to all-embracing eternity. In this music you can easily discern the descending motion, a departure into the deep-going strata of the subconscious and at the same time an elevated exploration of the universe, not only of the sensorily perceived Cosmos but also of the astral, supersensitive layers of human entity. And it involves the extreme slowing down of the musical time, yet verging on its complete stopping, when it comes within close proximity of a certain boundary line beyond which the pace of time merges with the infinity. Such approach becomes evident from the first bars of this Symphony. As soon as the basic note passes to its adjacent one lying off just by a minor second, the other voice takes up the initial note, which produces the effect of pulsation. In the same way precisely, the third voice joins in with retarding five seconds later after the beginning (according to the composer's remarks to his score, each voice is to be played by several instruments joining in approximately 2.5 seconds later, one after another).

As a matter of fact, in this case we have a *canon*, but it is of the unusual type, not to be subjected to equal tempered pulsation, which is just discarded; a canon in which the introduction of imitations is governed by pure, physical time measured in clock-wise intervals, if without striving for particular precision.

In the same way the next line is introduced here, representing a free variation on the initial one, likewise the third line introduced later. The absolute asynchronous superposition of these ramified musical lines leads eventually to the perception of the moving, or to be more precise, "crawling" block of sounds wherein its component voices fail to be clearly discerned.

In this block, however, the extended lines of two solo violins stand out, which makes its texture somewhat similar to the classical combination of a melodic relief and a harmonic background. Only in this case a flow of melody is extremely slowed down while the motion of harmony is reduced to vibrations in the degree of density, combinations of registers and changes in the timbre. As a result, there arises not just a lingering sonoristic block but a musical background living its own inner life, summing up the comprehensible voices and acquiring the quality of "singing har-mony," sort of the "music of spheres" filling up the boundless space. This imagery of the immeasurable, illuminating, starlit radiant space is unfolding in the third move-ment of *A Symphony of Elegies*. This space is visible and tangible and at the same time invisible, complemented by many dimensions inaccessible to the human eye. This music is not intended for universal view, for it creates an acoustical *symbol* of some multidimensional space within which the habitual unidimensional flow of time dis-appears and the listener could glimpse the unbounded horizons of eternity.

In the latter half of the 1970s another domain of Vyacheslav Artyomov's creative quests in the sphere of material sounds came to the foreground as the composer found himself attracted to the percussion instruments.

20th-century music is known to attach an ever increasing role to this singular group of instruments used by humans as far back as prehistoric times. But with Artyomov a turn to the percussion instruments was not a tribute to be paid to the avant-gardist fashion. He discovered for himself some different, latent resources of that sound production wherein an attack was more essential and impressive than the lingering and comparatively soon dying out resultant tone. The goal he set before himself may be defined as "melodization of the percussion instruments," even through those incapable of producing the sounds of definite pitch.

Moreover, a combination of percussive sounds can express most vividly the rhythmic nature of music and disclose the symbolic implications of concrete rhythms, their ritual and even cosmic meaning. Such of his work as *Totem* (1976), *Sonata Ricercata* and *A Sonata of Meditations* (both written in 1978) and especially *Invocations* (1979) by their very titles reveal the character of the composer's messages, their magical essence hypnotically suggested to the listener (Musical Example 2).

In this respect his *Totem* in one movement is the most revealing composition. Starting with the quiet, rustling tone, this piece becomes gradually more and more energetic through involving over and over some novel rhythmical figures. Along with the purely background blocks of sounds, its music gradually brings into relief some definite pitches, up to the statement of the old-time sequence *Dies irae*. The Christian ritual motto theme is enveloped by repetitions of the pagan invocative formulas unrelated to, the reproduction of any concrete rites but rather depicting the general atmosphere of magical solemn performance. Eventually the thickening of the space filled up with the rainbow-colored tonal nuances is set off by the rarefactions wherein separate, isolated notes reproduced by the percussion instruments seem to be suspended in the multidimensional field of sounds.

In the early eighties Artyomov's interest in mixed non-standard ensembles mounted, with the composer being captivated now by not their purely concertante idea of contest and confrontation of timbres but their harmonic concord in intricate polyphonic structures. To this category belong the following compositions: *Mattinate* (1979–83), *Star Wind* (1981), and *Hymns of Sudden Winds* (1985–85), with their titles being expressive of frank refinery.

Perhaps, the composer's best achievement in this sphere is a comparatively short piece entitled *Tristia* (1983). A group of solo instruments (piano, trumpet, organ, and vibraphone) come into foreground in turn as if complementing and specifying the idea expressed by their partner. But their individual statements are unfolding against the refined, carefully elaborated background of the strings "illuminating from beneath" the solos by their finest accompanying sounds and complementary elegant nuances. It is evident that the composer has been looking for the means producing the effect of non-materiality, weightlessness of the acoustic aura enveloping the earthly and quite tangible sound utterances. The earthly and the incorporeal, the struggle of passions and unearthly resignedness and purity — such opposites have become fundamental in Vyacheslav Artyomov's creative work.

The human voice is treated by the composer as a musical instrument in the following works: A *Hymn to Jasmine Nights* (1979) and *Moonlight Dreams* (1981). In these pieces one can feel the organic relationship of Artyomov's music with the early 20th-century Russian symbolist poetry and the spirit inherent in Alexander Scriabin's muse.

But Scriabin was known to attach great importance not only to the supreme finesse but also supreme grandiosity. In its own way the art of this great symbolist is heroic, though his heroism has nothing in common with the boring-to-death image of a champion of the absurd social utopias, which was imposed upon the Russian intelligentsia first by the *Narodnik* (Russian populist) ideology and then by the Bolshevik dogmas and myths. Artyomov inherited the special type of heroism intrinsic to

Scriabin; he also associated heroism with a spiritual feat and a noble impulse to *overcome* and *overpower* the passivity and feebleness that like a shadow follow a person immersed in pure contemplation. And an artist is capable of realizing his striving for vigorous activity and get engaged in a fight of cosmic magnitude exclusively within an extended musical form.

Vyacheslav Artyomov's bent for monumental canvases is his intrinsic trait. But it took him some time to write a large-scale composition for symphony orchestra — *Way to Olympus*, the first part of the composer's preconceived tetralogy (1978–84). This symphony has turned out to be the first composition to implement his idea of the *road* with sufficient clarity and consistency.

The idea of incessant, unflagging development designed to overcome the obstacles and temptations and therefore being difficult and full of tense thoughts and feelings is the spiritual core underlying the symphony *Way to Olympus*. This idea is disclosed through elaboration of sounds — from a separate note to multilayered blocks of sounds filling up the musical space. Olympus is treated by the composer as a symbol of the unattainable ideal of perfection, as a goal of spiritual aspirations.

The symphony starts with an extended serene exposition based on the sole musical note. This immutable note, a symbol of inertia, presents itself in diverse manifestations as regards harmony and timbre, becoming covered with layers of sounds. More and more striking and clear-cut turns of melody are gradually introduced, with the musical texture getting more and more dense, and the countless number of new voices and timbres being set into action, up to the first climax perceived as a herald of attaining the desired goal. There arises an obvious parallel between the architectonics of *Way to Olympus* and the conception of Scriabin's grand one-movement works, primarily with his *Poem of Ecstasy,* wherein the final climax is also achieved through the unfolding of stretched dynamic waves.

The ascent to the general (second) climax with the rigid repeated rhythms arising shortly before it is marked for the mounting inner energy and dynamism. The forcefulness of both climaxes makes a contrast to the episodes of short digressions immersing into pure contemplation, lending a singular effect to the chorale-like sounds of the organ and the fine melodic lines of the solo violin.

The utterances of solo instruments are combined with their joint actions, the changeable correlations of various timbrs and rhythmic combinations giving an impression of an integral entity. Such multidimensionality of complex sonority reflects the deep-going perspective opening up before the human mind both in the persistent spiritual clashes and in the immersion into contemplative meditation.

It is easy to observe that the symphony *Way to Olympus* follows in the basic traditions of Russian spiritual culture whose best achievements invariably call for ascension and moral purification. At the same time, Artyomov's symphony organically blends with the current developments in European music, allowing to appraise the value of its characteristic tendency to cognizing that infinity which opens up through immersion into the depths of man's inner world, and simultaneously to penetrating the higher, supersensitive otherworlds which could be glimpsed while contemplating the boundless spaces of the Universe. Herein lies the religious message of the symphony created by the artist consciously believing in God and striving for his listeners to partake of the Orthodox teaching.

The symphony *Way to Olympus* did not close up the ascent to the cherished goal, becoming just a first landmark in a new wandering that seemed to be endless. Since then the ascension designed to conquer a chain of heights has become the purport of the composer's entire artistic activity. Here are the main landmarks on this road: the ballet *Sola Fide* (1985–87), *Requiem* to the martyrs of long-suffering Russia (1985–88), the symphony *On the Threshold of a Bright World* (1990), and his latest symphony subtitled *Gentle Emanation* (1992), the third one in the composer's preconceived tetralogy.

The remarkable music of the ballet *Sola Fide* and its libretto based on a bulky novel written by Count Alexei Tolstoy, who came to replace Maxim Gorky in his status in Soviet literature and was treated kindly by the leader of the peoples — these things would seem incompatible.

Yet, a miracle occurred and there emerged a composition to expose the true meaning of the tragic events involved in the fratricidal civil war and depict the destinies of the people drawn into its bloody vortex. Running contrary to Alexei Tolstoy's apologetic treatment of Bolshevism, this ballet asserts the idea according to which faith alone is capable of illuminating to road to the truth, comforting the sufferer at a time of trials and mortal torments and helping him to withstand under the onslaught of evil bringing Death to all who still retained the human dignity. Probably, this inner understatement of the story, almost imperceptible in Alexei Tolstoy's novel, attracted Vyacheslav Artyomov in the first place and made him to create a work devoid of any daily vanities, spite, and the raging of low passions. As for its association with the plot of Alexei Tolstoy's novel, it served sort of indulgence to by pass the censorial obstacles and secure for his work the right to existence.

As we know, a requiem means the mass for the Dead. It would seem that it has little in common with the world-view of an artist inspired by the Russian religious philosophy, with the Orthodox teaching being its Alpha and Omega. It should be added that in this case the Orthodoxy implies not the official religion, dispirited under the pressure of the Soviet power, but the authentic Orthodoxy that came to be revived in Vladimir Solovyov's treatises and further elaborated in the works by Nikolai Berdayev, Ivan Ilyin and many other Russian religious philosophers who had been banished by the Soviet government and had to seek shelter in the foreign lands. Moreover, Artyomov set his *Requiem* to the complete canonic Latin text keeping it intact.

The success scored by this work upon its performance in the composer's homeland makes one to ponder over the universal human message of Christianity, irrespective of one's creed, when the differences in the religious dogmas lose their sense and to the foreground comes the idea of spiritual transformation in a man embarking upon the unknown road and ascending through grief and despair to elevation and transfiguration. Such apocalyptic message of Artyomov's *Requiem*, where the death is lamented over not only as the decease of the wanderings on the part of a unique human soul but as an event of cosmic magnitude, removes the traits of limited, local belonging to the concrete, in this case Catholic confession, from the canonic Latin rite. Artyomov's *Requiem* represents an experience of the purely Christian values purified of the birthmarks of the religious sub-divisions fatal for the human history. The Russian national fundamental principle discernible in this composition is not guarded against anybody in a striving to uphold its dogmatic sovereignty — it is open to the universal human values and close and dear to any Christian heart.

At the same time, Artyomov's *Requiem* reveals the views of a modern artist making use of the universal European "musical idioms". Among the conventional musical symbols vested with their long-established expressive meaning of the greatest import-ance is the archi-traditional tonality of adjacent seconds — the simplest sign of human suffering. The matter involves the *lamento* tonality which imbues the whole of European music both secular and sacred. This elementary cell turns out to be capable of embracing the open outcries of heartrending anguish and serene grief intrinsic in a humble doleful lament.

Vyacheslav Artyomov's *Requiem* discloses two qualities inherent in the current approach to this primary, symbolic tonality. The first one involves elaboration of its horizontal relationship giving rise to short chains of brief leading melodies. The other characteristic is to redouble the polyphonic *lamento* tonality up to embracing all the layers of the actual soundspace. It eventually gives an impression that even the smallest atom of the music recurring over and over again in various tonal guises resounds throughout the concert hall, as in a cathedral. Such multiform reflection of an elementary melodic line-symbol that acquires, along with spatial tridimensionality, a polytonal coloring is born of the thinking of a musician who has mastered and assimilated the accomplishments of 20th-century music. It is the meditative music of our century that could attain a psychological sensation of the incorporeality of sounds and the unearthly lucidity of sound production either by the singer's vocal chords or by quite tangible musical instruments. Artyomov in his *Requiem* managed to lend a sound the effect of a light both in the physical and purely spiritual sense, which allows to discern in it the radiance of the other, unearthly emanation. The fifteen settings of his *Requiem"* depict the road of a man descending into the abyss in order to elevate himself then to the state of bliss, which is epitomized in its final setting called *In Paradisum*. The incorporeal effect of musical sounds transformed into emanation, which is accomplished in this setting, could be traced back to the world musical practice: it is attained by removing the sharp accents, smoothing the rhythmic thrust and by enhancing a free flow of melody, excluding any possible clashes of separate notes. The melodic lines are brought together in such a way as to produce the sensation of ascending a ladder built up of the soaring notes devoid of any sensuality and impassioned pulsation. These voices gradually fill in the previously rarefied space, coming up from its faraway depths. And the music becomes similar to a cosmic symphony of the singing heavens, turning into a symbol of eternal harmony and supreme accord.

The above discussion is not to imply that the composer stays aloof from the current problems of this world and its fatal disorder. The best evidence to the reverse is his symphony entitled *On the Threshold of a Bright World* (1990) in which the ultimate goal is glimmering somewhere at a distance never to be attained in the long run. And the attainment of a bright world is blocked not by the pressure of satanic forces, nor by the persecution and reprisals of the inhuman tyrants — the symphony depicts the tragedy of those who have lost their touch with God, delivering the desparate voices of those facing the dark abyss ready to engulf them.

The principal distinction of the second symphony making part of the yet incomplete tetralogy is the absence of the clearly visualized musical elaboration of the *summing up* of life's wanderings. A bright world is failed to be attained and the human soul remains just on its threshold — on the boundary line which opens up both the road to ascending the faraway summits and the road to descending into the pitch-dark abyss of eternal sufferings. This time the composer is disinclined to persist in or suggest anything, analyzing by his own means the state of a man at a time when it has gone out of joint, when the false values came to be rejected but the true ones not yet defined. In this respect his symphony mirrors the current situation when people are scared and apprehensive of the morrow holding nothing but new trials and unavoidable disasters.

In this symphony one can clearly trace the consistent, albeit not straightforward, ascension to the general climax followed by a comparatively concise epilogue-an afterword. On the road to this ascension there arise intermediary climaxes similar to the pointed tops in a mountain-range. These are set off by the retarding pitches where the time seems to linger before to renew its endless run with redoubled forces. At the same time, the true building up of the musical form occurs through the developments reflecting the struggle of light and darkness, — obscurity and enlightenment, the emotional tension of passions and resigned serenity obtained by a soul purified of all transient vanities.

This unstable equilibrium in gravitation of two opposing poles underlies the moving force governing the developments unfolding within the gigantic soundscape. Here you can observe the activation of tempos and rhythms; their retardation; an interchange of the confronting tone-colors similar to a certain dialogue, their super-positions making up a multicolored sound field; the explicit materialization of the musical texture, its tangibility; its dematerialization and dissolution into weightless sounds; and, finally, a change of these obviously dispersed sunds into their flowing where it is hard to capture the clear-cut facets of separate tone-structures. But a particular role is now assigned to the invocative repetitions with alternation of stable rhythmic elements, accentuated beats giving an impression of a procession, a measured pace of a walking giant. The elevated contemplations are combined in this music with the primitive ritualism which has been bewitching the musicians since Stravinsky's *The Rite of Spring*.

Nowadays many composers are inclined to apprehend the outcome of their own work and exercise a conscious approach to the tasks they set before themselves. Their statements could not be taken for granted in all the cases, for without being suspicious of the creators' insincerity or their wish to conceal their true intentions, one has to take into consideration a gap between the desired and the actual, the preconceived and the accomplished.

What are the objectives of music in the present-day world — is it dispassionately recording down the state of the human spirit in the wicked society far from becoming perfect or it is striving to elevate people and suggest them the idea of their need for personal salvation and regeneration? Is music destined to guide those seeking a road to the temple sanctified by the Creator or it gives them a free hand in their choice without indulging in preaching? What are the lessons of music and has it to teach anything at all, being self-sufficient in its nature? And in case it offers a vivid depiction of the artist's *road* to the illuminating truth, is it in its power to kindle the eternal light of hope in the listeners' hearts and carry them along onto this road, too?

Indeed, all the above questions are posed in Artyomov's music. But does he provide the answers to them? It is not so simple to reply to the latter unambiguous question. For his music offers no ready-made solutions, it just helps anybody feeling in tune with it to perceive how difficult and agonizing is this road to the transformation and what temptations one has to overcome on this road. And the impassioned expectation of renewal and enlightenment — for herein lies the message of *wanderings* aimed at the divined, albeit not so easily attainable, goal, — such expectation is neither to remove nor shroud in the rose-colored spectacles the really existing evil with its universal satanic power.

Throughout the Universe and in the boundless world of a human soul — everywhere you can feel the confrontation of goodness and evil, the abyss of infernal obsessions and the multicolored glamour of the other higher worlds inaccessible to the sensory perception but divined by the spiritual eye. The overcoming of darkness and overpowering of evil can be attained only through the personal efforts of man seeking the support in the living God. Hence the underlying meaning in the creative work of Vyacheslav Artyomov as a *Christian* artist striving to grasp the original message of Jesus Christ's teaching as a guide for salvation.

Herein lie the roots of the properties inherent in the natural matter of his music. It focuses on meditation, the state of a human soul immersing into the invisible and inaudible world to be discovered in symbols manifested in material sounds. Artyomov's music embodies a certain *process*, but it is a process of special kind, quite dissimilar to the dynamics that have become firmly established in European music since the times of Beethoven. Instead of the impetuous dynamism and purposive attainment, his music is characterized by pure contemplation with its intrinsic seeming sluggishness and self-sufficiency of any moment of a lingering sound delaying a wonderful instant, but at the same time changeable, modulating, multicolored in its nuances and at times full of the greatest agonizing tension. His music reflects neither the outward onslaught of the evil forces nor the violence reigning in this world, but the state of a human soul discovering the hell in one's own self, and looking for the causes of the earthly disasters not in the aggressive and vicious nature of the other people but in one's own thoughts and motivations. To save the world, it is necessary first to save oneself — this idea commanded by Jesus Christ finds its embodiment in material sounds representing the spiritual substance of music.

For this reason the pitch structure of music in which harmony merges with timbre makes the basis of Artyomov's style. In its symbolic embodiment manifested in the harmonic equilibrium of each momentary sound you can feel the reflection of some other, higher harmony to be opened up only to the transformed and purified soul. These sounds may be extremely dense, multilayered as if reproducing the structure of a natural note-row involuted in each atom of music and each separate sound; but they may be also extremely rarefied and interwoven out of separate musical threads; or they may be now static and immutable, and again changeable and unstable to reflect the changing states of the human spirit.

Such correlation of the changeable and the immutable underlies the inner rhythm wherein the stability of the immutable combines with the unpredictability of the changeable, with its sudden breaks, outbursts of sounds and the ringing silence. The regular measures of the invocative repetitions with their cyclic motion marking a return to the initial point of departure, set off the onward development closed up by a leap onto a new level and a new step.

The general integrity of a composition in an extended one-movement form is similar to a building marked by its symmetrical proportions. It looks like a temple being erected in music, though not in the tangible stones but in the incorporeal matter of sounds. Vyacheslav Artyomov is a *builder*, an architect who erects both the unassuming chapels and the cyclopean structures in the vein of a grand cathedral. It is construction, rather than destruction, assertion and not negation that underline the true message of his music.

Ex.1 *Concerto of the Thirteen,* Second movement

PRINCIPAL WORKS

1964   *Funny Songs* for soprano and piano to folk texts
1966   *Northern Songs* for soprano, mezzo-soprano and piano to folk texts
1966   *Four Duets* for soprano, mezzo-soprano and piano, text by Ashot Grashi
1966   Sonata for Solo Clarinet
1967   *Concerto of the Thirteen* for wind and percussion instruments. Released by Melodia: C10 15059–60
1968–1984   *In Memoriam*, Concerto for solo violin and Orchestra.
                R10 00129 (Russian Disk)
1970   *Scenes* for mixed ensemble
1971   *Confession* for solo clarinet
          Tempo Constante for orchestra
1974   Variations: *Nestling Antsali* for flute and piano
1975   *Autumn Sonatina* for saxophone, or flute, or oboe, or clarinet, and piano
1975   *Capriccio for New Year's Eve* for soprano saxophone, baritone saxophone and vibraphone
1975–1981   *A Garland of Recitatives* for flute, oboe, clarinet or saxophone, bassoon and orchestra. R10 00133 (RD)
1976   *Totem* for percussion. C10 18981–82 (Melodia)
1977   *Sunday Sonata* for Bassoon and Piano
1977   *Litany I* for saxophone quartet
1977   *A Symphony of Elegies* for two solo violins, percussion and strings. C10 20241 003 (Melodia)
1977–1978   *Woodland Sketches* for two pianos
1978   *Sonata Ricercata* for percussion
1978   *A Sonata of Meditations* for percussion. R10 00131 (RD)
1978   *Awakening* for two solo violins. C10 18981–82 (Melodia)
1979   *Invocations* for soprano and percussion. C10 18981–82 (Melodia)
1979   *A Hymn to Jasmine Nights* for soprano and piano
1979–1983   *Mattinate* for soprano, flute, violin and guitar
1981   *All' Rondo* for alto saxophone and piano
1981   *Litany II* for flute quartet
1981   *Preludes to Sonnets* for solo piano
1981   *Star Wind* for mixed ensemble
1981   *Moonlight Dreams* for mezzo-soprano, alto flute, cello and piano. R10 00133 (RD)
1982   *Romantic Capriccio* for French horn and piano. R10 00133 (RD)
1983   *Tristia* for trumpet, piano, vibraphone, organ and strings. A10 00385 006 (Melodia)
1983–1985   *Hymns of Sudden Winds* for mixed ensemble.
                R10 00131 (RD)
1984   *Way to Olympus*, symphony for orchestra. A10 00385 006 (Melodia)
1984   *Expectation*, ballet-nostalgia
1985–1987   *Sola Fide*, ballet in three acts after Alexei Tolstoy's novel *The Road to Calvary*
1985–1988   *Requiem* for two or three sopranos, tenor, baritone, descant, the boy's choir, chorus and orchestra. A10 00547 006 (two discs, released by Melodia)

1986   *Gurian Hymn* for three solo violins, percussion and strings. R10 00129 (RD)
1986   *Litany III* for organ
1989   *Ave atque vale* for percussion
1990   *On the Threshold of a Bright World*, symphony for orchestra
1991   *Gentle Emanation*, symphony for orchestra
1992   *Pietá* for solo cello and orchestra

Ex.2   *Totem*

Faraj Karayev:
genug or not *genug*

Vladimir Barsky

Faraj Karayev

Prelude

EACH WORK OF ART, MUSIC INCLUDED, IS A MODE OF AUTOBIOGRAPHY.

THE COMPOSER CANNOT RECONCILE HIMSELF TO HIS MUSIC.

MUSIC IS INFINITE; A COMPOSER HAS JUST TO DISCOVER IT.

THE SOLE TRUE CRITERION IN APPRAISING A PIECE OF MUSIC IS THE COMPOSER'S DESIRE TO BE ITS CREATOR. LUCKY IS HE WHO CAN ACKNOWLEDGE AT LEAST SEVERAL BARS AS HIS OWN.

ONE CANNOT BE SERIOUS IN APPRAISING ONE'S OWN ENDEAVORS: ONLY THOSE WRITE MUSIC WHO COULD NOT FIND IN THEMSELVES WILLPOWER ENOUGH TO GIVE UP THIS USELESS OCCUPATION.

ALL MUSIC HAS ALREADY BEEN WRITTEN.

Such an introduction seems to invalidate any attempt at drawing a creative profile of a composer since further discussion, no matter how detailed and argumentative it may be, would fail to add anything essential to the characteristics of his artistic personality. Or it should be equaled in its text to the notorious preface to *The Picture of Dorian Gray*, unfolding within the range of similar aesthetic poles from its initial phrase ("The artist is the creator of beautiful things") and its final line ("All art is quite useless"). And in this case it would be quite adequate to start the narration with the following lines borrowed from the same source.

"The studio was filled with the rich odour of roses, and when the light summer wind stirred amidst the trees of the garden there came through the open door the heavy scent of the lilac, or the more delicate perfume of the pink-flowering thorn."

For the obvious reasons we would not even venture undertaking anything like that. The more so as by the close of our century too many things have changed, beginning with our environment to the self-sensations of a man living on this earth.

Counterpoint I

Vladimir Barsky: I have no doubt that there are two composers going under the name of Karayev. It is another point that the matter now involves the final outcome. In the ordinary human consciousness there exists a certain set of clichés on this matter such as: the nature seems to take a rest with the children, and scions of the great men could feel quite protected under the magic of their name. As for the reality, one has nevertheless to pass this road on one's own, without relaying on the accumulated experience, and finding the appropriate arguments inside oneself rather than from the outside...

Faraj Karayev: I have always regarded myself as a minion of fortune, since I was the son of the outstanding composer, Kara Karayev; I have been living in Baku and, by virtue of the circumstances beyond my power, could feel undoubtedly quite safe. On the other hand, one has to meet one's bills, and it often got me into a lot of trouble. I was invariably introduced to all as the son of Kara Karayev.... True enough, once during my talk with an old score copyist in Baku she asked me: 'Is your father's name Karayev?' I answered in the affirmative and got prepared for the usual question... But all of a sudden it came somewhat revised: 'Aren't you the grandson of Professor Abulfaz Karayev, the pediatrician?' I confirmed this fact, too. — 'You know, he used to treat me.' It was unexpected and pleased me very much. And for the second time, during my stay at the guest house for composers in Ruza I happened to catch the following phrase in a talk between two local cooks when one of them said pointing at me: 'Do you know who is this man?' I strained myself inwardly. But then she added: 'It is little Ashdar's dad.' The fact is that my son used to go there for his summer holidays when he was a little boy...

V. B.: Though the musical atmosphere in Baku in those years was quite conservative, your musical education seemed to be oriented from the outset onto the Western tradition, wasn't it so?

F. K.: During some period in my life it was so exclusively thanks to my father. His library and his erudition were just great. I remember how in 1951, when I was just eight years old, in our country house near Baku, taking precautions against seeing it be anyone, even by the other members of the family, he showed me the score of *Petrushka* and said: 'It is a work of a genius, 30 or 40 years later this music is sure to be played.' In those times it was quite a feat on his part, which left its imprint on my child's memory. When I started writing music at the age of ten or twelve, the range of my musical interests was confined to Mozart, Chopin, Scriabin, and the study of the period form and other fundamentals of the metier. Once my father called me into his study, got a pile of scores and said: 'In addition to the music you already know, there is something else.' Those were Shostakovich, Prokofiev, Ravel, Debussy, Casella, and Schoenberg... In 1957 we stayed in a country house near Kiev where Father was working for 15–16 hours a day, which was natural for him, on the orchestration of his ballet *The Path of Thunder*. He had a copyist who had arrived expressly for this purpose from Baku and who could not keep pace with him while I sat nearby watching all this. In this way I came to learn the purely practical attitude to the composer's work. While studying at the conservatoire I virtually never attended the classes in instrumentation. Besides, I had a remarkable tutor in harmony, Ella Markovna Nikomarova, who also taught me a lot. And not only from the viewpoint of harmony, but also as regards the sense of style and musical taste. This made the basis for developing my ability to play jazz, and many other things. During the years following my graduation from the conservatoire I learned quite a lot from my friend Oleg Felzer. Together we made two left-wingers, both acting as the number eleven, to use the football terminology.

Nevertheless, there was no full guaranty for leading a peaceful life. Following the premiere of my *Sonata for Two Players*, which took place in March 1977 in Baku, some sneaking person informed Suslov, the communist party chief ideologist, about an act of 'ideological subversion' committed allegedly by myself, demanding that this case should be duly 'investigated'. It was not so amusing in those days. The inertia of this wave was somehow stopped because it was quite faraway from Moscow, nearly two thousand kilometres...

When in the late seventies I set up a chamber orchestra at the operatic workshop of the Baku Conservatoire designed to play 20th-century music, all the repertoire problems were settled in the following way: a draft programme was sent to Moscow to my father on which he used to put down his approval, with no problems arising afterwards. But two weeks after his death a scheduled concert was cancelled in Baku. The rector of the conservatoire thus explained his decision: 'You are planning to play a composition by Oleg Felzer, and yours, there is no need to do it here. When you go on tour in Moscow, you can play whatever you like over there'.

V. B.: And how was your father taking what you were doing?

F. K.: Our relationship was not so simple, particularly during my first two student years at the conservatoire. I wished to do what I was unable to do yet, and he made me learn the fundamentals of the metier. But by the end of my third year at the conservatoire we found common ground. Sometimes for several months running we were not on the speaking terms because of the purely professional problems. Even when I tried to raise at home some point concerning my current compositional matters, I could get a curt reply: 'Tuesday and Friday at the conservatoire, no home lessons'. True enough, I changed my attitude to the educational process just before graduating from the conservatoire. And then he let me go and have a free hand. Upon listening to the recording of my *Sonata for Two Players*, Father asked me: 'What are you going to do now? Have you got any ideas?' I told him that I had some. 'Well, I hope so,' he said just that. At any rate, he displayed neither negative response to my music nor attempted to guide me into 'a proper way'. I got the impression that Father believed in me, which was encouraging and very important to me. It was a real school of life that Father has taught me. Thanks to him I early came to realize in what way a true musician should work and what an honest attitude to one's own endeavors meant.

Stretta I

... One of my first encounters with Faraj Karayev's music was *Goya*, a film to which he had written the incidental score, produced in 1971 by the German film director Konrad Wolf. As early as then I glimpsed in it the polemic and paradoxical character of his inner perception of the reality. The subsequent years only confirmed this initial impression. This composer is constantly in motion, his music is restless and full of contrasts. The sensation of stability and serenity becomes quite an unattainable ideal hidden beyond the horizon. His compositions, irrespective of their instrumental cast, in most cases present a certain scenic action whose characters walk about, quarrel and argue, they put down their instruments only to take them up again, then they play and shout, the members of the ensemble scan and cry out separate phonemes while the pianist beats the lower soundboard of the piano by a beetle...

One could treat Faraj Karayev's style as a customary manifestation of the avant-gardist mind and let its inner understatement be buried in some conventional notions. And yet, something in your soul resists such approach to his music. For a stereotype evolved within many years habitually fixes down a certain field of common aesthetic aspirations and the common foundations of style and techniques. But an incessant ramification of creative trends leads to formation of particular multidimensional musical soundscape within which the concept of "the avant-garde" could hardly be defined in any unambiguous terms. Therefore, the treatment of compositions written by some major representatives of modern trends emerging in the second half of this century as the avant-garde looks quite problematic. On the one hand, they seem to reproduce some definite archetype, passing through the conventional stages in their development as the avant-gardist composers — from the perpetual search for novel, uncommon devices through the expansion of the tangible horizons of the soundscape, up to taking an interest in the music of non-European cultures, conducting experiments with the musical time and striving for "autohermeneutics" and theoretical substantiation of their own compositions. On the other hand, aesthetics often differ from the reality whereas some concepts by their very nature imply in many cases not the elucidation of their meaning but obscurity and ambiguity. The avant-garde came to be replaced by the Post-avant-gardism and Postmodernism. The pace of time has got accelerated. To quote Sergei Averintsev, an eminent Russian writer, "our time calls itself by several names whose inner structure seems to be based on paradoxes. Post-modernism, post-industrialism, post-totalitarianism, etc. — all these word-formations sound like saying: after the end of the world, after the Judgment Day."

To my mind, a singular feature of Faraj Karayev's music and his style consists in that it represents something more than a purely musical phenomenon. His compositions invariably involve a certain wider artistic field embracing painting, literature, dramatic and plastic art. His creative work is rooted in the cultural sources past and present, with the aesthetic phenomena of the past to be easily identified in the modern artifacts: the poetry of René Char, Carl Sandburg, Edward Estlin Cummings, Nazym Hikmet, Jacques Prévert, Thomas Stearns Eliot, Giuseppe Ungaretti, and Ezra Pound; James Joyce's *Ulysses* and Samuel Beckett's Theatre of the Absurd, the paintings of Marc Chagall and Pablo Picasso, the films of Fellini and Antonioni, and the music of Charles Ives, Igor Stravinsky and Luciano Berio.

In my opinion, his early Piano Sonata No. 2 bears the hallmarks of Faraj Karayev's now well-established musical language. Within its quite conventional instrumental two-movement framework, representing a sample of sonata cycle widely employed in modern music, one can discern the theatrical imagery and tangibility of its "plot line" and dramatic collisions, which came to be so naturally developed in his later works.

The first movement embodies the idea of harmony and well-balanced proportions inherent in the truly beautiful world of stable spiritual values. The natural flow of the mutually complementing voices fill in the entire musical space. The logic of their development is aesthetically self-sufficing and significant. Like three Dorian Columns, the "vault" of its form is supported up by the chordal progressions in G-sharp minor arising at its outer facets-expressive of nostalgia for the "Golden Age" and an attempt at synthesizing the past and the present day.

The mood prevailing in its second movement is alarm, uncertainty and anxiety. The musical matter falls into separate "dots," "flashes," and "spots." Its aesthetic prototype — Webern's music — is transferred by the composer onto a different musical soil and mediated by the latest devices, which finds its manifestation in the invasion of rigid urbanistic structures of the middle section and the nostalgic reflections inherent in the recurrences from the first movement....

The initial period in Faraj Karayev's work could be defined in full justice as the "Sturm and Drang": the composer was looking for the relevant aesthetic sources, trying his hand at diverse genres, as if seeking his own "ecological niche," his own place in the musical world where his voice would not be lost in the intricacies of innumerable trends and styles. In his endeavors he relied on the experience of his great predecessors — Webern (*Concerto grosso*), Bach (Concerto for Piano and Chamber Orchestra), Scarlatti and Stravinsky (the ballet *Kaleidoscope*). He acquired the invaluable experience from his contacts with the theatre when he was writing his ballet *The Shadows of Kobystan* based on the Eastern tradition of musical thinking and embodying the idea that was to become most important to his further progress as a composer: the birth of man through the birth of an artist.

Yet, according to the composer himself, the first opus to adequately convey his vision of the world was his *Sonata for Two Players*, which had been conceived during his work on the opera *Morning of the Third Day* after Jean Anouilh's play. Lord Byron's following verses, used by the great Russian poet Alexander Pushkin as an epigraph to his poem *Poltava*, provided an additional impulse for his work:

> The power and glory of the war,
> Faithless as their vain votaries, men,
> Had pass's to triumphant Czar.

The score of this composition makes a kind of journey into the microworld of sounds, meditation, and an attempt to render the unrenderable, to embody the idea (in Plato's meaning) and to express its beauty and appeal adequately as possible in human power. The musical time seems to stop its run in this intransient world, with the artist just for a few minutes penetrating within its boundaries....

By the close of the 1970s Faraj Karayev wrote his vocal monodrama *Journey to Love*, the most uncommon composition as regards its conception and its acoustic and visual aura.

... On the stage you see a singer and an orchestra most uncustomary for our time — three grand pianos (the ordinary one, the electric and the prepared), accordion, vibraphone, bells, electric guitar, bass guitar, the percussion battery, flute, bass clarinet, and twelve strings (without the double-bass). Moreover, the performers constantly change their habitat, taking irregular seats and getting engaged in quite Brownian motion. The line of the solo voice intoning in the instrumental manner the verses by modern British, French, Spanish, Italian and Turkish poets (in the original language) is unfolding against the background of the carefully elaborated "scenography" of taped sounds (the murmur of the sea, the cries of seagulls, the howling of the wind, the rustle of grass, the honks of motor-cars, din and hubbub, and the recorded improvisations of the American Jazz organ-player Emerson and a melody from the mugham *Segyakh*, this mode of love, played on an Azerbaijan folk instrument). And the whole of this intricate fusion of the sounds associated with modern civilization and the voices of nature is interwoven into the eternal, albeit a sad narration about Romeo and Juliet, Tristan and Isolde, Pelléas and Mélisande...

Interlude I (*Journey to Love*) *

Once upon a time there lived a lonely and unhappy man.

One wouldn't say that he was too unlucky in his life, but in real earnest he had only once a stroke of luck — he met a woman he had been looking for all his life, they lived together and he felt happy.

Within a very short span of time he came to realize that his current life was nothing else but an illusion, a myth he had created himself. Or to be more precise, it was just false.

The finale was quite predictable: all ended in a vile betrayal and they parted.

At first he took it very hard, feeling grieved and miserable.

But gradually he reconciled himself to the idea that "you cannot lose what you don't have."

His contacts with this woman, for he was still unable to go without seeing her, were now confined to rare and chance encounters when two persons, once so close to each other, had nothing in common any longer.

Yet, at times he got very sad, feeling some bitterness tinged with insincerity from the life he has been leading now.

And at such moments everything went dark before him and he saw everything in the worst possible light, and the fact that this woman was not near him and his desire to see her merged together.

And in his innermost he puzzled at himself: how can one love so blindly.

***

Without you, my darling,
Paris is just summer heat,
Dry noise, and unhappy river.
I'm bored to stay here
In Paris, missing and
Calling you, my darling.
   Nazym Hikmet

Drowsing in my chair of disbelief
I watch the door as it slowly opens —
A trick of the nightwind?
Your whisper is too soft for credens,
Your tread like blossom drifting
 from a bough,
You touch even softer.
And though a single word
 scatters all doubts
I quake for wonder at your
 choice of me:
Why, Why and Why.
   Robert Graves

---

* The verses in this section are recited in any order, not necessarily in conformity with the sequence they arise in Faraj Karayev's composition; they may be also recited against the background of the initial text recorded on tape.

Dans les manèges du mensonge
Le cheval rouge de ton sourire Tourne
Et je suis là debout planté
Avec le triste fouet de la réalité...
                    Jacques Prévert

...L'ignominie avait
l'aspect d'un verre
              d'eau...

Le soleil en disparaissant
avait coupé ton visage. Ta tête
avait roulé dans la fosse du ciel
et je ne croyai plus au lendemain...
                    René Char

Ma le mia urla
feriscomo
come fulmini
la campana fioca
del cielo

Sprofondane
impaurite
              Giuseppe Ungaretti

...
a cloche tolled twice
once for the birth

and once to the death of love
that night
Lawrence Ferlinghetti

Stretta II

In the early 1980s compositions for orchestra and for voice and orchestra, in some or another way associated with the name of Kara Karayev, predominated in Faraj Karayev's creative work. The symphony *La Quinta del Sordo (Goya)*, written in collaboration with his father and based on the above mentioned incidental score to the film *Goya*, embodies the eternal collision of "the artist and the world" throughout his entire "hard road to cognition." His symphonies *Tristessa I* and *Tristessa II* may be viewed as a kind of cycle. The dramatic pattern of the first composition is built up on a confrontation of symphony and chamber orchestras, manifesting the perpetual struggle of goodness and evil, the beautiful and the ugly, the humane and the hostile to man. Correspondingly, the composition is noted down in two scores to be rendered by two conductors while the thematic material of the episodes in an extended rondo-like form, with their refrain coming to be second in importance, is made up of Kara Karayev's three piano preludes to be played by the conductor: B (Prelude in G-sharp minor)-A-C (Prelude in A major)-A-D (Prelude in C-sharp minor, either behind the stage or in taped recording).

Tristessa I, dedicated to the memory of "Father, Teacher and Friend" and subtitled *Parting Symphony*, has been preconceived as its world-famous predecessor: the orchestra players leave the stage while Kara Karayev's taped prelude remains alone on the empty scene with the curtain drawing back up to the sizes of the surrounding world wherein there is room for the intransient and the beautiful — for Music.

The next symphonic cycle written in the eighties is the serenade *I Bade Farewell to Mozart on the Karlov Bridge in Prague* (and its version, *The year 1791*, a serenade for small symphony orchestra). The dramatic pattern of this composition, similar to the one described above, is explained by fact that it was written shortly after the father's death and dedicated to Mozart's death anniversary. The thematic material of its outer movements (Prelude and Postlude) incorporates the newly orchestrated and transposed fragment from *Lacrimosa*, "submerged" into a more gloomy tonality. The central Chorale enhances the tragic tone of the composition while the bell measuredly beating the pace of time stresses the intransient character of its plot, moving already beyond the earthly time and space....

Faraj Karayev's Suite for string quartet *In memoriam* dedicated to Alban Berg, also belongs to that group of works in which the composer pays homage to the great musicians of the past. In conformity with the device used by this neo-Viennese classic himself, the tonal vocabulary of this suite is based on Alban Berg's personal motto (a-b♭-a-b♭-e-g) and mediated through the fragment of The Rhythm of Destiny from his opera *Lulu*, and quotations from his Violin and Chamber Concertos.

In the same vein was written the chamber concerto *Alla Nostalgia* for eight instrumentalists, dedicated to the memory of Andrei Tarkovsky. Its premiere took place in January 1990 in Switzerland (performed by the Soloists Ensemble of the Azerbaijan State Symphony Orchestra under the baton of Rauf Abdullayev, who had commissioned the composer to write this work). Its basic form-building element is a tritone to be used in one or another shape throughout its four movements.

In the first movement the tritone makes the basis of serial structure to form eventually a chorale that may be so defined only tentatively.

In the second movement the tritone stays motionless in somewhat paralysed state to dissolve then in the extended quasi-arpeggio chords of the third movement.

In the finale the basic idea seems concentrated as if summing up the previous development and representing a kind of epilogue-afterword of the entire cycle (see Example 1).

"This composition embodies mugham as an idea, as an emotion, as a perception of time, and, perhaps, as an abstract principle of working with melodic models. The individuality of the composer's tone is indeed impressive, for the national is fused here in full measure with his own style" (*Tages-Anzeiger*).

However, Faraj Karayev has been preoccupied not only with the past but also trying to correspond with his contemporaries, too. In his composition *A Crumb of Music for George Crumb* the following poetic lines of Emily Dickinson act on a par with the musical material, making its integral component and lending some mournful and mystical aspect to its general atmosphere:

> If I shouldn't be alive
> When the Robins come
> Give the one in red cravat
> A memorial crumb
> If I couldn't thank you
> Being fast asleep,
> You will know I'm trying
> With my granite lip!

This piece by Faraj Karayev provides a mixture of diverse expressive means lying quite apart from one another: the poetical theatre and "pure music" are presented in various combinations, producing the convincing artistic imagery.

Ex. 1 *Alla Nostalgia*

"Faraj Karayev's *A Crumb of Music for George Crumb* copied the American master only in using special effects, whispered poetry, amplified breathing and the sympathetic resonance of the open piano. The Dorian flavour and the strong sense of evocation make it, in contemporary sense, a typically Russian product" (*Independent*).

Interlude II, or Instrumentation of Scriabin's Tenth Sonata

...with the profoundest veneration for Music, without losing the perception of the Personality, neither imitating, nor following in his footsteps, for "you cannot enter the same river twice".

He always remained his own self, and His line came to a tragic rupture together with his music.

Why the Tenth Sonata in particular?

As compared to the striking Ninth Sonata, it may seem just a draft copy, rather than composition chiselled in all of its parameters, "merely" an insight of a genius, "eureka" — like an uncut diamond discovered in the boundless diamond-placer of the richest deposit awaiting its time to be properly cut;

besides, it contains a great amount of slips as regards its voice-leading, texture, and notation —

any yet, it is so easy to communicate with!

there is no need to cast bridges into the past, the present day is breaking in, it is still too far until the sunset, and the future is not so near at hand;

and with the profoundest reverence for the Personality, without losing the perception of Music...

Counterpoint II

V. B.: What ideas are predetermining your current work?

F. K.: Today I feel myself to be fully exhausted and in an intellectual vacuum. Nonetheless, I've lately completed a few pieces which are of major importance for me.

Fifteen Minutes of Music for the Town of Forst were expressly written for the piano duo Akif and Marina Abdullayevs, who played this composition on their tour in Germany. It is a short suite: the first piece lasts one minute, the second-two minutes, the third-three, the fourth-four, and the last fifth-five minutes. Conventionally speaking, Prelude, Canon, Interlude, Farce (a conglomeration of quotations from Beethoven, Chopin, et al, with the whole piece played on one pedal, *fortissimo* from beginning to end), and Postlude.

Der Stand der Dinge, written in 1990 on a commission of the Modern Ensemble, offers a certain projection of Webern's Five Pieces for Orchestra, Op. 10, ephemerally arising in the labyrinths of the orchestral texture and making up the core of the composition. In the process of playing the orchestra repeatedly falls into several self-contained ensembles: the string and wind quartets, a trio of brasses and strings, a duet of double-bass and bass clarinet, and so on. On a par with Webern's music, at times ringing but then invisibly existing exclusively in the conductor's mind, the musical texture is developing according to its own laws. The ensuing intricate complex of mutually penetrating structures at each new coil of development achieves a different quality, leading to a climax in its statement, which quite often fails to coincide with the culmination point in its dynamics. Such horizontal shift makes the musical form somewhat unstable, becoming still more dispersed owing to such episodes as the recitation of Max Frisch's prose and of Ernst Jandl's verses, an irrealistic funeral procession, and other similarly illogical interpolations in the spirit of the absurd theatre. The quasi-quotation from Kara Karayev's *A Haunting Idea*, a piano piece for children, which emerges in the first, third and, in a concise harmonic block, in the fifth movement, adds to all the above ambiguities inherent in this composition another *unanswered question* that could be unravelled by MUSIC alone. Anyone who finds quotations, or something else of interest, in my composition should not look for any hidden meaning behind all this and cherish any illusions. "You are looking the wrong way, for there is nothing hidden over there," to quote Khoja Nasreddin, the immortal hero of the Oriental epos.

"Karayev in this composition embodies the idea of spatial music reminiscent of Kagel's instrumental theatre. Snatches of words are hovering in the air, at a certain moment the entire composition, after a cradle song with its string flageolets, comes to a close. An Alpine dream? At any rate, an upside down world..." Achim Heidenreich (*Die Welt*).

Recently I completed quite a big composition, lasting for about 40 minutes, entitled *Ist es genug?*, which I believe needs no translation. It was written on a commission of the Schoenberg Ensemble of Amsterdam where it had its premiere on March 29, 1993. This is a vast collage from my various on compositions, having not a single new note. You see, I was fifty last birthday, hence the question: is it enough or not? In this case it is not even a play of words (if we take into consideration Bach's celebrated chorale quoted by Berg in his Violin Concerto), just a question addressed to himself. In conformity with the conception the use has been made of many ideas underlying my earlier opuses, with a great amount of dedications summing up all of them in the quoted pieces.

This composition may well be entitled in some other way to convey more authentically my message, say, "An Attempt at a Self-Portrait with the Untouched Ear" or, perhaps, "A Profile of the Baffled Biography."

. . . Summing up the experience accumulated over many years in overcoming the fear of facing a blank sheet of paper.

. . . Revising the absurd conceptions and unwise ideas implemented in the earlier compositions.

. . . Prologue and Epilogue with five principal movements in-between, each movement representing a spiral, a motion deep down and inward; with clots of "pure" music discernible behind the chaos and phantasmagoria of quasi-meaningless structures...

. . . And each clot-postlude is a quotation while the entire composition presents an endless postlude concluded by the tragicomical outcome:

— *Genug, es ist genug!*...

And yet, I don't like the idea that all my best pieces have already been written...

V.B.: And what pieces do you regard as your best accomplishments?

F. K.: These are certainly my *Sonata for Two Players*, then *Small Music of a Sad Night* dedicated to my daughter, and the Second Piano Sonata, written many years back, the first after my graduation from the conservatoire. There are some pieces that I have no wish to ever listen to, though at times I can look through their scores.

V. B.: What ideas do you entertain today?

F. K.: I hope to write *Es ist genug* without the question mark, it will be my last composition. Besides, I would like to write a Violin Concerto and dedicate it to the memory of my mother. But it will hardly be in the nearest future.

V. B.: Do you usually write guided by your own urge, or your writing depends on the commissions you get?

F. K: For the last few years I have been writing mainly on commission, but not more than one piece a year, which is, in my view, not so bad if you have a valuable idea for at least one composition.

V. B.: Now you live in Moscow but go on teaching composition at the Baku Conservatoire, don't you?

F. K.: From time to time I have to cover two thousand kilometers to get to my alma mater... In Moscow it was Edison Denisov who helped me very much. Once I received a letter from him; it was, as far as I remember, in 1987, in which he wrote that upon listening to one of my recorded compositions he got convinced that my music should be played in the West-European concert halls and that he would do all in his power to promote it. And he kept his word. Likewise did Alexander Ivashkin and the Soloists Ensemble directed by Alexander Lazarev, and Rauf Abdullayev, who started performing my compositions throughout the world.

Postlude

> ...es ist genug...
> ...ist est genug?..
> ...genug! es ist genug...
> ...genug or not genug?..
> ...that is the question...
> ...unanswered question...

Faraj Karayev was born in 1943 in Baku, graduating from the Baku Conservatoire (1966) and completing a postgraduate course there (1971), studying composition with his father, Kara Karayev. His works have been repeatedly performed within the programmes of major music undertakings, both at home and elsewhere, such as: the International Ballet Festival (Paris, 1966), the Soviet-American Festival "Making Music Together" (1988), within the framework of the Kara Karayev International Music Festival held under the motto "20th-Century Music" (Baku, 1988, 1990); "Almeida" (London, 1989), "New Beginnings" (Glasgow, 1989), "Alternative" (Moscow, 1989, 1990), the Prokofiev Festival (Duisburg, 1990–91), the Biennial in Berlin (1991), and the "Schönheit" — eine Utopie?" in Frankfurt (1991)

In 1979 Faraj Karayev set up the chamber orchestra at the operatic workshop of the Baku Conservatoire; since 1986 he has been Artistic Director of the Soloists Ensemble of the Azerbaijan State Symphony Orchestra. He has been one of the sponsors of the Kara Karayev International Music Festival.

Since 1966 Faraj Karayev has been teaching composition at his alma mater. He currently resides in Moscow.

PRINCIPAL WORKS

1965 Piano Sonata No. 1. 11'

1967 Piano Sonata No. 2. 8'
      Moscow: Sovetsky Kompozitor, 1982

1967 Concerto grosso in memory of Webern. 17'

1969 *The Shadows of Kobystan*, ballet in two acts, libretto by M. Mamedov and V. Yesman. 45' Melodia: M10 27271 004

1970 Suite from the ballet *The Shadows of Kobystan* for full symphony orchestra. 18'
      Moscow: Sovetsky Kompozitor, 1974

1971 *Kaleidoscope,* ballet in one act on themes of Scarlatti's sonatas, libretto by R. Akhundova and I. Dadashidze. 25'
      Suite from the ballet *Kaleidoscope* for small symphony orchestra. 18'

1974 Concerto for Piano and Chamber Orchestra. 26'

1975 *Morning of the Third Day (Orpheus and Eurydice),* opera in three acts, libretto by F. Karayev and O. Felzer after Jean Anouilh's play *Eurydice.* 120'

1976 *Sonata for Two Players* (two pianos, prepared piano, bells, vibraphone, magnetic tape). 45' Melodia: C10 15175 76

1978 *Journey to Love,* monodrama for soprano and Chamber orchestra, verses by 20th-century poets. 60'

1979 *La Quinta del Sordo (Goya),* symphony in three movements for boy's choir, mixed chorus and symphony orchestra, (written jointly with Kara Karayev). 21'
      Moscow: Sovetsky Kompozitor, 1984

1980 *Tristessa II,* symphony for full symphony and chamber orchestras. 38'

1982 *I Bade Farewell to Mozart on the Karlov Bridge in Prague,* serenade for full symphony orchestra. 24'
      Tristessa I (Parting Symphony) for chamber orchestra. 34'

1983 *The year 1791,* serenade for small symphony orchestra. 20'. Melodia: C10 22547 002
      Waiting for Godot, music for performance on the theatrical stage for four soloists and chamber ensemble after Samuel Beckett's drama. 41'

1984 *In memoriam....,* suite for string quartet dedicated to Alban Berg. 23'

1985 *... A Crumb of Music for George Crumb* for chamber ensemble. 18'

1986 *Waiting for Godot,* revised for four soloists and chamber orchestra

1987 *"1967–1987",* Piano Concerto No. 2 (after Kara Karayev's Violin Concerto). 23'
      Terminus for solo cello. 14'

1988 Chamber Concerto for five instruments (Wind Quintet). 25'

1989 *Small Music of a Sad Night* for chamber ensemble. 18' Four Postludes for symphony orchestra. 22'
      Alla Nostalgia (In Memory of Andrei Tarkovsky), chamber concerto for eight instrumentalists. 30'

1990   *The [Moz] art of elite* for symphony orchestra. 12′
       Postlude I for piano. 12′
       Postlude II (revised for piano, double-bass and string quartet)
       Aus . . ., three Fragments for bass clarinet and percussion. 15′
1991   *Der Stand der Dinge* for ensemble and magnetic tape. 35′
1992   *Postlude III* for two pianos eight hands. 12′
       Fifteen Minutes of Music for the Town of Forst for two pianos. 15′
1993   *Ist es genug?* for ensemble and magnetic tape. 35′
1993–1995 *Postludes IV–VI* for various ensembles.

The magic of Alexander Knaifel's message

Svetlana Savenko

Alexander Knaifel

Alexander Aronovich Knaifel was born on November 28, 1943 in Tashkent (Uzbekistan) where his parents, then students of the Leningrad Conservatoire, had been evacuated during the war. In September 1944 the family moved back to Leningrad. In 1950 Alexander Knaifel was admitted to the Central Music School at the Leningrad Conservatoire, finishing it in cello playing in 1961. During the period from 1961 to 1963 he studied cello with Mstislav Rostropovich at the Moscow Conservatoire, but had to give up playing because of a hand injury. In 1963 he entered the Leningrad Conservatoire where he studied composition with Boris Arapov, graduating in 1967. Worked as a teacher and music editor. He is married to the singer Tatiana Melentyeva, and they have a daughter and a grandson.

Alexander Knaifel's creative work may be in full justice ranked among the most singular phenomena in modern art, and it is owing not only to the composer's highly original language — the very matter of his music, but also its unique spirit — the conception, the atmosphere, the inner sense and message. Each of his mature works is intended not merely for performance but, first and foremost, for its accomplishment as a genuine existentialistic happening in a state of utmost concentration on the part of the interpretative artists and listeners. Knaifel's maximalism is certainly rooted in his avant-gardist quests, nevertheless, of no less importance in his following the traditions of Russian art with its high ethical and uncompromising spirit. One of the underlying ideas inherent in his work is the idea of a dialogue with the audience, but not in the conventional sense of "direct speech," nor as a sermon or public statement calling for immediate response. What he is doing may be more adequately defined as the creation of a *situation for a dialogue,* which in some mysterious way could kindle a spark of mutual understanding and in this case the listener would glimpse the innermost

* Партию литавр следует исполнять деревянными палочками.
* The kettle-drum part should be executed with the wooden sticks.

Ex. 1 *Two Pieces for Flute, Viola, Piano and Percussion Instruments*

message of an artistic utterance. "Beauty is a moment of burning, and only as a result of self-immolation the released energy may produce beauty"[1].

His first recital was given in 1974 in Leningrad, when the composer just turned thirty, moreover, the programme included the pieces written even earlier, at the age of nineteen to twenty-five, i.e. according to the conventional standards, these compositions could be regarded as still immature and raw. However, there was not a trace of

---

[1] Cited from: Alexander Knaifel. Auf der Suche. Ein Programmheft der Frankfurt Feste '92. Texte und Gespräch mit Alexander Knaifel von Tatjana Porwoll / Alte Oper Frankfurt. Hereinafter referred to as: Knaifel, 1992.

apprenticeship in them, quite the reverse, they revealed a chiselled style to be gained, as a rule, much later.

A retrospective appraisal of Alexander Knaifel's earlier compositions makes it possible to identify in them some intrinsic traits in his work. First of all, it is a powerful suggestive impact of his most plastic and laconic utterances, devoid of any ambiguity and verbosity, which are pardonable in a budding composer. Second, concrete features of his musical language such as cultivation of the rhythmics and a highly individual approach to timbre. "Rhythm for me is an essential, decisive component of musical material... But I treat rhythm in a broad sense — as form of motion and motion as form of life"[2]. In this respect the most illustrative example is his first of Two Pieces for flute, viola, piano and percussion, written when the composer was just nineteen. It is rhythmically based on a figure exposed by the viola in its first bar to be repeated persistently, i.e. *ostinato*, throughout this short piece to the accompaniment of other *ostinato* patterns-rolling of a side drum and the beating of kettled-drums and piano chords. Repeated only is the rhythmical figure like *talea* of isorhythmical motet; pitches have a self-contained structure asymmetrical to the rhythmical one and predetermined by a dodecaphonic series. The latter, however, is also treated as a kind of *ostinato*, since it is stated throughout the piece exclusively in one and the same pitch. But metrically the *ostinato* is not sustained, for the rhythmic pattern is constantly shifted within the perceptible units of measurement.

Another piece, *Musique militaire* for piano, written some time later, is based on free metrical accents. It has been notated without bar-lines, and the regularly repeated *ostinato* patterns are juxtaposed with the metrically unstable ones. In its tone *Musique militaire* is still more homogeneous than the above mentioned piece for an ensemble of instrumentalists, owing to the specifics of its basic twelve-note series consisting exclusively of major and minor thirds. These two traits-structured rhythmics and the use of few tones, at times up to the point of asceticism, — are characteristic of Alexander Knaifel's other compositions written also in the 1960s, including his crowning achievement of this period — *Monody* for female voice.

Monody was set to the verses by George Buchanan, a Scottish humanist poet, who provided the Latin version of Psalm 22, a prayer to be read at the times of trial. "A fighter against Catholicism, Buchanan wrote his verses while he was in the grips of the Inquisition, and this detail from his biography turns a poetical text into a documentary evidence"[3]. The existentialistic essence of the situation has been depicted by the composer with rare authenticity: the scenic expressiveness of every detail is combined with a strict selection of sound elements. These are simple and ritualistically clear-cut: psalmody-like recitative, modal cantilena-like phrases, *glissandi* descending in quarter-tones (akin to excessive *lamento*), and wide skips, sometimes embracing two

---

[2] Cited from: Alexander Knaifel. In: Fünfzig sowjetische Komponisten. Fakten und Reflexionen. Eine Dokumentation von Hannelore Gerlach. Ed. Peters, Leipzig/Dresden, 1984. Hereinafter referred to as: Knaifel, 1984.

[3] Tatiana Voronina and Boris Katz. A Profile of the Composer. Sovetskaya Muzyka magazine, 1975, Issue 4, p. 53.

octaves. The metric freedom of a monologue, prevailing in the first two sections, is replaced by a rigid *ostinato* pattern in the finale, which accentuates the variations of the repeated phrase from the verses.

The monody of the concluding section is multifaceted in its inner structure owing to the intrusions of the expressive elements from the preceding sections of the composition. A clash of the possessed *ostinato* "rubbing in" with the increasingly tense, texturally augmented and accelerated quarter-tone *glissando* makes the voice resound at its utmost mounting intensity to be broken at the culmination point.

Alexander Knaifel's *Lamento* for solo cello may be regarded as a kind of paired sequel to *Monody*. This piece dedicated to the memory of Leonid Yakobson, a remarkable choreographer, with whom the composer was closely associated in his creative work, is also built up on an alternation of contrasting sections in the vein of toccata, recitative and chorale. However, the dynamic "profile" of *Lamento* is quite reverse: the music moves from the spasmodical toccata-like initial *ostinato* to the expressive chromatic overtones and then to the doleful chorale-like aloofness imitating quite authentically the sounds of the Orthodox liturgy (the cellist delivers the middle voice of triadic chords through the closed lips, which enhances its "chorale-like" timbre).

As regards the most exacting demands set before the soloists, *Monody* and *Lamento* are akin to the avant-gardist virtuosic pieces in the spirit of Luciano Berio's *Sequenza*. Alexander Knaifel uses the widest possible range of sound production devices, including quite uncommon ones: for instance, in the middle section of *Lamento* the cellist is prescribed to play separate notes by tapping on the strings by the fingers of his left hand (*senza arco e non pizz.*). But these novel virtuosic techniques involve neither timbre alienation nor the violation or overcoming of the customary expressive "roles" usually assigned to the voice and particular instruments, which are intrinsic in the avant-gardist virtuosity. Quite the reverse, Knaifel stresses and places an expressionistic focus on the natural qualities of vocal and instrumental intoning to render the concrete, almost programmatic, messages of his compositions. To all appearances, the invention of new sonorities for coloristic effects seemed hardly to attract the composer even in his early endeavors. Later on he spoke about timbre as "a most effective means of form-building," implying his "striving to lend a certain timbre its symbolic meaning" (Knaifel, 1984).

His contacts with operatic and ballet art proved very important in the early period of Alexander Knaifel's creative career. He wrote his most known composition in this line when he was still a conservatoire student. It was the opera *The Canterville Ghost* after Oscar Wilde (there is also its abridged version for two soloists and chamber orchestra). This opera still promising to become truly popular some day abounds in humor and youthful ardor, telling the story of the ill-starred ghost inhabiting an old castle. It is tackled in an ironical and grotesque spirit inherent both in the scenic action and the opera's musical language. A noticeable feature is a parody of hackneyed genre situations as regards separate details in musical characteristics and the whole items (the aria of revenge, a ballade). The palette of timbres in this opera is most inventive, for instance, the xylophone and the tuba engaged in a dialogue with the singer's voice act as doubles and "partners" to the part of the Ghost. The comical and the lyrical are closely intertwined in this opera devoid of any straight forwardness and too simple dramatic solutions. It primarily concerns its main protagonist: the Canterville Ghost looks not just ridiculous and absurd, but rather touching at the same time, appearing somewhat like a Don-Quixote, especially in the "duet" version of the opera justifiably defined by the composer as "romantic scenes." The serious understatement of the action unfolding on the stage is best exposed by the orchestra; the culmination episode is delivered by the organ's passacaglia acting the part of the composer's commentary (existing also as a self-contained piece).

By the late 1960s direct contacts with the musical theatre were superseded in Knaifel's artistic quests by more indirect, mediated and individual ones. There arose so called "genre modulations," which is most evident in his composition that was destined to become a milestone in his creative career. He started writing it in 1970, and it took him eight years to complete it. In its final version it was entitled *Joan, passione for 13 groups of instruments (56 soloists)*. The composer makes a point of this work lasting for an hour and a half and first performed only in 1992: "It may be said that every single note in *Joan* has been paid for by my own blood" (Knaifel, 1992). Originally, it had been conceived as a choreographic piece for a ballerina, with its plot associated with the French heroine Jeanne d'Arc. In June 1970, Knaifel completed its first movement. When in 1975, after a five-year break, the composer resumed his work on *Joan*, it turned into a purely instrumental piece, though its subtitle *passione*, no doubt, retains its association with the initial conception. "Joan of Arc's Passions" with their concrete developments transform into a mystery of sounds to be experienced in some symbolic space remote from any plot line. Beginning with *Joan*, Knaifel evolved a new, highly individual style to be cultivated ever since, with most of his works bearing the hallmarks of conceptualism — the creation of a certain unique existentialistic situation to be actualized through the seemingly quite conventional instrumental playing or singing.

Alexander Knaifel regards *Joan* as his major work also because it gave rise to his idea of number, which turned out to be extremely important in his creative work. He had hit on it purely by intuition, and this idea has acquired the dimensions of the rational organizing principle. "In my view, the decisive factor in the structural organization of a composition and its realization belongs to the number as an abstract universal model intimately associated with the art of music. My basic constructive principle is the principle of relationship... Various numerical relationships provide for a simple but universal model of development" (Knaifel, 1984). Any relevant parallels with the numerical systems inherent in serialism could be assumed only as a purely outward, limited analogy: "Dodecaphony constitutes merely a particular case of its relationship to the number. I fail to understand why it is precisely twelve notes that should make a basis for any composition?" (Ibidem). The similarity of such approach with the tradition of Pythagoreanism, which is currently revived in modern art not by Knaifel alone, is more essential. Nevertheless, we should underline the spontaneity with which this idea of numbers had taken shape in the composer's mind: it arose not as a result of his erudition but rather as a manifestation of his "genetical memory." The number for Knaifel, as in the archaic mythological poetical systems, symbolizes its inner semantics, a qualitative characteristic latently intrinsic in it, which may be disclosed in the most varied and heterogeneous elements of a composition such as pitch, rhythm, the structure of a whole and its parts, the cast and disposition of performers, the manner of their conduct on the stage, and the like. This kind of creative thinking is apparently to be rooted in the philosophical and psychological underpinnings of a rare endowment for intuitive grasping of the cosmic relationship between being and the symbolic essence of phenomena appearing quite ordinary and common at first sight. All things are interrelated and significant: "...one should be aware that the intricate innermost sensations which are hard to express coincide with the simplest situations in life" (Knaifel, 1984). Another outcome of such notions is the ascetic elementary nature of musical material which should not by its too excessive concreteness and variety "diverge" one's attention from the symbolic meaning of universal concepts. His musical units are not just simple but there are few of them, too: since his *Joan* Knaifel's music has been distinguished for the prevalence of one-or two-part writing, restrained dynamics, and prolonged sustainment of one and the same register.

From the viewpoint of compositional techniques a numerical structure is of primary importance for the composer: "Until I find a key number or definitive number order I cannot start composing" (Knaifel, 1992). "A numerical structure is already a composition, but at the same time it is its framework. A structure may be filled in with 'flesh and blood', something intuitive, improvisatory, spontaneous, something beyond one's conscious control. In this way there arises 'a second composition'. The first one is some definite law, not to deprive you of the freedom of breathing, but quite the reverse, providing for a chance of living. Such method excludes following certain chords, timbres, turns of melody (no matter how good they may be in their own right), it forces you to follow the course of a musical idea" (Knaifel, 1984). Presumably, the composer's numerical system emerged as a result of the evolution of his innate sense of rhythm in its broadest meaning mentioned above. Numerical proportions, also in the broad sense, serve to manifest the inner and external order, this is "mathematics becoming an art that allows to apprehend the world..." (Knaifel, 1992).

In his music Knaifel employs some other elements, too, for example, letters, in their symbolic and ranking meaning. Thus, his piece *Ainana*, subtitled as "Seventeen Variations on a Name," is based on the numerical series 3, 2, 1, which corresponds to the three letters "a," two "n" and one "i" making up this exotic Chukcha name; his chamber miniature *Da (Yes)*, based on the conjugated concord of the notes *d-a*, presents, according to the composer, a kind of manifesto asserting the idea of two-fold unity. And in general, Knaifel attaches major importance to the titles of his pieces, invariably as individualistic as the composition an integral part of which they make.

Naturally enough, the concrete form of numerical proportion fails to be discerned by the listener; what is most important to the composer is the general sensation of the idea of order, the proportional and symmetrical nature of separate parts in his compositions. At the same time, as the classical composers, he is well aware that the precise symmetry is dead: "symmetry always involves, in my view, some deviations like in a human body" (Knaifel, 1992). The inner spontaneous growth of musical matter, similar to a biological process, is no less important to the composer than a strictly calculated structure.

Some features of the sound organization, characteristic of Knaifel's mature style, can be illustrated by his short piece *Vera* for string orchestra (14, 12, 10, 10, 9 plus two harps and harpsichord). This composition was dedicated to the memory of Vera Komissarzhevskaya, the legendary Russian actress, and its title, as in the case of his piece *Da*, is also polysemantic: in the name of the addressee (translated into English as "Faith") the composer stresses the deep-going understatement of his opus.

The general compositional idea of this piece marked for its singular purity and elevation inherent in the classicist art of St. Petersburg is disclosed in its subtitle: "Variations and a Stanza of Dedication." Its movements are presented in the following free symmetrical order:

1. Prelude
2. Chorale One
3. Interlude One
4. Monologue One
5. Interlude Two
6. Interlude three
7. Monologue Two
8. Monologue Three
9. Chorale Two
10. Postlude
    A Stanza of Dedication

As we can see, there are eleven movements which, together with the dedicatory strophe, actually make up a variational cycle, though treated in a most unusual way. The theme in the form of the cellos' monodic line emerges only in the eighth movement, Monologue Three, i.e. at the point of golden section. The previous monologues (Movements 4 and 7) are also "quasi-themes" owing to their sparse accompaniment and detailed instrumental exposition (*tutti* of first violins in the fourth movement and solo violin playing in the seventh one). The chorales are also akin, being fully identical in their pitch organization: both representing harmonization of the theme placed in the bass by triads, mainly in the minor key (Chorale Two, however, presented in a much denser statement). In contrast to the melodic texture of the monologues and the homophony of the chorales, the interludes are based on the "diagonal" texture — the instruments canonically joining in one after another, in Interlude One at the note $E_\flat{}^1$, in Interlude Three — in succession (though, not in mechanically precise order, but with departures) and intoning the sounds of the theme.

Interlude Two is interrelated with the framing (Prelude and Postlude) and in a certain way it makes the axis of symmetry in the entire composition.

The above discussion is certainly enough to reveal the well-thought-over architectonics of this refined piece. However, there is something else: like a sculpture or a temple, it rests on the rigid framework of numerical correlations based on the numbers 6 and 11. Let us point out some of the most striking indications: the theme comprises 66 notes; in Prelude it falls into separate phrases — four with 6 notes each, and four with 11 notes each (in a sum total it makes 68 notes because of two notes being repeated, but the composition of the groups is more important to the composer in this case than their precise sum). Each chorale consists of 6 phrases, each comprising 11 notes; in the central, third, interlude the theme is divided into segments of unequal length (by the number of notes): 6 8 7 5 10 1 9 4 3 2 11 and, as we can see, the number of these segments also makes 11, framed by the same key figures. The rationalistic nature of such system is obvious; however, it no less evident that its concrete version is composed every time anew, almost without any preconceived data, parameters and methods of calculation to roam from one opus to another. The framework is shrouded in the composition itself, making its secret, and the listener perceives only its outcome, in the same way as a passer-by fails to think about the mathematical laws of proportions when he stops in admiration at the Palace Square in St. Petersburg.

Against the background of rationalistic systems gaining ground in 20-th century art Knaifel's method looks quite typical and, yet, it is highly singular. Most probably, its singularity is due to the coexistence of calculation and intuition: the numerical structure, a "first composition," leaves much room for a "second composition" — free individualization of the concrete soundscape. These two aspects of a creative process make up, paradoxically enough, an indissoluble intricate unity, and the composer is not inclined to exaggerate either of them. Each creative undertaking invariably involves a risk, with each new opus taking shape under the imminent danger of failing to be realized and accomplished. "An abstract law-governed regularity gives rise to an organic, sensorily perceived life" (Knaifel, 1992).

The composition of music, as a priestly art in the ancient times, turns out to be an esoteric occupation and a metier for the initiated. However Knaifel is by no means an advocate of an elitist art, for each person is free to enter into a dialogue with a composition and unravel its existentialistic mystery in the same way as one unveils the riddles of being. But the cherished knowledge cannot be shared directly, being accessible exclusively through figurative expression and indirect allusions. The listener has to be worthy of an opus.

. . . "The musical material as it were ceases to be important any longer, with the chief point staying beyond the musical texture. Its organization is at times misleading since it calls to mind the deceptively familiar structures." In these terms Knaifel wrote about Shostakovich's last quartet[4], but these words may be virtually referred to his own work as well. Indeed, his compositions may be described as "misleading," though on the outward they do not seem to discard the traditional forms of music-making, easily blending with the customary concert ritual. Take, for instance, *A Silly Horse*, written in 1981, with its subtitle reading as follows: "Fifteen Tales for a Singer (Female) and a Pianist (Male)".

This song-cycle was set to the verses by Vadim Levin, a talented poet and translator, famous for his highly successful adaptation of the popular English child's rhymes; his book *A Silly Horse* had become a favorite with at least two generations of Russian children and their parents. It also attracted the composers who repeatedly wrote songs and choruses set to Vadim Levin's verses, intended for little performers and their audiences. Alexander Knaifel's cycle looks like children's music, too: outwardly, it is simple and transparent, captivating the child audiences by its theatrical liveliness and unexpected twists of plots. However it is just the external layer.

A more attentive ear would reveal in this music some peculiarities, primarily in treating the text. On the one hand, its meaning seems not to be distorted anywhere,

---

[4] Alexander Knaifel. "And the truth like a star sparkled in the night sky" / Sovetskaya Muzyka, 1975, Issue 11, p. 78.

being distinctly intoned and sometimes nearly depicted by the music. On the other hand, the ordinary and even habitual characters and situations seem to be quite often shifted into paradoxical dimensions governed by quite different laws. *A Silly Horse* is essentially traditional music that found itself in Wonderland seen by Alice through the mirror. Many of the composer's findings in this piece are rooted in his fine understanding of the British eccentricity keeping its balance on the verge between the real and the imaginable. "The British mind is very close to me. When I visited Great Britain I came to understand why traditions are so strong there. People resist any change over there. And since nothing changes, there is chance to retain one's inner freedom" (Knaifel, 1992).

The idea of paradox determines virtually all the specific features of the music in *A Silly Horse*. All begins with the first piece telling "A Simple Story" about a little puppy who had trotted down the street until he grew into a big pooch. However it is not just "a piece of information" to be learned: multiple repetition of the word "trotted", the weightiness of each note, the magnitude of the "ringing" rests in the ascetic texture of this music makes the listener physically experience the seemingly real time unfolding in this story.

This sensation is still more perceptible in the second story, "The Chest," telling about a dispute between two stubborn characters, the Gobbler and the Cow, and treated by the composer as a collision of perpetual expectation. The piano sounds here as a gentle magic casket with the "endless" winding mechanism, with the enchanted singer drinking in the sounds coming from it. And in each subsequent story the composer identifies its understatement, the hidden existentialistic message. The dramatic center of the cycle is the story about Joe More, an odd fellow who took upon himself to teach a goat to sing the notes at sight and who was very fond of stewed fruit, quite a "harmless" poem treated as a scene of violence full of convulsions and hysterics. The tragic mental and physical exhaustion is felt in the piece crowning the entire cycle, "A Sad Song About an Elephant," with an almost complete predominance of the monotonous, slowed down recitation at a single note. The childishly naive, ingenuous pieces, as a matter of fact, embody the archetypes of human existence with its vortex of births and deaths, carefree comforts and dramatic life experiences, joyous vigor and doleful paralysis. And in this context the composer's seemingly mysterious definition of *A Silly Horse* as a symphony in six movements becomes quite understandable and justifiable. The philosophical genre is shrouded somewhere in the depths of a composition reflecting its true meaning which, however, may exist exclusively as the submerged part of an iceberg, as a commenting allusion. Upon its exposure to the surface, it loses its meaning.

The stylistics of *A Silly Horse* are also paradoxical. Its musical texture is extremely sparse but not at all simple. Brief tunes in fourths and fifths, recitatives at one and the same pitch, and separate sounds of the piano are presented in a context of chromatic structures and refined variations in metre and rhythm. The precisely gradated rests are particularly significant. The composer makes use of diverse noise elements, including, in addition to the more conventional ones such as tapping on the piano, the beating on the pedal (as a culmination point), tongue-clicking to imitate temple-blocks, "hand whispering" (rhythmically precise rubbing of palms, one against the other), whistling the pianist's singing, and the like. The noises enhance the theatrical effect which is quite essential in the cycle, though not too excessive. All the factors pertaining to musical sounds, noises, and scenic action are reduced here to the seemingly authentic "elementary units" neutral in their style and devoid of any individuality. For one could hardly trace the origins of the recitative or progressions in triads. To all appearances, Alexander Knaifel in this piece, as in his other mature compositions, was primarily striving for a musical language purified of concrete stylistic coloring and the transient associations. In this respect his music may be treated as belonging to the minimalist phenomenon. However there are some substantial differences. First, Knaifel's style is not at all characterized by, and in some respects even opposed to, the repetitive technique; by the discrete nature of its musical texture and the significance attached to the rests his style may be only reminiscent of Morton Feldman's. Second, for all the "elementary" nature of musical units, his compositions are highly individual as regards their conception. The chimeric infatuation of some contemporary artists with "anonymous" writing is viewed by Knaifel as "the worst trend in art": "For me each piece of music is the most concrete crystallization of my own destiny and my personality... A composition should be marked by a specific tone..." (Knaifel, 1992).

The composer's conceptual daring achieves its utmost manifestation in his two opuses written in the mid-eighties: *Nika* and *Agnus Dei*. It is noteworthy that in both cases Knaifel gives up providing for the genre definitions, even most unconventional ones. Another unusual feature of these compositions in their duration (140' and 120' respectively) combined with the specific organization of time, which suggests a feeling of extreme retardation of the musical process. In his letter sent to Pierre Boulez on October 29, 1992 Knaifel wrote about his *Nika* as a composition which "by all external parameters could be hardly integrated into the current musical practices" (Knaifel, 1992).

The conception of *Nika* arose from "a desperate and bold attempt to enter into a dialogue with Heraclitus of Ephesus" (from the above cited letter). An excerpt from Heraclitus' treatise *On Nature* makes up the content of this composition. This text in Old Greek is "uttered" by an unusual ensemble of seventeen "sphinxes"-instruments mumbling and whispering; with each sound produced meaning a word. In the primordial galactic "noise of Creation" there gradually emerges a motion leading to the formation of the earthly world, mankind and human individuality. And the instrumental wealth of sounds gradually gives birth to a voice — the phrase uttered by the little poetess Nika Turbina "It is not me who writes my verses" making the basis of the finale. "I have discovered number in *Joan*, and word — in *Nika*..." (Knaifel, 1992). One of Knaifel's most complicated conceptions, his *Nika* epitomizes the idea of cosmos in a paradoxical unity of all the existent — divine, natural and human entities of the world. The voice of individuality resounding in the finale carries the memory of its origins.

The life of a word becomes the core of the composition in *Nika*. But its conceptual, substantive aspect is not the sole one here, moreover, it is relegated into the background and overcome by its symbolic, "liturgical" meaning, according to the composer. (By the way, in this respect its similarity with the "unassuming" *A Silly Horse* is easily observable.) The word may at times go deep down into a composition to form its inaudible but the most vital layer, a kind of inner tuning-fork for the entire work.

To this category belongs his large-scale opus *Agnus Dei* for four instrumentalists a cappella (1985).

This composition arose from quite a conventional commission to write a work for the musical theatre based on the short novel *Agnus Dei* by Francisko Tanzer, a modern German poet and prose-writer. Eventually nothing remained from this project save for its title and the inner theme of the work dedicated by the composer to "the memory of all who died, were killed and tortured to death in all past wars." On the face of it, such orientation puts down this composition within a range of anti-war conceptions quite developed and habitual in Soviet music. However, it seems so only at first glance, for the socio-historical, genre and any other concrete characteristics are fully dissociated from it. As a matter of fact, the composer makes an attempt to create an authentic ritual which would be similar in its function, and not only thematically, to a funeral rite — not to any specific one (Catholic or Orthodox) but rather its archetypical model. The universal character of this conception is stressed by a selection of texts inscribed into the score and intended for the musicians "to sing them in their minds" (these texts may be also read aloud before the performance or placed in the programme as a commentary to a concert). These texts include an excerpt from the diary of Tanya Savicheva, an eleven-year-old girl who died of hunger with all her family in besieged Leningrad; the Latin prayer "Agnus Dei" combining the versions of the Catholic mass and a requiem; the ancient Greek formula soma-sema (the body-the grave), and Jesus Christ's last words on the cross "It is accomplished" (The Gospel According to St. John, 19:30). The textual layer remains outside the musical embodiment, and not this layer alone: you have an impression that the composer in his *Agnus Dei* discards all sounds of life, plunging the listener into an experience of pure existentialistic time on the other side of being. The musical tone (the motto theme, melody, and harmony) appears to be "involuted" into a note, mainly it is a single note, with two notes running, or all the more so, sounding simultaneously looking like quite a happening here; the musical rhythm being transformed into a pure extent and duration of a note or a rest; with the changes in timbre and register becoming in this context the principal means for unfolding the musical material and, as a result, this composition lasting for two hours seems to be absolutely static. It is timbre and register (*Agnus Dei* involves the use of a piano, an electric organ, a harpsichord, a saxophone, a double-bass, a large set of percussion instruments, a synthesizer, and magnetic tape) that remain the main resource for conveying the traditional expressiveness, or to be more precise, its shadows discerned in the ascetic semantics of descension and ascension, in the cooly resigned clanging of the chimebells, the hollow beating of tam-tam, and the unbelievably low, as if coming up from an abyss, sounds of the synthesizer. This funeral ritual is devoid of either tears or consolation — it takes place sub specie mortis. In the earthly life among the living there is neither such time counting when separate sounds are hanging in the air as if deprived of terrestrial attraction, nor such slow motions which the musicians, action as a cappella chorus, are prescribed to make while being engaged in this solemn performance.

Agnus Dei, Joan and *Nika*, calls for exceptional concentration on the part of the listeners. The composer is fully aware of this fact: "Frankly speaking, I feel that my time has not come yet. But there is still another problem: perhaps, it is never to come..." (Knaifel, 1992). Indeed, this problem does exist. The elitist nature of his endeavors (though, unintentionally) makes part and parcel of Alexander Knaifel's creative work. Of course, with a passage of time the situation may become not so acute, but it would hardly change fundamentally. Yet, it is needless to say how important is such music in the present-day cultural context. Like the ancient hermetic teachings, it deepens the perspective of man's self-awareness, offering scope for a fundamentally new artistic experience.

It is not an easy task to discuss the stylistic context of Alexander Knaifel's creative work, its roots, and parallels with the other phenomena. In contrast to his early compositions in which some influences can be clearly discerned — the most powerful of them, undoubtedly, being that of Shostakovich, later on these become not so obvious materially, getting more and more generalized and typological. The conceptual cosmos of Knaifel's mature compositions, on the one hand, involves the avant-gardist aesthetics of the "uniqueness" of an opus and its law; on the other hand, it could be traced back to the monumental symphonic "pictures of the world" inherent in the late Romantic period and once more in Shostakovich's style, despite all dissimilarity in the material actualization. Alexander Knaifel's daring and uncompromising spirit reveals in him an adherent of the Russian artistic tradition, especially as regards Russian literature and philosophy. Neither does Knaifel seem to stand alone among his contemporary composers. The stylistic purity and aloofness from the musical "daily occurrences" bring him close to Xenakis or Boulez, while his asceticism and the inner "liturgical" nature of his creative work are akin to Arvo Pärt's style. Neither does Stockhausen's prophetic maximalism seem to be alien to him altogether, again for all contrasts in their stylistics orientations. As for minimalism, it has already been mentioned. One could hardly resist the temptation to "inscribe" Knaifel within the framework of "new simplicity" because, as far as this trend is concerned, there arise not just typological, but also stylistic parallels since, as mentioned above, Knaifel exhibits, quite conspicuously, his striving to severely limit the "vocabulary" of his music. However in contrast to "new simplicity," Knaifel's "elementary units" have no historical correlations, being unprecedented as regards the styles of the past, and in their ultimate manifestation they can be traced back to nothing else but the proto-forms and proto-tones, though not archaic but independent of the conventionalities of time and location. Knaifel's artistic thinking, again in contrast to that of Luciano Berio, Valentin Silvestrov, Alfred Schnittke and some others among his contemporaries, is not historical but rather metaphysical. The cultural layers should be reduced to a minimum or even removed altogether to make it possible for the listeners to comprehend the existentialistic, symbolic meaning of the sound elements. Herein lies the hidden spirit of Alexander Knaifel's art devoid of any pathetic spirit and unique in its own way.

PRINCIPAL WORKS

Musical Theatre

1964–65   *Aspiration*, ballet-symphony in two acts. Libretto by Yuri Stankevich and Alexander Knaifel. MSS piano and full scores. 60'

1965–66   *The Canterville Ghost*, opera in three acts with a prologue, for soloists and chamber orchestra. Libretto by Tatiana Kramarova after Oscar Wilde's like-named story. MSS vocal and full scores. 90'

1966   *Disarmament*, choreographic strip-tease. Libretto by Leonid Yakobson on the subject of Herluf Bidstrup's cartoons. MSS piano and full scores. 5'

1967   *Magdalene Repentant*, choreographic scene. Libretto by Leonid Yakobson on the subject of works by Titian and Rodin. MSS piano and full scores. 10'

1968   *Medea (A Colchis Sorceress)*, ballet in two acts. Libretto by Georgy Alexidze. Score. Moscow / Leningrad: Sovetsky Kompozitor Publishers, 1988. 35'

Vocal-Symphonic Works

1962   *Fling It Into My Garden*. Fugato for symphony orchestra and mixed chorus. Text by Herve Bazin. MS score. 2'

1965   *The Canterville Ghost*, Romantic scenes for two soloists (low bass and soft soprano) and chamber orchestra. Libretto by Tatiana Kramarova after Oscar Wilde. English text by V. Paperno. Score. Moscow / Leningrad: Sovetsky Kompozitor, 1977. 45'

1966   *150,000,000*, dithyramb for mixed chorus, six piccolos, six trumpets, six trombones, twelve double-basses and three groups of kettledrums, set to Vladimir Mayakovsky's like-named poem. MS piano score. 12'

1967   *Petrograd Sparrows*, suite-phantasmagoria for boys' choir and chamber orchestra. Text by B. Semyonov. Score. Moscow / Leningrad: Sovetsky Kompozitor, 1981. 35'

1969   *Argumentum de jure, Lenin's Letter to the Central Committee Members*, in unisons of bass chorus and eleven-voice symphony orchestra, MSS piano and full score. 10'

1979   *Early Cranes*, farewell music in twelve minor keys for symphony orchestra and two choirs (male and boys'). MS score. 20'

1982   *A Chance Occurrence* for mixed chorus, string orchestra, organ and girl-soloist. Text by Tadeusz Sliwiack, Russ. translation by Vadim Levin. MS score. 90'

1982   *Pagan rock* for bass chorus, percussion and rock group, MS score. 8'

1982   *In Twice-Two Mirrors* for two instrumental ensembles and two choirs (male and boys'). MS score. 13'

1984   *Opposition*, suite-memoria for full symphony orchestra and bass chorus. MS score. 20'

1986   *A Serf's Wings*, vocal-choreographic fresco for mixed chorus and instrumental ensemble after David Samoilov's like-named poem. MS score. 13'

Works for Orchestra

1963   *Burlesque* for trombone and string orchestra. MSS piano and full scores. 3'

1963	*Dream,* fantasia for chamber orchestra. MS score. 8'
1964	*131* for viola, double-bass, wind and percussion instruments. MS score. 9'
1965	*Seeking for the City of the Future,* two fragments for full string orchestra, percussion ensemble and organ. MS score. 25'
1970–78	*Joan,* passione for thirteen groups of instruments (56 soloists). MS score. 80'
1980	*Vera,* Variations and a stanza of dedication for string orchestra. Score Moscow/Leningrad: Sovetsky Kompozitor, 1990. 25'
1980	*The Storm Petrel's Call* for trumpet (trumpets), piano and orchestra, MS score. 3'
1987	*Madness,* white music for chamber orchestra, after Kornei Chukovsky, Gustav Mahler, Fyodor Tyutchev and Anna Akhmatova. MS score. 33'
1988	*Litania* for orchestra. MS score. 35'
1991	*Voznosheniye (The Holy Oblation)* for chorus of stringed instruments. MS score. 60'

Chamber Instrumental Music

1961	Small Piano sonata. MS. 9'
1962	*Diad* (two pieces) for flute, viola, piano and percussion. Score. Moscow/Leningrad: Sovetsky Kompozitor, 1975. 7'
1963	*Confession* for recitalist and percussion ensemble. MS score. 8'
1963	*Classic Suite for Piano.* Moscow/Leningrad: Muzyka, 1976 (in: Modern Composers for the Young, Issue 2). 11'
1964	*Ostinati* for violin and cello. MS. 7'
1964	*Musique militaire* for piano: Moscow/Leningrad: Sovestsky Kompozitor, 1974. 4'
1965	*Passacaglia* for organ. Hamburg, Hans Sikorski, 1990. 10'
1967	*Lamento* for solo cello. Moscow/Leningrad: Sovetsky Kompozitor, 1979; St. Petersburg, Kompozitor, 1992 (2nd version). 14'
1967	*Tournament Music* for soprano, piccolo clarinet, trumpet, bassoon, harp and piano. Moscow/Leningrad: Sovetsky Kompozitor, 1976 (in: Pieces by Leningrad Composers for French Horn and Piano; the version for French horn and piano). 1'
1967	*Tertium non datur* for harpsichord. Hamburg, Hans Sikorski, 1990. 1'
1969–71	*Constanta* for French horn and six percussion groups. 21'
1972	*A prima vista* for five percussion groups (four players). MS score. Free duration
1980	*Rafferti,* suite for jazz ensemble. MS score. 10'
1980	*A Stannza of Dedication* for soprano, harp and organ. MS. 3'
1980	*Solaris,* fragment of *canticum eternum* for 35 Javanese gongs. MS score. 13'
1980	*DA (Yes),* composition for an ensemble of soloists. Score. Hamburg, Hans Sikorski, 1980; Moscow, Muzyka, 1991. 15'
1983–84	*Nika* in 72 fragments by seventeen performers. MS score. 140'
1985	*Agnus Dei* for four instrumentalists a cappella. MS score. 120'
1992	*In a Half-Conscious State,* Postlude in memory of Mikhail G. Orlovsky. MS. 12'
1991–92	*Once More on Hypothesis* in a dialogue with J.S. Bach's Prelude and Fugue [WTK, I-22 (in B-flat minor)] for an ensemble of soloists. MS score. 21'

1992	*Jacob's Ladder (Scalae Iacobis), glossolalia* of thirteen. MS score. 42'
1993	*Cantus (from Silence to Darkness)* for percussion and a distant piano. MS score 33'
1995	*Psalm 51* for solo cello. MS. 23'

Chamber Vocal Pieces

1963	*A Song of Robert Burns* for baritone and piano. Russ. translation by Samuil Marshak. MS. 2'
1964	*In Memory of Samuil Marshak*, six lyrical epigrams to verses by Samuil Marshak, for baritone (high bass) and piano. Moscow/Leningrad: Sovetsky Kompozitor, 1971. 9'
1968	*Monody* for female voice. Latin text by George Buchanan. MS. 14'
1981	*A Silly Horse*, fifteen tales for a singer (female) and a pianist (male). Texts by Vadim Levin, English version by Faina Solasko. Moscow/Leningrad: Sovetsky Kompozitor, 1985. 70'
1988	*Through a Rainbow of Involuntary Tears*, trio for female singer and cellist. Verses by Anna Akhmatova and Fyodor Tyutchev. MS. 100'
1991	*Svete Tikhij (O Gladsome Radiance)*, Song of Saint Mary, the Mother of God for Tatiana Melentyeva. MS. 30'
1995	*Amicta sole* (a woman closed with the Sun) for soloist (female) of soloists, MS score. 30–35'

Choral Works

1964	*Five Poems of Mikhail Lermontov* for a cappella mixed chorus. Score. Moscow/Leningrad: Sovetsky Kompozitor, 1978. 10'
1964	*The Angel*, a setting of Mikhail Lermontov for a cappella mixed chorus. MS score. 4'
1964	*On Foolishness* in chorus and fugue. MS score. 2'
1973–75	*Status nascendi* for three groups of performers. MS score. 7–8'
1978	*Ainana*, seventeen variations on a name for chamber choir, percussion and tape. MS score. 45'
1985	*GOD*, Gavriil Derzhavin's ode for two choruses (mixed and children's). MS score. 60'
1993	*Chapter Eight, canticum canticorum* for temple, choruses (four) and cello. MS score. 96'

Incidental Scores to Films, Plays and TV Programmes, Music for Children Recordings

A Silly Horse, fifteen tales for a singer (female) and a pianist (male). Released by Melodia Recording Company, Moscow, 1988. A10-00377-004

Monody for female voice. Released by Le Chant du Monde. Anthologie de la mélodie russe et soviétique, Paris, 1990. LDC 278972/73

The Canterville Ghost, opera for soloists and chamber orchestra. Le Chant du Monde, Paris, 1991. LDC 288009

Lamento for solo cello. Le Chant du Monde. Oeuvres du XXe siècle pour violoncelle seul, Paris, 1991. CDM/LDC 2781059

Secrets of the moscow composition school in Vladislav Shoot's "pure music"

Valentina Kholopova

Vladislav Shoot

As the struggle was going on in the USSR for recognition and the legal status of the greatest composers from the generation of the sixties, primarily the three of them residing in Moscow — Alfred Schnittke, Edison Denisov and Sophia Gubaidulina, all the meanwhile their junior colleagues were staying far in the shade, waiting modestly and of their own free will in the wings for the time to come when they could get their share of the public notice. And since this struggle for the above mentioned greatest names had lasted for nearly three decades, up to the 1990s, their time came too late, with the best years of their creative lives spent in utter oblivion. Vladislav Shoot, a composer from Moscow, was one among those who had deemed it impossible for himself to go ahead of his highly esteemed senior friends and who seemed even to resign himself to his unlucky lot.

By the early 1990s there remained no trace in Russia of any bans imposed on modern music, which had been the invariable policy of the Communist Party in the artistic matters in the Soviet state. Nevertheless, the name of Vladislav Shoot, who ranked along with the names of Dmitry Smirnov, Yelena Firsova, Alexander Vustin and other composers of his generation, still remained overshadowed. It may be explained by the very character of his creative and his personal traits.

In his creative quests Vladislav Shoot has not been following the avant-gardist trend: he is neither inclined to strike the listeners with any challenging findings, nor to shock them with any spectacular extravagance, not to make sacrifices of the acknowledged musical values. Neither does he belong to those staunch "right-wing" composers who drag the musical language inherent in the 18th and 19th centuries into the 21st century. He is rather a "centrist," being vitally interested in the fundamental, stable and invaluable trends in 20th-century music. This interest may be well compared to Brahms orientations in 19th-century music. Some kind of esoterism intrinsic in Vladislav Shoot's compositions arises from his concentration on the purely acoustic character of musical imagery. It is apparent that 20th-century musical culture is currently striving for the predominance of visual, spectacular, theatrical and gestural elements, which finds its manifestation in the emergence of such new genres as "instrumental theatre" and "directed concerto," in the noticeably expanded experimentation with and a wider use of light-and-color projectors, motion pictures, and the like. The visual aspect made the musical art so graphic and multidimensional as to promote its natural contracts with the allied arts and to attract the ever increasing number of listeners.

As for Vladislav Shoot, he is a principled adherent of pure, absolute music in his creative work (Once again one may recall Brahms, went against the background of general movement to programmatic music and a synthesis of arts in the 19th century). For Vladislav Shoot the initial impulse of music lies exclusively in sounds, rather than in a literary text, a picture, a dance, or any other factor. Despite the fact that he has to his credit a number of vocal pieces, his approach to this genre remained purely musical (in the 19th-century traditions), but neither verbally musical not theatrically musical (let us recall the experience in working on verbal text by Stockhausen, Berio and other modern composers).

Moreover, living in the world of pure, absolute music, Vladislav Shoot is drawn not to the monumental performing bodies on the concert stage but to the chamber genres and chamber ensembles. Even when he writes symphonies, these are chamber symphonies. He loves the expressiveness of various instrumental duets, trios, quartets, and quintets, and he devotes most of his endeavors to such groups of instruments.

However, his music written in a fine chamber texture and very often unfolding in a slow tempo captivates primarily by its elevated romantic lyricism, and its heartfelt warmth which is commonly associated in Russia with soulfulness. The lyrical intersections in his music reveal the traditions inherent in the 19th-century Romanticism and the deep-rooted Russian perception of music as a highly emotional experience. It is most significant that Vladislav Shoot has entitled one of his major compositions for full symphony orchestra, rather than for a chamber ensemble as *Ex animo*.

Vladislav Alexeyevich Shoot was born on March 3, 1941 in the town of Voskresensk, Ukraine. He started learning music on a regular basis only when he was thirteen, taking lessons in the bayan-accordion (a Russian folk instrument) playing. He entered the Gnesins Music College in Moscow to study bayan playing, but shortly afterwards he passed over to the composition department, making rapid progress and catching up with his fellow-students in musical tastes and interests. He became a member of a small circle of modern music fans, which was set up on the basis of the Scriabin Museum in Moscow. There the young musicians had a chance to attend the recitals of Vladimir Sofronitsky, a brilliant pianist, and discover for themselves the music of Stravinsky, Hindemith, Berg, then Webern, Messiaen, and Boulez. Vladislav Shoot studied composition with Nikolai Peiko, an eminent Russian composer and pedagogue, at the Gnesins Music Teachers Training Institute (now called the Gnesins Russian Academy of Music), graduating in 1967. In those days his tutor was one of the few musicians who actively promoted the new trends in art, made a scholarly study of the latest compositions appearing in the West, delivered reports on the subject, encouraging the budding composers and protecting them against the Soviet reactionary officials. During the period from 1967 to 1982 Vladislav Shoot earned his living by working as a music editor with Sovetsky Kompozitor Publishers. He used this occupation, among other things, to promote the publications of the then officially censured works by the "Soviet avant-gardists" — Edison Denisov, Sophia Gubaidulina, Tigran Mansuryan, Leonid Grabovsky *et al.* In 1982 Vladislav Shoot decided to abandon his boring and purely mechanical job as a music editor in the hope of getting regular commissions for writing film scores. In fact, this type of job he has offered proved a milestone in his life and in the Russian cinema.

Being a composer of pure music, Vladislav Shoot for the first time faced a need to subject himself to a visual series in his creative work. Having found himself in an uncustomary artistic situation, he became preoccupied with the elaboration of specific principles underlying a film score. His undertakings in this sphere appeared to be so successful that during the period from the mid-eighties to the early 1990s Vladislav Shoot was acclaimed in Moscow as the most prominent composer of incidental scores to films, in this respect succeeding Alfred Schnittke, who was gravely ill at the time and then left for Germany. However, in the former USSR ideological obstacles to artistic development very soon came to be replaced by economic problems. The film producers had to virtually give up the services of highly qualified composers and use instead cheap computerized and other commercial substitutes.

In the 1990s composers of serious modern music found themselves in difficult situation with the dissolution of the official organizations that had previously provided the composers with paid commissions, no matter how occasionally it happened, and with the work of the creative structures, such as the publishing houses and film studios, getting out of order. In Moscow there remained only two possibilities for performing modern music-within the programmes of the concerts sponsored by the AMM (the Association of Modern Music which was set up by Edison Denisov) and within the framework of the annual music festival "Moscow Autumn," which has been saved thanks to the efforts of the Moscow branch of the Composers Union.

As many composers from the former USSR, Vladislav Shoot got substantial aid from the West — through the organization of concerts, publication of relevant information, and the performance of his works in the course of the 1980s and '90s in Zurich, Budapest, London (repeatedly), Lugano, Cremona, Boston, Brussels, Glasgow, Vienna, Duisburg, Schleswig-Holstein, and in other cities. His *Sinfonia da Camera No. 5* scored a great success in Paris within the framework of the music festival of the Moscow Association of Modern Music in 1993.

Because of many years spent in the shadows and his loathing for pushing himself forward and making a show of his own abilities, as well as a certain tendency of the entire Moscow-based musical press to depreciate and ignore everything Russian, as it turned out, there have been virtually no special publications devoted to Vladislav Shoot in Russian, since the Soviet mass media had only mentioned his name on rare occasions in general music reviews. Therefore, the sole radio programme prepared by the author of the present article and broadcasted by the Moscow-based music radio station "Orfei" in 1992 appeared as a discovery of a new talent.

Vladislav Shoot's "centrist" and at the same time neo-romantic style is quite diverse and highly original as regards the elements it incorporates. First of all his music reveals the tradition initiated by Alban Berg in the character of its harmony with the beautiful romantic extraneous thirds intensified by the spicy chromatic dissonances. This harmonic texture combines in his compositions, on the one hand, with the tense rarified pointillistic writing of Webern's later works and, on the other hand, with the archaic diatonics à la Stravinsky and even Rimsky-Korsakov (take, for example, his *Warum?* or his Trio for two clarinets and bass clarinet). And this stylistic synthesis of German and Russian elements dating back to the first decades of the 20th century leaves room for quotations from Bach, Mozart, Schumann, and Wagner, a singularly treated serial technique, sonoristics, and the novel sounds produced by the players of the woodwind instruments, which have been summed up in Bruno Bartolozzi's famous book *New Sounds for Woodwind*.

Here is a typical musical episode taken from Vladislav Shoot's Trio for Bassoon, Cello and Percussion (Movement two — *Adagio*) in which the bassoon delivers a melody full of romantic "sighs" that are most impressively enhanced by "Bartolozzi effects" — quarter-tones, *glissandi,* and polyphonic flageolet chords, while the cello accompanies by the dissonant waltz-like chords in *pizzicato*.

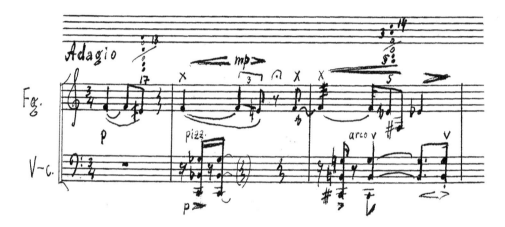

Ex. 1 *Trio for Bassoon, Cello and Percussion*

Despite the introvert nature of his music, confined exclusively to sounds and avoiding any extramusical factors (such as word, scenic action, dance, etc.), the musical material of his compositions is imbued with all kinds of associations, programmes, symbols, and latent plot-lines. However, as the composer himself stresses, all these associations are of purely musical character. He names only one of his works in which, as an exception, he employs action on the part of the performers — *Parable* for percussion. Nevertheless, even in this composition the "action" involves no participation of any concrete characters, with its plot based on the development of a musical idea. The purely musical nature of Vladislav Shoot's thinking manifests itself, among other things, in the fact that in most cases he provides verbal definitions to his compositions when he is coming to an end in his work, rather than at the outset.

Various associations and semantic symbols arise in his music owing to the stylistic quotations and allusions. But Vladislav Shoot works on the styles in a different way, as compared to the composers of the preceding wave — Alfred Schnittke, Luciano Berio or Arvo Pärt. He is striving to stay away from frontal collisions of a collage, smoothing the polystylistic contrast and employing allusions as close to monostylistics as possible. In this respect the most illustrative example is his chamber piece entitled *Romantic Messages* for bassoon, strings, flute and piano (1979).

A specific feature of *Romantic Messages* (in three movements) is a major part assigned in the musical texture to a theme from Mozart's celebrated symphony in G minor. The title of Vladislav Shoot's work is associated with the quoted principal theme from Mozart's work is associated with the quoted principal theme from Mozart's symphony, since this theme, in the composer's view, is purely romantic in its spirit and in general one of the first romantic themes in music. Vladislav Shoot had no preconceived idea of using this famous melody in his music, but when he set down to writing a certain romantic composition based on the quivering "sigh tones," he involuntarily associated it with Mozart and felt an urgent need to use his theme. And he introduced the quotation not through a collage but in some reverse way. As his music developed from the first to the second movement, a minor second got more and more intensified in different voices, with the Mozart theme arising from the melodics of modern composer according to the principle of "derivative contrast" (in the second Movement). Below we cite two moments in his approach to the quotation in the second movement — at the beginning of the strings' part and then continued by the bassoon (Fig. 13, m. 4, see Musical Example 2a,b).

Ex. 2a *Romantic Messages*

Indeed, the romantic, lyrical rendering of the theme from Mozart's symphony in G minor makes an antithesis to the dramatic part of the bassoon, a restless and suffering hero of Vladislav Shoot's composition. In its third movement the elevated melody of

Ex. 2b

the flute, joining in here for the first time, appears as an allusion to the Mozart theme. As for Mozart's melody as it were, it emerges later on, shortly before the final Coda, in a transformed form against a background of the strings' sonoristic block. In the Coda itself there arises its continuation in the tragic slow and gradually still slower movement (*Adagio*) as a symbol of burying and mourning for the most beautiful of musical themes. Another specific feature of *Romantic Messages*, also in contrast to the customary collage-like citation of a theme, is the utilization of pitch and structural devices defined by the composer as "a garland of series," which could hardly be employed either by Mozart or Romanticists.

Vladislav Shoot makes use of diverse styles in his piece for chamber orchestra *Warum?* This title evocative of Schumann's famous piano piece bearing the same name contains a stylistic allusion to the finale of the given composition. It beings with a trichord associated with the Stravinsky style, but it concludes, as a kind of external coda, by the orchestra's conductor playing on the so far silent piano a pseudo-romantic theme à la Schumann, providing a sudden "change for the last time" against the background of the modern music.

A noteworthy element inherent in Vladislav Shoot's style is a melodic turn based on the interval of a sixth. As is known, a broad and consonant "lyrical sixth" is an attribute of 19th-century musical romanticism. Vladislav Shoot as a neo-romanticist reinstates this turn of melody with its forgotten beauty in his music. But being a 20th-century composer, he illuminates it in colors associated with diverse styles. For instance, when in the finale (in Movement Five) of his Trio for Bassoon, Cello and Percussion there appears a sixth (in E-flat major) imbued with deep intimate feeling, it evokes reminiscences of Glinka's romances, Chopin's nocturnes, Liszt's *Liebesträume*, and Wagner's *Tristan und Isolde*. At the same time, since Vladislav Shoot belongs to a generation of composers writing at the close of the 20th century, who have imbibed Shostakovich's music and the ideas propounded by the Second Viennese School, his sixth (in various compositions) also reflects the emotions inherent in the beginning of Shostakovich's Fifth Symphony and the calculated austerity intrinsic in the exposition section of Webern's Symphony Op. 21. By elaborating on these fine stylistic allusions, Shoot in his neo-romantic sixth gives a slight glimpse of this rainbow of styles, combining at the same time all coloristic nuances into the single "white color" of his own music.

To a certain extent it is owing to stylistic allusions that some turns of melody acquire a stable symbolic meaning in Vladislav Shoot's music. Thus, according to the composer himself, the motto theme BACH (in various transpositions) bears the symbol of a cross in his music, and while introducing this symbol he proceeded from its conventional musical meaning, which can be exemplified by his *Offering* for violin, cello and piano and his symphonic *Ex animo*.

A major key to Vladislav Shoot's musical thinking lies in the understanding of his approach to the dramatic principle in his "absolute music." Having rejected the external dramatic patterns — theatrical and scenic, he developed a multifarious system of inner, purely musical, dramatic patterns. And in this respect he followed the principles evolved by Mozart, his favorite composer, whose instrumental music is permeated throughout with a dialogue, dialogism — between themes, leading melodies, registers, timbres, textures and so on. Since European artistic culture, musical culture included, had been founded on dramatic principles, the dramatic type of thinking based on a contrast of the opposite fundamental elements, over the course of centuries came to figure prominently in the musical art.

Vladislav Shoot had reflected a lot upon the dramatic principles, coming to the conclusion that the supremacy of the dramatic factor in music was fraught with certain dangers. In his view, if the composer devotes prime attention to directing, it may affect for the worse the clear-cut elaboration of details and the musical texture as a whole. He feels it to happen sometimes even to the greatest artists. For example, he believes that Fyodor Dostoyevsky's novels reveal in their texts some kind of "gaps" arising, to all appearances, in a haste, with the great writer having sacrificed such moments for the sake of producing a large-scale entity. As for music, such *ramplissages* may be found in Stravinsky's music, and they have been even preconceived in some of Lutoslawski's compositions (e.g. in his *Livre pour orchèstre*). The antipode to such thinking is the work of Webern, with his departure from the dramatic principles, and the magnitude of each separate sound. Vladislav Shoot regards the constructive explicitness of each detail as a conscious and indispensable precept in a composer's work.

Nonetheless, his compositions contain their own "plots," though their nature and the character of their elaboration, as it has been stressed above, are purely musical, which reveals the traditional tenets of Russian music, too. Thus, Pyotr Tchaikovsky believed that any genuine music was programmatic. We have already mentioned the "plot" of Vladislav Shoot's *Romantic Messages* wherein an essential part was assigned to a theme from Mozart's Symphony in G minor — its emergence, the purity it conveyed, its burial and mourning for it. Vladislav Shoot's *Parable* for percussion (1983), written for the celebrated Moscow-based percussion ensemble directed by Mark Pekarsky, involves not only a programme but also even some action on the concert stage in the vein of "instrumental theatre." The "plot" of this composition is based on a parable about an idea. The composer in his annotation to this work elucidated his message; the soloist — the generator of an idea — inspires by it all members of the ensemble, one after the other. Each player comes onto the stage, joining in at a certain moment in the development of the idea. In the *tutti* of the percussion ensemble the idea reaches its complete triumph. The soloist, having realized that the idea became self-sufficing and uncontrollable, tries to stop its further development. The music is interrupted by a whistle and then by a siren. Finally, a shot of a starter's pistol symbolizes the death of the idea's bearer. In a quiet coda (a dialogue between bells and the vibraphone played backstage) the idea retreats into the domain of reminiscences, losing the ominous meaning it had acquired at the climax of its development.

And here is a purely musical "plot" in *Metamorphosis* for alto saxophone, harp, double-bass and percussion (1979). In the score released in Moscow by Sovetsky Kompozitor Publishers in 1985 this composition was defined as "Chamber Concerto" for the same cast of instruments. The solo part is assigned to the alto saxophone, a typically jazz instrument, accompanied by the double-bass and percussion, also invariably associated with jazz, and complemented by the classical harp. Throughout the four movements of the concerto use is made of separate popular jazz and jazz waltz-like details delivered in the ironical distorted mirror in quite dense polytonality — as a solo of either the alto saxophone or the double-bass, to the accompaniment of either the harp or the beat-group of the percussion instruments. In the third movement the composer provided the following remarks for the part of the alto saxophone: "to be played in a special weak tone, at times as if dying down and slightly out of tune." In the finale, to quote the composer's annotation, "there occurs a visible process of regeneration: the players in turn take up the percussion instruments, which leads to a great climax of a new quality." In the Coda, according to the score, the double-bass player takes up the bells, the harpist plays the maracas, the alto saxophonist-the bass drum, and instead of the languorous accompanied "singing" you hear a purely rhythmical polyostinato.

Guided primarily by intuition in recreating the dramatic principles and plot lines in his compositions, Vladislav Shoot has evolved a singular approach to the culmina-tion points. The musical forms of this composer, though well balanced in their architectonics, are distinguished at the same time by a dynamic and vigorous character of their development reaching a climax at the critical, destructive point. Such climaxes are followed in his works by a special stage which he calls an "anticlimax" treating it as a passage to a new quality in the development of the idea and the musical material; as a rule, this stage has a static character and involves the use of sonoristic effects. According to the composer himself, he employed this contrast between a climax and an "anticlimax" for the first time in his *Sinfonia da camera No. 1* for four cellos, double-bass and kettledrums (1973). This composition falls in two movements unfolding in *attacca*, entitled respectively "Introduzione" and "Azione." A strong dramatic climax (*Molto intensivo*) reached shortly before the end of the second movement is built up on a transformation of the thematic material from the first movement. Upon its exhaus-tion there enters a sonoristic block of the string quintet — four cellos and a double-bass, making use of the flageolets with *glissando non tremolo* and *tremolo*, playing beyond the bridge with alternation of *pizzicato, arco, col legno*, and the like. The "anticlimax" beings in *crescendo* from ppp to ff, and then — *Furioso prestissimo possible*. As the composer points out in his annotation, a contrast between a climax and "anticlimax" is a device he used to resort to in some of his later works to intensify the tension and secure a passage into a new quality.

Another major composition in which Vladislav Shoot employed the same device is his *Largo-sinfonia* for chamber orchestra and organ (1981). It is in six movements, with the zone of climaxes falling on Movement Four. In the key, most lingering climax the sonoristic blocks are based on "quasi-clusters" — a speical kind of tone-groups acting as elements within the harmonic system of the given composition. In the following sonoristic "anticlimax" there arise traditional clusters not used anywhere else in this symphony.

The study of the role the dramatic factor plays in Vladislav Shoot's creative work discloses two essential, deep-rooted aspects in his musical thinking. The first one is characteristic of all serious modern music in general: it is the philosophical, conceptual treatment of music as a type of thinking about the eternal problems of human existence. The second aspect pertains to some definite feature of the composer's musical language, though it is not inherent exclusively in him alone — what he himself calls "dualism" and what we have defined above, while discussing the Mozart tradition, as "dialogism."

Conceptuality is quite characteristic of contemporary Russian composers in general: suffice it to mention Alfred Schnittke and Sophia Gubaidulina with the great musical scope of their works. Vladislav Shoot believes that an intrinsic feature of Russian music is its great (even too excessive) seriousness and a heightened sense of responsibility on the part of Russian composers for each of their musical pieces. The composer has always been interested in the conceptual, philosophical underpinnings of fiction literature, too; he tells of the strongest impression made on him by Thomas Mann's *Doctor Faustus*, Mikhail Bulgakov's *The Master and Margarita*, Fyodor Dostoyevsky's novels, as well as the works by Anatoly Kim, a modern Russian writer of Korean origins. And as regards his major compositions, such as *Largo-sinfonia* for chamber orchestra and organ and *Ex animo* for full symphony orchestra, he stresses his conscious "aim at conceptuality."

The "dualism" of "dialogism" of Vladislav Shoot's musical language are indicative of the dramatic method with its perpetual interaction of the opposite poles and the universal linguistic principle of "binary oppositions" which is revealed in his music, lending logical clarity to the novel musical devices he employs in his compositions.

Vladislav Shoot points to some analogies with the dramatic methods in the anno-tations to his works. Thus, as regards his *Romantic Messages*, he indicates that the instruments are treated as participants in a dramatic action, appearing with their own monologues and getting engaged in tense dialogues. The main protagonist is the bassoon, restless, suffering, reaching nearly the limits of its expressive and technical resources. The same dialogue between the main hero and the other members of the ensemble may be observed in his *Sinfonia da camera No. 1* (juxtaposition of the double-bass and four cellos) and in *Metamorphosis* (juxtaposition of the alto saxophone and the other instruments), and in some other compositions. A dialogue may also be multiple. Thus, as regards his *Sinfonia da camera No. 3* for flute, oboe, two string groups and percussion, the composer outlines the following two types of interaction between two types of instruments: (1) juxtaposition of the first and second string groups and (2) juxtaposition of the soloists (flute, oboe, vibraphone, and marimba) and two string groups.

The principle of "binary oppositions" discovered by the linguists as a law underly-ing verbal language without exception finds its manifestation not in very musical style in the form of concrete musical devices. Quite the reverse, many artistic ideas that have emerged in the 20th century are striving to depart from the linguistic dialectics of contrasts, among them, for instance, "the idea of mainstream" in literature, cinema and music, "the idea of biological growth" and "the idea of the expanding Universe," which are put forth as models of musical compositions. In Vladislav Shoot's creative work "binary oppositions" are crystallized in the form of devices embracing the musical dramatic pattern of his separate works, the stylistic structure of his musical language and numerous elements within his composition structures.

Let us go on with discussing the dramatic procedures and assess the latter in light of binary opposition as well. It is characteristic of Vladislav Shoot to base his conceptions on an initial contrast of two principles. Thus, in his two-movement *Sinfonia da camera No. 1* there are two initial principles: the impersonal, outwardly static, which is defined in the score's remarks as *ingenuo* and *indifferente*, and the personal, immediately responsive, which finds its manifestation in the following remarks: *espressivo, dolce* and *molto intensivo*. At a climax in the second movement the contrasting principles come to be transformed: the impersonal acquires a menacing look while the personal becomes extremely dramatic (the restless, "unrestrained" solo of the double-bass). At this culmination point the initial pair of principles comes across another opposition, which is exposed in the "anticlimax" following immediately after the climax. In *Sinfonia da camera No. 2* the initial dramatic pair presents itself as a contrast of spatially rarified music, with a great number of rests, and the controlled, rhythmically energetic music. In *Sinfonia da camera No. 3*, with its two kinds of juxtapositions mentioned above, of the instrumental groups and solo instruments, the dramatic principle underlies two types of musical expressiveness: gentle, lucid, seemingly joyous tone-colors of four solo instruments (flute, oboe, vibraphone, and marimba) and the ostensibly sad and tense polyphonic blocks of the strings. And this opposition in the types of expressiveness comes across the opposition of the symphony's two principal movements contrasting in tempo (slow–fast). As regards *Ex animo* for full symphony orchestra, the composer in his annotation discloses the initial duality underlying a superposition of a drama unfolding in the traditions of a symphony and a tragedy occurring simultaneously in reality.

Binary oppositions also determine the stylistic structure of Vladislav Shoot's musical language. It is characteristic of this composer to make a synthesis of the latest avant-gardist devices with the habitual, classical romantic devices. The composer reveals this tendency of his in the following commentary to one of his works (cited from the manuscript score granted as a courtesy to the author of the present article): "I have always been preoccupied with the ideas of combining and interpenetrating the novel and the customary, the unreal and the real, the imaginal and the actual... The assimilation of and search for adequate means and systems to solve the newly arising tasks dialectically aggravated my nostalgia for tonal expressiveness. These two streams merged together in a varying proportion in my compositions..."

And the more vivid his composition, the greater is the number of opposed pairs incorporated in its stylistics. A contrast of opposites skilfully combined in a composition by the master's experienced hand creates in it a wide range of artistic purport extending from one to the other pole and, paradoxically enough, remaining unsolvable. Let us take, for example, one of his most frequently performed compositions, *Warum?* for chamber orchestra. At first the composer wanted to leave only the question mark in the title of this short piece in two movements. Then he added the German word "Warum" to remind therewith of Schumann and his style. As the composer believes, he has combined in this piece quite incompatible phenomena: the relaxed and mechanical rhythms, the Oriental layering of a sound and the European discipline of microstructures, the Bach and Webern tonal cells and a romantic theme played by the conductor on the piano as a finishing touch to the entire composition, with these contradictions remaining unsolvable since it ends not with a full stop but with the question mark.

Let us turn back once again to the composition in which Vladislav Shoot revealed his ideas most profoundly — *Largo-sinfonia* for chamber orchestra and organ in six movements (1981). As the composer himself stresses, in this symphony "dualism manifests itself at various levels." As regards its emotional expressiveness, its general tragic tone is permeated with gentle, mellow sounds and lucid ringing. As regards its form, it combines the centrifugal romantic tendencies with the precisely calculated centripetal forces, and a juxtoposition of a climax and an "anticlimax" (in its fourth movement). The harmonic structures become polyphonic while the polyphonic ones get imbued with harmony. The blocks of quasi-clusters are embellished in the clearly discernible joyous or sad tone-colors. The composer's complex style displays in this work its various facets, bringing into contrast the dissonant style prevailing in the 20th century and the style inherent in the Bachian chorales, the clear-cut triads of the classicist style and the intricate linear chromaticism of the Baroque period. The "dualism" imbues the timbers as well: the dark, amorphously lingering sounds of the organ and the lucid, clearly articulated phrases of the harpsichord. In the same way are contrasted the extreme registers, slow and fast movements, the chordal and one-voice texture, the frozen sounds of the "non-breathing" organ and the energetical rhythmics of the percussion. Within each pair of poles there is an invisible force field of their mutual gravitation, producing an intricate and multidimensional semantic space of the composition. And over all the semantic fields there towers the main antithesis, conventionally speaking, of Darkness and Light, which accumulates its forces throughout the work until it dissolves in the Coda into a quiet tune, based on a romantic sixth played by the celesta and a funeral tolling of the bells and the vibraphone. Even the concluding trill-like melody (a distant allusion to the finale in Berg's *Wozzeck*) seems to be an interplay of opposites: yes-no-yes-no...

Vladislav Shoot is a master musician who reveals to the best advantage the professional qualities of the Moscow composition school. Among other things, this school is distinguished for the structural explicitness of a composition. As regards the composition craft, Vladislav Shoot is firmly convinced that a professional composer should have a perfect command of all the techniques in harmony, polyphony, rhythmics, melodics, and orchestration, for any gaps in his training are impermissible. Even if he has no need for all these structures at the moment, his proficiency should be evident. For his compositions Vladislav Shoot has worked out various harmonic systems (sort of series made up of tonal elements, the functionally differentiated chords), the non-traditional canons with varying transpositions of voices, his own types of poly-rhythmics, his own musical forms based on thickening and thinning of the texture, and many other devices. At the same time the composer insists that music should be clearly discerned no matter how complex it is. In case a composition is too unintel-ligible, it inevitably leads to depreciating its entity and weakening its integrity. This trust in two indispensable aspects of a composition — the chiselled techniques and intuitive hearing — is a characteristic feature of the Russian music school.

As for his personal creative process, Vladislav Shoot contributed the most revealing lines published in a booklet released within the framework of the music festival held in Schleswig-Holstein in 1991. Below is quite a longish extract from this text offered as a conclusion to this article:

"I've noticed that the best things in my music often turned out to be those preconceived and even heard by my inner ear at the moments when I was in a 'semi-conscious' state, when in my mind's eye, with the unbelievable visual clarity, there emerged some fantastic figures, plots and lines of sounds, arising one after another in a transformed shape. All this happened when feeling intellectually calm and cheerful in general, I was suddenly overpowered with inward trembling and yearning, like in a fit of fever arising from the wind blowing on a bright day! ... Of course, for such moments not to slip away as a shapeless and fruitless experience, it is desirable to equip one's subconscious with some preliminary drafts and designs...

"I love music which, for all its beauty and perfection, implies, like in Bluebeard's castle, some unreal door, a "black hole," the receptacle of chaos and grief. Sometimes the less it is apparent the better, but nonetheless its presence is imperative. Undoubtedly, a true artist would not cultivate deliberately the breath of the abyss in his creative work, being more inclined to build bridges and safe roads between the wittingly incompatible categories; he is engaged in a perpetual search for harmony and the supreme message, but the greater his personality the more difficult for him to attain the desired goal. One has to be a Dostoyevsky to feel wholeheartedly that it is possible to elevate oneself while falling too deep and low, and vice versa. And one has to be a Bach to erect, amid wild and dangerous nature, a kingdom of harmony without transforming the forest into a park and without the taming of the roaring beasts."

PRINCIPAL WORKS

Instrumental Compositions

Sinfonia da camera No. 1 for four cellos, double-bass and kettledrums (1973)
Silhouettes, eleven piano miniatures (1973)
Sinfonia da camera No. 2 for flute, oboe, clarinet, alto saxophone, bassoon, viola, cello and double-bass (1975)
Sonata breve for solo flute (1977)
Sinforia da camera No. 3 for flute, oboe, two groups of strings and percussion (1978)
Trio for Bassoon, Cello and Percussion (1978)
Solo per fagotto (1978)
Romantic Messages for bassoon, strings, flute and piano (1979)
Metamorphosis for alto saxophone, harp, double-bass and percussion (1979)
Largo-sinfonia for 15 players and organ (1981)
Trio for Two Clarinets and Bass Clarinet (1982)
Parable for percussion ensemble (1983)
Quintetto d' ottoni (1984)
Espressivo for flute, oboe, violin, cello and piano (1984)
Warum? for 14 players (1986)
Ex animo for symphony orchestra (1988)
Four Versions for bassoon and string quartet (1990)
... it is a long sleep for percussion ensemble (1990)
Offering for violin, cello and piano (1991)
Sinfonia da camera No. 4 for strings and tam-tam (1992)
Sinfonia da camera No. 5 for 16 players (1992)
Confession for Organ (1993)
Serenade for String Quartet (1994)
Serenade for String Orchestra, version of serenade for String Quartet (1995)
Con Passione for piano Quintet (1995)
Pantomime for flute and harpsichord (1995)

Children's Music

The Call of the Cuckoo (20 miniatures for children) for violin and piano (1969)
Youth Album for violin and piano (1971)
Talyanochka (accordion of Italian make), album of piano pieces for children (1974)
Children's Album for piano (1975–1995)
Ten Children's Pieces for French horn and piano (1976)
Two Lyrical Miniatures for flute and piano (1980)
Pieces for saxophone and piano (1987)

Vocal Compositions

Six Poems to verses by Sergei Gorodetsky for voice and piano (1986)
A Gleam of Light to verses by Boris Pasternak (1988)
Vorgefühl (Premonition) for soprano, bass clarinet, viola, cello and double-bass to verses by Rainer Maria Rilke (1993)

Four Songs on words by P.B. Shelley for soprano and string quartet (1994)
Three Songs on words by O. Mandelstam for high voice, flute, clarinet and string quartet (1994)

Alexander Vustin: the battlefield is the soul

Valeria Tsenova

Alexander Vustin

> *"Alexander Vustin is a very serious composer who tackles his work with a great responsibility. Each of his compositions bears the stamp of his inimitable individuality. He does not belong to any school, and what is particularly valuable in our time — he does not follow fashion, always remaining true to himself."*
>
> Edison Denisov

No doubt, Alexander Vustin, who just turned fifty, is one of the most singular of modern Russian composers. He works thoughtfully and unhurriedly, without seeking commissions and self-publicity, and this is perhaps the reason for him remaining little known both in this country and elsewhere[1]. Yet, the work of this composer devoted to lofty artistic ideals and uncompromising in creative matters deserves close attention and scholarly appraisal.

Alexander Vustin was born in 1943 in Moscow. He studied composition first with Grigory Fried at a music college, and then with Vladimir Feré at the Moscow Conservatoire, graduating in 1967. Since 1974 he has been working as music editor with the Kompozitor (formerly the Sovetsky Kompozitor) Publishers. During his student years he was influenced by Dmitry Shostakovich, Arnold Schoenberg, Iannis Xenakis, Sophia Gubaidulina and Arvo Pärt. Among those closest to his heart now are the 19th-century Russian composers, Schubert, Beethoven, Mozart, and Bach. Showing an obvious preference for chamber ensemble music, he writes predominantly for non-standard combinations of instruments, involving the percussion (primarily membranophones).

Alexander Vustin's earliest compositions already revealed two lines to feature prominently in his future work: *Three Poems by Moisei Teif* and *Cantata to Wartime Poems*

---

[1] His compositions were mainly performed within the framework of music festivals the most significant of which are the Sergei Prokofiev Festival in Duisburg (1991), the festival of the Association of Modern Music in Paris (1993), and the annual "Moscow Autumn" festivals.

were devoted to the theme of war and therefore saturated by the dramatic imagery, whereas his *String Quartet* and *Symphony* were evocative of the lyrical streak. These two sphere-effective and lyrical-merged together in his subsequent compositions.

In the early 1970s Alexander Vustin turned his attention to folklore. He regards his folkloric trips to the rural areas as landmarks in his creative career, for these helped him to recreate the primordial purity of music. The composer believes that "folklore is a natural phenomenon"[2]. During that period he wrote *Toropets Songs*, which appeared in two versions, one for the piano and the other for a chamber ensemble. These instrumental songs are far from being mere arrangements, though the composer used in them the authentic folk material. In their style they are rather akin to Stravinsky's music of the Russian period, which is primarily manifest in the employment of various types of polystructures — polytonality, polyrhythmics, polymetrics and polymodality (Musical Example 1).

During the period from 1969 to 1974 Alexander Vustin worked as a music editor at the USSR Radio where he gained access to the collection of most interesting recordings. There he ran into the compositions for percussion instruments by Boulez, Xenakis and other avant-gardists. Their soundscape made a great impression on the young composer and encouraged his own reflections on the resources inherent in these instruments. He came to realize that it was possible to give a fresh light to these instruments, treating them first and foremost as a self-contained group, as a thematic element, rather than merely as a certain coloristic or rhythmic means. Of particular interest for him was the thematic treatment of the percussion instruments of indefinite pitch: "There exists a number of certain clear-cut themes, melodies and whole lines which we cannot sing. There is some magic in it, which could be hardly explained. This section may be even juxtoposed with the rest of the orchestra, being self-sufficient and developing according to its own laws. The beauty of the matter arises from this self-contained nature of the percussion instruments, which has its own invaluable and self-assertive line within the orchestra." The ideas he evolved in those years as regards the percussion instruments, becoming an indispensable part of Alexander Vustin's compositions, have been consistently elaborated on to date.

His composition *The Word* for the wind and percussion instruments opened up a new page in Alexander Vustin's creative work. It is in *The Word* with its solemn and elevated character that the composer first introduced his conception of "effective music". Its dramatic development is based on the gradual accumulation of the dynamics, the key role in which is assigned to the percussion instruments: the exposition is played exclusively by the woodwinds, with the brasses and the percussion joining in at Fig. 3. The growth in the dynamics and the number of the instruments involved leads to a contrasting second section (beginning with Fig. 14), wherein disappears the monorhythmic movement of the initial section. The recapitulation arises at the peak of the middle section; in it the initial material recurs in the monorhythmic movement

---

[2]   All the composer's statements cited hereinafter have been made during his talks with the author of the present article.

Ex. 1 *Toropets Songs* for Piano

of all the wind instruments with the participation of the percussion, with the latter being juxtaposed with the former both in their rhythmic and melodic material. The development is based on the ostinato principle underlying the reiteration of notes, brief melodies and chordal blocks. The instrumentation is designed to produce a lapidary, direct sonority.

This composition was to become the first part in Alexander Vustin's tetralogy, a cycle of pieces similar in their dramatic message and the principles he followed in his treatment of the percussion instruments. In addition to *The Word*, this tetralogy comprises *Memoria-2*, *Homecoming* and *Dedication to Beethoven*.

Alexander Vustin's *Memoria-2*, which the composer subtitled as a concerto for percussion, keyboard and stringed instruments, is actually an extended version of his piece for strings and percussion entitled *Memorial*, moulded after Bach's chorale prelude on a *cantus firmus*. Its role is assigned to the part of the bells in the first movement. The structure of this composition is similar to that of *The Word*, the only difference being that in *Memoria-2* the contrasting material is played solo for a very long time by a huge percussion ensemble (33 membranophones). The orchestra is divided into two groups: membranophones of indefinite pitch (the concertizing group) and all the rest of the instruments.

Memoria-2 is a polyphonic concerto with three percussionists leading the fugal theme (it starts at the end of the eighth measure by the first percussionist). Beginning with Fig. 6, it involves all the rest of the percussionists, playing the same fugue but in retrograde inversion. With the introduction of the second voice (Fig. 1) the strings and keyboard instruments stop playing to appear again in Fig. 11 at the moment of the highest intensity in the beating of the drums. This introduction of the strings and keyboard instruments produces a theatrical effect preconceived by the composer: the playing of the orchestra is seen rather than heard as all the music is drowned in the powerful beating of the percussion. According to the composer, "The strings in this composition play the part of a curtain: at the beginning it rises and at the end it falls. As for the concluding section, the introduction of the strings here produces not so much of new sonority as the sensation of spaciousness."

The performance of *Memoria-2* at the Composers Club in Moscow in 1978 marked a turning point in Alexander Vustin's creative career, for it corroborated his conception of treating the percussion instruments as an independent force within the orchestra, capable of self-development.

Homecoming for baritone and thirteen instrumentalists (two string quartets, two pianos, French horn and percussion) is set to the verses of Dmitry Shchedrovitsky, a Moscow-based poet and philosopher, whose work turned out to be very close to Alexander Vustin and proved a highlight in his life. In this piece the composer adheres to a similar dramatic model while shaping a different type of imagery: its development proceeds from serene contemplative mediation to very dynamic and dramatic outbursts at the climax. The outer movements are sustained in B-flat major tonality. The chordal tonal pedal in the strings supported by the piano's bass is getting gradually more and more complicated and dissonant. Shortly before Fig. 3 there joins in the second piano with the dissonant supporting voice played in *staccato* and lingering through pedalization. Its sounds are ringing as if rendered by the metallic percussion instruments. Everything develops in *crescendo*, reaching the orchestral climax (m. 163) which quite soon collapses passing into recapitulation (m. 169). However following this culmination point the music in the recapitulation section becomes more tense than at the beginning, with the piano's supporting voice also sustained. The chords of the string quartet are triadic, but nevertheless more intensive in their function: the initial chord being B♭-C-B♭-e-E♭, and the tonic in B-flat major.

Dedication to Beethoven, a concerto for percussion and orchestra, is written in the form of variations on a theme in the style of the great classic. From the very first bars the theme in B-flat major gets complicated through the wind whining and the beating of the percussion instruments. The variations are most diverse in character: the initial one is a lyrical Adagio, then come *misterioso* (Fig. 1), *poco misterioso* (Fig. 2) , *con anima* (Fig. 3), *con energia* (Fig. 4), and *con fuoco* (Fig. 5). Gradually the percussion are spreading with an impressive drive until, shortly before Fig. 9 they oust all the other sections of the orchestra. This movement presents a kind of cadence in the concerto, which is outlined by harmonic chords as well: the last preceding chords include the Subdominant, its alteration, a cadential four-sixths chord and the Dominant whose bass note is delivered by the Kettledrums and then disappears altogether. At the end of the cadence developing according to the principle of mounting intensity the dominant harmony reinstates itself, getting its resolution in the tonic of the closing variation. Herein all the instrumentalist are called upon to him the initial theme while some of them are still playing. The composition ends in a sonoristic cadence which washes off all the previous development in B-flat major. All the sounds are terminated suddenly by switching off the electronic siren.

In 1987 Alexander Vustin's tetralogy was replenished by one more composition — *Festivity*, which was set to the texts borrowed from the collections of Russian chants. It is a kind of concerto of chimes (it arose from the short piano piece written earlier and entitled *Reverberations*). In contrast to his previous works, the composer makes use here of the percussion instruments of definite pitch. The orchestra, in addition to the string, woodwind and brass sections, also includes bells, a marimbaphone and a bass guitar. The strings duplicate the vocal part. The wind instruments appear only in the final *tutti* at Fig. 11, also duplicating the choral part. Hence the chorus is on both sides duplicated by the orchestral groups. At the beginning there emerges an ostinato four-voice layer: the little bells and bells (in the concert version — the vibraphone), the bass marimbaphone and the bass guitar are delivering their material in different rhythms throughout the composition. The ostinato in varying rhythms relieves the monotony of the single-rhythmic movements of the chorus and the orchestra. The work's key tonality is C major. The tonal choral part is superimposed by the overtones of the chimes. The key chord, C major with B-flat and F-sharp, is gradually expanding, first melodically (the appearance of new notes) and then in its harmony: the final *tutti* is built up on a colorful contrast of triadic chords: E-flat major, C-flat major (B), E-flat major, A major, E-flat major and C major. At the end the initial scale is reinstated.

The artistic and constructive ideas underlying this supercycle made the basis of Alexander Vustin's creative programme, and it took him nearly a decade to implement it (beginning with *The Word* written in 1975 and completed by *Festivity* in 1987). All the compositions in this cycle are grounded on the elaboration of his conception of effective music, on his approach to music as an act that involves not only the performers but the listeners as well: "Both performers and listeners find themselves participating in a certain Action whose meaning they cannot describe in words, though being fully preoccupied with it."

Alexander Vustin's conception of effective music has been technically founded on the principle of 12-fold restatement, a singular method of sound organization. Since this principle makes the core of the composer's creative process, it calls for more detailed consideration.

It all started with the composer's work on the traditional twelve-note technique: "I was striving to explain to myself what was the need for this technique, being guided by the rule of contraries in its assessment. Could I, pursuing the purely technical tasks and confining myself exclusively to the serial technique, produce something musical to satisfy my quests? Stravinsky used to say that nothing inspired him so much as a limitation. It gave him a sense of freedom he lacked when facing the boundless possibilities making him feel at a loss among them." This kind of limitation attracted Alexander Vustin, too. In the early 1970s he evolved a twelve-note series that made the basis of the music he was to write for nearly eighteen years, and a point of departure in his technical quests.

The composer was looking for a certain universal law of development to be defined in numbers and conducive to its free employment at all levels of a musical structure[3]. So he passed from the 12-note technique to 12-fold restatement.

The most conventional of his twelve-note compositions is *Sonata for six Instruments*; it displays the influence of Webern (its two movements lasting for merely six minutes). Another major work dating back to those years, *Nocturnes*, is a serial composition, too. But by the mid-seventies Alexander Vustin felt it insufficient to apply the twelve-note principles exclusively to the pitch organization. He was interested in time, striving to apply the principle of 12-fold restatement to the musical form.

For the first time it was consciously employed in his *Memoria-2*[4]. The figures in this piece are placed at the end of the sections. By Fig. 12 the twelve sections equal in the number of their measures come to a close. Each section contains 24 measures (12 double measures). Each double measure is arbitrarily symbolized by some definite note from the above mentioned with the double-measure structures repeating the latter in diverse variations coinciding with the modifications of the twelve-note series. By the end of the concerto (by Fig. 12) the note-row is exhausted. The two last measures in the finale appear as a sheer arbitrary rule so indispensable for "breathing" of the music.

Alexander Vustin transfers the serial principle both onto the sequence and the statement character of the note-row. If we arrange the note-row in the following order: b♭ d e d♯ f♯ c a b f g a♭ d♭, its second statement will start with the second note, the third statement will third one and so on. In this way, together with the initial series, a total makes twelve statements the initial notes of which correspond to the order of the series. The composer calls such sequence a series of second order (the basic set-form is a series of first order). It just the first stage in the composer's work.

The next stage involves the designation of all the conventional modifications of the series by figures: 1 for the basic set-form, 2 for its retrograde-inverted statement, the farthest from the basic one, 3 for a retrograde statement, and 4 for its inversion. Then these variations of the series are rearranged in such an order as to avoid the same numbers in the adjacent notes. The transposition is arbitrary: the basic note-row is followed by the farthest one and then by the two nearer ones. As a result, there arises the following sequence:

---

[3] Alexander Vustin believes that the number 12 is actually related to some general-governed regularities. It is rooted in the human subconscious, for man has originally divided time into 12 months and 12 hours.

[4] The division of the soundscape into twelve elements could be also observed in Alexander Vustin's earlier composition, *The Word*, though not throughout the entire piece but only in its second section: a rhythmic variation consists of a theme and its eleven statements.

1 2 3 4   3 1 4 2   2 4 1 3

The arbitrary sequence of figures justified only by the composer's aesthetic flair was to become eventually a certain law-governed regularity in interweaving his musical texture.

Further on, Alexander Vustin develops the idea of a series of third order wherein each system made up of twelve statements is equated with one element in the microseries. As a result, there arise twelve sequences of such systems embracing in their total 144 note-rows, with these systems comprising twelve note-rows interrelated also according to the discovered numerical formula. The composer defined his system as a formula of infinite development (if one willed it so, the following table could be continued to get the series of fourth and fifth order). Below is a fragment of this table granted by the composer as a courtesy to the author of the present article. It reveals the principle underlying Alexander Vustin's work on the numerical series (and, correspondingly, the serialization of pitches) both in their horizontal and vertical relationships.

1.	1 2 3 4	3 1 4 2	2 4 1 3
2.	4 2 3 1	1 3 2 4	3 4 1 2
3.	1 3 2 4	4 2 3 1	2 1 4 3
4.	4 3 2 1	2 4 1 3	3 1 4 2
3.	1 3 2 4	4 2 3 1	2 1 4 3
1.	1 2 3 4	3 1 4 2	2 4 1 3
4.	4 3 2 1	2 4 1 3	3 1 4 2
2.	4 2 3 1	1 3 2 4	3 4 1 2
2.	4 2 3 1	1 3 2 4	3 4 1 2
4.	4 3 2 1	2 4 1 3	3 1 4 2
1.	1 2 3 4	3 1 4 2	2 4 1 3
3.	1 3 2 4	4 2 3 1	2 1 4 3

Alexander Vustin's principle of 12-fold restatement in its description may seem too mechanical while the compositions written on its basis too mathematically calculated. However the touching sounds of his music and its high emotional charge dispel such assessment in no time. He uses this principle virtually in all of his compositions, but he varies and complicates it with great enthusiasm: "My series is infinite, going into space and abounding in latent potentials."

The emotional and diverse nuances of his imagery are particularly felt in the compositions belonging to the lyrical sphere in Alexander Vustin's work, primarily associated with the images of nature and "birds" singing, which appeared for the first time back in the 1970s in his *Nocturnes* and in the second piece ("My Nightingale") of his *Toropets Songs* (see Musical Example 1).

In his *Nocturnes* written for a chamber ensemble the folk echoes merged with the voices of nature. The composer made use of his son's ability to imitate birds and introduced his voice, the treble in the highest register, into the instrumental texture of its second movement entitled "Improvisation." Here the wind instruments, and then the strings are playing in an improvisatory manner. Its culmination point is a virtuosic cadence for a very high voice (Fig. 18).

The above mentioned *Sonata for Six Instruments* is notable not only for the twelve-note technique used here for the first time, but also for the meticulous elaboration of birdsong motives, thus combining pantheistic images with the strict laws of dodecaphony.

Alexander Vustin's composition *Dedication to the Son* for flute and ensemble, written much later, was also inspired by his son's voice improvisations. In the course of seven or eight years (up to the voice's mutation) these improvisations developed from mere imitation of birds' singing to the sonoristic compositions devoid of any naturalism. One of the last compositions in this vein, recorded by his son, Yuri Vustin, in 1982, features in addition to singing the boy's playing on the strings and resonant components of the piano, accompanied by his father's playing on the keyboard. This joint composition of father and son is entitled *Voice*. The role of "voice" in *Dedication to the Son* is assigned to the flute. The composer strove to retain the spirit of spontaneity and freedom of a creative act in the context of the well elaborated and quite rigid structure. As he writes in the annotation to this composition, "The flight of 'improvisation' is attended by rhythmic agility, and its easiness by tension. As a matter of fact, herein lies the message of this composition evocative of the delight at a mystery of the creative spirit." Thus, the "birdsong" theme that had preoccupied Alexander Vustin for a long time found its unexpected continuation in his son's creativity, which evoked a deep response in his heart.

His vocal pieces, with their highly original treatment of voice and instrumental accompaniment, also bear out most vividly Alexander Vustin's inimitable style. Among those of major importance for the composer is his *Capriccio* for female voice, chorus of basses and instrumental ensemble (comprising piano, violin, double-bass, percussion and the jazz batteria). This composition is noteworthy first and foremost for its singular instrumentation. Thus, for instance, in its first movement ("Tune") the voice is accompanied by the piano playing *pizzicato*; in the second movement ("Capriccio") the chorus of basses — by the piano, double-bass and percussion with the jazz batteria (with the percussion predominating at its climax), while in the outer sections of the third movement ("Dedication") the female voice is accompanied first by the kettledrums and then by the bells (Musical Example 2).

Capriccio is based on three authentic Hebrew wordless folk tunes borrowed from Mikhail Beregovsky's collection *Jewish folk Songs* (published in Moscow, 1962).

The following four vocal instrumental compositions — *In Memory of Boris Kliuzner, Idle Thoughts of Kozma Prutkov, Zaitsev's Letter* and *Blessed Are the Poor in Spirit* — make up a kind of another supercycle in Alexander Vustin's creative work. In the first place these four compositions are similar in their treatment of the literary source, with the composer being particularly interested in a selection of non-rhymed texts for, as he admits, he is more fond of prose than verses: "The prose is more captivating because in it you are to reveal its hidden layer, not the external one obvious to everyone, but its latent rhythm. For any speech is musical."

This idea was first subject to verification in his vocal piece *In Memory of Boris Kliuzner* for baritone, violin, viola, cello and double-bass set to Yuri Olesha's text (*From Literary*

Ex. 2 *Capriccio*

Diaries). The brevity of the twelve-note piece became an element of its content —
comprehension of a whole life as a momentary experience (a boy — an old man). The
vocal intoning is diversified from mere singing to musical intoning of speech and
whisper.

The colloquial speech features prominently in Alexander Vustin's composition
Idle Thoughts of Kozma Prutkov. Thus, in its second part, "Thoughts and Aphorisms,"
the percussion's phrases are alternated with the recitation of Kozma Prutkov's

witty aphorisms[5]. This piece unexpectedly calls to mind the songs by Modest Mussorgsky who also used to set to music the prosaic texts on the topical social subjects.

As for *Zaitsev's Letter* for voice, strings and bass drum, Alexander Vustin set to music the original text of the letter sent by Sergei Zaitsev, a seventeen-year-old boy, to the *Ogonyok* magazine telling about the horrors of his life in a corrective labor colony[6].

While reading this letter in the popular magazine, the composer felt deeply touched with this story about the humuliations, brawls and the ruin of human dignity, which that boy had to go through. Moreover, he was impressed not only with this outburst of emotions, but also with the prosaic manner in which this text, devoid of any poetical tinge, was written. It urged him to produce a sonoristic composition devoid virtually of any normal sounds but the beating on the soundboard of the instruments, palm tapping on the strings, the highest notes (at the upper limits of auditory faculties), all kinds of *tremolo*, and the highest flageolets. And beginning with Fig. 37, it involves the taped recording of natural noises: the buzzing of human voices, foot stamping, wind roaring, and the engine's distant din. At the climax (Fig. 36) the string players simultaneously sing in chorus the text form the Gospels: "My God, my God, why hast thou forsaken me?" (St. Matthew, 27:46).

Zaitsev's Letter is not a musico-journalistic work; first and foremost, it is a musical composition confined to an abstract musical form, which corroborates Alexander Vustin's tenet that all is music and any phenomenon in life, even the most horrible one, is musical.

His piece *Blessed Are the Poor in Spirit* for voice (desirably, children's) and ensemble, though differing in content, is also set to the prose text from the Gospel according to St. Matthew (5:3). It is a quiet, serene composition, with its vocal phrases divided by the chorale of the strings (*PP misterioso*), gradually becoming longer and wider in diapason with the distance between them decreasing (the device used to make the form more dynamic). By the end of this antiphonic piece, with a view to retaining its integrity, the composer introduces new contrasting material in the strings while the concluding vocal phrase is delivered at a different pitch. The change occurs only within the last few measures: the note E becomes a Dominant for A major.

Alexander Vustin spent a lot of his creative effort and time (14 years) on his sole scenic composition — the opera *The Devil in Love* based on Jacques Cazotte novel's *Le Diable amoureux* written in 1772. He began working on it in 1975, but he had often to interrupt his work for long periods of time. Coming across some definite task, the composer put the opera aside and experimented in his other pieces. This opera turned out to be a synthesizing work and at the same time a source of impetus to his subsequent compositions.

---

[5] Kozma Prutkov was the pen name and the satirical image of a team of the Russian writers who, in the mid-nineteenth century, published under this assumed name their verses of parody, fables and aphorisms.

[6] This composition is dedicated to Edison Denisov who commissioned Alexander Vustin to write it for the chamber ensemble which was then just set up in Moscow under the auspices of the Association of Modern Music.

Originally, it was preconceived as a chamber opera both in its cast and length. But gradually it got overgrown with the additional characters and plot lines, coming to incorporate some conventional operatic scenes such as a carnival, fortune-telling, a rural wedding, and a duel with the main protagonist's friend. The composer then had to introduce the chorus and the ballet. The instrumentation had also to be expanded. The selection of instruments was influenced, among other things, by Stravinsky's experience, with the orchestra seeming to grow out of the core of Stravinsky's *L'histoire du soldat*; namely, in addition to the clarinet, trumpet, trombone, percussion, violin and double-bass, the use was made of saxophones, a piccolo, a flute, a bass clarinet, piano, celesta, harpsichord and electric organ (later on synthesizer was also added). A special role, as in Alexander Vustin's other "effective" compositions, was assigned to the percussion instruments. As a result of all the modifications and additions, the opera by the moment it was completed became quite impressive in its scope, though still retaining its initial "chamber-like" tinge.

Jacques Cazotte's novel tells the story of a young man making advances to the evil spirit. This is the eternal subject-matter in European art — a sin, punishment, and pleading mercy. The two main characters are Alvare, a young officer, and the devil who, upon several metamorphoses, appears eventually as the charming girl Biondetta. In the course of the plot and musical developments in the opera Biondetta, "the devil in love," gradually acquires the human look; her love sets her free from the power of supernatural forces.

The composer provided his main characters with their individual instrumental timbres: Alvare with the violin and the trumpet, and Biondetta with the saxophones (alto, tenor, and baritone). At the beginning of the opera the saxophones depict the character of the devil's messenger. But Biondetta changes as she falls in love with Alvare. His timbre penetrates the heroine's music, with their instrumental characteristics coming closer to each other. Meanwhile Alvare's vocal part, built up at the beginning mainly on declamation, is drawing nearer to Biondetta's in its songfulness. This interpenetration is most evident in their extended love scene (No. 42).

Alexander Vustin defined the genre of *The Devil in Love* as scenes for voices and instruments with games and dancing *ad libitum*. The style of the opera is light-spirited, somewhat in the vein of a farce. At first the events are developing rapidly: a game of billiards, a dispute, temptation by a mystery, a dangerous adventure, various miracles and metamorphoses. However, as early as in Scene Three, the action is transferred into the main protagonist's inner world and his soul.

The opera falls into three acts, each divided into seven scenes. On the whole, there predominates the through principle: the recurrence of a scenic situation entails the recurrence of the musical material[7].

Below is the distribution of the opera's numbers throughout its acts and scenes:

Forewarning (Nos 1 and 2)

---

[7] The sound organisation of the opera involves the series of fourth order. However 144 sequences of the note-row multiplied by 12 appear to have exhausted themselves by the beginning of Scene Four. Then, starting with m. 22 (No. 26), the composer used the entire sequence in its retrograde inversion.

Act One :
I. The Pupil (Nos 3–10)
II. A Dangerous Adventure (Nos 11–18)
III. A Sham Page (Nos 19–25)
Act Two :
IV. The Attacking Spirit (Nos 26–31)
V. A Wounded Passion (Nos 32–34)
Act Three :
VI. Revenge (Nos 35–40)
VII. Desperate Efforts (Nos 41–43)
VIII. Bolero (Nos 44–52)

The main message of the opera is rendered by the stage managing director in his introductory speech (No. 1): "... here is an instructive story presented in the allegorical style wherein the characters' principles are competing with their passions. Herein **the battlefield is the soul**; the moving force behind the whole action is curiosity." In the last number of the opera (No. 52) the managing director repeats the same words. This episode is called "Allegory." Alvare and Biondetta appear in the masks to stress the point that all the developments are imaginary, a lesson to be learned, a scenic action. At the end of the opera the figures on the stage, the director and all the performers, stand rooted to the spot. Assessing his sole composition for the musical theatre, Alexander Vustin emphasized that he was generally attracted by a show performance, a farcical scenic action to be perceived as a kind of ritual (like in Stravinsky's *L'histoire du soldat*). The developments are treated as a parody while the imaginary nature of the action is underlined by the endless disguises. Thus, Alvare's friends, Bernadillo and Soberano, appear either as surgeons or as gypsy-women singing in male voices. The Demon's voice from Anton Rubenstein's opera *The Demon* (singing "And you will be the Queen of the world...") also sounds like a parody at the moment when Biondetta utters: "You will be the king of the Universe and me, its Queen" (in No. 42).

In some sections of the opera the listener feels involved in the atmosphere of mystical premonitions and the devilish metamorphoses. A major part in such episodes is assigned to the percussion ensemble to convey the action of supernatural forces: thus, for instance, in No. 14, "Metamorphoses," the ceiling is drawn apart and Alvare sees the Camel's head asking "Che vuoi?", and then the Camel turns into the Spaniel. The orchestra includes some noise-producing instruments, such as the washing board and the self-made percussion instruments handled by the opera's characters, such as tambourines and rattles. In No. 51 there appears a ballet-dancer with the mule's jaw (quijada) in his hands, dancing to his own rhythm and beating it at the same time by his feet on the instrument as well.

In Jacques Cazotte's novel the devil eventually turns out to be the winner while Alvare pleads mercy. As for Vustin's opera, it provides no definite denouement, with everyone being left to one's own judgment: either Biondetta's love for Alvare has transformed her completely, making her to side with her lover, or the appearance of the devil's head at the end of the action is designed to imply the hero's defeat. The composer is not striving for the resolution of the conflict, leaving it beyond the scope of his work; the plot line is cut short, and the opera ends with the question addressed to the audience ...

Alexander Vustin's *Music for the Ten*, a short piece lasting for six minutes and written two years later, came in some curious way to be linked both with the plot and the musical images of his opera *The Devil in Love*. Their relationship proved to be so close that the composer allows of its performance in two forms: as a separate piece and as an entr'acte before the opera's Act Three (in the latter case, presented on a film-strip).

Music for the Ten is set to the text of *Cazotte's Prophesy*, written by Jean-Franis La Harpe in the 18th century and freely arranged by the composer. This piece resembles a musical spiritualistic séance with its characters representing the spirits of the dead persons now engaged in joint reminiscences about an evening party once spent together ("it seems to me that it all happened just yesterday, though it actually took place early in 1788... On that day a lot of people gathered together at the house belonging to one of our fellowmen from the Academy..."). The culmination point of that party comes when Jacques Cazotte (to be performed by the conductor) starts predicting who and how could end his earthly existence (on the scaffold, from a poison, or in some other way). Following the last words of the piece — *Kyrie eleison*, the conductor and the orchestra players stop dead in their postures at the moment the last syllable is uttered (its end similar to that of the opera).

Music for the Ten is intended for ten performers including nine instruments (flute, bass clarinet, trumpet, French horn, piano, violin, viola, cello, and double-bass) and the conductor. The musicians not only play their instruments but also talk among themselves and with the conductor, freely passing from recitation to playing. According to the composer's remarks. "The instrumentalists while performing the *Voce* part are to recite the text 'expressionlessly' as if playing the words at sight. Any imitation of the actors' manner of reciting or any attempt to make the text sound dramatic are excluded, for it runs counter to the composer's message." Besides, the conductor introduces a recorded episode from Alexander Vustin's *Dedication to Beethoven*, with the flutist and the viola player having also to tackle the sirens. The composition incorporates some quotations from Scriabin's *Prometheus* and the Catholic chant *Dies irae*.

The musical resolution of *Music for the Ten* is similar to some sections of the opera. It is a spectacular sonoristic piece based on an indefinite musical tone, whisper, sounds between whisper and speech, glissando played with closed and open lips. It gives rise to certain associations with Alexander Vustin's other vocal instrumental compositions, especially with his expressionistic *Zaitsev's Letter*.

In the early 1990s some new tendencies came to the fore in the composer's work, revealing themselves for the first time in his *White Music* for organ. This composition is based strictly on the twelve-tone technique, but in its first movement the composer deliberately avoids to the last moment to use D-flat, the last note in his series (the twelfth note seems to be implied, though it is not actually taken). This D-flat, note is very important, since within the series, according to the composer's conception, there occurs a kind of modulation from B-flat to D-flat.

The second case of combining the diatonics and twelve-tone procedures is his Sextet for French horn, piano, bass drum, violin, viola and cello, entitled *Heroic Lullaby* and dedicated to his friend — the composer Alexander Raskatov. It is an extended *Andante*.

Only in the latter quarter of the piece the tempo becomes slightly more energetic with a view to replacing, to quote the composer, "the measured solemn 'pace' by something like the striking of the wall chiming clock." The static mode conforms with the stiffened tempo. The piece is built up on the *obikhodny* (ritual) scale, earlier used exclusively in the old Russian church music (g-a-b c^1-d^1-e^1 f^1-g^1-a^1 $b^1_\flat$–c^2-d^2). The scale is prolonged to the ultimate limits up and down, embracing eventually all the diatonic and chromatic tones.

The turn to the *obikhodny* mode appears to be another landmark in Alexander Vustin's creative career. The composer appraises this modal structure as one of possible ways to depart beyond the somewhat automatic, in his view, European chromaticism based on the equal-temperament system: "I felt myself confined within the framework of the tempered system associated for me with a certain loss of purity. I see a way out of it in turning to the pre-tempered system when the chord was pure. But to write just in the old-time modes is too simple. It is necessary to preserve all the achievements in the history of music and, first and foremost, its functionality," The harmonic conception of the Sextet is based on a combination of the diatonic *obikhodny* mode and the twelve-tone procedures. The temporal organization of this piece corresponds with its pitch organization, which is also 12-fold (but owing to the size of 12-fold blocks of its form these are stated only three times).

Alexander Vustin attaches particular importance to the departures form the initial form-building principles in pitch and temporal organisation (treating a departure as a component of musical form). Thus, he departs from the *obikhodny* mode at the moment when the instrumentalists' voices are set into action, using the notes non-existent in the initial scale (from Fig. 31). The instrumentalists sing in overtones (each note producing overtones providing for these additional sounds). By the way, the instrumentalists sing a lullaby (this partly explaining the piece's title). As for the Coda, here the 12-fold rhythmics are also violated because of the "wrong" concluding measures.

This Sextet contains some quotations from Schoenberg's *A Survivor from Warsaw*, Mussorgsky's *Boris Godunov*, Mahler's Fifth Symphony, from Beethoven (the often recurred rhytmical figure of his motto-theme of destiny), as well as the quotations from Alexander Vustin's own compositions cited here not in their literal form but somewhat revised and delivered tentatively as if from memory. And what was most important for the composer all these allusions arise spontaneously from the very texture of his music and its logical development.

In the early 1990s Alexander Vustin was also preoccupied with further development of his constructive ideas, his principle of 12-fold restatement in particular. His latest approach is to treat twelve notes as a single monolithic sound (a kind of compound "twelve-element sound"). Any subsequent manipulations with this compound sound are subject to the above discussed numerical set-form. This novel creative idea is still in the process of its elaboration. . .

PRINCIPAL WORKS

1966 *Three Poems by Moisei Teif* for baritone and piano (translated from Hebrew by Yunna Moritz). 9′

1966 *String Quartet.* 26′
Moscow, Sovetsky Kompozitor Publishers, 1977

1967, Three Choruses: 1. *Lament for Armenia's Victims* for
1976, male chorus and bass drum, 2. *Lamento* for mixed chorus
1988 and flute, 3. *The Star* for mixed chorus to lyrics by Mikhail Lermontov. 10′

1969 *Symphony* for full symphony orchestra. 30′

1971 *Cantata to Wartime Poems* for soloists, chorus and orchestra to verses by Boris Pasternak, Alexander Surkov and Paul Eluard. 30′

1972 *Three Toropets Songs* for piano. 7′
Moscow, Sovetsky Kompozitor, 1977

1972, *Nocturnes* for chamber ensemble in three movements. 15′
1982 Moscow, Sovetsky Kompozitor, 1985

1973 *Sonata for six Instruments* (piccolo, flute, clarinet, viola, cello, double-bass) in two movements. 6′.
Piano version. Moscow, Sovetsky Kompozitor, 1980

1975 *Toropets Songs* for instrumental ensemble (flute, bass clarinet, piano, violin, viola, cello). 10′

1975 *The Word* for wind and percussion instruments. 9′
Moscow, Sovetsky Kompozitor, 1986

1975 *Memorial* for strings, keyboard and percussion instruments. 2′

1977 *In Memory of Boris Kliuzner* for baritone, violin, viola, cello and double-bass to words by Yuri Olesha. 4′.
Moscow, Sovetsky Kompozitor, 1988

1977, *Capriccio* for female voice, chorus of basses
1982 and instrumental ensemble (on three Hebrew themes from Mikhail Beregovsky's collection) in three movements. 15′. MELODIA, 1989

1978 *Memoria-2.* Concerto for percussion, keyboard and stringed instruments. 14′
Moscow, Sovetsky Kompozitor, 1988
Released by OPUS, Bratislava 9110 1448

1979 *Fairy Tale* for solo oboe. 3′
Moscow, Sovetsky Kompozitor, 1982

1981 *Homecoming* for baritone and 13 instrumentalists to lyrics by Dmitry Shchedrovitsky. 13′. Moscow, Sovetsky Kompozitor, 1988

1982 *Idle Thoughts of Kozma Prutkov* for baritone and percussion ensemble in three movements, to Kozma Prutkov's texts. 12′

1983 *Three Settings of Alexander Pushkin and Dmitry Shchedrovitsky* for baritone and piano. 9′
Moscow, Sovetsky Kompozitor, 1988

1984 *Dedication to Beethoven.* Concerto for percussion and small symphony orchestra. 18′. Moscow, Sovetsky Kompozitor, 1988

1987 *Festivity.* Composition for children's and mixed choruses and symphony orchestra, to texts from Russian 17th-century chant collections. 13′

1988   *Blessed Are the Poor in Spirit.* Piece for voice and ensemble, to the text form the Gospel according to St. Matthew. 7′

1989   *The Devil in Love.* Scenes for voices and instruments. Libretto by Vladimir Khachaturov after Jacques Cazotte's short novel *Le Diable amoureux*

1990   *Zaitsev's Letter* for voice, strings and bass drum, text by Sergei Zaitsev. 7′

1990   *White Music* for organ. 10′
        Hans Sikorski, Hamburg, 1991

1990   *Action in the Spirit of Luigi* for percussion ensemble. 7′

1991   *Music to a Film.* Suite for percussion and orchestra in four movements. 45′

1991   *Music for the Ten* (flute, bass clarinet, trumpet, French horn, piano, violin, viola, cello, double-bass, and the conductor). Text by Jean-Franis La Harpe. 6′

1991   *Heroic Lullaby.* Sextet for French horn, bass drum, piano, violin, viola and cello. 17′

1992   *Three Songs from Andrei Platonov's Novel "Chevengur"* for voice and ensemble (clarinet, bass clarinet, viola, cello and double-bass). 5′

1992   *Dedication to the Son* for flute and ensemble in two movements. 18′

1992   *Piece for organ.* 6′

1993   *Music for Solo Bassoon* in two movements. 10′

1994   *The Birth of a Piece* for string quartet in three movements. 7′

1994   *A Sacred Story, or the Son Humanity,* suite from the film score.

1994   *For the Flame* for bassoon and piano. 7′

1994   *Little mass for the dead* for soprano and string quartet. 15′

1995   *Music for Angel,* trio for saxophone, vibraphone and cello. 12′

1995   *Song from Platonov's Novel* for male chorus and orchestra. 6′

1995   *Disappearance* for bayan, cello and stringed orchestra. 17′

1996   *Fantasy* for violin and orchestra. 12′

A lyrical digression with commentary or, that 'notorious' Ekimovsky

Vladimir Barsky

Victor Ekimovsky

. . . I began composing when I was thirteen, and very soon it was Sergei Prokofiev who became my idol. Perhaps, his influence on the formation of my creative personality was the greatest as compared to other composers, though several years later I departed quite far from his stylistics towards newer more radical music.

The evolution of my creative work is virtually the evolution of cognition as it were. Whenever I came to learn something new I invariably tried to embody it in my music. As a matter of fact, a purposeful change of guidelines, i.e. a successive preoccupation with some definite tasks, is out of my line.

The inner world of Victor Ekimovsky's musical labyrinths has so far remained inaccessible, waiting for their adequate comprehension notwithstanding the current hard times unconducive to concentration on spiritual matters. And yet, sometimes it is necessary to forget about the current daily problems and try to get through the paling of abstract notational symbols erected according to some definite design known to the composer alone. In this universe of sounds made up of the "consciously" moving musical atoms, which seem to be striving from the very outset for some ultimate goal, one's craft turns out to become a destiny, whereas the profession of a composer becomes a means of grasping the perpetually slipping truth unattainable even with a passage of years.

. . . From the time of its inception music was developing through gradual accumulation of separate local discoveries; in the course of the latter's exploration it was steadily moving towards an increasingly complex inner organization. This accumulation in quantity lasted until the 20th century, which came to be distinguished by an abundance of qualitative leaps making it possible to produce most intricate music bypassing the previously inevitable gradual maturity. Hence a great variety of schools, trends, stylistic individualities and eventually compositions unique in some or another of their qualities. As a result, nowadays it is extremely difficult, if ever possible, for a composer to produce something radically new.

In this vortex of the current developments each modern composer invents his own creative guidelines. A majority of them, including Shostakovich, Hindemith, Webern and Edison Denisov, work out for themselves a certain stylistic stereotype, mercilessly employing it throughout their life. Some others (and there are far less of them) are striving to make a synthesis of diverse achievements in world music, fusing them into a singularly individual panstylistic conglomerate, e.g. Messiaen, Alfred Schnittke, et al. To the third category belong those (the fewest of all) who set for themselves the periods of some definite style, Igor Stravinsky being the forerunner of this tendency...

20th-century music history has borne out that progress in art is not a unidimensional notion; that a motley tangle of aesthetic trends and musical fashions could be uncoiled endlessly, with the innovations sometimes before our very eys becoming archaic, and the avant-garde turning into the rearguard immediately labelled "a step back" into the past. Only those things prove to be of lasting value which, not ignoring the perpetual motion of musical substance to the unexplored domains, elevate this objective motion to a certain spiritual level, allowing us to speak about the reasonableness of the musical language, which cannot be learned and which should be accepted once and for all.

...Finally, there may be the fourth type of a modern artist who in his creative work embodies in each concrete case the stylistic characteristics, means of expression and techniques selected exclusively for a given composition. As a result, there emerge unique compositions that could neither be imitated nor give rise to a certain trend or school. The most vivid examples of such compositions are Stockhausen's *Stimmung*, John Cage's 4'33", and Alexander Scriabin's incomplete *Mystery*.

I believe that this creative approach is the best suited to the spirit of our times, for it stimulates the search for the "new," perhaps to the point of attaching absolute significance to the idea of "novelty," and it is on this road alone that discoveries and genuine revelations of true artistic value are possible today.

For me this approach is not theoretical, but evolved spontaneously; upon merely analyzing the list of my compositions, I came unexpectedly to reveal its intrinsic feature: each new one, as compared with the previously written compositions, had far more distinctions than similarities in all the basic parameters making the essential characteristics of a musical work.

Two piano quartets — *Compositions 1 and 2* — were based on the principles of atonality and orthodox dodecaphony respectively. *Composition 2* for violin, clarinet, cello and piano was written expressly for a concert that presented, for the first time in Moscow, Olivier Messiaen's *Quatuor pour la fin du temps*, which explains its non-conventional instrumentation. Its three movements — Theme, Counterpoint and Variations — embody respectively the idea of thesis, antithesis and synthesis. The means of musical expression used in this composition as regards its rhythm, texture, dynamics, etc, deliberately depart from the conventional stereotypes of dodecaphonic style.

Cadenza for solo cello (*Composition 5*) was written for Alexander Ivashkin who appeared as its first performer. The meaning of the term "cadenza" is two-fold. On the one hand, it is an extended self-contained solo piece (following the extended cadenzas in the concertos of Beethoven, Tchaikovsky and Rachmaninov, there appeared cadenzas as separate movements — in Dmitry Shostakovich's Violin Concerto and Alfred Schnittke's *Concerto grosso* No. 1). Subsequently, it remained to make just one more step to turn a cadenza into a separate composition as it were. On the other hand, it is a virtuosic episode in a non-existent cello concerto. Its structure is free, though imitating the structure of a typical cadenza — with a faster motion at the end and the indispensable closing trill according to the classical specimens. (I wouldn't object if any cellist has taken it into his head to insert my *Cadenza* into a cello concerto written by some other composer.)

Composition 7 for string quartet is an experiment in aleatory texture (quite uncommon for the year 1970 in this country), though combined with the classical principles of thematic development: each of the four instruments has its own textural theme. Its structure is based on the serial principle, the exposition of themes being followed by the development section built up on separate elements of themes and their accompanying counterpoints and introducing nothing new as regards its texture and tone-structure. The recapitulation representing solos of each instrument leads to the Coda with its resolution of the work's message.

The aleatory principles are also used in *Sublimations* for orchestra.

Victor Ekimovsky is like a monument always looking forward. His music rests on the perpetual, albeit unsteady, foundation of an experiment, producing quite often most striking results inexplicable from the viewpoint of his previous compositions. Each new work is based on a novel idea involving into the sphere of its gravity a particular range of artistic and compositional techniques inherent in it alone.

And this has been going on from the outset of his creative career, beginning with his Lyrical Digressions that marked the end of his academic training and scandalized his colleagues at the time...

...In *Lyrical Digressions* for a solo group of cellos and orchestra I elaborated on the collage technique. The underlying idea was to juxtapose two contrasting principles: my own music deliberatley unmelodious and built up on the general forms of movement, and the lyrical quotations from the classical works by Mahler, Barber, Brahms and Tchaikovsky. In the finale, at its climax, there occurs a direct confrontation of these two different stylistic layers — my own music and that of Tchaikovsky.

Balletto for a conductor and an ensemble of musicians is graphic music (in the score) and a kind of the instrumental theatre (in concert performance). It is a type of composition that should be not only listened to but also seen. The score is written for the conductor alone, presenting in graphic symbols all of the maestro's movements (not only of his hands but also his head, shoulders, feet and other parts of his body); the music is being born out of the conductor's gestures, making each performance looking differently. It had its premiere eight years after it had been written, with the challenge taken by Mark Pekarsky and his Percussion Ensemble. It could be virtually performed by any cast of musicians — from a few players up to an orchestra. In my practice I came to see its various interpretations, among them quite extravagant, such as by a rock group or a full symphony orchestra.

"... *there was the slapstick humour of the totally silent cadenza for the conductor*" (*Glasgow Herald*).

"*Ekimovsky's Balletto formed the latter part of the programme and most successful due mainly to the acting abilities of Mark Pekarsky.*

"*The work is written for a conductor whose movements are carefully choreographed and to whose gestures the players improvise.*

"*Pekarsky's gaunt and angular figure was just right for this piece of absurd theatre to which he brought an excellent sense of comedy*" (*Scotsman*).

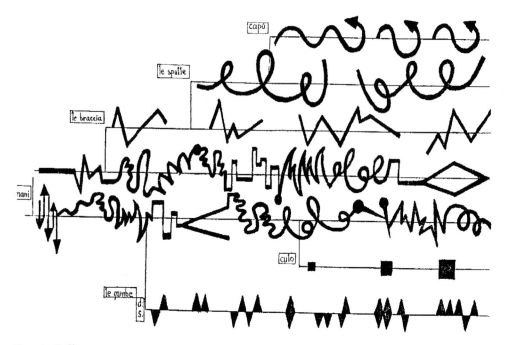

Ex . 1 *Balletto*

. . .*Kammervariationen* for thirteen performers is an attempt to reproduce the total serial effect. It is based on Anton Chekhov's short story *So Sleepy*, hence its psychologi- cally lyrical mood. In structural terms, Chekhov's poetic style also played a decisive part: the complete text of his story may be recreated if some definite words (in syllables as in the vocal part) are placed under each of its musical phrases. The emotional charge and meaning of each word is embodied in the greatest possible degree. And since the writer used to repeat the same words and situations in his stories, you get variations. In technical terms this piece is outwardly reminiscent of Webern's style, hence its dedication to the two Antons.

The string *Quartet-cantabile* is based on the unitary structural principle sustained from beginning to end: alternation of a motto-theme evocative of the sighs and entreaty, and a rest. This nearly speaking tone symbolizes man's inner state.

The Trumpets of Jericho for 30 brass instruments overwhelm the listeners with a powerful avalanche of sounds sometimes producing a horrible effect. And this is what underlies its message — the destruction of a city.

Ave Maria for 48 violins epitomizes a synthesis of spiritual and material aspects of a musical work. The very idea being projected far ahead calls for its "untwisting." I avoid situations when the musical material has to be confined to some definite principle of development. I believe the very word "development" has nothing to do with what is going on in my music. In modern music a composition arises from its texture. You have to invent a texture to make a composition a reality, and if you failed to do so, there will be no composition at all. Simultaneously with an impulse and an idea, you have to preconceive a texture, not a separate sound, tone, theme or harmony, but texture. As soon as I have generated an idea and the rules of the game, the composition is unfolding on its own, irrespective of me and without my further involvement in it. My task is just to provide some minor technical details, but in general it is inessential for the entire composition.

In *Cantus figuralis* for 12 saxophones I was looking for new potentials inherent in non-conventional and unusual combinations of instruments. I had never before heard such sonority and it aroused my interest. I began inventing sonorities and selected a texture in which you could hardly discern anything definite, being only able to imagine how it would sound in reality. As a result, some acoustic effects produced during its performance turned out to be unexpected. Of course, I had presumed that something should be in there but what exactly it was I did not know. In this case I was guided in my writing primarily by the constructive factor. Besides, I felt confident that a beautiful structure should produce beautiful sounds. Each movement had its own constructive idea. At first something had to be preconceived and then it just involved filling in of the outlined idea.

Any system is far from being perfect, always calling for some corrections. However, all the changes should be taken into account in preliminary designs. At the same time I do not consider myself confined in my composition work. I am free to do with the material whatever I wish. But I do not violate what has been designed beforehand. No doubt, there may be some technical corrections. Besides, in such cases I consciously try not to depart from my initial conception.

And in general, a composer has to be feeling free in his endeavors, otherwise he or she is not a composer at all. The granted freedom delivers only the composer's environment, changing the public attitude to him, allowing his compositions to be performed in the concert halls and providing for his physical survival. No doubt, freedom in any manifestation is always a positive fact, but what we witness today in this country is just anarchy. Indeed, Zarathustra was right when he said: freedom *from* rather than *for* something ...

The *Brandenburg Concerto* is based on the principle of stylization, with the focus on those moments in Bach's style which went beyond the framework of the period traditions: the voice-leading giving rise to the dissonant vertical and intricate harmonic relationships more inherent in the later periods. Basing myself on the quasi-Bachian stylistics, I somewhat exaggerated these moments but without borrowing a single authentic intonation. My turn to the idea of "imitating" is not a stylization in the spirit of Stravinsky, but rather a restoration. I was interested not in the conventional image of Bach well familiar to anybody, but in the Bach who tried to depart from his own style. The non-traditional and uncustomary vision of Bach arises from some minor details in his music, and I was keenly interested exclusively in these details.

Farewell for piano is a typical case of kitsch music. It is not stylization but "merely music" in mock-pop style. The use has been made of the three following genres: Nocturne, Elegy and Waltz (in 4/4 time). The Nocturne follows a through principle in its development, each time diminishing in its size, as if keeping something back, and herein lies the main idea of this piece...

Die ewige Wiederkunft, a composition for bass clarinet, was written at the request of the Dutch bass-clarinettist Harry Spaarnay. The idea of semi-fixed pitch organization struck me while I was under the impact of his virtuoso playing. The title of this piece is associated with one of major philosophical categories evolved by Nietzsche, his idea of eternal recurrence, an inevitable return of all and anything to one's own circle. An additional distinctive mark of this composition is the instrumental theatre delivered virtually in sonata form.

The return is indeed inevitable: in the process of playing the performer leaves the stage to return again, as if taking a second round; the piece's principal motto-theme, a symbol of "return" recurrs over and over again; with each new performance the circle (or a spiral?) is not closed up. The artistic idea once again remains unresolved...

...The underlying idea of *Sonata with a Funeral March* is the absence of the march stated in its title. There are separate allusions to this specific rhythm, making the basis of the aleatory episode in the second movement. The initial chord is the basis of the second movement and the finale. No concrete events are associated with this composition, just an artistic idea (Beethoven, Chopin).

A sample of minimal music is "Māndāla" for nine instruments. Its title derives from one of the symbols in Indian philosophy, which epitomizes a whole system of specific mentality and world-views. But I was interested not in its philosophical aspects but in the embodiment of the very idea of "māndāla" in a drawing, i.e. the "life" of the symbol as a visual artistic image. It represents a circle placed within a square. The square itself is divided into four sectors, each having its own symbols. Inside this drawing you see a great amount of additional symbols which say a lot to the initiated person. This drawing evocative of the idea of "māndāla" makes the object of meditation.

I ran into this symbol owing to the graphic works by the painter Gennady Sukhanov, known for his extensive experimentation in this domain: some of his works are associated with the idea of a circle, a square and graphic lines. The painter showed me the famous illustrations of this symbol, which are kept in museums throughout the world. It stirred up my interest and I began thinking how this idea of the unity of the world, the Oriental idea, could be expressed by musical means; moreover, I wanted it to be perceived as if it were my own view of the East.

This composition was commissioned by the Yugoslavian *Ansambl za drugu novu muziku* comprising many pianists, percussionists, and some other instrumentalists. Out of this ensemble I selected nine musicians who made up four groups, each containing necessarily a keyboard instrument added by some other instrument (eventually these made two percussion instruments, a cello and a saxophone).

In "māndāla" there is a key moment seeming to be inviolable and sacred to embody a certain vital, personal principle. I even tried to depict it visually by placing the four groups of instrumentalists within a circle, with the flutist seated in the centre (the ninth player). Since this centre represents a mystery, the flutist plays only at the very end.

Each instrumental group is playing synchronously, though irrespective of one another, the episode prescribed to it and consisting of separate dispersed chords, at first precisely deciphered but then given to the discretion of the players who are invited to improvise on them. Having played his own episode, the musician by the ear orienting himself to any other performer beats off his rest and then joins in again with a new episode. At the end of the composition all the groups meet together in one and the same rhythm.

The number of chords in each episode is carefully calculated, differing throughout and never repeated. This is to convey the idea of irrationality rendered in an exaggerated form by technical means as well.

In the original score all the time values had the precise rhythms. However in the process of recording the rhythmical idea retreated into the background. All the qualitative measurements were exclusively based on the number of chords, rather than duration. As a matter of fact, absolute rationality served as a point of departure for eventual irrationality.

Stanzas for two violins were named after a poetic genre characterized by its lyricism and laconic form. In its musical rendering this genre is embodied in seven short parts ("stanzas") contrastive in their imagery but making up an integral and indivisible cycle. It combines in a definite order both the rhytmically organized and freely aleatory pieces. The even-numbered stanzas are not scored but notated in the form of separate voices.

Ex . 2 *Stanzas*

This set of two violins was a challenge owing to a wide range of timbres and dynamics, and its most expressive and unusual textural resources. The technical complexities it involves call for high professionalism on the part of interpretative musicians. The composition was written for the International Festival of Chamber Music held in the Polish town of Luslawice at the request of its sponsor Krzysztof Penderecki.

Prelude and Fugue for Organ is a sample of meditative music. The first movement of the traditionally two-movement cycle signifies the triumph of harmonic vertical relationships-the chordal clusters on the tonic organ point seem to measure up the root notes of musical space, turning into its audible coordinates. The figure, as it often happens in Ekimovsky's music, constitutes a Kunststück making even the most sophisticated musician look for the laws underlying the life of this time-honored genre in a different sound environment. The polyphonic horizontal is reduced to a single tone which fails, strictly speaking, to give birth to a theme. In our bizarre world the stable values and categories very often turn out to be unattainable...

...*Composition 43* for two pianos is one of the large-scale works written in recent years. In technical terms its governing idea is to elaborate most diverse tempos, which implies the metrical and rhythmical independence of each part in this piano duet and their vertical asynchronous development. It lasts for nearly twenty minutes and follows the purposeful, mathematically calculated dramatic pattern leading to a powerful general climax (at this moment the taped recording joins in the action).

In the Hunting Dogs Constellation for three flutes is minimal music based on the same type of figures in all three instruments, elaborated against a background of the recorded radio interferences, noise and crackling, with arbitrary vibrations of dynamics ranging from *pp* to *mf*. The live noises are introduced by a fader several seconds before the start of the playing and withdrawn several seconds after it ends. The score is notated down in the form of a circle with separate bar-lines bearing the musical phrases with the encoded names of the constellations. Each flutist plays his whole part in succession and in full, then repeating its separate fragments in an arbitrary order. The composition ends at any place agreed upon by the players beforehand, but it necessarily involves their simultaneous transition to the concluding phrase. The score presents a kind of celestial map. The duration is optional, the performance may take from five to ten minutes (open time).

Three flutists are wholly engrossed in meditation, bending over a small round table fully in line with the form of the notational text lying on it. Outbursts and twinkles of the soundscape against the background of the infinitely lingering temporal and spatial continuum...

...*Doppelkammervariationen* for twelve players is a composition in six short movements, each being based on one and the same invariable pitch block. All the other means of the musical language (timbre, rhythm, dynamics, etc.) are subject to gradual variation. Besides, the first half of the composition (three variations) is scored in the precise, conventional notation whereas the latter half (the other three variations with absolutely the same music) is presented in graphic symbols. Hence its title defined as "double." It has been my long cherished idea to employ the stable and mobile techniques within one composition using the same musical material.

Assumption for percussion ensemble has been written at the request of Mark Pekarsky and dedicated to this remarkable musician. It is not a direct illustration of the plot inherent in the old Russian icon painting, but the general idea of this piece is associated with apprehension of the sacrament of a departing earthly life. The minimalist technique in this case, in my view, is conductive to setting up the atmosphere of strict meditation. Its asceticism is stressed by the usage of muffles by all the drums without exception, to avoid the characteristic and customary stereotype of loud and rhythmic playing associated with percussion instruments: the entire composition is unfolding within the range of *pp* nuances, without any common rhythmical vertical relationships.

"The sight of the instruments being painstakingly draped in shrouds injected an inevitable element of black comedy into the performance".

"The barely audible opening, the fastidous rhythms, the muffled drums — not to mention the audience's absolute silence while the players slowly tapped and clicked their notes — nevertheless made this piece of funeral music theatre the highlight of the evening" (Scotsman).

...*Deus ex machina* for harpsichord, written at the request of the Swiss harpsichordist Petja Kaufman, is marked by the uniform texture, rhythms, dynamics, and techniques, with a new quality in rhythmic accents and textural rests appearing only at the very end, providing the key to comprehending the message of this composition and its title.

The piece's modal development is rooted in six-note chordal modes with foreign sounds gradually injected hereinto and imperceptibly transforming one mode into another. The rhythmical procedures are strictly calculated, with differences in the recurrence of the chords following the intricate quasi-serial logics.

Trippelkammervariationen is the concluding piece in the quite conditional cycle of variations embracing *Kammervariationen, Doppelkammervariationen* and *Trippelkammer-variationen*. All the three pieces have some common features as regards their musical language, the principles of development and their style.

The term "triple" implies not three themes but three movements: the composition falls into three extended sections, three variations of the initial material exposed at the beginning. Written for the *Modern* Ensemble, it is characterized by a deliberate avoidance of any melodic structures, harmonic functions, dynamic waves and any-thing that may be associated with so called emotional music.

In my compositions I'm trying not to repeat the previous findings, striving in each of them for elaboration of some novel means of expression, technical and stylistic devices. Therefore, one piece may reveal the prevalence of the collage principle, another — stylization, and still others are marked for either serialism, aleatory, graphic notation or minimalism, kitsch or the instrumental theatre. In retrospective view, each piece in my output is singular, for I never know beforehand what procedures I'm going to employ in writing my next composition.

As for repetitions in my works, I should stress once again that I'm consciously avoiding them, being guided primarily by a search for something novel and pre-viously unexplored, for I'm not in the least interested in repeating myself. And it puzzles me when somebody finds anything immutable in my compositions. Perhaps, repetitions occur unconsciously, at some deep-going level in my thinking.

Of course, I'm far from believing that all my endeavors are actually "singular" on a global scale, nevertheless, in retrospection each one becomes for me really new, absolutely dissimilar to all my previous compositions. By the way, this explains why it is so easy to criticize my music, which has been done quite often, for "the lack of a style all his own," "too prolonged quests for his own individuality" and the like. However, I'm still confident of my guidelines: the new should be really novel in all conceivable respects.

It is another point how well I manage to cope with this task, and I hope I'm not ever going to sit in judgment of my own compositions ...

In the hierarchy of current occupations in Russia the profession of a composer ranks last. As a matter of fact, it has always been so, but the circle seems to be currently narrowing down. True enough, to "reform" an artistic personality has so far remained unfeasible for anybody. A serious composer have invariably his own firm convictions irrespective of social cataclysms. For his life in music is concentrated on the quests for its inner sense identified by means of sheet

Ex. 3 *Composition 43 for two pianos*

music and the acoustic environment. Victor Ekimovsky does not claim for the exclusiveness of his world-view, but neither is he to be guided by the rules of the game so often imposed by the life around him. Therefore his position is so natural and convincing.

Born in 1947 in Moscow, Victor Ekimovsky graduated from the Gnesin Music Teachers Training Institute (1971) where he studied composition with Aram Khachaturyan, and music history with Konstantin Rozenschild; he completed his postgraduate education at the Leningrad Conservatoire (1978) where he majored in the history of foreign music with Galina Filenko.

Victor Ekimovsky took a master's degree in musicology (1983) and has to his credit numerous articles on modern music and the first Russian monograph about Olivier Messiaen (published by Sovetsky Kompozitor in 1987); he has also edited several volumes of Dmitry Shostakovich's *Collected Works*.

Many of his compositions have been written on a commission from the well-known musicians and performing bodies (among them Harry Spaarnay, the International Saxophone Ensemble directed by Jean-Marie Londeix, and the *Modern* Ensemble). His music has been performed at the international music festivals in Zagreb, Warsaw, London, Duisburg, Frankfurt and in Moscow.

PRINCIPAL WORKS

1969 *Composition 1* for violin, viola, cello and piano. 8' Moscow: Kompozitor, 1994.
Composition 2 for violin, clarinet, cello and piano. 9' Moscow: Kompozitor, 1994
Composition 4 for piano. 12' Moscow: Sovetsky Kompozitor, 1989
1970 *Cadenza* for cello. 6'
Composition 7 for two violins, viola and cello. 8' Leipzig: VEB, 1985
1971 *Trio-sonata da camera* for violin, piano and cello. 11'
Lyrical Digressions for cellos soli and orchestra. 18'
Sublimations for symphony orchestra. 10'
1974 *Ave Maria* for forty-eight violins. 5'
Balletto for conductor and ensemble. 13'
Kammervariationen for thirteen players. 8' Moscow: Muzyka, 1986 Melodia: C10
15747-8 CD: Le Chant du Monde, LDC 288062, CM 210
Nocturnes for three clarinets. 8' Moscow: Sovetsky Kompozitor, 1979
1977 *Quartet-cantabile* for two violins, viola and cello. 9' Moscow: Sovetsky Kompozitor, 1991 CD: Le Chant du Monde, LDC 288062, CM 210
The Trumpets of Jericho for thirty brass instruments. 18'
1979 *Brandenburg Concerto* for flute, oboe, violin, string, orchestra and harpsichord. 13'
1980 *Farewell* for piano. 12'
Die ewige Wiederkunft for bass clarinet. 7'
Cantus figuralis for twelve saxophones. 13'
1981 *Sonata with a Funeral March* for piano. 12' Moscow: Muzkya, 1985 Melodia: C10
21917 000 CD: Olympia, OCD 295
1983 *Māndālā* for nine players. 10' Moscow: Muzyka, 1991 CD: Le Chant du Monde,
LDC 288062, CM 210
1984 *Stanzas* for two violins. 15' Moscow: Sovetsky Kompozitor, 1989 Melodia: C10
26479 009 CD: MLD 32131
1985 *Prelude and Fugue* for organ. 8' Moscow: Sovetsky Kompozitor, 1988 Hamburg:
Sikorski, 1990 CD: Le Chant du Monde, LDC 288062, CM 210
Composition 43 for two pianos. 18' Moscow: Kompozitor, 1994
1986 *In the Hunting Dogs Constellation* for three flutes and magnetic tape. 5'–10' CD:
Le Chant du Monde, LDC 288062, CM 210
1989 *Doppelkammervariationen* for twelve players. 12' CD: OLYMPIA, OCD 282
Assumption for percussion ensemble. 10'
1990 *Deus ex machina* for harpsichord. 12' Hamburg: Sikorski, 1992
1991 *Trippelkammervariationen* for fifteen players. 20'
1992 *Kite-Flights* for four recorders. 8'
1993 *Moonlight Sonata* for piano. 10'
1993 *Symphonic Dances* for piano and orchestra. 25'
1994 *From Escher's catalogue.* Theatrical piece for seven musicians. 16'
1994 *La Favorite — La Non favorite* for harpsichord. 13'
1995 *27 Destructions* for percussion ensemble. 16'
1995 *The Mirror of Avicenna* for fourteen players. 7'
1996 *Swan song* for string quartet. 16'
1996 *Swan song* for string quintet, conductor and tape. 12'

Alexander Raskatov's apologia

Vladimir Barsky

Alexander Raskatov

The formation of an artist is one of the most mysterious processes in the earthly realization of a human personality, even if it takes place before your eyes. Indeed, a unique combination of many components, both external and internal, is involved to make ring out that innermost string whose vibrations determine the inimitable "timbre" of a composer's voice and the latter's harmonic incorporation in the universal "music of spheres".

This somewhat solemn introduction in the Hellenic spirit is due to the impressions gained long time ago from meeting Alexander Raskatov, then just a budding musician, before the author of the present article had actually a chance to listen to his compositions. The talks, as it always happens with young persons, concerned mainly existential matters, with references quite often made to Plato's texts, for the symbolism inherent in the mythological aesthetics of this ancient Greek philosopher seemed to provide the intellectual medium for an adequate perception of the world. It may well be asserted that the *Aufhebung* of these ideas, perhaps even subconsciously, in many respects predetermined the parabola of Alexander Raskatov's creative career (for the same reason the further discussion will sometimes follow the pattern of "Socratic dialogue," combining the voiced opinions of the composer himself, music critics, and some commentary offered by the author of the present article).

Alexander Raskatov's road in art was not so straight and easy. And the point is not in winning recognition, for as early as during his conservatoire years his serious attitude to artistic matters came to the notice of the people around him, and today his compositions are regularly performed in concerts and within the programmes of music festivals both in Russia and abroad. They are played and recorded by distinguished interpretative artists, and published and appraised by music critics. The point is that Alexander Raskatov's road to self-cognition and overcoming of the perpetual aesthetic problem arising from the assumption that "any idea once uttered sounds false" called for passing a certain artistic distance (by the way, his compositions include one symptomatically entitled *The Road*).

It would be fully justified to say that in the beginning of Alexander Raskatov's creative work there was word; primarily, because a circle of books he had read embraced a vast amount of strata involved in a dialogue of world literatures. Hence a diversity of a "circle of songs" — a play on words is predetermined in this case by the title of his composition written in the mid-eighties. Secondly, according to the composer himself, a word may become for him "a supporting device helpful in defining a reliable criterion in choosing a subject-matter of a composition". Alexander Raskatov's vocal music ranges from the refined score of his cantata *Courtly Songs* based on the haiku by early medieval Japanese poets, his *Stabat Mater* for voice and organ, rooted in the Gregorian canon, to his vocal instrumental cycles: *Circle of Songs* to verses by Vasily Zhukovsky and Yevgeny Baratynsky, recreating the atmosphere of home music-making in 19th-century Russia; *Book of Spring* for tenor and chamber orchestra to verses by Vasily Zhukovsky, and *Let There Be Night* to verses by Samuel T. Coleridge; the lyrical oratorio *From Spring, From the Grass, From the Heavens* to verses by the singular Russian poetess Xenia Nekrasova, marked for a subtle penetration into the elements of her poetry and its adequate interpretation in musical tones.

"Raskatov's musical world is most often an intimate one; from the early Courtly Songs (1976), a chamber work to texts by Japanese poets, to the recent Let There Be Night (1989), Raskatov has showed himself an artist of medieval refinement, producing brilliantly crafted jewels and miniatures and shunning the grandiose and vulgar" (Gerard McBurney, musicologist).

Chamber music for a long time remained the main sphere of Alexander Raskatov's interests. It is in this domain that the composer was looking for the melodic formulas which, as the time passed, came to prevail in his musical language (Musical Example 1). For their evocation he selects quite unusual combinations of timbres and the closest to his style composition techniques and devices out of the 20th-century vast musical vocabulary. However he consistently follows his own principles in the organization of musical space in his vocal and instrumental compositions, regarding them as the logically arranged and dramatically verified musical speech subject to the general laws of rhetorics in their highest sense. Hence a dialogic nature inherent in most of his composition; you seem to discern behind them Socrates' voice guiding his pupils: "Well, Protarch, look what kind of discourse you are going to borrow from Phileb and what of our arguments you intend to question if you dislike any of them". Such a type of dialogue may involve different interlocutors, for instance, three flutes, two cellos and a harpsichord, voice, a percussion ensemble, *Cassa musicale*, a synthesizer, and a baby grand, but the main point invariably lies in the dialectical development of the initial premise, the imagerial and emotional elaboration of a musical idea.

Among Alexander Raskatov's major instrumental works written in the 1980s mention should be made primarily of his concerto for piano and chamber ensemble entitled *Night Hymns, Sentimental Sequences* for thirteen performers, and his Concerto for oboe and fifteen stringed instruments. The first of these compositions in its very title formulates the uncustomary "nocturnal" idea embodied by the modern aleatory and minimalist devices and actualized by an unusual combination of the instruments: the low registers of bass clarinet, bassoon, double-bassoon, trombone, and bass electric guitar, presenting a kind of paraphrased trio of low male voices from the introduction to Mozart's *Don Giovanni* to convey the atmosphere of night visions, fears, rustles, and obscure movements, which is so typical of the aesthetical views held by many 20th-century composers, Alexander Raskatov included. The cycle *Sentimental Sequences* with its "neo-romanticism", genre allusions and latent quotations continues to elaborate on the idea of a dialogue between the epochs wherein the limited span of a human life poses no obstacle for perpetual unfolding of an idea and its material realization. The last of the above mentioned works lends somewhat a different color to the composer's imagery. It consists of the following three movements: (1) "Voice of Grass," (2) "Voice of Water," and (3) "Voice of Birds." Here the solo instrument acts as a certain ideal voice of nature. The parts of the stringed instruments envelop it, merging into unitary musical environment. The motto idea — the core of the concerto — passes through several stages in its development — emergence, maturity and decline at the end of each movement. This kind of "dying" nature imparts an ecological understatement to the composition.

"Most impressive amongst his instrumental works is his piano concerto, Night Hymns (1984), written for his wife, the distinguished young pianist and composer, Olga Magidenko" (Gerard McBurney, musicologist).

"By far the most substantial work in this recital is the set of seven Sentimental Sequences. Raskatov appears far less prone to 'effect'-seeking per se, evoking his insinuating, claustrophobic sound world instead by the highly inventive juxtaposition of relatively conventional timbres. Particularly memorable in this respect are the ghostly, Janacek-like ostinati of No. 2 and the multi-layered pedal-pointing of No. 3. The entire set possesses a nightmarish quality, increasing in intensity until the mad wailing of No. 7, which abruptly and tantalisingly leaves one staring right over into abyss" (Olympia Compact Discs Ltd.).

". . . Sentimental Sequences is a series of seven firmly etched character sketches, slowly rising in pitch to end punishingly high (a brilliant demonstration of the group's technique). This piece was shown to be a remarkable feat of integration. Raskatov's piece also recycled older styles in modern context, but it gave the listener something recognisable to hold on to-a bit of Mahler in the fourth movement, and romantic snatches, of the sort it is impossible to play without an affected pose, elsewhere" (Glasgow Herald).

Alexander Raskatov's pieces for percussion instruments stand apart in his creative work, all of them written expressly for Mark Pekarsky's unique ensemble and inconceivable, at least today, without their conductor's striking personality taken into consideration: his inventiveness, rich fantasy, immaculate proficiency combined with his fine musicality and subtle emotionality. *Invitation to a Concert* offers a kind of journey around the halls of the museum of rare and non-European instruments from Mark Pekarsky's collection. *Reminiscences of the 'Alpine Rose'* explores the potentials of a dialogue between a "musical box" and more traditional representatives of the musical world. The last part in the triptych for percussion instrument — *Gra-ka-kha-ta* — has been designed, moreover, to exhibit the resources of the singer and violinist Alexei Martynov who got a chance to appear here in both roles (Musical Example 2).

"Raskatov has also produced a triptych of works for the Percussion Ensemble of Mark Pekarsky, which have become one of the most successful and popular parts of the ensemble's repertoire" (Gerard McBurney, musicologist).

"Mark Pekarsky commissioned Invitation to a Concert from Alexander Raskatov for his collection of exotic percussion instruments. It is a piece of instrumental theatre in which the listener is not only a spectator but a participant of the drama that is played out before him. A

carnival of changing instruments pass before his eyes, called into being by the soloists' bell. The ironic and grotesque, the serious and the comic are bizarrely combined in this 'play in seven scenes'.

"*Gra-ka-kha-ta for tenor, violin and percussion uses a text by Velimir Khlebnikov, the Russian futurist poet who experimented with language in an attempt to find a new, more direct expression of feelings through invented language. Raskatov's primary impetus for this work, which he wrote in 1988, was his desire to use a text which would not require translation into another language. The sounds were to be understandable to any listener.*

"*Alexander Raskatov wrote Reminiscences of the 'Alpine Rose' in 1982 especially for Mark Pekarsky's collection of percussion instruments, including a musical box which is the piece's main hero. A public-house barrel-organ waltz, an echo of a vanished epoch, unexpectedly gives birth to a doppelganger, vainly striving to be like its model. This is the synthesizer, our contemporary musical box. The nostalgic note becomes screamingly penetrating. The image of which we dream not only will not be resurrected but itself catastrophically loses its outline. The winding mechanism has run down — the box has fallen silent forever*" (New Beginnings).

"*... the empty stage with only a slowly winding-down musical box, which ended his Reminiscences of the 'Alpine Rose' was a neat, if purely visual, sign of our time*" (Fergus Black, musicologist).

It is not in vain that "people value the newest chants delivered recently by the singers" (Homer). So it would be quite natural in this case to address the composer himself, though in recent years we almost lost touch with each other. Below is the actual, rather than "artificial," dialogue we have had:

Alexander Raskatov: Upon my return from the USA late in 1990 I made up my mind to do everything possible not to lose time on any outside matters. I believe that for the last two years I have managed to accomplish something quite important to myself: I've almost completed the opera *The Pit and the Pendulum* after Edgar Allan Poe (the libretto in English has been provided by Alexei Parin). It was not a commission but a purely altruistic urge with which I infected the librettist as well. Besides, figuratively speaking, I managed to catch the last carriage, so to speak, since the former system of subsidized guest houses for composers today, with the commercialization of this sphere too, has collapsed, which excludes any chance to write anything you just like, without getting a commission. The opera remained unfinished, for I had to put it aside for a time being because of some other commitments I took up: on the initiative of Mark Pekarsky I wrote *Commentary on a Vision* for percussion ensemble and orchestra (1991). The underlying idea of this one-movement composition is musical decoding of a certain hypothetical vision. The soloist surrounded by the orchestra throughout the entire piece moves in a circle trying vainly to leave the confines of its closed space. The constructive feature of this piece is a system of timbre reflections, sort of an echo. The orchestra's sonority is immediately reflected in the soloist's part while occasionally some definite timbre of the percussion calls for its imitation by the other sections of the orchestra.

By the close of the piece the soloist in a somewhat bizarre cadence unfolding against the background of the striking clock once more, this time in a fast tempo, makes the same circle as if parting with the instruments.

Vladimir Barsky: Freud's *Traumdeutung* seems to be your primary impetus for this work, wasn't it?

A.R.: I wouldn't say that it was so direct, though I felt a keen interest for some relevant ideas. I would rather treat it as a commentary on a certain hypothetical vision. On the other hand, all the structural units of this quite longish piece, as it seemed to me, should be based, as far as their musical elaboration concerned, on the principles that were indeed discovered by Freud: the shifts in the musical layers and distortions in timbres in this case reflect the indirect links between the conscious and the subconscious, reality and its psychological perception. Then I wrote, on a commission from the Frankfurt Festival, a piece entitled *Xenia* for twenty-six performers (1991). It was first performed in September 1992 by the Deutschekammerphilharmonie Orchestra. The meaning of this title is two-fold: (1) it is associated with the name of the Russian poetess Xenia Nekrasova, who died in the fifties in utter oblivion and poverty. She used to write blissful, naive verses in an absolutely singular style, and her poetry definitely impressed me; (2) as is known, the word "xenia" means "wanderer," and the idea of wandering and roaming — audible and even almost visible — was very important to me.

The whole composition sustained in a very quiet, subdued and lucid tone, nearly to the point of insinuating sounds that emerge and immediately disappear, was to evoke the idea of blissful wandering. The entire piece grows out of the simplest proto-elements which I would define as proto-diatonic.

The sonoristic aura of this piece is based on the employment of such instruments as a temple gong, a jews' harp, Javanese gongs, a baby grand, and singing within the orchestra. It's performance was to be accompanied by a video film showing a succession of semi-abstract static landscapes. These two pieces *(Commentary on a Vision* and *Xenia)* are so intercomplementary that they should be performed together; I hope this could be arranged sometime in the future. I associate their interrelationship with the medieval paintings that used to depict paradise and hell on two halves of the same canvas.

V.B.: In this case it would be logical to insert in between a sort of aesthetic purgatory, don't you think so?

A.R.: Its role could be assigned to the environment in which these pieces have been written, I mean the surrounding reality. These are two halves of a single musical entity, at first sight seeming to be absolutely unrelated, in which *Xenia* embodies a certain ideal vision, an attempt to go back (in conformity with the meaning of its title implying "wanderer") where it is impossible to return — to the images of the unattainable proto-existence or childhood. With this message predominating, even the instrumentation was to convey it, up to using a baby grand and special kinds of percussion instruments. Both pieces were performed in 1992: *Xenia* in September in Frankfurt, and *Commentary on a Vision* in November in Moscow. I consider these two performances as the most important events in my recent life. Simultaneously I went on with working on another composition: some years ago Natalia Gutman and Yuri Bashmet commissioned me to write for them a concerto in memory of Oleg Kagan. Thus, I got engaged in writing my third large-scale composition in recent years.

V.B.: It is a double concerto in its genre, isn't it?

A.R.: Strictly speaking, it is not so much a double concerto (even though a concertante element here is very important) as a composition in twelve movements (according to the number of setting in a Requiem) whose whole musical spirit is imbued with the imagery of sacred music, though not quite in its customary meaning. The matter involves sort of proto-religious music in the spirit of old Byzantine or ancient Judaic music, taking us back to its proto-language. It is of vital importance for me to restore this immutable proto-language which is most likely going on to exist in our subconscious and imagination.

V.B.: Perhaps, it is worthwhile to discuss in greater detail the state of musical creativity when under the above mentioned current crisis everyone runs for his life, looking desperately for any hook or a straw to keep oneself afloat.

A.R.: I think that the current problems in composition matters arise from too excessive adherence to separate procedures or trends; avoiding any attempt at a synthesis, some particulars are treated as the sole device in music. As a result, music is still further divided into a vast amount of stylistic and technical trends to the detriment of its unity and integrity. By and large, our time, in my view, is a time of synthesis to be made under the guidance of one's own inner individuality or some other motivations.

Music history and the old masters set us the examples of fusing separate trends and "streams" into a certain integral whole, a common "suspended" state. Regrettably, modern composers almost never turn to the past experience or hardly attach any importance to it and herein lies the deficiency of modern music. As a rule, modern opuses come to the notice just for the sake of information, which produces the effect of a "disposable needle" in music when a composition serves a substitute for a momentary aesthetic injection. To revert to it is not at all necessary, which is doubtful per se. As for the composers who managed to elevate themselves over this state, such as Arvo Pärt, György Ligeti, and Alfred Schnittke, their music invariably holds a certain lasting mystery that could be hardly unraveled.

V.B.: Perhaps, for this reason precisely one is inclined to go back perpetually to their compositions?

A.R.: You always feel an urge to listen to such things over and over again, and perhaps, one should strive to attain the level of these composers (though there are very few of them). As a matter of fact, festivals of modern music feature quite a number of purely informative compositions creeping away like oysters without leaving any trace. True enough, the current professional level in purely technical terms is high as never before. At some major festivals of modern music you would virtually find no weak or poorly written compositions.

V.B.: Let us go back to the early Byzantine music, the old masters and the problems of a tradition in general.

A.R.: In this matter you observe a moment of hypnotic attraction to early music, a moment of interpretation. Complete authenticity is, of course, out of the question, but it is not the chief point. I'm interested not so much in the original form of the proto-language as in its possible existence, viewing it as a certain point of departure. I feel that this music is imbued with great power akin to that permeating the notations of the ancient synagogal chants. Admittedly, I'm not a connoisseur and cannot claim to possess certain systemic knowledge, but it is not so important to a composer. It is far more important what impressions you gain from this music and the imagery it evokes. While composing a concerto dedicated to the memory of Oleg Kagan I studied very carefully the specimens of the early Jewish music. I cannot appraise the final result, but my reliance on these sources in the process of my work just saved me.

V.B.: Schnittke was also proceeding in this way in his Fourth Symphony.

A.R.: And it is in his Fourth Symphony that Schnittke has embodied one of his most profound artistic ideas.

V.B.: Do you mean the oecumenical idea?

A.R.: As a matter of fact, this idea has been eventually and strikingly declared in the Coda of his composition. Most likely, I'm not being quite original, but I always believed that all sacred music had grown out of the common core that could hardly be defined. All is rooted in the same sources and any attempts to oppose one to another are not honest in most cases and therefore fruitless. This source belongs to no particular nation. Our current resources to penetrate so far back into history are limited, but to a modern composer it is perhaps far more important to create a certain myth and try to realize it in music, which is much more productive than keeping up with the current fashions in the musical world.

V.B.: Besides, it is hardly possible anyway.

A.R.: You are quite right. An attempt to recreate the idea of the musical proto-language, if it is impossible to find evidence in historical documents or in music, is not a creative panacea, but it is undoubtedly a way to a far fresher atmosphere than the one imposed on us by our current realities.

V.B.: It is justified even from the logical point of view, for all innovations like any objects of technical progress in no time turn into the attributes of history, with the present immediately turning into a past.

A.R.: Formerly, we could excuse ourselves by the unavailability of relevant information and, in our ignorance, we could go on devising a long-invented bike. Today, when we have access to such information, there arises a problem of retaining one's individuality. Of course, individuality based on semi-illiteracy is quite dubious. To retain one's individuality in the context of information explosion is far more difficult but it is more esteemed. Now as we have got involve in the world musical process, composition is likely to become a more complicated matter.

V.B.: And yet, to my mind, it won't do to overestimate the current situation, either. In the final analysis, a breakthrough into the informational space is not tantamount to the discovery of a musical America.

A.R.: Nevertheless, a chance to travel around the world, as Messiaen or Orff did, and to familiarize oneself with the specimens of world culture in the highest sense of the word, is invaluable for a composer. It may overwhelm, but at the same time it may become a powerful impetus. Of course, the point is not in the geographical movement. It would be nice to believe that the same may be attained through self-appraisal. Herein lie the potentials for inner renewal, but this is the most difficult road.

V.B.: It is possible to compile a song catalog of all the birds inhabiting our earth, and yet some basic categories won't change therewith. And quite the reverse, sometimes it is enough to hear a single bird singing...

A.R.: It is another evidence that movement towards one's own inner proto-language is quite possible. Every person is endowed with such striving for it, no matter in music or in any other type of human activity. Every person has one's own individual code, for it is no accident that we use the expression "know thyself." I believe that for this reason precisely the most signal successes have been scored by the composers who could find power enough in themselves to live, so to speak, beyond the control of time, for instance, Charles Ives. Today speed is marked by self-negation, producing a bizarre effect of self-elimintion. In the past, people used to travel in horse-driven cabs and yet during their lifetime they managed to accomplish so much that for a modern composer it seems incredible. And today people fly by plane and nevertheless they could have hardly time enough to write anything. In this respect much also depends on the working conditions, a possibility to concentrate on the prime things in some secluded place close to nature ...

V.B.: Leo Tolstoy lived in his estate at Yasnaya Polyana but Mikhail Bulgakov was writing on the edge of his kitchen table ...

A.R.: Everyone accommodates himself to the actual conditions, but nobody wishes to worsen them consciously. Rather to the contrary. We all need quietness and simple things in our daily life, but somehow even the minimal requirements to improve the living standards look too excessive against the background of our current realities. At the same time, plenty and abundance hamper the composer's self-realization. According-to the conventional long-established views, anything produced in Western music has been achieved thanks to the local conditions while our accomplishments have all been gained in spite of the prevailing domestic realities. Hence many compositions written in this country bear the stamp of much suffering.

V.B.: Life in general, judging from music history, was not so easy for good composers, and much suffering is quite inherent in their compositions.

A.R.: To all appearances, this factor has a wholesome effect on our work, though it does not make our life easier. It is very difficult to work in a large city, and not everybody can afford to live in a bungalow on a Fiji island.

V.B.: And what do you think about the line of your creative career? How did you start and what did you come to by this time?

A.R.: I can only repeat the poet's words that I have written nothing foul and mean. But I'm far from self-love when one considers anything he has written to be invaluable for mankind. I'm rather prone to another extreme. I have always shunned being classified as a composer. The only thing that I regard as very important to myself is to have serious inner grounds for writing a composition. Life with its commissions introduces certain changes but, as an ideal, weighty inner motivations are required for the emergence of a composition. Only in this case it is worth writing. Otherwise, especially if you come to think how much has already been written, it occurs to you that perhaps it is not worth to multiply the existing number over and above what is required. Those of my compositions that I appreciate most of all are united in my attempt to unravel some mystery, carrying a certain mystical moment. I was never able to make a rational analysis of composition I have written, neither before nor afterwards. It seems to me that as soon as I learn too much about it, it will die. In my case it is a purely intuitive process. That's another matter if your intuition is basically right, if you can trust your intuition, carrying a rational core in itself. No matter what techniques has been employed in writing a composition, I have invaribaly been striving for such intuitive comprehension of a musical form, the means of developing the musical material, etc. As far as I'm concerned, this approach appears to be most natural to me.

My recent compositions unite in some intricate way separate elements of diverse techniques — be it minimalism, aleatory, sonoristics or modality. It is by no means polystylistics, but rather an attempt to perceive various components of modern music through my own inner self, guided by intuition alone. Some of these components are quite alien to my nature, for example, I virtually write no purely dodecaphonic music. My prime concern is to interpret diverse, mutually unrelated, layers in modern music and try to fuse them into an integral whole. An individual combination, in each separate case, of different feature and their synthesis produces a singular effect. I always shunned sectarianism and concentration on a particular phenomenon, which is often fraught by too excessive detachment from a wealth of sounds. You owe nothing to anybody and you are entitled to dispose of anything you need in each concrete case. It is another point that sometime you may fail in your initial intentions.

V.B.: And what about the corporate interests for, as far as I know, you are a member of the Association of Modern Music (AMM)?

A.R.: Yes, I'm a member of this association of musicians who regard one another with great piety. Within this group you find different personalities, some close to you and others not so close, but man should feel responsible only for himself and for his own musical endeavors. If some composition is going to live on, it will be due to its own value and not because its creator was a member of a certain flock. I don't overestimate the significance of the AMM for myself; it is important to me because it unites people whom I really value best of all in artistic matters, but the more dissimilar we are, the better for the AMM at large. Incidentally, it is in this way precisely that the joint elaboration of a new musical mentality is taking shape. It involves no concrete language but something far more important that could not be defined as yet. But the fact of its happening is obvious. All of this is gradually accumulating in the creative work of many persons who take the trouble to think over it. These reflections are indeed imperative, which was virtually non-existent under such phenomenon as "Soviet music" that has been deprived of its spinal cord but still goes on in its last, purely physiological contractions, which makes one feel nothing but irritation.

V.B.: It is indeed worth thinking over, for we are living in a crucial age for music, going through the 300-year cycle of its regular metamorphosis.

A.R.: But it is also the age of a special kind of synthesis based on a different perception of time, space, etc. There is no need to come forth which more technical novelties, for a new musical mentality is not necessarily associated with an external innovation. It is far more difficult to make use of what is already at hand. If everybody thought along these lines, it could guarantee at least the absence of routine which plunges you into gloom when you hear many modern compositions. At the last music festival in Frankfurt I had a chance to listen to many pieces by John Cage, who had a stable reputation of a paradoxical composer in this country, and I made a new discovery for myself. It turned out that this man at the age of eighty showed a far fresher approach to many things than some young people. It was absolutely pure music revealing a new, refreshing and thrilling quality. This is one of the possible facets of new musical mentality. Or take, for instance, Alexander Knaifel, irrespective of your attitude to his music, he sets an example of gaining a new, emancipated, musical mentality. Such music makes one to realize that it does not matter what technique has been used for its composition, thereby destroying the houses of cards erected by the sectarian apologists both on the right or left wing.

V.B.: And when they fail to classify music, they stay puzzled or, which is more often, display irritation.

A.R.: As far as I'm concerned, with a passage of time I attach greater importance to the intuitive search, even if at my own level, for a new musical mentality. A retrospective view of music history, which should teach us something, reveals that none of the 20th-century great masters has ever departed from the great tradition of striving for the creation of musical mentality, not on the ruins of the previous epochs, since music takes revenge for any attempt to destroy it, but precisely thanks to all the previous accomplishments.

. . . Progress is inconceivable without perpetual correspondence with the past, with all its errors and deadlines, but also with its milestones and lodestars that have been reached through much suffering. And the truth is approaching, a glimpse of light in the incessant advance towards the cognition of laws undergoverning arts and life.

***

Alexander Raskatov was born in 1953 in Moscow. He graduated from Albert Leman's composition class at the Moscow Conservatoire in 1978, completing his postgraduate course there in 1982. Since 1979 he has been a member of the Composers Union, and since 1990 a board member at the Association of Modern Music (AMM). In 1990, as a composer in residence, he read a semester course of lectures in Russian and Soviet music at Stetson University (Deland, Florida); in 1991 he took part in the symposium "Espace Europeen des Sciences et des Arts" in Strasbourg (France) devoted to the problems of future urban and cultural development. In 1989 Alexander Raskatov participated in the shooting of the BBC film about Soviet music in London and Moscow. He was awarded *World Intellectual of 1993* by the International Biographical Centre, Cambridge, Great Britain. He currently resides in Germany.

PRINCIPAL WORKS

1976 *Courtly Songs* for soprano and instrumental ensemble to words by early medieval Japanese poets. 13′
Moscow: Sovetsky Kompozitor, 1990
Melodia: C10 13247-8

1979 *Dramatic Games* for solo cello. 11′
Moscow: Sovetsky Kompozitor, 1984

1981 Piano Sonata. 17′
Moscow: Sovetsky Kompozitor, 1986
Invitation to a Concert for percussion. 12′

1982 *Reminiscences of the 'Alpine Rose'* for percussion ensemble, musical box and tape. 11′
CD: Mobile fidelity MFCD 911

1984 *Night Hymns,* concerto for piano and chamber ensemble. 24′
Moscow: Sovetsky Kompozitor, 1990
Circle of Songs for mezzo-soprano and chamber ensemble to verses by Vasily Zhukovsky and Yevgeny Baratynsky. 16′
Moscow: Sovetsky Kompozitor, 1990
CD: Saison russe / CDM Chant du Monde, LDC 288059 CM 210

1985 *Books of Spring* for tenor and chamber orchestra to verses by Vasily Zhukovsky. 27′

1986 *Muta in...* for three flutes. 12′
Sentimental Sequences for thirteen performers. 18′
CD: Saison russe / CDM Chant du Monde, LDC 288059 CM 210
CD: Olympia OCD 283

1987 *The Road* for two cellos and harpsichord. 12′
Concerto for oboe and fifteen stringed instruments. 25′
From Spring, From the Grass, From the Heavens, lyrical oratorio for mezzo-soprano, boys choir and orchestra to words by Xenia Nekrasova. 40.

1988 Sonata for Viola and Piano. 22′
Gra-ka-kha-ta for tenor, violin and percussion ensemble to verses by Velimir Khlebnikov. 20′
Moscow: Sovetsky Kompozitor, 1990
Stabat Mater for high voice and organ. 30′

1989 *Let There Be Night* for counter-tenor and string trio to words by Samuel T. Coleridge. 17′
Moscow: Sovetsky Kompozitor, 1990
CD: Saison russe / CDM Chant du Monde, LDC 288059 CM 210
Consolation for piano. 9′
Punctuation Marks for harpsichord. 11′

1990 *Sixty-Sixth Sonnet by William Shakespeare* for soprano and ensemble. 11′
Dolce far niente for cello and piano. 10′
CD: Saison russe / CDM Chant du Monde, LDC 288059 CM 210
Illusion (in memory of Luigi Nono) for six percussions. 10′
Ricordi

1991 *Commentary on a Vision* for percussion ensemble and orchestra. 31′
Xenia for chamber orchestra. 25′

1992   *Misteria-brevis* for piano. 14'
  CD: Saison russe / CDM Chant du Monde, LDC 288059 CM 210
  Urtext for soprano and chamber ensemble on texts from the Old Testament. 4'
  CD: Saison russe / CDM Chant du Monde, LDC 288059 CM 210

MAJOR PERFORMANCES

Invitation to a Concert	1988	"Autumn in Warsaw"
	1989	"Almeida," London
	1989	Days of Soviet Culture in Zurich
Reminiscences of	1989	Soviet Arts Festival, Glasgow
the 'Alpine Rose'		
Night Hymns	1988	Opole, Poland
Circle of Songs	1990	RADIO-FRANCE, Paris
Sentimental Sequences	1990	Cremona (Italy), Glasgow, Amsterdam
	1991	Frankfurt
Oboe Concerto	1989	Moscow, K34 sponsored by National
		Endoment for the Arts, USA
Sonata for Viola	1991	Bonn, Bashmet-Festival
and Piano		
Gra-ka-kha-ta	1989	Glasgow
Stabat Mater	1991	Heidelberg (Germany)
Let There Be Night	1989	"Almeida", London
Consolation	1989	Buffalo
	1991	Tokyo, Amsterdam
Punctuation Marks	1991	Montreal, Vancouver, Zurich
Illusion (part of the team	1991	Cremona, Vienna
composition in memory	1992	Munich
of Luigi Nono)		
Dolce far niente	1992	Frankfurt, Geneva, Berne
Misteria-brevis	1992	Tokyo
Urtext	1992	Dartington, Great Britain
Xenia	1992	Frankfurt

In February 1993 in Paris, within the framework of the Russian Music Festival, RADIO-FRANCE presented two compositions by Alexander Raskatov: *Reminiscences of the 'Alpine Rose'* and his Concerto for oboe and fifteen stringed instruments. Le Chant du Monde timed the release of his personal CD for this event. Franck Mallet in his review published in *Le monde de la musique* wrote that "the composer managed to find his own style based on a certain variety of imaginable folklore remote in time and space. His strange music is often puzzling, as the music by Alfred Schnittke. The name of Raskatov should be remembered".

Currently, the composer is working on *Miserere* for viola, cello and orchestra to be dedicated to the memory of Oleg Kagan (on a commission from Natalia Gutman and Yuri Bashmet), as well as on his opera *The Pit and the Pendulum* (after Edgar Allan Poe, libretto in the English by Alexei Parin). Alexander Raskatov has to his credit numerous incidental scores to films and plays. In 1989 the film *F.I.P. (Freedom Is Paradise)* with his music won Grand Prix at the America-89 festival in Montreal. He completed and provided an instrumentation for the Chamber Symphony by the Russian composer Nikolai Roslavets, which the latter started to write early in this century but left unfinished (CD: Saison russe / CDM Chant du Monde, LDC 288055); Alexander Raskatov also completed and revised Nikolai Roslavets's Sonatas Nos 1 and 2 for viola and piano (CD: Saison russe / CDM Chant du Monde, LDC 288047).

Ex. 1 *Dramatic Games* for solo cello

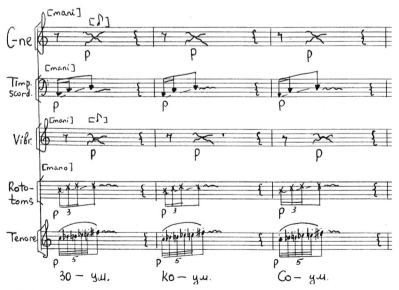

Ex. 2 *Gra-ka-ha-ta*

Sergei Pavlenko:
on the way to simplicity

Vladimir Barsky

Sergei Pavlenko

In Lieu of Introduction

"I believe that I follow my own definite line in my creative work, as anybody else does. At the very beginning, when I first came to Moscow, my contacts with Edison Denisov proved very important to me. In his class I could get the musical information previously unavailable to me, learn about the latest events in the world of modern music, and familiarize myself with the new scores and recordings, Denisov's own compositions included. Naturally enough, for several years I remained under his influence, though always striving for my own inimitable 'voice'. I recall how once, already after my graduation from the conservatoire, Denisov during one of our talks expressed a curious thought: 'You must come to hate my style to become a good composer'."

. . . Edison Denisov, that recognized leader of the national musical avant-garde (for all the ambiguity of this term) for the last three decades, captivated by his uncompromising attitude to his profession, discarding anything transient and commonplace. His classes at the Moscow conservatoire were always overcrowded with neophytes looking for his support after they had to face for the first time the severe realities of our musical life. And they could find consolation in a simple and quite customary phrase he used to draw their attention, for example, to the good sonority of low flutes in a score under analysis. The true scale of life's values got established by itself, though liberation from the impact of the master's powerful and energetic personality, and going beyond the confines of the narrow and dogmatic educational approach were not so simple in the case of Sergei Pavlenko.

"In the course of approximately two years I actually 'overcame my own self', and then in the late 1970s — early 80s a definite turning took shape in my style for a certain simplification of my musical language. It became most evident in my Second Symphony, though it was wholly performed just ten years after it had been written. I have never been particularly striving for winning somebody's notice and love. Frankly speaking, in modern music there are not so many things that I really care for. In the music written by the composers of my generation I like the

artistic ideas of Victor Ekimovsky, Alexander Raskatov, and Nikolai Korndorf whose creative work I find extremely interesting."

In Lieu Of Profile

...Sergei Pavlenko marked the completion of his formal musical training by writing the Cello Concerto whose premiere took place in the Grand Hall of the Moscow Conservatoire, the most prestigious concert hall in the Russian capital. It evoked a warm and well-deserved response in the audience who appreciated the composer's assured hand felt throughout the development of its musical pattern, his exploration of a wide range of emotional states in this one-movement composition, and his inventive employment of diverse expressive devices. The concerto opens with the soloist's cadenza, a point of departure in its dramatic development, presenting a sharp contrast by its lyrical mood to the austere and dynamic middle section. The part of the solo instrument is treated as the main character in an instrumental drama, revealing a theatrical bent in the composer's thinking, a quality to distinguish many of his future opuses. Therefore, Sergei Pavlenko's musical language with its idioms inherent in the late 20th century, in each concrete case, changes its "timbre" — the employment of these idioms is rigidly, often to the detriment of the outside effects, subject to a selected goal, a supertask.

Guided predominantly by the tone-structure and treating it as the most essential component of an artistic entity, the composer pays particular attention to the tone-color. Hence his inventive orchestration and individual approach to every instrument. In particular it concerns a series of his compositions for saxophone ensembles including his virtuosic Quartet in the concertante style and the *Concerto breve*, comprising the entire saxophone range from sopranino to bass. Written on a commission from Jean-Marie Londeix, this work is distinguished for logical development in its dramatic pattern, clear-cut structure, and vivid themes, which is enhanced by the unusual methods of sound production and utilization of the latest techniques including microchromatics, chords, and playing on the mouthpiece. As a result, the chorus of saxophones sounds like a truly orchestral ensemble, with the monotimbre changing its color in the sound palette of the composition with regard to various twists in the development of its "plot."

Sergei Pavlenko's composition manner is characterized by a singular thoroughness in his work, a striving for producing natural and comprehensible musical utterances, and an unhurried gradualness of the creative process. All these qualities seem to be hidden behind the quite earthly and routine mode of his daily life. He speaks reluctantly about the details of his craft, getting off with meaningless phrases and shunning any theorizing about his music. And only a person who has known him for a long time is aware of the existence of a second plane behind the fade of his routine work. The key problem for Sergei Pavlenko is still the moment of fixing down his artistic conception, its adequate material embodiment and a harmonious combination of its inner message and a compositional form.

To attain the above, you have to see the uncustomary in the most habitual things, to perceive the world as if anew, and to be able to reveal the unconventional relationships between various phenomena. Only in this case you could create your own

inimitable and memorable musical world combining improvisation and strict calculation, the graphic stretched lines of sounds and colorful harmony...

Another step on this road was made by Sergei Pavlenko in his Chamber Concerto
for seven instruments in which the subtlety of musical expressive means and the inner
logic underlying the development of its motto theme produce a singular emotional
atmosphere, making this composition coherent and well-proportioned.

His virtuosic *Hommage* for bassoon and string quartet, dedicated to the distinguished bassoon player Valery Popov and designed for the latter's technical potentials,
displays a chain of emotional states from the lyrical and romantic mood at the
beginning through restlessness and rhythmic instability in its middle movement to the
concluding mediation and apprehension of the past developments. The formula
discovered by the composer in this piece is most characteristic for correlation between
the solo part and its accompaniment by the string quartet (mostly muted) epitomizing
the objective principle and entering into a dialogue by playing its weighty phrases in
counterpoint with the solo part.

Sergei Pavlenko's Piano Trio, the most condensed in its emotional tone, seems to
be developing in two musical dimensions. The first, lyrical, movement, the dynamic
second with its vivid climax, and the summing-up finale in this work are rotating
around their common axis — C-sharp, following a kind of "Ariadna's thread" now
emerging to the surface and then lost from the view, which lends multidimensionality
to the musical space, and symbolic ambiguity to the aesthetic message of the whole
composition.

The heartrending *Concerto-Serenade in Memory of Vladimir Vysotsky* for clarinet and
strings is one of Sergei Pavlenko's most popular works. Formally presenting one of
the endless memorial compositions written after the tragic death of the famous
national poet and singer, this Concerto-Serenade bears out the deeply-felt message of
the composer's personal grief. The voice of Vladimir Vysotsky personified by the
clarinet, no matter how paradoxical such solution may seem, conveys the latent nerve
of his poetry, which is hard to describe and which could be only perceived by a kindred
soul. Wrath and protest, lyricism and irony, elevated and noble impulses and daily
routine are all interwoven in the *lamento* of the strings setting off the graphic part of
the solo instrument by their extended, most impressive commenting phrases. This
composition concludes one of the stages in Sergei Pavlenko's creative career. It equally
concerns the means of unfolding the thematic core, the type of orchestral writing, the
treatment of solo instruments and methods of sound production, i.e. all the essential
components of the musical language to determine a composer's style.

Beginning with his earliest compositions, Sergei Pavlenko revealed his striving for
dramatic integrity — hence the condensed character of exposition and development
of the musical material, preference for one-movement forms in his chamber and
orchestral instrumental compositions, and logic and naturalness of thematic elaboration. Irrespective of a concrete composition technique employed, in his language there
predominates the common approach to the building up of horizontal and vertical
relationships based on threading of uniform melodic formulas and intervalic units
under the clearly discerned tonal center acting as a director of dodecaphonic, modal
and aleatory structures. All of this stems from the musical embodiment of the clearly
perceived artistic principles evolved as a result of meticulous preliminary analysis and

selection. In each concrete work the composer finds a new solution through a search for a unique artistic form, which explains a keen interest his compositions arouse in the music-lovers.

It is most unlikely that Sergei Pavlenko has ever given special consideration to all the above reflections, for in his composition work he is guided rather by intuition. Man does not reflect on how he breathes until the adequate natural environment surrounds him. When it disappears, it has to be recreated anew...

At times Sergei Pavlenko's musical world appears to be so shockingly uncommon and bizarre that it may evoke a negative response. But anybody devoid of prejudice and inertia could easily penetrate it.

Perhaps, it is all owing to a different sort of mentality and a different perception of the world. And the point is not even so much in his selection of genres, themes and plots for his compositions as in his treatment of a particular method of sound production in such of his pieces as *Pas-de-trois* for flute, violin and piano, *Games* for clarinet, trombone, cello and piano, and *Message* for solo clarinet. The most conventional musical instruments, particularly the wind ones, seem to produce uncommon sonority in Pavlenko's instrumental concertos, his *Lacework* for wind quintet, and *Konzertstück* for three flutes.

The period from the late 1970s to the mid-eighties saw the emergence of expansive symphonic canvases in Sergei Pavlenko's creative work. In addition to the concertos for solo instruments and orchestra (for the saxophone, the violin and for the oboe), he wrote within this period four symphonies marked for their large scope (the last symphony falls into five movements, lasting about an hour) and impressive musical content. In his symphonies the composer is not striving to strike the listeners with the techniques and originality of the newly invented forms, often using the devices well elaborated in the 20th-century musical practice, and sometimes turning to the archaic layers in the national musical culture. Nevertheless, his symphonies create a sensation of being fresh and singular.

The revival of the traditional instrumental genre of European art on the Russian soil by drawing on the expressive resources of traditional instruments and combining this tradition with the 20th-century musical idioms requires from a composer to be most inventive in his treatment of the means and devices he uses: a flexible and fastidious metric organization, subtle, yet contrasting dynamic tone-colors, characteristic modes, and a diverse orchestral texture. Only in this case you would get an impression that the music has not been invented but given a lease of life by its creator.

The best known of Sergei Pavlenko's symphonies is his Third Symphony timed for the centenary of Igor Stravinsky's birth, which was introduced virtually simultaneously in Russia and the USA. Being subtitled as a "Symphony of Laments," it reproduces the characteristic features of the traditional Russian musical mentality through using some melodic phrases from the Russian laments and dirges. The chamber cast of the orchestra in this case is treated as an ensemble of soloists, with their vertical relationships following the laws of collateral-part polyphony. The musical texture organized as a developing variation of the motto-chord block abounds in refined flashes, picturesque tone-combinations and their subtle nuances.

During the same period Sergei Pavlenko wrote such memorable compositions as *Farewell* for string quartet (pure, beautiful and piercingly lucid music) and *Orgelwerk* ("a double fantasia with a fugue and a piece in the minuet type," dedicated to the 300th anniversary of J.S. Bach's birth).

In the late 1980s, the composer's style showed some definite change, which first outlined itself in his Violin Concerto, his Fourth Symphony and the choreographic fantasia *Rothschild's Violin* (his first experience in stage music). His tendency for greater simplicity became more evident in his *Pastorale* for saxophone quintet, *Katzenmusik* for the ensemble of French horns (another version of Haydn's *Abschiedsymphonie / Farewell Symphony* / which involves the musicians' exit from the stage and the use of mouthpieces as instruments), and *Lilac*, an instrumental postlude inspired by Mikhail Vrubel's painting (Musical Example).

It would be hardly appropriate to draw the final conclusions on Sergei Pavlenko's music, for he is still in motion and the parabola of his creative road may be defined as "individualization of consciousness." Against the background of the current stylistic delimitation in modern music, rapprochement and intercrossing of polarly different trends when you can witness the fast changes in the principles of composers thinking, the new often appears as the well-forgotten old. The attempts to synthesize in one's creative work the most different styles are highly individual, with each composer having to pass this road on his own. Hence a unique nature of conceptions, artistic messages, and dissimilarity inherent in works written by one and the same composer. In the context when the atom of musical matter, previously believed to be indivisible, has been split, when this matter ceases to be regarded as a given prime element of music and has to be created anew, composition involves not only a form, but also a sound, timbre, musical time and space, and each time anew as for the first time.

As far as the musical substance of Sergei Pavlenko's vocabulary is concerned, one would hardly find anything to stand it apart from that of his colleagues. However a singular relationship of its component elements, and their unique combination allows us to speak about his individual style and his individual perception of the world. This is the road chosen by this composer in his creative work.

In Lieu of Afterword

"The essential prerequisite of fruitful composition work, in my opinion, is the development of one's own unique idea of a dramatic message and its convincing embodiment in music. And it does not matter what composition technique you employ. Except for the notorious Resolution of the Central Committee of the Communist Party adopted in 1948, no ban has ever been imposed on any technique to be utilized in one's creative work. I'm striving to combine various composition procedures, and recently the musical material I use has been founded on a certain tonal bases (in the broadest sense of the word). Some definite artistic task underlies each concrete composition, even if it is a short piece. To my mind, of the greatest value is the uniqueness of an aesthetic idea.

For several years now I have used the free serial technique and tried at the same time to rely on the root-tone foundation. Besides, in my compositions there often arise aleatory structures based rather on some definite forms of motion than on the concrete sounds. In this respect I have derived a lot from the compositions by Edison Denisov, Alfred Schnittke and Sophia Gubaidulina. As for the foreign composers, I got the essential impulses for my work from the music by Luciano Berio, Karlheinz Stockhausen, György Ligeti and some others."

Ex. 1 *Lilac*

One of Sergei Pavlenko's latest works, *Treversium* for percussion ensemble and chamber orchestra, providing for its performance either by the complete cast, or separately by chamber orchestra, or by the percussion ensemble alone (all three versions being equally valid), is based on a simple and eternal plot unfolding between two poles: the world of harmony, proportion and stable spiritual values, and the opposing world of rigid urbanistic structures and disintegration of the musical matter. This plot is symbolic while the conflict is perpetual. The pendulum of time is mercilessly swinging, and at its poles apart you face either a possibility of attaining an ideal or the impending universal disaster. The future is mediated by the past and the perspective by a retrospection. At the crossing of musical epochs, in a dialogue of cultures and world-views there arises the artist's inimitable language in which he speaks with his contemporaries.

* * *

Sergei Pavlenko was born in 1952 in the Ukrainian town of Sumy. He graduated from the Moscow Conservatoire in 1977 and completed a postgraduate course there in composition under the guidance of Nikolai Sidelnikov in 1980.

During the period from 1977 to 1982 Sergei Pavlenko was musical director at the Taganka Theatre, taking part in Yuri Lyubimov's most popular productions; he wrote the incidental score to the play *A Complaint Book* (after Anton Chekhov).

The main sphere of his interests is symphonic and chamber instrumental music. Some of his compositions were written on commissions from the International Saxophone Ensemble directed by Jean-Marie Londeix, the Dutch Clarinet Quartet directed by Henri Bock, the "Westdeutsches Hornen" ensemble, the clarinettists Harry Spaarnay (the Netherlands) and Jacques Merrere (France), the harpsichordist Petja Kaufman (Switzerland), and the wind orchestra of Tallahassee University (Florida, USA).

Sergei Pavlenko's compositions have been performed at national and foreign music festivals in Bulgaria, France, Germany, and the USA. His *Pastorale* for saxophone quintet won First Prize at the International Composers Contest in Paris (1988) and his Hymn *Jesu Redemptor omnium* for soprano and chamber orchestra won the main Prize at the International Composers Contest "Musique du Sacrée" in Switzerland (1995).

PRINCIPAL WORKS

1973   *The Vologda Wedding*, song-cycle to folk texts. 15′ Moscow: Sovetsky Kompozitor, 1980

1975   Concerto for Saxophone and Orchestra. 15′
      Sonata for Saxophone and Piano. 9′ Moscow: Sovetsky Kompozitor, 1982
      Piano Sonata No. 1. 8′

1976   Quintet for Flute, Clarinet, Violin, Cello and Piano. 11′
      Quartet for four saxophones. 13′ Moscow: Sovetsky Kompozitor, 1986
      Cantata in Memory of Marina Tsvetayeva for voice and chamber orchestra. 11′

1977   Concerto for Flute and Orchestra. 12′ Moscow: Sovetsky Kompozitor, 1984
      Chamber Concerto for Seven Instruments. 11′

1978   *Portraits* for flute and piano. 8′ Moscow: Sovetsky Kompozitor, 1981
      Cantata in Memory of Osip Mandelstam for voice and chamber orchestra. 18′

1979   Cello Concerto No.1. 15′
      Hommage for bassoon and string quartet. 12′ Melodia: C10 18407 005
      Piano Trio. 11′ Moscow: Sovetsky Kompozitor, 1985 Melodia: C10 18255 001
      Symphony No. 1. 30′
      String Quartet No. 2. 9′
      Pas-de-trois for flute, violin and piano. 14′

1980   *Sonata-continuo* for bass clarinet. 8′
      Concerto breve for twelve saxophones. 12′
      Concerto-Serenade in Memory of Vladimir Vysotsky for clarinet and strings. 10′
      Games for clarinet, trombone, cello and piano. 8′
      Quartet for four clarinets. 10′
      Christmas Capriccio for bassoon and strings. 12′
      Message for solo clarinet. 7′

1981   Piano Sonata No. 2 (*Fantasia quasi una sonata*). 8′ Moscow: Muzyka, 1985
      Adagio for orchestra. 13′
      Symphony No. 2. 45′
      Duo a tre for bass clarinet, vibraphone and marimba. 8′

1982   Symphony No. 3 (*Symphony of Laments*) for chamber orchestra. 15′

1983   Violin Concerto. 17′
      Farewell for string orchestra. 13′
      Sonata for Solo Cello. 15′

1984   *Orgelwerk* for organ. 40′

1985   Symphony No. 4. 60′
      Intermezzo for alto saxophone, harp and percussion. 12′

1986   Concerto for Oboe and Strings. 33′
      Konzertstück for three flutes. 10′
      Water Suite for bass and organ (verses by Federico Garcia Lorca). 15′

1987   *Rothschild's Violin*, choreographic fantasia in one act, based on Anton Chekhov's short story. 45′
      Lacework for wind quintet.

1988   *Perestroika in Retrospection* for ensemble.
      Pastorale for saxophone quintet.

1989   Trio-Nocturne for flute, bass clarinet and piano.
        Quasi Toccata for harpsichord.
        Sinfonia humana for strings.
        Concerto for wind and percussion instruments. 20'
1990   *Lara,* composition for piccolo clarinet and percussion.
        Katzenmusik for 6/12 French horns.
1991   *Re-Markus* for percussion ensemble
        Lilac, Postlude inspired by Mikhail Vrubel's painting for piccolo clarinet, viola
        and piano.
1992   *Treversium* for percussion ensemble. 30'
1993   *Res Facta* for cello quartet. 16'
1993   *Ives Composition,* concerto No. 2 for cello and strings. 24'
1994   *In the manner of Gauguin* for clarinet, violin, cello and piano. 17'
1994   *Princess Dream,* symphony poem. 20'
1994   *In imitation of Denisov* for bassoon and piano. 12'
1994   *Stanzas,* concerto No.2 for saxophone and orchestra. 20'
1995   *Jesu Redemptor omnium,* hymn for soprano and chamber orchestra. 14'
1996   *Chansons sans paroles* for soprano, clarinet and piano (verses by P. Verlaine). 20'
1996   *Venice Stanzas* for soprano, viola and piano (verses by I. Brodsky). 15'

The "culturology" of Vladimir Tarnopolsky

Valeria Tsenova

Vladimir Tarnopolsky

"Once I asked Tarnopolsky what single score he would have taken with himself if he were to live on an uninhabited island. He answered that it would be Mozart's *Jupiter* Symphony; it says a lot about him".

Gennady Rozhdestvensky

In 1982 in a concert held at the Grand Hall of the Moscow Conservatoire within the programme of the cycle "From the History of Soviet Music" the symphony orchestra directed by the outstanding conductor Gennady Rozhdestvensky played the *Cello Concerto* by the unknown composer Vladimir Tarnopolsky, who had just graduated from the conservatoire. Gennady Rozhdestvensky had selected his concerto out of many other compositions submitted for his judgment, as the most spectacular and talented opus. The performance was preceded by the conductor's short witty commentary to present a new name to the audience: "I wouldn't deliberately speak about the structure of this composition which abounds in many interesting finds both in the cello part and in its orchestral accompaniment, and the value of these findings is primarily due to the fact that these are neither hidden deep in the texture, nor draped in any subtleties but openly and, I would even say, visually demonstrated to the listeners. This lively music brims over with youthful ardor and congenial expressiveness"[1].

It was a stroke of luck for the young composer to have his work, written during his postgraduate years, played in the best Moscow concert hall under the baton of a prestigious conductor before the mass audience. This performance gave a start to the creative career of the composer whose inimitable style took shape within the next decade.

---

[1] Gennady Rozhdestvenksy's commentary to his recitals cited in the book Gennady Rozhdestvensky's Preambles. Moscow: Sovetsky Kompozitor Publishers, 1989, p. 148.

Vladimir Tarnopolsky was born in 1955 in the Ukrainian city of Dnepropetrovsk where he studied at a local music college. It was Edison Denisov who came to play a major-part in his musical career. While still a college student in Dnepropetrovsk he wrote a letter to Edison Denisov who regarded the young musician with great favor. In the early seventies Tarnopolsky came to Moscow from Dnepropetrovsk to show Denisov his compositions. He got qualified consultations and the invaluable advice upon following which he was able to attain his artistic aspirations. In 1973 he entered the composition department at the Moscow Conservatoire[2].

Here is an excerpt from Edison Denisov's letter addressed to Vladimir Tarnopolsky: "Dear Volodya, I heartily congratulate you on your entering the conservatoire. I was sure that you would pass all the exams, though I still worried" (August 16, 1973). Denisov advised him to apply for the composition class of Nikolai Sidelnikov, a notable composer and pedagogue, belonging to Denisov's generation: "At least, he would't interfere with your self-development, for some teachers just spoil one's soul, and it is dangerous." Tarnopolsky followed his advice, though Nikolai Sidelnikov appeared to be his opposite as regards his individuality. But, as the composer believes, this fact precisely proved to be essential for the development of his creative abilities. It was thanks to Sidelnikov that Tarnopolsky kept away from imitating Edison Denisov who was very popular among the budding avant-gardist musicians, often quite captivated by his style.

Vladimir Tarnopolsky studied composition with other teachers. First of all, he attended Edison Denisov's classes in instrumentation. These were no ordinary lessons in score reading and instrumentation, for the students got there the truly professional approach to their future craft, and technical proficiency: "Denisov has given me the most accurate lessons in composition in my life. He was devoid of any didactics. He just set his students on the right way. His appraisals were tactful and to the point. He merely indicated some details while his pupils were to recreate the entity. I regard Edison Denisov as the best master in orchestration. He helped to grasp the orchestral style of a composer and tried to reconstruct his ideas most artistically"[3]. By the way, the young composer failed to fully avoid the influence evoked by Edison Denisov's strong personality, which made itself evident in some of his opuses written during his conservatoire years. Thus, his Three Romances for soprano and piano, *Alexander Blok's Italian Poems*, even in their title reminded of Edison Denisov's *Italian Songs* (also set to Blok's verses), while his *Girls' Songs* for female chorus set to the folk Russian texts came as a response to Denisov's folkloric *Wails*. Denisov's quests for novel instrumental combinations found their reflection in Tarnopolsky's composition *The Reed-Pipe Singing* for soprano, flute, harp and viola, another setting of Alexander Blok.

According to Vladimir Tarnopolsky himself, he got invaluable information pertaining to the composition techniques from the lectures in musical theory — harmony,

---

[2]

    This story is strikingly reminiscent of what had actually happened to Edison Denisov himself two decades ago. Back in the early 1950s Denisov wrote a letter to Dmitry Shostakovich and then sent him his early compositions (see p. 67).

[3] From a talk with Vladimir Tarnopolsky on March 3, 1988.

polyphony and musical form — delivered by Professor Yuri Kholopov, an eminent music scholar. On a par with Edison Denisov and Nikolai Sidelnikov, he invariably mentions Yuri Kholopov among his teachers. It is a noteworthy fact that his first published composition appeared in Yuri Kholopov's book *Tasks in Harmony*[4], a set of home assignments for students majoring in composition. One of these tasks was to write a piece in the twelve-tone technique. The *Piano Scherzo*, written by Tarnopolsky in 1976 as his home assignment in harmony, was cited by Yuri Kholopov as a sample in the Supplement to his book. It was to remain for a long time the composer's sole published work.

In 1978 Vladimir Tarnopolsky graduated with honors from the Moscow Conservatoire, presenting the *Symphonic Prologue* as his diploma work. And his completion of the postgraduate courses in 1980 coincided with the appearance of his neo-expressionistic *Cello Concerto*, representing a modification of the conventional sonata form on the basis of the basic chord technique.

Vladimir Tarnopolsky's musical style is distinguished by the well-thought-out elaboration of details, clear understanding of the tasks undertaken, an accurate idea of the entity, and the associative musical material. He may be called a composer, who thinks structurally. When he just starts working on a composition, the key point for him is to find a structure which would convey his musical idea in the most adequate way, bearing its message in itself. Of no less importance for him is the stylistic and concrete substance of musical material. Most of his compositions (including those purely instrumental) carry no general genre definitions such as a quartet or sonata, but the concrete titles, among them *Cassandra, Jesu, deine tiefen Wunden, Eindruck-Ausdruck,* and *The Echoes of a Past Day.* These titles imply no literary programme in an instrumental composition, but being quite concrete, they virtually exclude any arbitrary interpretation on the part of the listeners. This distinctive trait of Vladimir Tarnopolsky's compositional thinking led to his frequent employment of the collage and stylization techniques in his music.

A vivid example of a whole collage form is his *Music in Memory of Dmitry Shostakovich.* The idea of this composition for recitalist, chamber orchestra and two tape recorders belongs to Gennady Rozhdestvensky, who was the first to perform it in the Grand Hall of the Moscow Conservatoire, acting himself as a recitalist. In its genre it is a collage melodeclamation. The verses devoted to Dmitry Shostakovich by four Soviet poets (Anna Akhmatova, Mikhail Matusovsky, Alexander Mezhirov and James Patterson) are recited against the background of the quotations from Shostakovich's music, as well as from the works by the other great symphonists Tarnopolsky reveres — Beethoven, Wagner, Tchaikovsky, and Mahler.

In this case the choice of a collage form is explained by its memorial genre. The musical texture is interwoven of short melodic structural units, i.e. quotations (more than 110!), in which the composer has revealed their deep-going tonal interrelationship: in particular, Shostakovich favorite personal motto-theme "DSCH" turned out to be "calling for" the closing cadence in the form of the destiny theme from Wagner's

---

[4] Yuri Kholopov. Tasks in Harmony. Moscow: Muzyka Publishers, 1983, pp. 280–281.

Valkyrie whereas the theme from the finale of Beethoven's Symphony No. 3 could be "discerned" in the invasion episode of Shostakovich's Seventh Symphony. Vladimir Tarnopolsky defines this composition as "an experiment in musical hermeneutics," implying his striving to retain "the letter and spirit" of Shostakovich's music in a novel compositional context through lending it a fresh interpretation.

His composition *Upon Reading Mussorgsky's Draft Notebooks* has been written in the traditions of the Russian choral concerto. Its dramatic pattern is based on the division of two layers: choral and orchestral. The chorus sings "Lord, make me to know mine end" (Psalm 39:4) in the spirit of the Orthodox service while the orchestra plays Mussorgsky's music from his draft notebooks, which has been orchestrated by Vladimir Tarnopolsky. Some of these drafts by the great Russian composer known for his innovative approach to harmony are conspicuously differing in their style from the music inherent in the latter half of the last century. Their stylistic uncertainty and extratemporal character allow Vladimir Tarnopolsky to avoid stylization of Mussorgsky's orchestration, treating these drafts in a later style. Thus, some of them have been orchestrated in the pointillistic manner à la Webern, and others in the multivoice heterophonic texture (in the vein of Lutoslawski). The composition ends with Mussorgsky's unfinished romance "Cruel Death," also in Vladimir Tarnopolsky's orchestration. This romance unites two layers — choral and orchestral — in their joint final cadence.

The concerto *Upon Reading Mussorgsky's Draft Notebooks* was adapted to the stage and produced by Boris Pokrovsky at the Moscow Chamber opera in 1989 to mark the 150th birth anniversary of Modest Mussorgsky. It was conducted by Gennady Rozhdestvensky who was also reciting the excerpts from Mussorgsky's letters in-between the music.

In general, many compositions written by Vladimir Tanopolsky have been associated with the name of Gennady Rozhdestvensky, among them *In Memory of Dmitry Shostakovich, Upon Reading Mussorgsky's Draft Notebooks*, and his opera *Three Graces*. As for his composition *Wahnfried* for six Wagner tubas, percussion, solo violin, piano and chorus. It quotes Richard Wagner's couplet engraved on the pediment of his villa at Wahnfried, which is sung by the invisible mixed chorus (backstage or taped).

Tarnopolsky's two operas similar in their genre and message reveal the composer's brilliant treatment of "playing with styles." Striving neither to provide a conventional operatic performance nor to lend the avant-gardist touch to this genre, he is just composing a parody of the opera, producing an opera-farce.

Three Graces is an opera-parody in three scenes to the libretto by Carl Maria von Weber based on his autobiographical novel *Weber: The Life of an Artist*. Weber's libretto makes a parody of the operatic stereotypes. The action involves three graceful ladies: Grace One — the Italian opera buffa, Grace Two — the French lyrical opera, and Grace Three — the German romantic opera.

Vladimir Tarnopolsky's opera is parodying everything: the plot, vocal and orchestral casts, forms, melodic turns, genres, and the structure of an entity (a separate number, a scene). All is imbued with the composer's satirical treatment. The music stylized after one of the European operas is suddenly invaded by the deliberately inopportune harmonic devices borrowed from another style, such as semitonal shifts, cross relations, and parallel clusters. The opera contains the quotations from Weber (his operas *Oberon* and *Der Freischütz*), Martin Luther's chorale, and the Baroque *passus duriusculus* used to express one's torments and death, which has also become one of the operatic cliches.

His second composition for the theatre, the chamber opera-farce *Ah, ces russes*, written expressly for the festival of Russian music held in 1993 in Evian (France), is stylized after Rossini. The libretto by Irina Maslennikova, a famous Russian singer, in the past — soloist of the Bolshoi Theater, tells about the adventures of new Russian "businessmen" in France. Its stage production was directed by Boris Pokrovsky.

It is a noteworthy fact that Tarnopolsky's both operas were inspired and commissioned by the two outstanding musicians of out time: the first one by Gennady Rozhdestvensky and the second by Mstislav Rostropovich. However the composer is inclined to be quite skeptical in his attitude to these two works calling them "light music" and entertaining operettas in which case he had to confine himself to stylization and employment of foreign musical material. Anyway, irrespective of such critical appraisal of his own work, it does credit to the composer's proficiency, for his operas proved to be most spectacular and inventive.

The compositions written within a decade following his graduation from the conservatoire could be united into a single period in his creative work, which is defined by Vladimir Tarnopolsky as *culturological*. What does the composer mean by this term? In the first place, he implies that the music written by him during that period sheds a fresh light on the cultural realities and symbols of the past centuries. Symbols play an essential part in it, though these symbols belong not to our times but date back to the other cultural periods. The best compositions written during that period in his life — *Choral Prelude*, Psalmus poenitentialis and *Troïsti muziki* — turned out to be further unified by the composer's conception to write four opuses devoted to different world religions — Protestantism, Catholicism, Orthodoxy.

His *Choral Prelude* was written for the Ensemble of the Instrumental Soloists of the Bolshoi Theater and dedicated to its art director — Alexander Ivashkin. The visual imagery of its music is associated with Passions of Jesus Christ inherent in the old-time chorales: derision, castigation, betrayal, imprisonment, humiliations, tortures, and execution. The Prelude is based on the 16th-century Protestant chorale *Jesu, deine tiefen Wunden*. The traditional idea underlying the genre of choral prelude of commenting upon the chorale's text with a view to producing the expressive effect of castigation has found its instrumental theatrical manifestation in this case. Protestantism is often associated with naturalistic expression of feelings, which acquires its theatrical aspect making the first layer in this composition. In the course of their playing two percussionists move from the backstage towards the conductor depicting castigation in various forms (by beating on their hands and on the instruments). The conductor himself eventually becomes an "object" of castigation (he is to be "hammered in"), stopping dead in the posture of the crucified Jesus Christ. The theatrical element is explained here by the need to carry through the idea of musical commentary to its logical end.

The second, antagonistic, layer is represented by the string trio (Trinity). Trinity means unity. Hence the violin and the cello are carrying on a mirror canon around the note F-sharp (up to the culmination point, then a simple canon; the viola has a free voice). The third layer is presented by the wind instruments engaged mainly in playing the chorale.

On the whole, the form of Vladimir Tarnopolsky's *Choral Prelude* is based on the crescendo principle, with its dynamics developing through a gradual ascending "growth" to a sharp rupture at the end.

The elevated repentance as the epitome of Catholicism is embodied in Tarnopolsky's Choral Concerto with solo violin, *Psalmus poenitentialis* (Psalm of Repentance) set to the text of Psalm 31 (in Latin). The composer offers a fresh interpretation of the old-time genre, drawing on the canonical type of *responsorio*. Canons are extended onto different levels: from separate elements of musical texture to the entire form. The following three principal layers are identified in this psalm: the first one pertains to the recurrences in its movements (each next movement repeats the material from the previous one); the second layer involves the responsive development in two extended movements of the form (the first movement recurs as a response in the second movement), and the third, minor, layer presents the canons and imitations of the musical material as it were, based on the psalmody-like vocabulary.

In this case the pitch centred at the note E-flat serves as an element of culturological symbolism. Vladimir Tarnopolsky views it as a special symbol of St. Trinity (three flats).

This psalm was performed in London and Oxford in 1990 by the "Schola Cantorum of Oxford" Choir.

The Piano Trio entitled *Troïsti muziki*[5] stands apart in Vladimir Tarnopolsky's creative work. Written in a free folk improvisatory manner, this trio in its style combines in equal measure folklore and minimal music, i.e. what is quite alien to the composer in general. The piano is prepared à la cymbals with the help of pencils placed on its strings, with the string players seeming to be engaged in amateur music-making. In his remarks to this piece the composer writes: "The pressure of the bow onto the string should be so light as to make it possible to discern overtones along with the clear-cut tones." His instructions stipulate that the musicians are to play on the bridge, *sul ponticello* arising as if by chance, with the musician's finger suddenly slipping into the wrong octave; all such devices are taken into consideration: "The score provides for all the details as regards the musical material. Nevertheless, the musicians should give an impression as if they were grouping for their way; this composition is just a draft, *opus non finita*." It starts with a long tuning up of the strings, imperceptibly becoming part of the music, then recurring again. By the end of this trio the violin is changed for the viola and tuned up once again.

Symbolism inherent in the culturological period of Vladimir Tarnopolsky's creative work manifests itself in this case in the fact that the entire trio is sustained in G minor.

---

[5] *Troïsti muziki* means in the Ukrainian a folk instrumental trio widespread in the Ukraine up to the middle of the 19th century. As a rule, it consisted of the violin, *basol* (a folk type of cello) and the tambourine, though there could be other combinations of three instruments.

The note "G" (sol) is the key sound here; incidentally, in the Russian language the word "sol" has one more meaning, which is fully explicit in the frequently used expression "the salt of the earth."

In the finale the instrumentalists along with their playing sing in simple voices "Hymn to Christian Poverty" by Grigorij Skovoroda, the Ukrainian 18th-century philosopher and poet. The profound symbolic message of this hymn lies in that

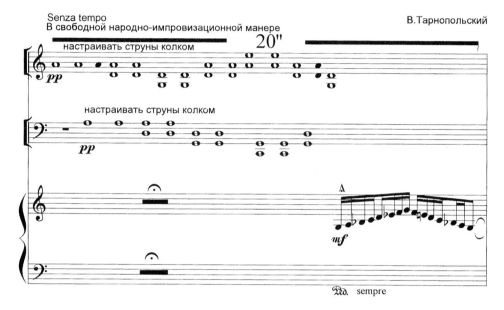

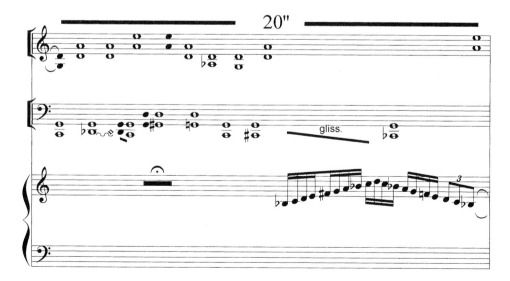

Ex. 1 *Troïsti Muziki*

poverty is one of the key philosophical concepts in the Orthodox teaching: "Oh poverty, the heaven gift! You are cherished by any sacred and honest person"[6].

Vladimir Tarnopolsky's "culturological decade" also includes his vocal instrumental cycle *Brooklyn Bridge or My Discovery of America* for soprano, tenor and instrumental ensemble set to the texts of Vladimir Mayakovsky's poetic cycle written during the poet's stay in the USA. In this case the composer has also resorted to some traditional symbols, though borrowed not from the time-hallowed philosophical or religious concepts of life but from the more recent realities. The underlying idea is to reveal something common between the Soviet, Russian and American ways of life. This idea is embodied, among other things, through a constant mixture of two languages — English and Russian, and the use of slang (its fourth part, "American Russians," depicts the Russian emigrants, their milieu and daily talks). The first section ("Brooklyn Bridge") incorporates the U.S. anthem and the national anthem of the former U.S.S.R. delivered in turn and clinging to one another, for example, the beginning of the Soviet anthem is followed by a cadence from the American anthem, and then both played in counterpoint. The composer sarcastically combines some elements of jazz (a symbol of the USA) and the free-and-easy Russian tavern songs, the bayan playing, a chorus of instrumentalists (in the second section, "Prohibition"), and a typewriter used here as a musical instrument.

This composition was written expressly for the "Making Music Together" Festival in Boston to be presented as concluding item at its closing concert, which partly explains its somewhat spectacular style.

The culturological period in Vladimir Tarnopolsky's creative work ended in the early 1990s, as the composer himself believes, with his trio *The Echoes of a Past Day* for clarinet, cello and piano, though it still carried some culturological moments. It is a kind of musical fantasia on the themes of James Joyce. The trio closes with the last phrases borrowed from his world-famous psychological novel *Ulysses*, whispered by the instrumentalists. The trio's ending delivered in a whisper is the key to the entire composition, coming as an outcome of the ideas propounded by Joyce. Whispering is not a theatrical device, it is used here to produce a sonoristic effect, for fifty percent of the composition has been built up on noises and subtle reverberations.

Moreover, the key idea of James Joyce is the stream of consciousness. Before just falling asleep in his heroine's mind there arise some isolated events from her past and remembrances of her lover. Tarnopolsky's Trio also represents a kind of such stream of consciousness. To quote the composer, "I was striving to exclude as much as possible my self-control and a priori reasoning and to engage the mechanism of the subconscious." In this respect of great interest is the closing section when the musicians, passing on to mere imitation of their music-making (the clarinettist plays without the mouthpiece, the cellist upon having reversed his instrument plays on the back side of its body and the finger board, and the pianist closes the lid of his instrument and goes on playing on it), at the same time start uttering last phrases from

---

[6] As a matter of fact, Grigorij Skovoroda spent the last ten years of his life in poverty as a wandering philosopher.

Joyce's novel: I put my arms around him and his heart was going like mad and .... Yes I said Yes I will Yes ...

During his work on this trio Tarnopolsky was touring Western Europe (Germany and Great Britain included). And the associations arising spontaneously in his musical subconscious were highly important to him. Those associations found their manifestation in some words and set expressions that came to be interwoven into the musical texture in the process of its development to become the substantive symbols and emerging in the stream of musical consciousness, outlining the reference points in the train of the composer's thought. Thus, beginning with Fig. 16 the players, in a march-like rhythm, repeat two words *rechts-links*. At first they recite the text with their lips half opened in a low register, and the last words are pronounced in a high register. To all appearances, the march *rechts-links* turned out to symbolize a German order. Before Fig. 28 the players unexpectedly ask the perpetual Russian question "What is to be done?" For the tonal development of the Trio major importance also attaches to the descending minor seconds, gradually arising from the obscure and shapeless sonoristic block of the exposition and then growing into the initial phrasing of Beethoven's piano piece *To Elise* (by the way, Tarnopolsky dedicated his Trio to the cellist Elise Wilson) (Musical Example 2).

Tarnopolsky is convinced that his Trio *The Echoes of a Past Day* has concluded a major stage in his creative career. In contrast to the earlier period in his life when he felt confined in the linguistic aspects (in addition to the subject-matter) to the cultures he tackled in his music, afterwards he has been trying to depart from the linguistic cliches, retaining only the symbols indispensable for giving tangible and definite form to his musical ideas.

Cassandra for chamber ensemble is a composition of exceptional importance for Vladimir Tarnopolsky, for it proved to become a landmark and usher in a new period in his creative work. The character of this piece may be defined as the heartrending and touching state of a tragic prophecy. According to the composer himself, in it he was aspiring to produce something unyielding to any formal traits, something more intuitive than his earlier written opuses.

Cassandra and *The Echoes of a Past Day* are illustrative of two opposite trends that could be observed in Vladimir Tarnopolsky's artistic thinking in recent years. These trends involve two types of material, forms and techniques, and even in a broader context, two types of music.

The first trend involves the independent, so to speak, natural development of musical material in a way similar to organic outgrowth. The most revealing example is the development of the basic chord in *Cassandra*, which passes through many qualitative estates: at first it is just taking shape, then undergoes a prolonged arpeggio treatment, coming in Fig. 11 to the chordal exposition as it were, and ultimately it dies down. From the point of development principles, it represents variations on a single chord. The composer characterizes his first trend in the following words: "I wanted to slacken the reins, let this material go on its own, developing anywhere, detaching itself and disseminating, all of this in the purely physiological sense producing an acoustic magma through its recurrences and transformation."

The second trend is based on the opposite idea: the musical material is not spreading about on its own to find its channel, but some conceptualistic ideas seem to be pressing

Ex.2 *The Echoes of a Past Day*

on it (meaning some concrete impulses, rather a general conception). In "*The Echoes of a Past Day*" the musical impulses seem to arise not from within the material but exclusively in the composer's mind. Tarnopolsky calls this method "a psychogram calling primarily for the use of the collage technique."

The above two trends find their embodiment in different types of musical texture. On the one hand, Tarnopolsky's strong point lies in harmony, its richness, colorfulness and full sonority. And in *Cassandra*, too, the composer elaborates on polyphonic chordal blocks. On the other hand, his soundscape comes to embrace all kinds of rustles, reverberations and some elements of concrete sounds. At the same time the musical and extramusical factors are not juxtaposed but merge together to create a common scale of musical development, as it is explicitly done in his trio *The Echoes of a Past Day*.

Naturally enough, the composer's creative quests are not confined to the above delineated trends, for his works are quite diverse in their style. However so far his preference for the trend outlined in *Cassandra* is quite obvious, which found its manifestation in *Amoretto* for soprano and chamber ensemble to the verses by Edmund Spenser, and in his piece *Eindruck-Ausdruck* with its aleatory cadence in the finale.

Rather unusual in this sense is the composition "Welt voll Irsinn" for recitalist and orchestra to the text by German Dadaist Kurt Schwitters. The composer transfers on a musical stage dramatic realities of Russian social life in 1993 — noise of crowd, shouts of demonstrators, sounds of loudspeakers and etc., finding in absurdist poems, which shout the musicians from the orchestra, direct parallels with our today's situation: "In image and in the purely structural plan I was interested here in making balance between pure accident and complete determination, just as our society balanced between chaos and dictatorship".

Nevertheless, Vladimir Tarnopolsky occasionally reveals some unexpected twists in his style as, for instance, in his piece for instrumental ensemble *O, Pärt — op art*, a kind of allusion to the music by Arvo Pärt, who left Estonia for permanent residence in the West. It is no accident that the title of this serene and short piece associates the name of this composer with the word-combination "op art" (optical art). On the one hand, Tarnopolsky employs here the minimalist technique, which is so characteristic of Arvo Pärt's style. The entire piece is built up exclusively on the C minor triad stated in the pointillistic manner with a great number of rests in-between the phrases. On the other hand, these three notes are rotated assuming various shapes like it happens in the op-art installations exposing an object under varied angles.

The major events in Vladimir Tarnopolsky's personal life in recent years include his participation in the activities carried out by the Association of Modern Music, which was founded in 1990 and headed since then by Edison Denisov[7]; his teaching of composition and harmony at the Moscow Conservatoire; and numerous trips and

---

[7]

  Both the principles and the name of this organization are reminiscent of a similar structural body functioning in Russia back in the twenties. The first AMM was dissolved in 1931. More than half a century later its ideas found their continuation in the activities of the second AMM. It was founded on the initiative of composers themselves as an artistic alternative to the official Composers Union.

commission from different performing bodies (*Cassandra* was written for the Modern Ensemble of Frankfurt, *The Echoes of a Past Day* for the Chameleon British Trio; he is currently writing a children's composition for recitalist and orchestra on a commissions from the Roald Dahl Foundation). On his initiative at the Moscow Conservatoire in 1993 the *New Music Society*, ensemble, *New Music Studio* and annual International music festival *Moscow Forum* were organized.

Vladimir Tarnopolsky's music is quite familiar to the musical communities in Germany, Great Britain, USA, Holland, Belgium, Italy, and Switzerland. His compositions are performed at major music festivals[8]. In 1989, following the Almeida Festival in London, the BBC Russian Agency transmitted a radio programme devoted to Vladimir Tarnopolsky, and this profile made a point of his vivid style not to be lost among the other eminent composers from Moscow. In May 1994, after the performance of his *The Breath of Exhausted Time* for full symphony orchestra at the 4th Münchener Biennale Vladimir Tarnopolsky was rated as "a discovery of the festival" (*Süddeutsche Zeitung*, May 13, 1994). In this slow and quiet composition in the esoteric style the composer is looking for new approaches to the orchestra (in addition to the traditional instruments, in this case use has been made of the electronic section comprising two synthesizers and two electric guitars), as well as to the problem of musical time. He writes in his foreword: "Music was born from breath. Breath is the first manifestation of life and also its last. On a boundless scale it is involuntarily thought that Time has its breath, huge phases of which we are not capable of comprehending, and today it seems that its important period is exhausted." The image of exhausted time produces a hypnotic effect on the listeners and opens up new prospects in Vladimir Tarnopolsky's creative work.

---

[8] Some of these festivals deserve special mention, among them "Making Music Together" (Boston, 1988), "Aktive Musik" (Dortmund, 1989), "Almeida" (London, 1989), San Diego Arts Festival (1989), Huddersfield Music Festival (Great Britain, 1990), Wien Modern (1991), Schleswig Holstein (1991), 41 Berliner Festwochen (1991), Panorama mit Löchern (Zurich, 1992), Frankfurt Feste (1991, 1992, 1993), the Sergei Prokofiev Festival in Duisburg (1991), The ISCM World Music Days (Warsaw, 1992), the Modern Music Festival in Moscow (1992), World Music Days (1992), Münchener Biennale (1994, 1995), Tage für Neue Musik (Zurich, 1994).

PRINCIPAL WORKS

1978   *Symphonic Prologue* for orchestra. 15'

1980   *Cello Concerto.* 20'

1982   *Symphony* for orchestra in three movements. 25'

1983   *Music in Memory of Dmitry Shostakovich* for recitalist and chamber orchestra. Collage to verses by Anna Akhmatova, James Patterson, Mikhail Matusovsky and Alexander Mezhirov in four movements. 17'

1984   *Wahnfried* for six Wagner tubas (or five trombones and one tuba), percussion, solo violin, piano and chorus (or taped choral singing) set to Richard Wagner's couplet. 9'

1986   *Psalmus poenitentialis.* Concerto for chorus, solo violin, organ and percussion. 28'

1987   *Choral Prelude "Jesu, deine tiefen Wunden"* for chamber orchestra. 10'

1987   *Three Graces.* Opera-parody in three scenes (fragments). Libretto by Carl Maria von Weber. 45'

1988   *Brooklyn Bridge or My Discovery of America.* Cantata for soprano, tenor and orchestra (or chamber ensemble) in four movements to the text by Vladimir Mayakovsky. 17'

1989   *Eindruck-Ausdruck I* for piano. 10'

1989   *Troïsti muziki.* Piano trio with singing Grigorij Skovoroda's "Hymn to the Christian Poverty". 23'

1989   *Upon Reading Mussorgsky's Draft Notebooks.* Concerto for chorus, soloists, recitalist and chamber orchestra. 25'

1989   *The Echoes of a Past Day.* Trio for clarinet, cello and piano. 18'

1990   *Per archi* for percussion quartet in memory of Luigi Nono. 10'

1991   *Cassandra* for chamber ensemble. 23'

1992   *Eindruck-Ausdruck II* for solo piano and chamber ensemble. 14'

1992   *O, Pärt — op art* for clarinet, violin, viola, cello and piano. 10'

1992   *Amoretto* for soprano, two clarinets, viola, cello and double-bass to the text by Edmund Spenser. 7'

1992   *Variations on Taneyev's Theme "Going Along the Unknown Road"* for two violins and chamber orchestra. In memory of Nikolai Sidelnikov. 15'

1993   *Ah, ces russes.* Opera-farce to the libretto by Irina Maslennikova. 45'

1993   *Welt voll Irsinn (This Crazy World)* for recitalists and orchestra to the texts by Kurt Schwitters. 15'

1994   *The Breath of Exhausted Time* for full symphony orchestra. 26'

1995   *Landscape after the Battle*, upon reading Rilke, for baritone and ensemble. 24'

1995   *Szenen aus dem Wirklichen Leben (Scenes from real Life)* for soprano, flute, French horn and piano to the texts by Ernst Jandl. 20'

1996   *Le vent des mots cu'il n'a pas dits* for cello and orchestra. 15'

1996   *Hommage a Kandinsky* for piano, flute, clarinet and string trio. 12'

INDEX*

---

* The Index is compiled by Valeria Tsenova